BLACKSTONE'S PHARMACY LAW AND PRACTICE

Kenneth Mullan

BLACKSTONE PRESS LIMITED

First published in Great Britain 2000 by Blackstone Press Limited,
Aldine Place, London W12 8AA. Telephone: (020) 8740 2277
www.blackstonepress.com

© K. Mullan, 2000

ISBN: 1 85431 940 X

British Library Cataloguing in Publication Data
A CIP catalogue record for this book is available from the British Library

Typeset by Montage Studios Limited, Horsmonden, Kent
Printed by Ashford Colour Press, Gosport, Hants

Contents

Four   The Licensing of Medicinal Products   73

Five   The Regulation of Drug Products — Prescription Only
Medicines   109

Six   The Regulation of Medicinal Drug Products — Controlled
Drugs   133

Seven   The Regulation of Medicinal Drug Products — Poisons   156

Preface

The practice of pharmacy has made a significant contribution to the development and process of health care over a period of centuries. Progress in the expansion of health care has relied on the contribution of all aspects of pharmacy for its success. Modern drug therapy remains one of the most successful interventions in individual patient treatment and the pharmacist, contributing significant expertise in the delivery of that therapy, performs a fundamental role as a provider within the health care team. The pharmacist's role in health care is therefore crucial.

Pharmacy is practised through the roles and responsibilities of pharmacists. In turn, the roles and responsibilities of pharmacists are necessarily shaped by law. The practice of pharmacy, therefore, has a legal reality which complements its parallel clinical, social, ethical and commercial realities. The purpose of this text is to describe, analyse and contextualise the legal reality of the practice of pharmacy by outlining the duties and obligations which surround the roles and functions of pharmacists. Such duties and obligations arise from the countless laws which apply to the organisation, administration and processes of the pharmacy profession.

The practice of pharmacy is going through exciting and innovative changes and developments. The current model of pharmacy practice is radically different from that which was in existence as few as thirty years ago. The principal aim of the prevailing (and still developing) model of professional pharmacy practice is to design, implement and monitor a therapeutic plan which seeks to achieve a set of desired therapeutic objectives. Increasingly this aim obliges pharmacists to share responsibility for individual patient outcomes with other members of the health care team. This modern, clinical role for pharmacists — using patient-specific evidence to monitor and manage the patient's care — equates with current expectations of the profession, applying existing knowledge of drug therapy in original and creative ways to improve patient outcomes.

The adoption of such innovative models of professional practice has distinct legal and ethical implications. The extent to which the new models will become accepted and recognised will be dependent on the reaction of the law and the legal system. In addition, the development and maintenance of new professional relationships with patients and other members of the primary health care team, necessitates a re-evaluation of existing legal and ethical responsibilities. The analysis contained in this text is designed to reflect such important and fundamental variations.

The systematic addressing of ethical issues, and the resolution of ethical questions and dilemmas form part of the professional responsibility of pharmacists. Because the practice of pharmacy is specifically concerned with the interests and welfare of other people, it necessarily has an ethical reality. The ethical reality of the practice of pharmacy is often ignored in texts such as this or is confined to an analysis of the contents of professional codes. However, an understanding of the concept of ethics, the place of ethics in the professional setting and the provision of a structured method for the resolution of ethical questions and dilemmas is essential for the effective implementation of professional health care practice. As such, specific provision has been made for this increasingly significant topic.

The pharmacist is a unique member of the primary health care team in having a further set of roles and functions, arising from but not necessarily linked to, the health care process. Foremost among these roles is the capacity to manage significant commercial interests. In addition, a pharmacist may be the employer of a substantial number of employees. The legal implications of the adoption of these further roles are important for pharmacists. Most of these legal rules are not unique to pharmacy but they can and do have a pharmacy context.

It might be added that it is equally important for the pharmacy profession to explore and analyse the tensions which may be created by the interaction of other roles (commercial, employment) with the professional health care roles, and any resultant legal, ethical and professional implications which may arise. As such the text provides for a specific analysis of the legal and ethical implications of the other roles and functions of pharmacists.

A main objective of this text is to provide an accurate and comprehensive description of the laws relating to the clinical aspects of pharmacy practice as part of the wider provision of health care. A parallel aim is to set those laws into the context of everyday practice. As the principal environment for the practice of pharmacy remains the community where pharmacists continue to contribute to the provision of health care for individual patients, the aim of contextualisation has been achieved by analysing the implications of the law for those involved in the practice of community pharmacy. Pharmacy is practised in other contexts, most notably in hospitals and in private industry. No separate provision is made in this text for these other frameworks in the belief that the comprehensive analysis of the laws relating to the practice of pharmacy can be easily adapted to the complexities of those settings.

The practice of pharmacy is primarily concerned with sharing responsibility for the competent provision of pharmaco-therapy for the purposes of achieving definite outcomes that improve or maintain a patient's quality of life. Some pharmacists involve themselves in contributing towards the improvement of the lives of other species, most notably through involvement with members of the veterinary profession or through their own small animal work. That aspect of the professional practice of pharmacy has its own legal reality which has not been examined in this text. The principal reason for this omission is the decreasing participation of pharmacists in this area of professional practice partly as a consequence of the profession's desire to increase its involvement in patient health care.

The substantive law relating to the practice of pharmacy is as dynamic and changing as most other areas of law. The laws described in this text are, as accurately as possible, those in force in England and Wales on 1 July 1999. Any significant variations for Scotland and Northern Ireland have been introduced where necessary.

I am extremely grateful to Professor David Brushwood for the significant contribution which he has made to my thinking on the subject of pharmacy law and practice. David introduced me to this subject and has been providing myself (and many others) with thoughtful and critical insights and academic leadership ever since. I am privileged to have him as a colleague, mentor and friend. I am also very grateful to my close friend Dr Bruce Weinstein for providing me with an introduction to pharmacy ethics and for his ongoing contribution to the systematic addressing of ethical issues and the resolution of ethical questions and dilemmas. I would also like to thank a number of individuals at Blackstone Press for taking on the subject of pharmacy law, for assisting in turning my ideas into this text, and for persevering with me through the usual delays and queries. In particular, I am grateful to Jeremy, Heather and Alistair, and to David, Ramona and other members of the editorial staff.

A number of close friends and family members have been extremely supportive and understanding through all stages of this text's production, and I am very grateful to them. However my greatest debt of gratitude is owed to my wife, Wilma. Without her guidance, motivation, humour, patience and love, this book would not have existed.

Kenneth Mullan
January 2000

Table of Cases

Table of Statutes

Table of Statutory Instruments

ONE

The nature of law and the legal system

1.1 INTRODUCTION

Pharmacy law can be perplexing for those who have to understand its rationale, comprehend its detail, introduce it as an essential element of professional practice, and cope with, and manage its direct effects and consequences. This is because the myriad laws which apply both to the practice of pharmacy, and to the administration of the pharmacy profession, and which give rise to specific legal duties and obligations, are complex and intricate and require close attention and study.

The process of understanding and implementing the detailed rules of pharmacy law is exacerbated by the nature of law and the legal system. Lawyers use specialised and complex language. Laws come from a wide variety of sources. Rules and regulations are written in intricate and bewildering detail. The legal system has a highly formalised and ritualistic structure. Legal advice and assistance is expensive and difficult to obtain. The law rarely seems to give a correct, or indeed any, solution.

Pharmacists are usually expected to comprehend the detail of the law, without being given any background information on its source, its form and structure, its use of language, and its practical and administrative implications. Typically a pharmacist might read that a new set of regulations has been introduced, a colleague is being sued in the courts, a judicial review is taking place, or that the European Union is implementing a new system. Before attempting to understand the technicalities of such legal developments, many pharmacists might ask 'What is a judicial review?', 'In which court will a pharmacist be sued?', 'Why is the law changing?'.

The purpose of this chapter is to assist the process of understanding the detail of pharmacy law, by giving a general insight into the nature of law and the legal system. This chapter will, first, explore the nature of law, and describe various concepts and theories which have influenced its development. Secondly, it will describe the two main divisions of law and show how the understanding of both divisions is crucial to an understanding of law in general, and pharmacy law, in particular. Thirdly, the chapter will examine the main sources of law, showing how individual laws are formulated and made and will explore the relationship between various law-making bodies. Finally, the chapter will explore aspects of the legal system, demonstrating how laws are implemented and enforced.

By the end of this chapter, the pharmacist should have a thorough and realistic understanding of the nature of law and the legal system which will facilitate the comprehension of the complex rules which will be described in subsequent chapters. The pharmacist should also have obtained a better perception of the foundations on which pharmacy law and pharmacy practice is based, and ought to have gained a practical insight into the operation of the law and the legal system which should lead to more effective professional practice.

1.2   WHAT IS LAW?

It is impossible to offer a definitive and authoritative account of what law is. Rather what is proposed is to offer one definition of the nature of law and outline various concepts and ideas included within such a definition. The nature and relevance of the law has been subject to a broad analysis by philosophers, lawyers, legislators, judges, politicians and academics over a considerable period of time, which reflects the comprehensive depth and history to the development of the law in the United Kingdom.

The issue of the nature and relevance of the law is not confined to those specialists however. The debate engages most members of society. Miscarriages of justice, the inappropriate sentencing of a convicted rapist, the introduction of controversial legislation, such as that on abortion, can stimulate extensive debate and discussion on the character of law, often closely managed by the media. Health care professionals are also concerned with the general issue of what law is, or ought to be. For example, the recent amendment to the rules on the sale of aspirin-based products to the public, precipitated significant analysis by the pharmacy profession of the purpose behind the changes, as evidenced in the widespread discussion in the relevant professional literature. 'What are the legislators up to?' is a question frequently asked by health care professionals.

Law is about the regulation of human affairs and human relationships. Every modern society has a legal system which includes a set of general rules regulating the conduct of the society's members. This general definition disguises a number of important concepts requiring further exploration, notably the concepts of rights, duties, rules, regulations, authority, morality, settling disputes and dynamism.

Some people believe that the law is all about legal rights. Certainly there are rights that arise from law. For example, we would all agree that we have the right to enjoy a good name or reputation. In addition, the potential exists for one individual to make accusations against another. If such accusations are false, then that other person may claim that their right to a good reputation has been infringed. Is the right to a good name or reputation a legal right then? The answer is 'Yes'. A rule in the legal system obliges individuals not to make false statements which damage the reputation of another. May that individual enforce that right in law? Yes, an action might be brought for defamation or invasion of privacy.

One person's legal right is often linked to another person's legal duty. Legal duties (or obligations) and legal rights tend to be found together. The existence of a legal right may mean that individuals are under a duty to act or omit to act. To return to the issue of defamation, the right to enjoy a good reputation might, correspondingly, imply that others are under a duty not to damage a person's reputation. The language of law is full of the notion of legal duty. As will be noted below, the whole basis of the law of negligence is that, in certain circumstances, we each owe a duty to those with whom we are in contact, to act in a certain way or indeed to omit to act.

For many people, the most attractive way to classify or define law is in terms of rules and regulations. The idea is that the law simply outlines a series of rules which we must obey or else we will be penalised. Implicit within this view is the notion of authority. The law is seen as the ultimate authority to be obeyed at all costs. There is much to this idea. For example, the law states that we should not physically assault other individuals and if we do we shall be penalised for our behaviour. So too there is a rule within contract law that one party to a valid contract is obliged to carry out obligations under the contract or face the penalty of paying damages to the other party. To an extent it could be argued that the law, in this sense, is absolute. If the law has been broken the penalty must be exacted and there is nothing further to discuss. Traditional analysis of pharmacy law (and traditional methods of teaching pharmacy law) has been in terms of rules and regulations. Pharmacists have often been provided with detailed lists of rules and regulations and have been advised that strict adherence to the letter of the law results in no liability and no sanction.

This is too narrow a view of the law. The regulation of human affairs and human relationships is about much more than the imposition of a set of rules to be obeyed. The dynamism and flexibility of the law also operates against its analysis purely in terms of absolute adherence to a set of rules and regulations. While laws have to be certain and consistent to allow individuals to conduct their affairs and their relationships they also have to be adaptable to reflect the variety of circumstances which they are designed to cover. Laws have to be dynamic to reflect changes in human affairs and human relationships, changes which were not foreseen at the time when the laws were drafted. Those changes may arise from social, political, economic or technological factors. Law is real, dynamic, ever-changing and has to be studied and practised in context.

The factors of adaptability and change also provide the reason why the solutions to legal problems are not always clear-cut nor can be clearly stated. Lawyers often reserve judgment on a particular legal issue, precisely because the wording of the law might be applied or interpreted in a number of different ways.

The law is also about the settling of disputes. Those disputes may be between individuals and society or may be between individuals themselves. The law provides a mechanism whereby society can resolve disputes with individuals who have infringed society's code of human behaviour and conduct. For example, society's current code of human conduct dictates that individual members of society should not possess nor use cannabis for personal use. An individual who violates that rule is in conflict with society as a whole. The law provides the framework for the resolution of that dispute. In a parallel way, the law also recognises that the regulation of human relationships necessitates the development of processes to allow individuals to settle disputes which have arisen as a result of those relationships. For example, an individual pharmacist may enter into a contractual relationship with an individual drug company. If the pharmacist does not pay for products supplied by the drug company, the two individuals will be in dispute. The law regulates the parties' individual relationship by ruling that mutuality of promise is an essential requirement of a valid binding contract and provides the method by which the dispute may be resolved, allowing the drug company to sue the pharmacist for breach of promise to pay. In this sense, the law regulates human relationships in which society has no individual interest.

As such, law, or rather the enforcement of law, in the United Kingdom is adversarial in nature. The settling of disputes is between two parties with the judge (sometimes assisted by a jury) acting as arbiter or umpire in between. One party will always assume the burden of proof and will try to adduce enough evidence to satisfy the standard of proof appropriate to the form of action. If that objective is achieved, that party will win the case. The judge, in most legal actions, is not supposed to assist the parties in adducing the evidence. The judge's role is to decide whether the party who has assumed the burden of proof has presented enough evidence to satisfy the requisite standard. In having an adversarial nature law, the legal system in the United Kingdom stands in contrast to other countries. For example, the system of law which exists in most European countries is inquisitorial in nature, allowing judges to call witnesses and ask them questions.

Law has a close link with morality. There are myriad laws which have their basis in the reflection of current or past moral trends — for example, the recent prohibition on the ownership of certain types of handguns. Equally, though, there are more laws which are morally ambivalent — for example, laws regulating the day-to-day management of public corporations. The development of law is influenced by a number of factors and morality is one of them, but it is not the only one. Past customs, current trends, society's needs, political expediency are examples of others. In turn, it is entirely possible for a course of action to be immoral without being illegal. Many individuals lawfully purchase magazines which might be regarded by many others as pornographic. Overall the individuals' behaviour might be regarded as being immoral but it is certainly not illegal.

Health care practice, and therefore health care law, has a close relationship with morality. Relationships in health care practice raise moral or ethical issues which may become problems or dilemmas or disputes requiring resolution. Where the answer to the problem or dilemma, and the settlement of the dispute, could be found in the law, that solution is often advocated as the most obvious, rational and intelligible. Strict adherence to the requirements of the law is deemed to be the most appropriate response to the moral or ethical dilemma. In this sense, the law is seen to encapsulate morals and ethics and to be the best representation of them. That thinking is reinforced by the further moral obligation to obey the law.

Compliance with legal standards (or with the profession's code of ethics) is often advocated as the best method for the resolution of ethical problems or dilemmas which arise in pharmacy. As will be seen below, in chapter eleven, the resolution of ethical dilemmas has something to with adherence to the law, something to do with observation of professional standards but much more to do with the development of a systematic procedure for ethical decision making. To adhere to the requirements of the law unquestioningly, involves the unquestioning acceptance of the moral or ethical basis of those laws. That is too narrow a view: the moral basis for some laws is clearly dubious.

Finally, law is necessarily limited in its effect. That might be because many individuals, as outlined above, might question its ethical or moral basis, and having done so, decide that their own moral standards justify an ignorance of the law's requirements. Unless and until the ignorance of the law, and parallel continued action in conformity with individual morality, results in the disruption of human relationships or the violation of society's code of behaviour, the law will be restricted in its effect. Individuals may therefore continue to act in an immoral fashion without infringing the law or legal requirements. Further the law is an inappropriate method for the regulation of all human behaviour and disputes which arise in human relationships. Quite clearly, there are aspects of human relationships which are better regulated by those involved in the relationship. In addition, it is not suitable for the law to regulate every minor violation of the law.

1.3   WHAT ARE THE MAIN DIVISIONS OF LAW?

The discussion of the enforcement of law, as outlined above, has hinted at the two main divisions of law, i.e., civil law and criminal law. The understanding of both divisions is crucial to an understanding of law in general, and aspects of law, including pharmacy law, in particular.

Criminal law is largely self-explanatory and is the division of law with which most people are familiar. That is largely due to the amount of media attention which the criminal law, or rather violations of it, attracts. Criminal law is concerned with the relationship between an individual and the state and relates to the regulation of human conduct. There is a certain code of conduct which society regards as fundamental to societal function and good order. Violation of that code of conduct necessitates the involvement of the state in the investigation of the violation, the detection of the offender, indictment of the transgressor, and, if the violation is proved beyond all reasonable doubt, the imposition of sanction or punishment. The purpose of the criminal law is to punish individuals for carrying out criminal activity and to deter others from carrying out such activity.

The key to an understanding of the criminal law is to remain aware that society or the state takes an active involvement in criminal law at a number of stages. It provides the resources for the agencies whose task is to prevent, investigate and detect crime, it prosecutes offenders, and provides the methods and systems by which convicted defendants are punished. In a criminal action, the state prosecutes the defendant or the accused and, in so doing, assumes the burden of proving that an individual is guilty beyond all reasonable doubt. The prosecution is usually carried out by the police but may be done by a number of other agencies; for example, some prosecutions may be commenced by the Royal Pharmaceutical Society of Great Britain. Finally, the state will occasionally allow an individual to take a private criminal prosecution but such instances are few and far between.

The criminal law is relevant to the practice of pharmacy. Of course, pharmacists are as obliged to conform to the general requirements of the criminal law as other members of society, so a pharmacist who drives through a traffic junction displaying a red light is as guilty of road traffic offences as is anyone else. However there are other aspects of the criminal law which have a direct bearing on the practice of pharmacy, many of which will be outlined in the chapters below. One example would be the requirement that a prescription only medicine may only be sold or supplied in accordance with a prescription given by a practitioner. Violation of this requirement amounts to a criminal offence. Equally there are other aspects of the criminal law which impinge on pharmacists in the variety of roles which they undertake in parallel with the practice of pharmacy. For example, all employers are under a duty to ensure the health, safety and welfare of all of their employees. Breach of this duty can amount to a criminal offence. Clearly this aspect of the criminal law is as applicable to the pharmacists as employers (which they frequently are) as to all other types of employers.

Civil law is concerned with the relationships between individuals and relates to the conduct of human relationships. The civil law recognises that each member of society has a number of individual and collective civil rights which regulate their relationships with each other. Further the civil law will protect and enforce those rights by allowing those individual members of society, who feel that one of their rights has been infringed, to sue the other individual who is believed to have infringed that right. The purpose of the civil law is to regulate human relationships, protect individual rights and to provide compensation to an individual where one of those rights has been infringed.

A crucial difference between civil law and criminal law is that society or the state takes no active part, on behalf of individual members of society, in civil law actions. It does have a direct involvement in the development of the laws which embody individual civil rights. It also provides the method and system (courts, judges etc.) whereby individual members can seek to enforce their specific rights. The decision to bring a civil law claim lies with the individuals who feels that their rights have been infringed. If they decide to do so they will sue, as claimants, the other individuals or defendants in the civil courts. A claimant assumes the burden of proof, and will have to prove, on the balance of probabilities, that the defendant is responsible for the problems which have arisen. If the claimant succeeds, the court will find that the defendant is liable to the claimant and will award compensation, or occasionally some other appropriate remedy, to correct the problem which has arisen.

It is important to remember that the same set of facts may give rise to actions in both the criminal and the civil law. For example, a pharmacist employer who fails to repair a set of stairs, after being alerted to the defect on a number of occasions, may be sued in the civil law, by an individual member of staff who is injured after falling on the stairs, and may be prosecuted (i.e., a criminal law action) for failing to ensure the health, safety and welfare of his or her employees. Actions in civil and criminal law are not interdependent. It is not essential to commence a criminal prosecution before bringing a civil action and vice versa. Further, success or lack of success in one action will not predetermine — although may help or hinder — success in the other. The alternate actions in criminal and civil law will be heard in separate courts. As will be discussed below, the court structure in the United Kingdom reflects the important separation of the law into civil and criminal divisions.

Sometimes lawyers classify the law into the divisions of public and private law. Public law encompasses all areas of law where society has intervened directly to regulate human conduct or behaviour. On the basis of the description given above, it necessarily includes criminal law, but also covers constitutional and administrative law. Private law, on the other hand, encompasses all areas of law which regulate human relationships.

1.4 WHERE DOES LAW COME FROM?

When most people are asked why they should not drive a car after having consumed a large amount of alcohol, they will respond that the reason is that such action is against the law. Yet when they are asked to outline the source of the law, most will struggle to find the answer. Such limitations are not confined to ordinary members of society. Health care professionals know that they must not act carelessly or negligently when treating their patients, will further realise that such an obligation is imposed by the law, but will usually be unsure of the direct source of the legal requirement.

1.4.1 Primary legislation

It is reasonable to suppose that each law has a ground of some kind. In a modern state many of the rules in the legal system will have their ground in acts performed by parliaments, regional assemblies, and the like, and written down as a matter of public record. This source is known as *legislation*. In the United Kingdom, legislation is one of the most important sources of law. Indeed, it is often suggested that legislation is *the* most important source of law. This is because Parliament is said to have 'legislative sovereignty'. This means that when Parliament passes or enacts a piece of legislation, it may only be reformed or repealed or struck out by another piece of legislation. Judges in the United Kingdom, under the doctrine of legislative sovereignty, are not permitted to strike out legislation, on the ground that Parliament was wrong to enact it. In this sense, the United Kingdom stands in contrast to a number of other countries, such as the United States of America and the Republic of Ireland, where judges may declare legislation to be invalid in that it offends or is contrary to the principles of the written constitutions of those countries.

In short legislation is law which comes from Parliament. Legislation is divided into 'primary' and 'delegated' or 'secondary' legislation. Primary legislation is essentially what we know as Acts of Parliament, created through a formal procedure to be outlined below. Because Parliamentary time is so limited, and because the demands for new primary legislation are increasing, Parliament usually cannot enact the full, detailed rules which it has in mind for a particular scheme of law. The solution which it has found is to establish the structure of the particular programme in, and through an Act of Parliament. That Act then gives power or enables another body, usually a government department, to make or enact the detailed rules to complete the scheme. The detailed rules, when eventually enacted, are known as delegated or secondary legislation. The fact that secondary legislation does not undergo the same detailed, formal legislative process as primary legislation, does not lessen its importance or applicability.

Parliament, or more accurately, the Queen in Parliament, has three important elements — the House of Commons, the House of Lords and the reigning monarch.

The House of Commons, as currently constituted, consists of 659 Members of Parliament (MPs), all of whom have been elected to represent a United Kingdom constituency, either at a general election or at a by-election following the death or resignation of an existing MP. Following a general election, the political party which has gained the greatest number of seats in the House of Commons is asked to form a government, and the leader of that party is appointed by the monarch to be Prime Minister. The government's role is to govern the country, a role achieved through administration by a large number of government departments, headed by a government minister. As will be noted below, the government also has the greatest influence over the form and content of legislation. The role of MPs is to represent their constituents' interests in Parliament, participate in government, and contribute to the law-making work of the House of Commons by participating in debates and committees. Because of the in-built majority which the government has in the House of Commons, that body has the greatest influence over the law-making or legislative process.

The House of Lords, as currently constituted, consists of approximately 676 members. None of these peers have been directly elected to the House of Lords but have either succeeded to their seats (hereditary peers, of which 92 remain), been appointed to their seats, usually only for their lifetime, as a reward for public service (life or 'working peers', of which there are around 547), senior members of the judiciary (serving Law Lords, of whom there are 11 together with the Lord Chancellor) and senior members of the established churches (spiritual peers, of whom there are 26). The role of peers is to participate in government and to contribute to the law-making work of the House of Lords by participating in debates and committees. Most of the important law-making work of the House of Lords is carried out by the life or working peers. Hereditary peers, while in the majority in the House, only have a major influence when it comes to important votes. The power of the House of Lords over the legislative process has been subject to a process of elimination during the twentieth century. The House of Lords may now only delay the enactment of legislation or make suggestions for reforms to the House of Commons. The role and participation of hereditary peers in the House of Lords was reduced by the House of Lords Act 1999. A number of hereditary peers remain in an interim capacity.

The monarch has a traditional, but now ceremonial role in the parliamentary law-making, or legislative, process. The monarch opens each parliamentary session at the formal state opening of Parliament. As part of this ceremony the monarch makes a speech, the Queen's Speech, which gives full details of the legislation which Parliament intends to enact during the following parliamentary session. The Queen's Speech is written for her by the Prime Minister's office and she has no influence over its contents. No legislation may be enacted without receiving formal agreement — the Royal Assent — from the reigning monarch. Despite the appearance of this wide power, the monarch now will never refuse to consent to a piece of legislation; indeed the 'Royal Assent' is now given on her behalf.

Most pieces of primary legislation begin their life as proposals from cabinet ministers, either on suggestion from government advisers, or as a result of a commitment to make new laws in an election manifesto. Proposals for new legislation may also be introduced by individual MPs using the private members' Bills procedure. The opportunity to introduce legislation in this way is very limited and a private member's Bill will not usually succeed unless it receives government support.

Proposals for primary legislation may be published for consideration by special interest groups, or by the public in general, through the production of a green or white paper. Individual cabinet ministers will then have to persuade the cabinet as a whole that the proposals are sufficiently important to be introduced to the formal parliamentary process and that time, in a busy schedule, should be found for their enactment. If the cabinet agrees, the legislative proposals are drafted into relevant legal terminology by specialist civil servants called parliamentary counsel. The proposals are then known as a Bill and begin their formal passage through Parliament.

A Bill is usually introduced into the House of Commons. However if the contents of the Bill are non-controversial, the Bill may be introduced in the House of Lords instead. In the House of Commons, the Bill will go through five stages. The first stage is called the first reading and is a formality when the existence of the Bill is announced and a date set for the second stage which is called the second reading. At this stage the minister responsible for the introduction of the Bill will formally propose its adoption. There then follows a full debate on the merits of the Bill followed by a vote of all MPs who are present.

The third stage is called the committee stage and is probably the most important stage of the Bill's whole enactment. The Bill is considered, word for word, clause by clause, by a committee of between 25 and 45 MPs, made up of Members in proportion to party weightings in the full House. Significant amendments to the Bill may be proposed and/or adopted at this stage. The committee reports on its findings to the full House of Commons at the fourth stage of enactment which is called the report stage. A debate takes place during which further amendments may be suggested and a vote is taken on the merits of the Bill. The final stage of enactment in the House of Commons is called the third reading. A final short debate takes place but few significant amendments will be introduced.

The passage of a Bill through each stage of the House of Commons may take a considerable length of time, or it may be rapid. To give an example, the first reading of the Medicines Bill, which was eventually to become the important Medicines Act 1968, was heard on 2 February 1968, and took just five minutes of Parliamentary time; the second reading took place on 15 February 1968 and lasted for five and a half hours; the committee stage took place between 12 March 1968 and 30 May 1968 when the committee met on 20 occasions lasting each, on average, for two and a half hours; the report stage took place on 24 June 1968 and took two and a half hours; and finally, the third reading took also took place on 24 June 1968 and lasted for one minute.

Following its passage through the House of Commons, the Bill will pass to the House of Lords. In the House of Lords it will go through the same five stages as in the House of Commons. As noted above, the power of the House of Lords to affect the form, content, and enactment of a piece of legislation has now been curtailed. The House of Lords may introduce significant amendments to the Bill during its passage through the House but it may not now delay any non-financial Bill for more than one year. Financial Bills may not be delayed for more than one month. Despite this, the existing delaying power, and the legislative and debating expertise contained among the working peers in the House of Lords, may mean that the House may exercise significant influence over the passage of a Bill and the its form and content when eventually enacted.

Again the passage of the Bill through its various stages in the Lords may take differing amount of times. To return to the Medicines Bill, which was to become the Medicines Act 1968, it was introduced to the Lords and received its first reading on 26 June 1968 (two days after completing its passage through the Commons) when the whole process took one minute; the second reading was taken on 4 July 1968 and lasted one hour and forty minutes; the Bill was then sent to a committee of the whole House of Lords, which stage took place on 18 July 1968 and lasted for two and a half hours; the report stage was commenced on the same date but was resumed on 30 July 1968 for two hours; the third reading stage also took place on 31 July 1968 and lasted for one minute.

Occasionally the House of Lords will propose significant amendments to the Bill during its passage through the House which may have to be considered further by the House of Commons. This happened during the passage of the Medicines Bill. Following its passage through the House of Lords, the Bill returned to the House of Commons on 18 October 1968, where the House spent two hours considering Lords' amendments. It was sent back to the House of Lords on 22 October 1968, when the Commons' replies to the amendments were considered for a further five minutes.

Formal enactment will take place when the Bill receives the Royal Assent. The Bill will then become an Act of Parliament. Royal Assent to the Medicines Bill was given on 25 October 1968 when it became the Medicines Act 1968. The Act may come into force of law immediately or its effect may be delayed to allow parties affected by its provisions to become accustomed to its provisions. For this reason, the Medicines Act 1968 was introduced in stages. When enacted, an Act of Parliament is given a chapter number for the particular year of its enactment. For example, the chapter number for the Medicines Act 1968 is 67 of 1968.

Primary legislation is usually enacted to introduce a new scheme of law for a particular area. However primary legislation often repeals or revokes or amends earlier legislation deemed to be out of date or otherwise in need of reform. For example, the Medicines Act 1968 repeals the Pharmacy and Medicines Act 1941 in its entirety and the individual section 19 of the Pharmacy Act 1954. Occasionally new primary legislation is used to 'tidy up' an existing scheme of law, enacted through a whole series of Acts of Parliament over a period of time. The new primary legislation consolidates the earlier legislation.

1.4.2 Secondary legislation

As noted above, most Acts of Parliament delegate power to other bodies, to make detailed rules to complete the scheme or programme of law which the minister or other proposer intended to introduce. The detailed rules created under the powers delegated by primary legislation are known as secondary or delegated legislation. In reality, secondary legislation has become a very important source of law, for the reasons outlined above.

Power to make secondary legislation is delegated to a body called a rule-making authority. Rule-making authorities are usually government departments but also include the Privy Council or local authorities. The primary legislation, sometimes called the parent or enabling Act, will determine the area in which law can be made; it may say something about the content of the law, but the details of that law will be left to the person or body to whom legislative power is delegated. This has certain important consequences. No secondary legislation can be enacted without a power being given by the enabling legislation. We shall also see that if that power is exceeded, the secondary legislation may be challenged in the courts. However it is important to make it clear that delegated or secondary legislation is just as binding on the general public as the primary legislation. Thus, despite the fact that most people are unaware of secondary legislation, it plays an important part in our lives, both in terms of its content and in its binding nature.

It is possible to identify three different types of secondary legislation: statutory instruments, Orders in Council, and statutory rules. Statutory rules are unique to Northern Ireland and Orders in Council have taken on a particular significance within Northern Ireland. It is important to note that while the secondary legislation may use the words 'rules', 'regulations' or 'order' this does not necessarily mean that the secondary legislation is of a particular type.

Statutory instruments are made under the authority of a United Kingdom statute. They are the most common and prevalent form of secondary legislation. An example of a statutory instrument is the Misuse of Drugs Regulations 1985 made by the Home Secretary under ss. 7, 10, 22 and 31 of the Misuse of Drugs Act 1971. Statutory instruments are given numbers for the year in which they are made and are referred to by that number. The number of the Misuse of Drugs Regulations 1985 is S.I. 1985/2066. As we shall see below in chapter six, the legislative requirements outlined in S.I. 1985/2066, relating to controlled drugs, are extremely important to all of those, including pharmacists, associated with the distribution of these medicinal products. This fact stresses the importance of secondary legislation as a source of law, and reinforces its significance, despite the fact that secondary legislation does not undergo the same formal methods of enactment as does the primary legislation which enabled its initiation.

A statutory instrument may repeal or amend earlier statutory instruments, and in turn may be repealed or amended itself. The Misuse of Drugs Regulations 1985 (S.I. 1985/2066) have been amended many times, for example by the Misuse of Drugs (Amendment) Regulations 1990 (S.I. 1990/2630). A statutory instrument may even repeal or amend primary legislation. As we shall see below, the use of statutory instruments to amend primary legislation is usually restricted to those situations where the primary legislation requires amendment to comply with European Union requirements. A good example would be the Medicines Act 1968 (Amendment) (No. 2) Regulations 1992 (S.I. 1992/3271) which introduced a new s. 58A into the Medicines Act 1968.

Orders in Council are, strictly speaking, another form of statutory instrument. The fact that a piece of secondary legislation is called an 'Order' does not necessarily mean that it is an Order in Council. A good example would be the Prescription Only Medicines (Human Use) Order 1997, made by the Secretaries of State concerned with health in England, Wales and Scotland, and the Department of Health and Social Services, under powers conferred on them by ss. 58(1), (4), (5) and 129(4) of the Medicines Act 1968. In recent years, Orders in Council, as a form of secondary legislation, have taken on a particular significance in Northern Ireland, where they are used to enact legislation under the legislative powers held by the former Parliament at Stormont. The vast majority of these Orders in Council are made under the Northern Ireland Act 1974. An example of an Order in Council enacted under these powers is the Health and Personal Social Services (Northern Ireland) Order 1991 (1991/194 (NI 1)).

Statutory rules are a form of secondary legislation enacted by a rule-making authority in Northern Ireland under powers given by an Act of the United Kingdom Parliament, or by an Act of the former Stormont Parliament or by an Order in Council made under the Northern Ireland Act 1974. Statutory rules have been described as the Northern Ireland equivalent to the statutory instruments made for the rest of the United Kingdom. Often the legislative content of the statutory rules is very similar to the equivalent statutory instruments made for the rest of the United Kingdom. An example of a statutory rule would be Health and Personal Social Services (Charges for Drugs and Appliances) (Amendment) (No. 2) Regulations (Northern Ireland) 1974 (NI 1974/83).

Secondary legislation is drafted by civil servants, usually located in the legal section of the government department responsible for the scheme of law with which the secondary legislation is concerned.

The exact method of enacting secondary legislation depends on how important it is deemed to be. The most important forms of secondary legislation must usually be laid in draft form before both Houses of Parliament and be approved by both Houses. The secondary legislation is then sent to the monarch for formal assent or agreement. For some forms of secondary legislation, therefore, there will be Parliamentary debate and a requirement for affirmation before formal enactment. The debate must usually take place within 40 days of the laying of the legislation and if no debate takes place then no further action may be taken on the legislation.

Urgent secondary legislation can be made without being first laid before Parliament but it will cease to have legal effect if each House does not approve it within the following 40 days. Alternatively the legislation will take effect or continue to have effect, if already made, unless it is specifically annulled in either House within 40 days. Under all these procedures, the secondary legislation cannot be amended. It must be affirmed or struck out entirely although it may be re-laid in a subsequent Parliamentary session in a revised form.

Less important secondary legislation may not be subject to the procedures for affirmation described in the preceding paragraph, but must be laid before Parliament. Although formal debate does not take place on such legislation, questions can be asked of the appropriate ministers about it and it cannot come into force before it is laid before Parliament. The least important secondary legislation does not need to be laid before Parliament at all, although questions can be asked about it.

Secondary legislation is controlled by the courts and by Parliament. Parliament can obviously control the content of secondary legislation through the extent of the powers to be delegated under the primary legislation. In addition, if the legislation is to be debated as part of the enacting procedures described above, then further discussion and scrutiny can take place. Secondary legislation may also be discussed by Parliamentary committees — a standing (or merits) committee of the House of Commons and, if the secondary legislation is in the form of statutory instruments, by a joint select (or scrutiny) committee of the House of Commons and the House of Lords.

Control by the courts over secondary legislation is exercised through the process of judicial review. An application may be made to the court that the secondary legislation is *ultra vires*, i.e., that the rule-making authority, in making the secondary legislation, has gone beyond the powers conferred by the parent or enabling Act. If the court agrees then it will strike out the secondary legislation as being void.

1.4.3 Judicial precedent
It is often thought that, because Parliament has legislative sovereignty, as described above, legislation is the most important source of law. Courts and judges also play a part in formulating laws. This type of law-making is called judicial precedent or case law, common law or judge made law.

The essential difference between legislation and case law is that the former may be described as a body of rules which have been formally enacted by the legislature or executive, whilst the latter is the statement of the legal position in a particular case or situation based on the decisions of previous courts in similar cases or situations. Judges *make* law in two main situations, namely where there is no legislation on a particular issue, or where there is legislation and its meaning is unclear. There are particular rules and principles attached to each form of judicial law-making.

Despite the fact that there have been Parliamentary structures in existence for centuries, there are large areas of law which have remained untouched by the legislators. The law of contract is an example of this, as is the law of negligence. In the absence of attention from Parliament, the courts are charged with the development of the law, and are under a duty to consider novel legal issues which arise in the cases which come before them. The courts make law as part of the process of dealing with cases initiated by individual litigants. Often those litigants will be aware that their factual circumstances, combined with a lack of development in the existing law, will mean that their case will be argued and decided on legal principles. Other litigants go to court with the simple intention of having their dispute resolved or their concerns addressed. Lack of development of the existing law might lead to unanticipated complications in their case, resulting in the removal of their case to courts higher in the judicial structure.

When judges and courts make law, they do so according to long-standing principles and traditions. Not all courts are continually involved in law-making, although all courts are charged with the duty of developing the law. The significant decisions, which formulate and develop the law, will be made in the higher courts in the hierarchy of the United Kingdom legal system, i.e., the House of Lords, the Court of Appeal and the High Court. In the lower courts, the dispute will usually be factual in nature and judges in these courts will rarely be called upon to make significant decisions in law. When important points of law arise in the lower courts, judges will usually make decisions of a preliminary nature, knowing that the case will be appealed further up the system. Some judges bypass the process by stating that individual cases involve important points of law worthy of further consideration by the higher courts.

In the United Kingdom legal structure, the highest court is the House of Lords. This body, which is different from the House of Lords as the second tier of Parliament, is made up of twelve of the most senior judges in the country, called Lords of Appeal in Ordinary, and the Lord Chancellor. The House of Lords hears cases involving points of law of public general importance, on appeal from the lower courts. The House of Lords has its own committee of three judges to decide whether a case is appropriate for hearing before it. The House of Lords usually sits as a court of five judges although, if the case is deemed to be particularly important, seven judges will sit.

The Court of Appeal, the court immediately below the House of Lords in the hierarchy of the courts, has two divisions reflecting the existing separation of the law into civil and criminal aspects. The Lord Chief Justice acts as the President of the Criminal Division of the Court of Appeal, while the President of the Civil Division is called the Master of the Rolls. Both divisions of the

Court of Appeal hear cases involving important points of law, usually on appeal from the lower courts. A case in the Court of Appeal will usually be heard by three judges, although some matters may be heard by a two judge bench.

The High Court of Justice has three divisions, namely the Queen's Bench Division, the Family Division and the Chancery Division, each with their own jurisdiction, which will be explained in more depth below. However, when exercising those jurisdictions, High Court judges, who usually sit on their own, formulate and develop the law. This is particularly the case when High Court judges sit as a Divisional Court to hear judicial review cases. Often the decisions of High Court judges will be appealed to the Court of Appeal and even further to the House of Lords. However there is a significant body of law which has been developed by the High Court and there are many important legal principles which have their origins in High Court decisions.

All judges and courts, when formulating and developing the law, follow the same principle of relying on previous decisions of other courts as authority for making a determination in the present case. This guiding principle is what gives rise to calling judge-made law 'judicial precedent'. The rules of judicial precedent oblige lower courts to follow the decision of higher courts in cases which are similar. The rules are dependent upon understanding the hierarchy and structure of the courts, finding previous decisions in similar cases and persuading judges that they are bound to follow these previous decisions.

As noted above, the United Kingdom court structure is hierarchical in nature. As such the decisions of the House of Lords are binding on all courts below it. In turn, decisions of the Court of Appeal, are binding on all courts below it, with a similar rule being applied to decisions of the High Court. It is important to remember that not all cases involving important points of law will reach as far as the House of Lords. Cases involving points of law are precipitated by individual litigants who may or may not be persuaded by their legal advisers that further appeal to the higher courts is merited.

For well over seventy years the House of Lords felt bound to follow its own previous decisions. As might be imagined, such a practice was clearly leading to a stagnation in the development of the law. In 1966 the House of Lords issued a statement, called a Practice Direction, which indicated that, for the future, the House of Lords would *usually* treat former decisions as binding, and would only depart from them when it appeared right to do so. Since 1966 the House of Lords has only rarely used this power, reinforcing the importance of the doctrine of precedent in the United Kingdom legal system.

The Court of Appeal also adopts the practice of following its own previous decisions but may refuse to follow them in certain limited circumstances. In practice the Court of Appeal strongly adheres to the principle of being bound to follow its own previous decisions. The High Court adopts a similar practice and will follow its own previous decisions unless persuaded that they are wrong, for example if the previous High Court decision has been overruled by a subsequent decision of the Court of Appeal or House of Lords.

Previous decisions of certain of the courts are to be found in the law reports. There are now several sets of both paper and electronic law reports, published both officially by a body approved by the judicial and court sector and unofficially for commercial profits by law publishers. Not all decisions of the courts are reported in the law reports although transcripts of almost all decisions are retained. Some cases are reported in the law sections of certain of the daily broadsheet newspapers.

The rules of judicial precedent involve lawyers persuading a court that a previously reported decision of a court at a higher or equivalent level is binding because it is similar. In doing so, the lawyers will seek to demonstrate that the essential facts of the previous case and the legal principles based on those facts are similar to the issues raised in the present case. The material facts and the legal principles on which a case is decided are often referred to as the *ratio decidendi*. Anything else said by a judge is often referred to as *obiter dicta* or 'other things said'. Only the *ratio decidendi* is binding on a subsequent judge.

As well as spending a great deal of time persuading judges that they are bound to follow previous decisions, lawyers will often also seek to convince judges that the previous decision should be distinguished and not followed. Distinguishing a case is the method most often employed to avoid the binding nature of the rules of precedent. Further, when a court does refuse to follow a previous decision, and declares it to be wrong, the decision will only apply from the date of the new decision. It is not possible for the party who lost the original decision to reach back and have the previous decision, with any associated financial implications, overturned in their favour.

As noted above, judges are obliged to make law in two main situations, i.e., where there is no legislation on a particular issue, or where there is legislation but the meaning of the wording of that legislation is unclear. An example of the former situation is provided in the case of *Prendergast* v *Sam & Dee Ltd, The Independent*, 17 March 1988. In this case, which will be discussed in greater detail in chapters ten and thirteen below, the Queen's Bench Division of the High Court was asked to determine the extent of the duty owed by a pharmacist to a patient in relation to the dispensing of medicinal products pursuant to a prescription. In arriving at his decision, Auld J referred to the earlier Court of Appeal decision in *Dwyer* v *Roderick* (1983) 127 SJ 805. The decision of Auld J in *Prendergast* was appealed further to the Court of Appeal (*The Times*, 14 March 1989) which confirmed Auld J's decision.

The process whereby a court formulates new law by determining the meaning of a particular word or phrase contained in a piece of existing legislation is often referred to as statutory interpretation. When legislators draft and enact both primary and secondary legislation they endeavour to ensure that the wording and formulations used will cover all circumstances and eventualities. For the most part they succeed in this task. However the imprecise nature of language, and the possibility of unforeseen circumstances arising following the enactment of the legislation, means that judges are charged with choosing the construction to be applied to particular words and phrases.

In carrying out the process of interpreting statutes, judges and courts follow the rules of precedent outlined above. However a series of guiding precepts and rules, known as the principles of statutory interpretation, have also evolved, and have been used by the courts and judges to assist them in the task of discovering the meaning of legislative words and phrases. In the past, judges and courts tended to apply the principles in a rigid and strict way, in the manner of a set of binding rules. The modern approach to statutory interpretation is to attempt to discover the intention or purpose of Parliament in passing or enacting a particular legislative provision, and that means considering any Parliamentary material, including *Hansard*, the official record of what takes place in Parliament, which may assist the interpretative process. The modern approach does not wholly reject the principles of statutory interpretation but rather subsumes them into a modern 'purposive' approach. Further guidance on the meaning of legislative words and phrases may also be found in the actual legislation or in specialist Acts of Parliament, including the Interpretation Act 1978.

An example of judicial law-making involving statutory interpretation may be found in *Roberts* v *Littlewoods Mail Order Stores Ltd* [1943] 1 All ER 271, which is discussed in more detail in chapter eight below. Here the King's Bench Division (as it then was) of the High Court was asked to determine the meaning of the phrase 'sale effected by, or under the supervision of, a registered pharmacist' as contained in s. 18(1)(a)(iii) of the Pharmacy and Poisons Act 1933.

1.4.4   European Union law

On 1 January 1973, with the coming into force of the European Communities Act 1972, the United Kingdom became a member of the European Community (now the European Union) and in consequence subject to an additional source of law. The 1972 Act was amended in 1986 by the European Communities (Amendment) Act 1986 in order to ratify and implement the Single European Act of 1986. The Single European Act was designed to remove any remaining barriers to the achievement of a truly 'common' market. Within the EU an area without internal frontiers which allows the free movement of goods, services, people and capital was created. The main method for the achievement of the elimination of the barriers to a single internal market would be a major programme of harmonisation. Further commitment to full economic and monetary union was achieved by the signing of the Treaty on European Union or, Maastricht Treaty, in 1991. The Treaty on European Union was ratified and implemented in the United Kingdom by the European Communities (Amendment) Act 1993.

There are four main institutions dealing with the functions of the EU, namely the European Commission, the Council of Ministers, the European Parliament and the European Court of Justice. The European Commission consists of commissioners nominated by member states. A president is appointed from the commissioners. The Commission is charged with implementing the Treaty of Rome (which had established the original European Economic Community), with bringing to the Council of Ministers proposals for furthering the aims of the Union, and with supervising the adherence to the Treaty by the member states.

The term of office of commissioners is four years, though they may resign or be compulsorily retired for misconduct by the Court of Justice before that period expires. Individual commissioners have special responsibilities, or portfolios, e.g., for agriculture and transport. The Commission consists of 20 members. France, Germany, Italy, the United Kingdom and Spain are allowed to appoint two commissioners each while the other member states appoint one each. In 1999, all of the European Union Commissioners resigned following continuing controversial allegations concerning the internal management of their offices. A new group of EU Commissioners, including some of the previous office-holders, has now been appointed.

The Commission initiates most Community legislation and, in some areas, the Commission can enact legislation itself where the Council of Ministers has delegated power to it to do so. As an additional function the Commission can bring any member state or commercial undertaking before the Court of Justice where it feels Community obligations, such as failure to implement a European Union Directive, are not being carried out. The Commission is also responsible for the implementation, through legislative action, of the policy objectives of the Council.

The Council of Ministers is composed of one representative from each of the member states. The representative is usually the Foreign Secretary but others may attend where a matter of importance in a particular field is involved, e.g., if health, it will be the Health Secretary. The Council enacts legislation on proposals from the Commission. For the implementation of some policies, more than a simple majority is required. Other decisions may be taken on a simple majority vote but the majority of decisions required to complete the internal market are decided by 'qualified majority voting' where the votes are based on relative populations.

The European Parliament represents the peoples of the member states, and sits in Brussels, Strasbourg and occasionally Luxembourg. Seats are allocated to member states on the basis of population. The members, who tend to act in political rather than national groups, are elected by the electorate of the state which they represent. The Parliament does not legislate, but advises. However, it is invariably consulted on proposals for legislation and its powers were greatly increased by the Single European Act and the Treaty on European Union. It provides a place where Community problems can be discussed and questions put to the Council and Commission.

The Court of Justice of the European Communities, which is often referred to as the European Court, sits in Luxembourg, and is charged with ensuring that Community law is observed in regard to the interpretation and implementation of the Treaties. The usual manner of achieving this objective is by giving preliminary rulings in relation to the interpretation of the Treaties or other European Union legislation, in cases referred to it by courts and tribunals of member states. The European Court deals with the interpretative aspect of the case, and then refers the case back to the domestic court or tribunal for further rulings on the substantive issues. An example of the operation of this process is to be found in *R* v *Royal Pharmaceutical Society of Great Britain, ex parte Association of Parallel Importers and Others* [1989] 2 All ER 758. In this case the Court of Appeal asked the European Court to make a determination whether certain national measures concerning pharmaceutical products supplied only on prescription were compatible with Articles 30 and 36 of the Treaty of Rome.

The decisions of the European Court must be accepted by the courts of member states and there is no right of appeal. Matters before the court are disposed of in front of all the judges, though some preliminary (or interlocutory) matters can be dealt with by a division of three judges. There are fifteen judges in total assisted by a number of Advocates-General. The role of the Advocates-General is to present a preliminary, objective opinion on the merits of the case. The European Court also has jurisdiction to hear cases involving actions against individual member states, other EU institutions and EU employment cases.

The European Court must not be confused with the European Court of Human Rights, which sits in Strasbourg. This was set up by the Convention for the Protection of Human Rights and Fundamental Freedoms to ensure the observance of the engagements undertaken by contracting states under the Convention. The United Kingdom is one of the states which have signed the Convention. The European Court of Human Rights deals with all matters concerning the interpretation and application of the Convention. One of the most significant amendments introduced by the Single European Act 1986 was the introduction of the Court of First Instance of the European Communities. The jurisdiction of the Court of First Instance is to decide, at first instance, certain specific classes of case. Appeals, on a point of law, lie from the Court of First Instance to the European Court.

The main source of European Union law are the Treaties which established the original Communities and which have been added to by a number of other international agreements. Some parts of the Treaties take direct effect in individual member states and thus create directly enforceable individual rights. The Treaties are sometimes referred to as the primary legislation of the European Union.

There are three principal types of secondary European Union legislation. *Regulations* are of general application in the member countries and, under Article 189 of the Treaty of Rome, in theory become part of domestic law without the need for UK legislation to implement them. *Decisions* are of more particular application, and are also immediately operative. Decisions may be addressed to a state or to an individual or a corporation. Decisions have the force of law but affect the recipient only. *Directives* are under Article 189 binding in principle, but it is left to the member countries to decide upon the means of giving them legal and administrative effect usually within a given time scale. In the United Kingdom, this is dealt with by s. 2 of the European Communities Act 1972, and the most common method of incorporating directives into British law will be by statutory instruments, subject to annulment by 'negative' resolution of Parliament.

The importance of the European Union as a source of pharmacy law cannot be underestimated. As part of the process towards harmonisation of laws between member states, a whole series of directives have been passed which have had a direct effect on the content of our domestic laws relating to aspects of the distribution of medicinal products. For example, Directive 92/27/EEC, which details a series of obligations with regard to the labelling of medicinal products and the provision of information leaflets, discussed in further detail below in chapter nine, led directly to the passing of the Medicines (Labelling) Amendment Regulations 1992 (S.I. 1992/3273) and the Medicines (Leaflets) Amendment Regulations 1992 (S.I. 1992/3274). The process of harmonisation is likely to continue, resulting in a plethora of new legislation implementing the European Union obligations.

Section 3 of the European Communities Act 1972 requires the courts to take note of the provisions of the Treaty of Rome (among others) and also the decisions of the European Court. Although there is considerable controversy about the subject, it is now probably beyond doubt that EU law is supreme. It could therefore be argued that the sovereignty of the United Kingdom Parliament, and the power of the courts, are thereby reduced.

1.5   THE LEGAL SYSTEM

We have already explored many aspects of law and the legal system. In particular, we have examined the methods employed by judges and courts in formulating and developing the law. During that discussion it was noted that the process of law-making occurs as part of the original functions which the courts have to perform. It would be appropriate to review those functions to give an indication of the sources for the resolution of legal disputes. The full court structure in the United Kingdom reflects the principal division of the law into civil and criminal law. Some courts have exclusive criminal or civil jurisdictions. Other courts can hear both civil and criminal cases.

At the lower end of the civil court structure is the magistrates' court. So far as civil jurisdiction is concerned it deals with matrimonial disputes, small debts, ejectment proceedings and licensing applications and renewals. Proceedings are by way of complaint, process and notice. Appeals on decisions of fact lie to the county court, while appeals on a point of law lie to the Court of Appeal. The county court is almost exclusively a civil court. It deals with contract and tort cases up to certain defined values, maintenance, divorce and adoption, licensing, rent and property and, of course, civil appeals from the magistrates' court. An appeal on a point of fact is by way of full re-hearing to the High Court. An appeal on a point of law lies to the Court of Appeal. There is a special county court procedure known as the small claims court which is presided over by district judges. They deal with claims for less than £1,000 by a process of arbitration, or, in certain circumstances, £3,000 by full hearing using the standard county court procedure. Rights of appeal are restrictive when the arbitration process is used.

The High Court has three main divisions. The Queen's Bench Division deals with tort and contract cases together with the very important judicial review process of inferior courts, tribunals and public bodies. The Chancery Division deals with land law, deeds, wills, trusts, company law, liquidations and bankruptcy. The Family Division deals with divorce, maintenance, custody, wardship, adoption and the affairs of the mentally ill. Appeals from the High Court lie to the Court of Appeal and the House of Lords. As noted above, the Court of Appeal and House of Lords on the civil side hear appeals from all the inferior courts on points of law.

To understand the jurisdiction of the criminal courts, it is necessary to have a grasp of the differences between types of criminal offences. A summary offence is a less serious offence which is triable by a judge alone, e.g., careless driving. An indictable offence is a more serious offence which is triable by a judge and jury, e.g., murder. In Northern Ireland some indictable offences, 'scheduled' offences, are tried by a judge sitting alone. A hybrid offence is one which may be tried either summarily or on indictment if certain conditions are satisfied, e.g., theft. This classification of criminal offences carries over to the criminal court structure. It is equally important to remember that a great deal of work relating to a criminal case, e.g., investigation, detection, evidence gathering, remand and bail applications, is carried out before the case comes to court.

On the criminal side, the magistrates' court deals with minor cases, basically those carrying a maximum of six months' imprisonment on any one offence or £5,000 prescribed fine. It is arguable that a magistrate may sentence an offender to more than six months' imprisonment where there are several offences involved or where the offender has a suspended sentence. The sentence may be increased to 24 months where the charge is criminal damage. The magistrates' court also deals with committal proceedings where a decision will be made as to whether to send the accused for trial to the Crown Court. Appeals usually go to the Crown Court or if an important point of law is raised, to the Court of Appeal and House of Lords. The Crown Court deals with more serious offences with a judge and jury. Appeals lie to the Court of Appeal and the House of Lords.

In addition to the civil and criminal courts described above, it is important to remember that there are other specialised courts, concerned with the resolution of particular legal disputes, e.g., juvenile courts, courts-martial and coroners' courts. It is also important to remember that just like courts, tribunals rule on certain issues and make certain pronouncements. They are a very important part of the legal system. In theory, the procedure in tribunals is supposed to be quicker, cheaper, less formal and more private. Tribunals are also supposed to be better suited to dealing with certain types of questions for which they have a specific skill — skills which would not be possessed by judges. The issues which are decided by tribunals are usually factual and so would not require the involvement of the complete legal process.

Tribunals are frequently composed of three members with the chairman usually being legally qualified. It is usual to disregard the formal rules of evidence and formalities identified with judges and professional lawyers. Applicants may be represented by persons other than solicitors or barristers although in some cases legal formality remains the norm. Legal aid for representation is generally not available although the legal advice and assistance scheme may be used. Decisions are usually given to the parties immediately to save costs. The courts do have a role to play in relation to tribunals. They deal with some appeals from certain tribunals and also control tribunals through the judicial review process. Certain tribunals are supervised by the Council on Tribunals, set up in 1958, following the Franks Committee Report. The Council keeps under review the constitution and working of administrative tribunals.

There are three types of legal aid, each of which has separate conditions for qualification. The first of these is the Legal Advice and Assistance scheme. This scheme extends to all legal work but does not usually include proceedings in court. The legal representative can undertake a variety of other work however including writing letters, negotiating, drafting documents, obtaining opinions from counsel and preparing a written case to help someone who has to appear before a tribunal. Eligibility for assistance is based on a financial test relating to an individual's income and capital which must fall within current financial limits. Individuals receiving certain benefits are automatically eligible for legal advice and assistance, provided that their capital does not exceed the relevant limit. The amount which can be claimed under this scheme by legal representatives is extremely limited.

Aid under the Legal Aid for Civil Court Proceedings scheme covers all legal services up to and including the court hearing and includes representation by a solicitor and by a barrister, if necessary. Legal aid is available for cases in all of the civil courts. Eligibility is again based on showing, through the completion of an application form, that the individual's income and capital fall within the appropriate financial limits. However a further test is added whereby the individual seeking civil legal aid must show they have reasonable grounds for taking, defending or being a party to the proceedings and that it is reasonable to receive legal aid in the circumstances of the case.

Legal aid may be free or a contribution may be payable. If the individual wins their case then the amount which will have to be paid will depend on whether the other side is ordered to pay costs, actually does pay those costs, or whether the successful party is awarded money or recovers property as a result of having been successful in the proceedings. If the individual loses their case, all that is usually payable is what is called the maximum contribution. However the court may also make an order for the successful party's costs which will usually depend on the financial circumstances of the losing party.

The Lord Chancellor has major plans for the reform of the Legal Aid for Civil Court Proceedings scheme. Gradually this scheme will be replaced by a contingency fee scheme which will allow lawyers to accept cases on a 'no-win, no-fee' basis. This means that unsuccessful claimants will not have to pay anything towards the cost of their civil action with the lawyer taking out insurance against the event of failure. Under the scheme, successful claimants will agree to pay a percentage of their damages or compensation to their lawyers.

Legal Aid in Criminal Court Proceedings covers representation by a solicitor, and, if necessary, a barrister in the magistrates' courts and the Crown Court, in all matters relating to the proceedings, including applications for bail. Unlike the other schemes, the granting of legal aid in criminal proceedings is entirely at the discretion of the court before which the individual appears. Eligibility in most cases depends on the court being satisfied that it appears desirable in the interests of justice that legal aid should be given and that the means are such that assistance is required. There are no formal financial limits and if criminal legal aid is granted then no contribution is necessary.

The barrister's two main roles are to represent clients in court and to give opinions on points of law. Barristers may not be consulted directly but must be instructed by a client's solicitor. Barristers have full rights of audience in all courts and tribunals. Senior members of the Bar are called Queen's Counsel and have been appointed to that position after a substantial background at the Junior Bar. The General Council of the Bar is the elected representative body of all barristers. It also controls discipline in most matters affecting barristers. Admission to the Bar is closely regulated.

The control of and admission to the solicitors' profession is regulated by the Law Society which also exercises disciplinary powers over solicitors. The solicitor's role is primarily to act as the first point of general advice to the public on all legal matters including conveyancing, wills and the administration of estates, matrimonial and domestic matters, commercial matters, consumer protection and social legislation and compensation awards for injuries. Unlike a barrister, solicitors do not have rights of audience in all courts and tribunals, although the situation is changing.

1.6   WHAT IS PHARMACY LAW?

Pharmacy law might be described as the application of legal rules and principles to the practice of pharmacy. At times those legal rules and principles are similar to those found in other aspects of both ordinary life and professional practice. So pharmacists owe similar duties to the patients with whom they interact as do other health care professionals such as doctors and dentists. Similarly, a pharmacist who has employees is subject to the same legal regulation as any other employer.

Pharmacy law is to be found in a plethora of UK legislation, both primary and secondary, case law and EU legislation. Pharmacy law can be difficult to find as amendments and changes are introduced on a regular basis. Once found, pharmacy law can be difficult to understand. There are aspects of pharmacy law which are highly complex and detailed and the grounding of some pharmacy laws in complicated rules and regulations exacerbates this difficulty.

Pharmacists are assisted in the task of identifying and understanding the detail of pharmacy law by the publication of textbooks such as this which seek to summarise and explain the main provisions. In addition pharmacists are given further guidance by the Royal Pharmaceutical Society of Great Britain, through the pages of the professional journals, and, more importantly, through the publication of *Medicines, Ethics and Practice* which is sent to all pharmacists twice a year. Publications such as this help to identify the principal amendments and assist in the complex process of implementing them into busy, clinical practice.

Pharmacists who have identified legal problems in practice (and they do arise on a regular basis), have a ready and accessible source of advice available in the Legal Information Division of the Royal Pharmaceutical Society of Great Britain. Where the matter cannot be resolved without further recourse to legal action, pharmacists might turn to other professional organisations, such the National Pharmaceutical Association, for assistance. Finally, it may be necessary to consult professional lawyers, particularly where the matter is so serious that the opposing party has already also done so.

1.7 CONCLUSION

The purpose of this chapter has been to equip the reader with the necessary skills to begin the process of analysing the detail of the remainder of the text. The content of the remaining chapters is written on the basis that the reader comprehends a series of basic ideas and theories about the law, and understands a number of fundamental phrases and terms associated with the law.

The material in the subsequent chapters is reasonably complex and detailed. It is to be hoped that the process of mastering that complexity will be facilitated by the analysis undertaken so far. It will also assist pharmacists to begin the task of integrating the law into professional practice. It is important to remember that good pharmacists take the law seriously, both because they are legally obliged to do, and because it is part of the reality of professional pharmacy practice.

TWO

The pharmacist's role in health care

2.1 INTRODUCTION

The practice of pharmacy has made a significant contribution to the development and process of health care over a period of centuries. During that time, pharmacy practice has evolved and expanded in correlation with the health care system of which it forms an integral part. The process is symbiotic. The development and growth of the practice of pharmacy has been necessitated by the parallel enlargement of the health care system; pharmacy having to respond to advancements and improvements in the primary structure in which it is located and operates. In turn, progress in the development of health care has relied on the contribution of all aspects of pharmacy for its success. Modern drug therapy, the most successful intervention in individual patient treatment, requires an effective and productive relationship between pharmacy and health care.

Pharmacy is practised through the roles and responsibilities of pharmacists. In turn, the roles and responsibilities of pharmacists are necessarily shaped by law and so the greater part of this textbook is concerned with analysing and describing the legal reality of the practice of pharmacy by outlining the duties and obligations which surround the roles and functions of pharmacists. Such duties and obligations arise from the countless laws which apply to the organisation, administration, and processes of the pharmacy profession.

However, the current reality of pharmacy and the contemporary roles of pharmacists cannot be described in isolation. Pharmacy, its practice, and its relationship with health care is, and has been dynamic. The existing roles and responsibilities of pharmacists are vastly different from those of their predecessors. Speaking about the changes which have taken place over the past thirty years, David Walker and Stephen Hoag (Foreword to the Symposium on the Evolving Pharmacy Jurisprudence: Changing the Law for a Changing Profession (1996) 44 Drake Law Review No 3 i) have said:

> From a professional practice model that focused almost exclusively on fast and accurate dispensing of prescription medications, we can now observe practitioners involved in planning specific drug therapy for individual patients and in sharing the professional responsibility for drug therapy outcomes.

Changes in the pattern of pharmacy practice, while necessary, are not radical and extreme. New models of practice have built on existing experience, acquired over a considerable period of time. For example, the prevailing model of pharmacy practice, as described by Walker and Hoag, compels pharmacists to use *existing* knowledge of drug therapy in original and creative ways to improve patient outcomes. Existing knowledge is based on centuries spent in its acquisition, so the current roles and responsibilities of pharmacists, which make up the reality of pharmacy practice, can only be understood by examining the origins and sources on which they are based.

An examination of the evolution of professional roles and responsibilities, by necessity, will include a parallel exploration of the development of the laws which have shaped and defined those roles and responsibilities and which make up the legal reality of pharmacy. The process of linking the development of laws to the evolution of roles and responsibilities (or professionalisation) puts the historical review into context. Further the examination of the origins and sources of the prevailing (and still developing) model of pharmacy practice allows for a more authoritative analysis of potential legal implications which might arise from its introduction. In addition, the extent to which new models of professional practice become accepted and recognised is often dependent on the reaction of the law and the legal system. As Walker and Hoag state:

> The extent to which pharmacy becomes under law the profession envisioned by the mission of pharmaceutical care depends significantly upon the extent to which such an expanded role is recognised by judges, legislators, and regulators. What duties pharmacists owe, to whom such duties are owed, what is the relevant standard of care, and what constitutes breach all define the role of pharmacists and the conduct expected of them.

The purpose of this chapter will be to provide a context for the description and analysis which appears in the remaining chapters. That context has three characteristics. First, an historical overview will show how the practice of pharmacy and the pharmacy profession have developed historically in line with the historical development of the pharmaceutical industry and the National Health Service. Secondly, an analysis of models of pharmacy practice, drawing on the historical review, will show how the prevailing roles and responsibilities of pharmacists have evolved and are continuing to evolve. That analysis will show that the pharmacist, as a major contributor to rational drug therapy, is closely linked with two other participants — the manufacturer and the doctor — in the drug distribution process. The nature, extent and relevance of the drug distribution process, and the contributions made to it by these three participants will then be explored. Finally, the chapter will seek to demonstrate how pharmacy is going through a period of re-professionalisation, and is seeking to redefine its role in health care.

2.2   A BRIEF HISTORY OF PHARMACY

The early history of pharmacy is necessarily linked with the early history of medicine. It is possible to trace the history of pharmacy back to biblical times and to early civilisations including those of Babylonia-Assyria, Mesopotamia, ancient Egypt and early Greece. The development of health care continued and indeed expanded through the later Greek, Roman and Arabian periods.

The aspirations of the Romans in the field of war led to the invasion of a variety of countries throughout Europe and beyond. The Roman invasion of Britain ensured that the Graeco-Roman influence over medicine reached this country. The Roman Empire began to break up around the fourth and fifth centuries AD and the following period is often referred to as the Dark Ages. This period saw a decline in the ordered practice of medicine with resultant destructive epidemics. The orthodox practice of medicine fell into the hands of the church and became known as monastic medicine.

At the same time, however, a trend developed in Europe to rely on the growing expertise provided by the Graeco-Arabic tradition. This trend resulted in the refinement of ancient Roman and Greek works, allowing the scientific study of medicine to re-emerge. In Germany, at the court of Frederick II, court apothecaries were involved in the translation into Latin of the main Arabic works of medicine and pharmacy. In or around 1240, Frederick II, no doubt due to the influence of the apothecaries at his court, issued an edict on the regulation of pharmacy which was to have a profound effect on the development of the pharmacy profession. The role of the pharmacist as an established and distinct member of the health care team was established by that edict.

In Britain, monastic medicine, based on the development of that mode of practice throughout the rest of Europe, did flourish for a while. However, unlike the developments in Europe, no separate profession of apothecary had emerged. Rather the function of physician, apothecary and surgeon were carried out by the same person. The real origins of pharmacy in Great Britain lay in the development of a trading community.

Trade with Continental Europe had continued from Roman times and began to take on a greater significance after the Norman invasion and the Crusades.

Commodities were introduced under the headings of 'mercery' and 'spicery' and certainly included drugs and medicines. Spicery in Britain was dealt with by traders known as spicers and pepperers. The development of increased trade brought with it a parallel development of the guild system as traders and merchants began to take on an increasing importance. Both the spicers and the pepperers, as important traders and merchants, formed their own guilds. Some spicers began to specialise in the dispensing and compounding of medicines and began to take on the mantle of apothecary.

Apothecaries mainly involved themselves with the practice of pharmacy and became more and more specialised in that function. By the end of the fifteenth century, an open conflict between the apothecaries, now specialised practitioners of pharmacy, and physicians began to emerge. Until then physicians had been keen to protect their own interests and establish a position in society which would reflect their growing professional status. The apothecaries were involved in the practice of medicine as well as in the preparation and dispensing of drugs and it was this drift into the spheres traditionally occupied by physicians which was to cause conflict. A Regulation, of Henry VIII, often referred to as the first Medical Act, attempted to resolve this conflict, by specifying that no person could practise medicine until he had been examined, approved and admitted by the Bishop of London or the Dean of St Paul's. This regulatory protection restricted the practice of medicine to the physicians.

This process by the physicians, of restriction of the right to practise and the maintenance of a privileged position within the health care system, continued through the early part of the sixteenth century. The College of Physicians was founded in 1518. A new Medical Act in 1543 acknowledged the position of the apothecaries, and others, as preparers of medicinal products and gave them the right to administer those products without the regulatory requirement of examination and licensing.

After being given a charter establishing a new guild, by James 1 in 1617, the apothecaries were organised into a Society of Apothecaries. However the continuing movement of the apothecaries into the practice of medicine led the College of Physicians to bring an action in the courts. The court found that it was in the public interest for apothecaries to add the function of giving medical advice to their traditional functions of compounding and selling medicines. The net effect of the decision in this case was that the majority of apothecaries turned their attentions to the practice of medicine or surgery leaving the maintenance of their shops in the hands of their assistants.

The assistants of the apothecary, who were left with responsibility for the running of the shop while the apothecary visited his patients, were either apprentices of the apothecary or were 'druggists', who received their name by virtue of their former trade in spices and drugs. These dispensing assistants acquired expert knowledge themselves particularly in relation to the *materia medica* of the day which allowed them to leave their apothecary masters and open their own shops.

Disputes arose between the apothecaries who had moved into the practice of medicine, the physicians whose monopoly they had sought to break and the chemists and druggists who wished to obtain control over the sale and dispensing of medicines. Concessions were given by the apothecaries to the newly organised chemists and druggists through the Apothecaries Act of 1815.

The 1815 Act gave powers to the Society of Apothecaries to control the professional standards and medical education in England and Wales. The Act recognised that the physicians would continue to practise medicine and imposed an obligation on the apothecary to dispense and prepare medicines as directed by a physician. That right and the right to inspect the shops and drugs of an apothecary, retained by the Society of Apothecaries under the legislation, was not exercisable against the chemists and druggists. Further the apothecaries were subject to rigid examination, qualification and admittance procedures.

The Apothecaries Act had the secondary effect of moving the apothecaries further towards the practice of medicine, leaving the practice of pharmacy in the hands of the chemists and druggists. Those chemists and druggists who did not have an interest in the practice of pharmacy developed into wholesalers and ultimately into manufacturers, leading directly to the formation of some of today's familiar names in the pharmaceutical industry.

Among these companies there was little commitment to pharmaceutical investigation or product development. The major developments were continuing in Europe, based on earlier work undertaken in France and Germany in the eighteenth century. The synthetic dye industry developed through companies such as Bayer and Hoechst in Germany. This industry was the basis of the evolution of a number of important pharmaceutical products by the end of the nineteenth century. Antipyrine for fever had been produced by Hoechst in 1883 with Bayer introducing phenacetin for fever and pain in 1888. Very soon Bayer made the major breakthrough in the development of aspirin. The work of Paul Erhlich at the start of century led directly to the development of products which could cure disease.

The recognition of the status of chemists and druggists as preparers and dispensers of drugs and medicines convinced some prominent chemists and druggists of the value of having a body to organise the practice of pharmacy, protect the interests of chemists and druggists and promote and advance the profession through the establishment of appropriate training, qualification and admission requirements. In 1841, a resolution for the formation of such a body was formally adopted. The laws and constitution of the new Pharmaceutical Society were adopted in June of that year.

Regulations were quickly formulated for examinations for admittance to the qualification of pharmaceutical chemist. The first candidates for examination were admitted in 1842 and a School of Pharmacy was formed in the same year. A royal charter was granted to the Society on 18 February 1843. The charter outlined in detail the requirements for membership, provisions for examination, regulations for the administration of the Society, the Constitution of the Society and by-laws for its administration and day-to-day running.

Members of the Society were instrumental in promoting the Pharmacy Act of 1852. This Act confirmed the charter and by-laws of the Pharmaceutical Society, established procedures for the carrying out of the statutory obligations of the Society and set up a system for the registration of chemists and druggists.

The grant of the royal charter of incorporation, the influence exercised in the passing of the Pharmacy Act 1852 and the introduction of relevant pharmacy journals increased greatly the status of the Pharmaceutical Society. This growing status was reinforced when the Society was asked to assist in the development of a British Pharmacopoeia which appeared under that title in 1864.

The 1852 Act did not ensure that the practice of pharmacy would be limited to those who were examined and registered by the Pharmaceutical Society. The wholesale chemists and druggists formed their own Society in 1861, the United Society of Chemists and Druggists. For the next seven years the United Society and the Pharmaceutical Society claimed to control the development of the pharmacy profession. A compromise was reached between both Societies which resulted in the passing of the Pharmacy Act 1868.

The 1868 Act made it unlawful for any person to sell or keep open a shop for retailing, dispensing or compounding poisons — a schedule in the Act listed the articles to be defined as poisons — use the titles 'Chemist and/or Druggist' or 'Pharmacist' or 'Dispensing Chemist' unless that person was a pharmaceutical chemist or chemist and druggist within the meaning of the Act and was duly registered under the Act.

A register of pharmaceutical chemists and chemists and druggists and assistants was to be maintained by the Pharmaceutical Society. Entry to the register was confined to pharmaceutical chemists and to those already in the business as chemists and druggists, subject to a certification that they were so in business and to a certification that they were suitable to be registered. Thereafter entry to the register would be subject to examination with the Pharmaceutical Society as the examining body.

The Pharmacy Acts Amendment Act 1898 made all chemists and druggists eligible for election to full membership of the Pharmaceutical Society. Other amendments were also made to the constitution of the Society which were to make it more representative of all aspects of the pharmacy profession.

The wording of the 1868 Act continued to create difficulties. One particular problem related to the increase in the development of the proprietary medicine trade and retailing by co-operatives, department stores and pharmacy chains owned by limited companies. These retailers often used the title 'chemist'. Matters came to a head in the case of *Pharmaceutical Society* v *London and Supply Association* (1885) 5 App Cas 857, where the House of Lords decided that limited liability companies might use the titles contained in the 1868 Act without penalty.

In 1896 the Proprietary Articles Trade Association was formed for the purpose of the establishment of resale price maintenance. In 1899 the Chemists' Defence Association was also formed for the purpose of regulating the pharmacy profession and for ensuring the right of chemists to dispense. The London Wholesale Drug and Chemical Protection Society had been formed in 1867 and the Drug Club in 1891.

The decision in the *London and Supply Association* case did not fully resolve the issue of the use of titles by limited liability companies. The problem was only resolved by the passing of the Pharmacy Act 1908. Under this Act, corporate bodies could use the title of 'Chemist and Druggist' provided that a pharmacist was appointed as a qualified superintendent to control and manage all aspects of the company's dealings in poisons. The superintendent also had to be a member of the Board of Directors of the company. The titles 'Pharmaceutical Chemist', 'Pharmaceutist' and 'Pharmacist' were restricted to the existing pharmaceutical chemists, including the former chemists and druggists.

Section 4 of the 1908 Act extended the Pharmaceutical Society's powers in relation to the education of those training for the pharmacy profession. The Society could make by-laws in relation to courses of study and examinations which were required of candidates seeking registration as pharmaceutical chemists and chemists and druggists. The Act also contained amendments to the previous legislative provisions relating to poisons, a matter which had been concerning the Pharmaceutical Society for some time.

The Pharmaceutical Society was able to convince the promoters of the National Insurance legislation that the pharmacist was the correct person to supervise directly the dispensing of national insurance prescriptions and that all contracts for the dispensing of such prescriptions should be restricted to those in business as pharmaceutical chemists. This development ensured that the principal functions for pharmacists after the passing of the National Health Insurance Act 1911, would be dispensing and compounding.

The extension and development of the pharmacist's role following the passage of the national insurance legislation had the incidental effect of bringing into question the role and powers of the Pharmaceutical Society in relation to the trading and employment conditions of its members. In a friendly action to determine the question, *Jenkin* v *The Pharmaceutical Society* [1921] Ch 392, the High Court indicated that the expenditure of the funds of the Pharmaceutical Society in the formation of an industrial council committee for the regulation of the trading and employment conditions of its members would have the effect of turning the Society into a trade union.

Such a course of action would be contrary to the objects of the Society as contained in its Charter. The net effect of this decision was the formation of an association for the express purpose of protecting the interests of employee pharmacists. This was known initially as the Retail Pharmacists Union, then the National Pharmaceutical Union and is in existence now as the National Pharmaceutical Association.

Following the government's proposals to introduce a Bill relating to patent medicines in 1919, a new group called the Association of Manufacturers of British Proprietaries was formed with membership open to the owners of British owned or manufactured proprietary medicines, appliances and foods. This association spent most of its first seven years of existence negotiating with the government over the possibility of the introduction of proprietary medicines legislation. When the possibility of this initially ran out in 1926, the association changed its name to the Proprietary Association of Great Britain. Under this title the association continued in its role of regulating the proprietary medicines industry in Great Britain. It is still performing this function today.

The Drug Club, which was the successor to the London Wholesale Drug and Chemical Protection Society, joined the Chemists' Supply Association in 1930 to form the Wholesale Drug Trade Association. This development had a significant impact on the formation of the Association of the British Pharmaceutical Industry which today represents the interests of the companies in Great Britain which produce prescription medicines.

The Pharmaceutical Society was now in a position to devote its attention to the development of the discipline of pharmacy. The period from 1920 saw the formation of a number of local associations and organisations to advance and promote pharmaceutical science. In addition it was proposed to have an annual meeting of the delegates of those associations to discuss developments in the science of pharmacy; a compromise was eventually reached with the existing British Pharmaceutical Conference to continue the annual meetings under that name. The Pharmaceutical Society was also instrumental during this period in developing journals, a codex, and revisions to the British Pharmacopoeia. Pharmacological laboratories were also opened to deal with the requirements of the Therapeutic Substances Act 1925 in relation to the control of certain substances.

During this period it was also thought necessary to consider amendments to the poisons legislation, the developments within medicine and science prompting the possibility of review. At the same time the Pharmaceutical Society saw the possibility of a review of the poisons legislation as an opportunity to review the pharmacy profession. The Pharmacy and Poisons Act was passed in 1933. Under the 1933 Act membership of the Pharmaceutical Society became compulsory. The distinction between registration and membership was abolished. Every person registered as a pharmacist became, by virtue of that registration, a member of the Pharmaceutical Society. Annual fees for membership became payable in addition to the registration fee.

A statutory committee was established with the power to supervise the functions and activities of registered pharmacists whether individuals or companies. The Pharmaceutical Society was given the power to enforce the provisions of the Act. These supervisory and enforcement powers included the disciplinary power to remove names from the register and inspect premises through inspectors appointed for that purpose. In addition to these provisions relating specifically to pharmacy a great deal of the Act was taken up with provisions relating to poisons.

The 1933 legislation reinforced the position of the Pharmaceutical Society in relation to the pharmacy profession in the UK. Pharmacy was recognised as a discipline concerned with dispensing and compounding, the control of drugs products and medicines and the advancement of the science of pharmacy and pharmacology. The Pharmaceutical Society was seen as a self-governing body which had control over its own affairs and was the principal regulator and administrator of the members of the pharmacy profession.

Following the passage of the 1933 Act, the Council of the Pharmaceutical Society established a committee to enquire into the future of pharmacy. When its report was published in 1941, it placed a strong emphasis on the discipline of pharmacy as opposed to its commercial aspects. The report also emphasised the requirement for a code of ethics for the profession. In the same year, 1941, the Pharmacy and Medicines Act was passed which made some minor amendments to the scheme governing the advertisement of remedies for a list of specific diseases.

Over the next thirty years the pivotal position of the pharmacy profession and the Pharmaceutical Society was strengthened by a number of pieces of legislation. The most significant of these was the legislation which introduced the new national health service.

2.3   THE NATIONAL HEALTH SERVICE

It is arguable that the history of the National Health Service may be traced back as far as the eighteenth and even the seventeenth centuries. Much of the poor law and public health legislation was enacted during that century and many of the 'voluntary' hospitals were built and financed by, largely, religious philanthropists to provide medical services to the poor at that time.

The starting point for the development of the modern day health service was the introduction of proposals for a National Health Insurance scheme by Lloyd George in 1911. While the National Health Insurance Act 1911, which implemented these proposals, ensured that a large percentage of the population would have some access to medical care, it was the problems associated with the administration and running of the scheme which led to a consensus view by the late 1930s that change would have to come about.

The administrative arrangements for the provision of the benefits under the 1911 schemes were too detailed; the range of medical benefits obtained was basic; problems existed with the range and distribution of hospital services, largely associated with the dual system for the provision of hospital services; there was little collaboration between the voluntary and public hospital systems; the hospital sector, both voluntary and public, quickly developed significant financial problems; there were significant shortages in the physical facilities available and in the skill of the practitioners within those facilities;

general practitioner services were geographically maldistributed; and clinical conditions were highly unsatisfactory.

The combined effect of all of the problems described above was a growing collective awareness that change was necessary. Following the end of the First World War — when the problems with the provision of medical services described above were greatly exacerbated — a number of reports, recommendations and interim reforms were published and introduced which were designed to address the issue of the state of the provision of health services.

These included the report of the Dawson Committee published in 1920, the Cave Committee in 1921, the Local Government Act 1929, the two reports of the Royal Commission on National Health Insurance published in 1926, the two reports of the British Medical Association in 1930 and 1938, the agenda of the Socialist Medical Association published in 1933, the Ministry of Health series of papers on reform of the hospital sector commenced in 1939, the report of the British Medical Association's Medical Planning Commission in 1942, and hospital surveys undertaken by the Minister of Health in 1941.

This series of background reports and recommendations formed the background for the report of the Committee on Social Insurance and Allied Services, chaired by Sir William Beveridge which is usually recognised as the most important factor leading to the formation of the National Health Service. The recommendations of the Beveridge Committee were based on a number of assumptions including comprehensive health services. In brief the government accepted the principle of this assumption, and after a series of discussions with a number of relevant interest groups, including pharmacists, sought to bring its policies into the open through the publication of a White Paper *A National Health Service* in 1944.

The victory for the Labour Party in the general election of 1945 brought Aneurin Bevan to the Ministry of Health. By early December 1945, the Minister was able to outline to the Cabinet proposals for the introduction of a national health service and was able to ask for authority to prepare a Bill for consideration. Early in January 1946, a further paper with an outline scheme which followed closely the recommendations contained in the 1944 White Paper was produced for the Cabinet and sent to a number of interested parties including representatives of the medical profession and pharmacists.

A draft Bill was introduced to the Cabinet on 1 March and approved by its members on 8 March. The National Health Service Bill was published on 20 March 1946. Accompanying the Bill was a White Paper which summarised the details of the implementation and administration of the new comprehensive health service. The National Health Services Bill went through its Parliamentary stages between 20 March and 6 November 1946. Because the new scheme would lead to such radical changes in the provision of health services, it was not due to come into operation until 5 July 1948.

In the interim opposition to the contents of the legislation continued and conflict with the medical profession seemed to be inevitable. The difficulty for the Government was that it still needed to enact detailed regulations to complete the scheme and establish an effective administration to run it, both of which would require the collaboration of the medical and pharmacy profession. The National Health Service (Amendment) Act 1949, was introduced to satisfy some of the concerns of both the medical and pharmacy professions and was sufficient to allow both to resolve to enter the new service.

2.4   THE DEVELOPMENT OF RELATIONSHIPS BETWEEN THE NHS, THE PHARMACEUTICAL INDUSTRY AND PHARMACY

In late March 1948, the first set of regulations governing the general medical and pharmaceutical services of the National Health Service were published. The National Health Service (General Medical and Pharmaceutical Services) Regulations 1948 (S.I. 1948/506) were the first official statement of the proposed arrangements for the supply of drugs, medicines and prescribed appliances to persons receiving general medical services.

The proposal for the introduction of the prescription charge was first mooted in October 1949 after the review of the first twelve months of the service. By that stage 187 million prescriptions at an average cost of 14p each had been dispensed, representing close to one-tenth of the total cost of the service and financial estimates for the second year of the service had been predicting a large increase in the running costs of the service. Enabling legislative provisions — through s. 16 of the National Health Service (Amendment) Act 1949 — were put onto the statute books.

However it was not until 1952 that the prescription charge was finally introduced. The National Health Service (Charges for Drugs and Appliances) Regulations 1952 (S.I. 1952/102) were made on 23 May 1952 and came into force on 1 June 1952.

The passing of the 1946 National Health Insurance Act ensured that the pharmacist's primary function within the health care scheme was the dispensing and compounding of medical prescriptions. The Pharmaceutical Society was anxious to ensure that the training of pharmacists should be carefully controlled and its 1941 Committee of Enquiry had recommended minimum standards of entry. By the 1950s these had become three years of academic study leading to the award of a pharmaceutical chemist diploma or a degree. By the late 1960s the minimum requirement for registration as a pharmacist had become an approved degree in pharmacy followed by a period of supervised practical experience.

The 1953 Pharmacy Act abolished the existing register of chemists and druggists and instead established a new Register of Pharmaceutical Chemists. By this time it was also felt that concentration of the existing charter of incorporation and the existing legislation was necessary. A supplemental charter was granted on 19 November 1953. This charter recognised the new developments in the profession of pharmacy and the movement away from the earlier ideas by having as a principal objective the maintenance of the honour and the safeguarding and promotion of the interests of the members in the exercise of the profession of pharmacy. In 1954 a new Pharmacy Act was passed to consolidate the existing legislation which was contained in a great number of Acts, regulations etc. The new Act also made certain changes in the classification of membership of the Pharmaceutical Society.

Although the pharmaceutical industry in the UK was slow to respond to the growing demands of the National Health Service as a new user of its products, foreign companies were quick to grasp the opportunity to take over existing, well-known United Kingdom companies and form new multi-national concerns ready to exploit the new opportunities. The new companies were soon involved in the large-scale production of innovative, complex drug products necessitating high levels of purity, consistency, stability and efficacy.

The important early work of Ehrlich had led to the development of chemicals which could be tailored to destroy the micro-organisms which caused disease. The impact took full effect in the 1930s and 1940s with the isolation of sulphanilamide and the synthesis and testing of members of the sulphonamide family. During and after the Second World War the development of antibiotics, as part of the research work on the limitations of penicillin was the priority. Streptomycin was developed in 1943 and the post-war period ('the golden age of drug discovery') saw the development of a wide range of new drug products from laboratories and from a rapidly developing industry.

The large-scale growth in the number of prescriptions dispensed had a dramatic effect on the work of the pharmacist. After the introduction of the National Health Service the pharmacist spent less time acting as the first point of contact for the patient and sold fewer over-the-counter medicines. As a corollary the amount of time devoted to dispensing and the income to be derived from it increased significantly. In 1937 the income obtained from the dispensing of 65 million prescriptions represented about 10 per cent of the total income of the 13,000 pharmacies in the United Kingdom. By 1984 the income from the dispensing of almost 400 million prescriptions by 12,000 pharmacies had risen to 70 per cent of the total turnover.

By the middle of the 1960s — and despite the impact of the thalidomide disaster — the pattern established following the rapid development of the pharmaceutical industry and the increase in the numbers of prescriptions being dispensed under the National Heath Service schemes was continuing. The Sainsbury Committee, established to examine the relationship of the pharmaceutical industry with the National Health Service, was able to note the increasing numbers of prescriptions being dispensed under the National Health Service, the effect that this growth was having on the pharmaceutical industry in the United Kingdom and the growing reliance by the pharmacy profession on this growth as the major element of their income. That pattern has been maintained through to the 1990s.

2.5 CURRENT PHARMACY ROLES IN HEALTH CARE

This historical analysis has shown that the pharmacist has a fundamental role in the provision of health care and the drug distribution process. As the historical analysis has shown, the pharmacist's role in health care is directly linked to the roles of two other significant participants in that system, i.e., the doctor and the manufacturer of drug products.

In the United Kingdom, although the position is changing, the doctor (as general practitioner) will be the primary source of health care advice for the vast majority of patients. The doctor's role in health care practice is to use his or her knowledge, training, clinical experience and acquired subjective and objective evidence from the patient, to assess the patient's health care problem and to develop and implement a therapeutic plan to alleviate the difficulty. Knowledge, training and clinical experience will necessarily include information and expertise in the practice and expected outcomes of drug therapy. That knowledge may have been acquired through initial and continuing education, clinical practice or, importantly, through the marketing endeavours of the manufacturers of drug products.

The development of the therapeutic plan will often involve the writing of prescriptions for drug products. Occasionally it may also involve the actual distribution of drug products, either in an emergency situation, or because of the particular geographical location of the health care practice. However, it is clear from the statistics that the therapeutic plans for the alleviation of health care problems frequently involve the writing of prescriptions for drug products, and that the vast majority of drug products distributed in the National Health Service are done by prescription.

Again, although the position is changing, the doctor's expectations of the patient are to assist the implementation and outcome of the therapeutic plan by presenting the prescriptions to be dispensed and to take the prescribed drug product as instructed. The doctor's expectations of the pharmacist are to interpret the contents of the prescription, check its validity, dispense the prescription and give appropriate verbal or written instructions as to how to take the medicine.

It is important to note, therefore, that while the doctor has direct clinical contact with the patient, it is often the case that he she does not have direct drug distribution contact. The sales of certain drug products are usually conducted by a pharmacist or other distributor with legal authority to sell. Certain other drug products must be distributed through an intermediary, i.e., the dispensing pharmacist.

The manufacturer's initial role in health care is to develop drug products through a variety of stages — discovery, test, trial and licence. The manufacturer's secondary role is to market the drug product to health care professionals and patients and the final role is to distribute and/or sell the drug product to patients. Distribution and sale may be undertaken either directly through sales, or via a health care professional through prescription disbursement.

It is important to note, therefore, that the manufacturer does not have direct distribution contact with the patient. Certain sales are usually conducted by a pharmacist or other distributor with legal authority to sell. Other drug products are distributed through two intermediaries — the prescribing health care professional and the dispensing pharmacist.

The pharmacist's primary role in health care is to use his or her technical expertise to interpret the details of the prescription, to ensure that the prescription is valid, to dispense the drug product which has been prescribed or, in certain circumstances, an equivalent drug, to give instructions to the patient on the use of the drug, including possible side-effects, through appropriate verbal or written directions. That role equates with the expectations of the prescribing doctor, as described above. The pharmacist's secondary role in health care is act as a source of advice for the patient who has a self-formulated, or doctor-assisted therapeutic plan involving the use of drug therapy. That drug therapy includes the provision of drug products available either exclusively through the pharmacy, or both in the pharmacy and other outlets.

2.6 CURRENT PHARMACY ROLES IN THE DRUG DISTRIBUTION PROCESS

The pharmacist's role in the drug distribution process can best be understood by reference to the classification of drug products.

Part of the rationale behind the passing of the Medicines Act 1968 was the control of the retail sales of medicines. The method by which this aspiration was to be achieved was the restriction of the supply of medicines through pharmacies. There are, of course, a number of exceptions to that general rule. Certain drug products have been classified as capable of being sold, with reasonable safety, to members of the public without the supervision of a pharmacist. Certain other medicines may be sold by a hospital or health centre where there is no pharmacy under certain restricted circumstances. Other drug products may be supplied directly by a doctor to a patient, either in an emergency situation, or because of the particular geographical location of the health care practice.

Those medicinal products which in the opinion of the appropriate Ministers can, with reasonable safety, be sold or supplied otherwise than by or under the supervision of a pharmacist, are known as general sale list (GSL or OTC (over the counter)) medicines and are listed in the General Sale List Order. The sale or supply of GSL medicines is not restricted to pharmacies. These drug products may be sold or supplied from other shops, subject to certain legislative requirements. Further details on these, and other legislative requirements relating to GSL medicines, are provided in chapter eight.

Prescription only medicines (POM) may only be sold or supplied in a registered pharmacy, by or under the supervision of a pharmacist, in accordance with the prescription of a doctor, or other health care professional. Such drug products are described in the Prescription Only Medicine (Human Use) Order 1997. The rationale behind such a restriction is that the use of such products in treatment needs to be supervised by a doctor or other health care professional because they may produce a toxic reaction or physical or psychological dependence, or may endanger the health of the community. There are detailed regulations on the nature and form of registered pharmacies, the training and accreditation of registered pharmacists and the form of valid prescriptions, all of which are described below in chapter five.

Pharmacy (P) medicines are a default category in that all medicines which are not GSL or POM are automatically P medicines. They must be sold in a registered pharmacy by or under the supervision of a pharmacist. Incidentally, a retail pharmacy business must be under the personal control of a pharmacist so far as it concerns the sale of all medicinal products, including products on the general sale list. Again, full details of the legislative requirements relating to P medicines are provided below in chapter eight.

What is clear from this analysis is that the pharmacist, unlike the other two participants in the drug distribution process, has direct distributive contact with the patient in relation to all three categories of medicinal drug products. The pharmacist may recommend and/or sell GSL medicines, has direct control over the sale and supply of P medicines, and is directly responsible for the distribution of the vast majority of POM medicines. It is clear that such an allocation of responsibility has direct legal consequences for the pharmacist. Some of these consequences are discussed below in chapter thirteen.

2.7   A CHANGING ROLE FOR PHARMACISTS

The pharmacist performs a fundamental role as a provider within the health care team. Without the technical expertise described above, patients would not be in a position to complete their treatment. The pharmacist's role is therefore crucial. The fundamental technical decisions which a pharmacist has to make in relation to the treatment of patients, are surrounded by a number of legal duties and obligations which the pharmacist must fulfil. These duties and obligations arise from the myriad laws which apply to the administration of the pharmacy profession.

The practice of pharmacy, therefore, has a legal reality and pharmacists have to consider carefully what their legal responsibilities are. The pharmacist's primary concern will be to satisfy specific legal duties with regard to the prescription which has been presented. However pharmacists will also have to consider a number of general legal obligations which affect not only them but other employees both within and without the health care system. Pharmacists may also owe legal obligations to employers and to the patients as individuals.

The legal issues facing pharmacists can themselves be complex and confusing but it is true to say that by 2000 both case law, legislation and international laws are extremely relevant to the practice of pharmacy. As we have seen, those laws relate to and indeed have been formulated to reflect the role and functions which pharmacists perform.

However it is true to say that the role and functions of the pharmacist have changed from those experienced as recently as thirty years ago. The modern pharmacist's primary role, as described above, is different from that experienced in the past. There is undoubtedly a great deal of professional skill and expertise involved in that process, reflected in the plethora of legislation surrounding the dispensing of drugs and the recognition by the courts of legal liability for failure to perform routine dispensing functions. However it is an adapted and altered role. To take an example, compounding would rarely take place in the modern pharmacy. Most drug products arrive in the pharmacy in a form and makeup which allows pharmacists, once they have established that all other requirements have been fulfilled, to dispense the product easily and quickly.

It is possible to trace the reasons for the change in the pharmacist's role to that of a dispenser of drug products. In the United Kingdom at least, the principal reasons why the community pharmacist has become a dispenser of medicines and drug products prescribed by medical practitioners are the advent of the National Health Service and the spectacular growth of the international research-based pharmaceutical industry.

As we have seen, the period from the 1940s to the 1980s saw the National Health Service changing radically the provision of health care within the United Kingdom. In parallel with and almost as a corollary to the birth of the NHS, the evolution of the pharmaceutical industry had the most significant technological and scientific impact on the practice of medicine within the National Health Service structure. These two determinants forced community pharmacy into accepting certain roles and functions as providers of health care.

The acceptance of those particular roles and functions led some to question the future of pharmacy as a profession and to criticise pharmacists' current standing and reputation. It would only seem natural that pharmacists would not take such criticism lightly. Pharmacists hardly see themselves as routine technicians counting pills and typing labels. Current literature on the pharmacy profession published by the profession itself, describes pharmacists as trusted and highly-organised health care professionals, ready and willing to undertake more and more health care functions and to play a vital part in health education, health checks and preventative medicine.

As a result, a major debate about the role which the pharmacist should take within the health care system has emerged — a debate which has been entered into by pharmacists themselves, by general practitioners, has been taken up by government, has led to the establishment of inquiries, and has been commented upon by a wide range of academics and others.

Everyone would appear to be agreed that pharmacists need to adopt some sort of new or at least, 'extended' role but are undecided precisely what that role should be. It is further agreed that the role should be one which builds upon the existing expertise of the pharmacist in relation to drugs and drug therapy (the basis of their technical training) but which would see the pharmacist becoming more actively and directly involved in patient care.

While the idea of a 'patient-oriented' practice for pharmacy has been around for some time, the debate has recently taken off in the United States of America. Current research on the role of the pharmacist in patient care is confirming that pharmacy should expand into new areas beyond those traditionally expected of the profession. The principal suggestion is that pharmacy practice should move a step beyond the traditional technical model where the primary function of the pharmacist is to process prescriptions, to a new model where the pharmacist is involved in rational drug therapy. The new model has become known as 'pharmaceutical care' which is defined as:

> The responsible provision of drug therapy for the purpose of achieving definite outcomes that improve a person's quality of life. (Hepler, C. D. and Strand, L. M., 'Opportunities and Responsibilities in Pharmaceutical Care (1989) *American Journal of Pharmacy Education*, No. 53, p. 12S.)

The practice of pharmaceutical care obliges the pharmacist to share responsibility for the design, implementation and monitoring of a therapeutic plan which seeks to achieve a set of desired therapeutic objectives. As an essential element of health care, the practice of pharmaceutical care must be carried out in co-operation with patients and other professional members of the health care team. It is clear, however, that pharmaceutical care is provided for the direct benefit of the patient and the pharmacist must accept direct responsibility for the quality of that care.

Pharmaceutical care moves the practice of pharmacy beyond the traditional model where the primary function of the community pharmacist is to dispense prescriptions, to a new model where the pharmacist is involved in rational drug therapy. Within this new model, pharmacists, in their professional capacity, continue to function as experts in the dispensing of drugs but also collect/find and interpret evidence relating to specific clinical questions and provide information that permits patients to assess risk, enhance their autonomy, and develop their own medication practice.

When patients obtain their medicines they may choose not to take the drug at all or to take it in a certain way based on their own individual social and familial circumstances. The patient has a great deal of autonomy in deciding whether or not to take a drug, is largely unsupervised in making that decision and has no one with the appropriate knowledge of their individual circumstances to assist them in making rational and careful decisions about self-administration and re-administration.

The community pharmacist is well placed to fill this void and assume a client-specific role with respect to decisions about drug taking. Pharmacists are highly trained in the science of drug therapy, are readily available in the community in which they live and are highly regarded and trusted by members of that community. As a result of this, pharmacists often have a greater access to information about the prescription process relating to a particular patient.

The pharmacist in this new role is still concerned with the initial choice of prescription and more concerned with patient outcomes, using patient-specific evidence to monitor and manage the patient's care. This role equates with the current expectations of the profession, applying existing knowledge of drug therapy in original and creative ways to improve patient outcomes. The new role naturally requires co-operation with patients and with the members of the primary health care team. However the pharmacist's intervention is provided for the direct benefit of the patient and the pharmacist must accept direct professional responsibility for the quality of that intervention.

The pharmacist in the pharmaceutical care system is less concerned with initial choice of prescription and more concerned with monitoring, management and patient outcomes. The pharmacist in such a system will use patient-specific evidence to monitor and manage the patient's care. Pharmaceutical care changes episodic drug therapy to coherent, continual care. Responsibility for patient outcomes is spread from the individual (doctor) to the team (all health care providers).

The consequences of this proposed expansion may be significant. The courts in the United States have begun to indicate that declarations of professionalism and expansion of function carry with them the likelihood of liability for failure to maintain professional standards or for failure to perform that function. Those findings have been augmented by the imposition of new duties by federal legislation.

Those involved with the regulation and control of the pharmacy profession in the United Kingdom have also begun to recognise that the adoption of new professional roles has important legal, as well as professional consequences. Further, those with the responsibility of representing the legal interests and welfare of those affected by health care decisions, have realised that judicial recognition of the expanded role is important in that careless performance of that role may result in the imposition of liability and the award of substantial damages. Some of the legal implications of the adoption of the extended role by pharmacists are explored below in chapters ten and thirteen.

2.8   PHARMACY ROLES AND THE NATIONAL HEALTH SERVICE

The historical analysis, and the overview of the pharmacist's role in health care undertaken above, demonstrates that the pharmacist is inextricably linked to the National Health Service. Over a considerable period of time, the pharmacy profession has negotiated for its members a virtually exclusive monopoly on the distribution of certain medicinal drug products. The distribution of those drug products (POM and P medicines) makes up a significant part of the professional role and functions of pharmacists, and incidentally, provides them with the greater portion of their income.

The National Health Service remains the most significant medium through which the pharmacy profession is able to exercise its exclusive monopoly on the distribution of certain drug products. The historical analysis shows that the pharmacy profession had a significant input to the initial structure and form of the National Health Service in the knowledge that the exclusive provision of pharmaceutical services would reinforce, augment and develop the pharmacist's existing professional role.

The significance of the continuation and furtherance of the link is demonstrated in the statistics relating to the dispensing of National Health Service prescriptions and the cost to the National Heath Service of that provision. In 1995 (the latest year for which such statistics are available), 545 million National Health Service prescriptions, costing £4,711 million were dispensed in the United Kingdom. Of these 83.8 per cent were dispensed exempt of any prescription charge.

The relationship between pharmacy and the National Health Service is not only a health care relationship, or an economic relationship, but is also a legal relationship. Exclusivity of role and participation has been recognised and enforced through a range of laws designed to prohibit others from participating in the process. In turn, the award of exclusivity is dependent upon the adoption of legal rights, duties and responsibilities for the provision of the service. The full extent of this legal relationship between pharmacy and the National Health Service is explored in the next chapter.

2.9   THE PHARMACIST'S OTHER ROLES

The pharmacist is a unique member of the primary health care team in having a further set of roles and functions, arising from, but not necessarily linked to the health care process. Foremost among these roles is the capacity to manage significant commercial interests. In addition, a pharmacist may be the employer of a substantial number of employees. The legal implications of the adoption of these further roles are important for pharmacists. Most of these legal rules are not unique to pharmacy but they can and do have a pharmacy context.

It might be added that it is equally important for the pharmacy profession to explore and analyse the tensions which may be created by the interaction of other roles (commercial, employment) with the professional health care roles, and any resultant legal, ethical and professional implications which may arise.

2.10   CONCLUSION

In the introduction to this chapter, we noted that pharmacy is practised through the roles and responsibilities of pharmacists. In turn, we concluded that the roles and responsibilities of pharmacists are necessarily shaped by law. The pharmacist's roles and responsibilities have evolved, altered and been modified over a considerable period of time. Rules and regulations to shape and mould both that evolution, and those changes and revisions have been formulated and implemented at the same time.

The pharmacist's function and purpose in health care has not only been shaped by the law. The economic determinant of the growth of the pharmaceutical industry and the health policy determinant of the development of the National Health Service have cast the pharmacist into particular roles. Those roles are crucial to the provision of health care and their importance is reflected in the degree of legal control and regulation attached to them. Much of that legal control is described in the chapters which follow.

However the pharmacy profession is not content to maintain its current position in health care. It has worked enthusiastically to re-professionalise and to redefine its purpose. The new model which has been advocated also has important legal implications and the consequences of this proposed expansion may be significant.

THREE

The pharmacist and the National Health Service

3.1 INTRODUCTION

The analysis undertaken in the last chapter demonstrated the pivotal role which the pharmacist plays in the provision of health care. The examination also showed that the National Health Service is the main method by which health care is provided in the United Kingdom. The pharmacy profession had a successful input to the development of the NHS, and has been effective in negotiating a key role for the pharmacist in the provision of pharmaceutical services.

It is important, therefore, to analyse the legal structure of the NHS, and to describe the NHS context and framework within which the pharmacist operates and functions. The difficulty of this task is exacerbated by the fact that, at the time of writing, the legal structure of the NHS is subject to important and far-reaching legislative reforms. These reforms have not yet been implemented. and so the legal structure remains as described below. The context of the new changes has also been analysed.

Productive negotiation and recognition of an exclusive role for pharmacy does not mean that the pharmacist's relationship with the NHS does not have a legal reality. As part of the regulation of the overall structure of the NHS, the provision of pharmaceutical services is subject to strict legal control which takes a number of forms. First, the class and description of persons permitted to provide pharmaceutical services is closely regulated. Secondly the methods by which those pharmaceutical services are provided, and are paid for, are also subject to significant restriction. The legal relationship between the pharmacist, as provider of pharmaceutical services within the NHS, is subject to the pharmacist accepting, and acting on, a detailed range of terms of service. Finally, important mechanisms exist for the termination of the legal relationship between the pharmacist and the NHS.

Some aspects of the legal relationship between the pharmacist and the NHS have been left to other chapters. For example, important legal structures exist for the determination of complaints against pharmacists, and others, within the NHS and these procedures have been considered in detail in chapter twelve. Equally it is important to remember that the obligations outlined in the terms of service supplement other extensive regulations on the provision of pharmaceutical services, which will be described in subsequent chapters.

3.2   THE LEGISLATIVE FRAMEWORK FOR THE NATIONAL HEALTH SERVICE

The main legislative framework for the National Health Service (NHS) is now set out in the National Health Service Act (the NHS Act) 1977. The NHS Act 1977 has been amended quite substantially by a number of other important pieces of legislation including the National Health Service and Community Care Act 1990, the Health Authorities Act 1995 and the National Health Service (Primary Care) Act 1997.

As we shall see below, under the NHS Act 1977, as amended, the NHS is essentially divided into two different systems. Under Part I of the NHS Act 1977, a responsibility is placed on the Secretary of State to secure the provision of health care in hospitals, and the services provided by district nurses, midwives or health visitors in clinics or individuals' homes, and medical services to pupils in state schools. The functions of the Secretary of State have, for the most part, been delegated to health authorities, created under the Health Authorities Act 1995. Health authorities enter into arrangements with NHS trusts, established under the National Health Service and Community Care Act 1990, for the provision by the trusts of hospital and community health services.

NHS trusts are bodies set up to assume responsibility for the ownership and management of hospitals or other establishments or facilities previously managed or provided by a health authority, or to provide and manage hospitals or other establishments or facilities which were not previously so managed or provided. A trust's functions are conferred by its establishment order made under s. 5(1) of and by sch. 2 to the National Health Service and Community Care Act 1990. All the NHS hospitals in the country are now run by NHS trusts.

The setting up of health authorities is provided for in s. 8 of the NHS Act 1977, as amended by the Health Authorities Act 1995. Specific provision for the structure, form and administrative procedure of health authorities is made under sch. 1 to the Health Authorities Act 1995, the Health Authorities (Membership and Procedure) Regulations 1996 (S.I. 1996/707), and the

National Health Service (Functions of Health Authorities and Administration Arrangements) Regulations 1996 (S.I. 1996/708).

Part II of the NHS Act 1977 governs the arrangements made by health authorities for the provision of services by general practitioners, general dental practitioners, ophthalmic opticians and ophthalmic medical practitioners, and chemists. They provide what are termed general medical services, general dental services, general ophthalmic services and pharmaceutical services respectively. Changes introduced by the National Health Service and Community Care Act 1990, allowed for the creation of fund-holding practices of general practitioners providing services under Part II of the NHS Act 1977.

The new fund-holding system did not alter the services they provide. Fund-holding practices are given, however, an allotted sum of money with which to purchase, on behalf of their patients, from whatever provider they see fit, some of the care under Part I of the NHS Act 1977 which would otherwise have been purchased by the local health authority. Thus, from 1990, there are two types of purchaser or commissioner of services, i.e., health authorities and fund-holding practices.

The National Health Service (Primary Care) Act 1997 introduced a new option for the delivery of family health services. Personal medical services and personal dental services may now be provided under agreements known as pilot schemes. These agreements are made between the health authority and NHS trusts, general practitioners, and NHS employees. Pilot schemes allow personal medical services and personal dental services, which can be equated with the old general medical services and general dental services, to be provided under the Part I system. Health authorities fund the services provided under a pilot scheme and enable them to agree with the local pilot providers the content of the services and the conditions under which those services will be provided.

3.3   PROPOSALS FOR CHANGE IN THE NHS FRAMEWORK

In December 1997 and January 1998, the government published white papers on its proposals for the National Health Service in England, Scotland and Wales (*The New NHS*, Cm 3807; *Designed to Care*, Cm 3811; *Putting Patients First*, Cm 3841). Further detailed proposals on the quality and partnership were set out in the consultation documents *A First Class Service* (HSC 1998/113), and *Quality Care and Clinical Excellence*, published in July 1998, and the discussion documents *Partnership in Action*, published in September 1998, and *Partnership for Improvement*, published in October 1998.

Following this, a new Health Bill was published, designed to implement those proposals, contained in the white papers and consultation documents, which require primary legislation. The Bill's main purpose is to make changes to the way in which the National Health Service is run in England, Wales and Scotland. The Bill abolishes GP fund-holding and amends the NHS Act 1977 to make provision for the establishment of new statutory bodies in England and

Wales to be known as primary care trusts, and provides for NHS trusts in Scotland to take on additional functions.

The Bill makes changes to the provisions in the National Health Service and Community Care Act 1990 concerning the establishment of NHS trusts, including retrospective changes to the purposes for which NHS trusts are established, and to the current NHS trust financial regime. The Secretary of State's current powers of direction in respect of NHS trusts are extended to cover all the functions of those trusts. The Bill also replaces the provisions about special hospitals to enable NHS trusts in England and Wales, with Secretary of State approval, to provide high security psychiatric services.

The Bill places a new statutory duty of quality on NHS trusts and primary care trusts and establishes a new statutory body for England and Wales, to be known as the Commission for Health Improvement, to monitor and improve the quality of health care provided by the NHS. The Bill creates new partnership duties within the NHS and between NHS bodies and local authorities and provides for local strategies to be developed for improving health and health care. New operational flexibilities allow NHS bodies and local authorities to enter into joint arrangements for the purchase or provision of health and health-related services. Allocation of additional funding to health authorities is permitted on the basis of their past performance.

New measures designed to tackle fraud against the NHS are also introduced. A new criminal offence of knowingly making false representations to obtain exemption or remission from NHS charges is created. The current functions of the NHS Tribunal, described in detail below, are extended to include imposing sanctions on family health service practitioners who have defrauded the NHS.

Importantly, the Bill provides for the Secretary of State for Health to make regulations and directions securing compliance with aspects of a negotiated pharmaceutical price regulation scheme, to regulate the profits of companies outside the negotiated agreement and to set maximum prices for medicines supplied to the NHS. The Bill also provides new powers to regulate health care professions by Order in Council.

3.4   THE PROVISION OF HEALTH SERVICES

Under s. 1, NHS Act 1977, as amended, it is the duty of the Secretary of State to:

continue the promotion ... of a comprehensive health service designed to secure improvement—
    (a)   in the physical and mental health of the people ..., and
    (b)   in the prevention, diagnosis and treatment of illness.

Under s. 1(2), NHS Act 1977 the services to be provided under s. 1 are to be free except in so far as the making and recovery of charges is expressly provided for. These legislative duties repeat the obligations owed under the National Health Service Act 1946, which had set up the original National Health Service.

Section 2 of the NHS Act 1977 confers wide-ranging powers for the Secretary of State to provide such services as are appropriate to, and to do any other thing whatsoever which is calculated to facilitate, or is conducive or incidental to, the discharge of any duty imposed by s. 1. Section 3 sets out those general services which it is the Secretary of State's duty to provide to such extent as he considers necessary to meet all reasonable requirements. These include hospital accommodation, accommodation for other services, medical, dental, nursing and ambulance services, facilities for the care of expectant and nursing mothers and young children, facilities for the prevention of illness, the care of persons suffering from illness and the after-care of those who have suffered from illness, and other services for the diagnosis of treatment of illness.

Section 4 imposes a specific duty on the Secretary of State to provide special hospitals for persons detained under the Mental Health Act 1983 who have dangerous, violent or criminal propensities. The services provided under this section are often referred to as 'high security psychiatric services' and are presently managed outside the normal hospital system by certain special health authorities established under s. 11 of the NHS Act 1977.

Further miscellaneous powers and duties are imposed on the Secretary of State by s. 5. These include the provision of school medical and dental inspection services, contraceptive services, the provision of invalid carriages, the provision of treatment and accommodation outside Great Britain for those suffering from respiratory tuberculosis, a microbiological service, and grants and assistance for the conduct of research into the causation, prevention, diagnosis and treatment of illness.

Although the main functions under Part I of the NHS Act 1997 are conferred on the Secretary of State, the Act provides a mechanism which enables the Secretary of State to devolve to health authorities the responsibility for performing these functions, whilst retaining the ability to control how those functions are performed. The Secretary of State may direct a health authority or special health authority to exercise his functions on his behalf under s. 13. He may also give directions about the exercise of functions by a health authority or special health authority under s. 17.

The Secretary of State has exercised his powers under these sections on many occasions but the main provision is the National Health Service (Functions of Health Authorities and Administration Arrangements) Regulations 1996 (S.I. 1996/708). Schedule 1 to those Regulations lists those 'specified health service functions' of the Secretary of State that he has delegated to health authorities. The Secretary of State has directed health authorities to exercise most of his functions under Part I of the NHS Act 1997, in particular ss. 2, 3, and 5. It is these Regulations by which health authorities have their functions in respect of Part I services conferred upon them.

As we have seen, the setting up of health authorities is provided for in s. 8 of the NHS Act 1977, as amended by the Health Authorities Act 1995. The setting up of special health authorities is provided for in s. 11, NHS Act 1977. Health authorities are established to act for the area set out in their establishment order and together cover all of England and Wales. Special health authorities are established for specific functional purposes which the Secretary of State directs them to perform on his behalf. Specific provision for the structure, form and administrative procedure of health authorities is made under sch. 1 to the Health Authorities Act 1995, the Health Authorities (Membership and Procedure) Regulations 1996 (S.I. 1996/707), and the National Health Service (Functions of Health Authorities and Administration Arrangements) Regulations 1996 (S.I. 1996/708).

3.4.1 Advice on the provision of health services

Under s. 12(1), NHS Act 1977, as amended by Part 1 of sch. 1 of the Health Authorities Act 1995, every health authority must make arrangements for ensuring that they receive advice from, amongst others, persons with professional expertise in and experience of health care.

Advice on the provision of general medical services is also received from bodies known as community health councils. The Community Health Councils Regulations 1996 (S.I. 1996/640) make provision for the establishment by the Secretary of State of community health councils, and provide for their membership, proceedings, staff, premises, expenses and functions.

It is the duty of each council to keep under review the operation of the health service in its district, to make recommendations for the improvement of that service and to advise any relevant health authority upon such matters relating to the operation of the health service within its district as the council thinks fit. In turn, it is the duty of each relevant health authority to consult a council on any proposals which the health authority may have under consideration for any substantial development of the health service in the council's district and on any proposals to make any substantial variation in the provision of such service.

The members of a council are appointed by the relevant local authorities, by the voluntary organisations, by the Secretary of State and hold a term of office for four years. Voluntary organisations are those organisations which, in the opinion of the Secretary of State, have an interest in the health service in the district of a council.

Under the provisions of the National Institute for Clinical Excellence (Establishment and Constitution) Order 1999, the Secretary of State has provided for the establishment and constitution of a special health authority to be known as the National Institute for Clinical Excellence (NICE). The function of the new special health authority will be to promote clinical and cost effectiveness through guidance and audit to support frontline health service staff. It will advise on best practice in the use of existing treatment options, appraise new health interventions, advise the NHS on how they can be implemented, and how best these might fit beside existing treatments. Detailed provisions on the membership and procedures for NICE are provided for in the National Institute for Clinical Excellence Regulations 1999 (S.I. 1999/260).

3.5   THE PROVISION OF PHARMACEUTICAL SERVICES

Under s. 41, NHS Act 1977, every health authority has a duty to arrange, in respect of their area, for the provision to persons in that area, of:

(a)   proper and efficient drugs and medicines and listed appliances which are ordered for those persons by a medical practitioner in pursuance of functions in the health service;

(b)   proper and sufficient drugs and medicines which are ordered for those persons by a dental practitioner in pursuance of the provision by a health authority, an NHS trust of dental services, or in pursuance of the provision by a dental practitioner of general dental services;

(c)   listed drugs and listed appliances which are ordered for those persons by a prescribed description of registered nurse, midwife or health visitor in pursuance of the functions of the health service;

(d)   such other services as may be prescribed.

Arrangements for the provision of pharmaceutical services are made through the National Health Service (Pharmaceutical Services) Regulations 1992 (S.I. 1992/662), as amended.

Under reg. 4 of the 1992 Regulations, a health authority is under a duty to prepare lists, called pharmaceutical lists, of the persons who undertake to provide pharmaceutical services from premises in the health authority's locality by way of the provision of drugs and appliances. Each list contains the addresses of premises in the health authority's locality from which those services are provided and particulars of the days and hours at which those premises are open for such provision and must indicate whether or not the chemist has undertaken to provide supplemental services under reg. 16, and to be described in more detail below under reg. 16.

Not everyone is permitted to provide pharmaceutical services. Under s. 43, NHS Act 1977:

(1)   with limited exceptions, a health authority may not make arrangements with a medical practitioner or dental practitioner under which that practitioner is required or agrees to provide pharmaceutical services to any person to whom he or she is rendering general medical services or general dental services; and

(2)   with limited exceptions, no arrangements may be made for the dispensing of medicines with persons other than registered pharmacists, or persons lawfully conducting a retail pharmacy business in accordance with s. 69 of the Medicines Act 1968, and who undertake that all medicines supplied

by them will be dispensed either by or under the direct supervision of a registered pharmacist.

3.5.1 Applications for inclusion on the pharmaceutical list

A person who wishes:

(a) to be included in a pharmaceutical list for the provision of pharmaceutical services from premises in a health authority's locality; or

(b) who is already included in a pharmaceutical list but wishes to open, within that locality, additional premises from which to provide the same or different pharmaceutical services; or

(c) to change the premises from which he or she provides pharmaceutical services to other premises; or

(d) to provide from existing premises in that locality pharmaceutical services other than those already listed in relation to him or her,

must apply to the health authority in the prescribed form set out in Part I of sch. 3 to the 1992 Regulations.

The health authority must grant an application where the applicant intends to change premises but intends to provide the same services. For such an application to be granted the health authority must be satisfied that the change is a minor relocation, and that the provision of pharmaceutical services will not be interrupted. The issue of what is a minor relocation was considered in the cases of *R v Cumbria FPC, ex parte Boots the Chemists Ltd, R v Yorkshire Regional Health Authority, ex parte Gompels, The Times*, 15 August 1994 and *R v Yorkshire Regional Health Authority, ex parte Suri, The Times*, 15 August 1994. The courts have held that the issue is a matter of fact and degree, with necessary consideration of factors such as geography, the distance of the move, the population affected, and the significance and consequence of the move as it affects users of the service. The courts are clear that the continuing viability of adversely affected pharmacies is an irrelevant factor.

In addition an application must be granted where the application is to provide pharmaceutical services at premises from which such services are already being provided. Again the health authority must be satisfied that the same services will be provided from those premises, and that the provision of pharmaceutical services will not be interrupted.

Otherwise an application will be granted by the health authority only if it is satisfied that it is necessary or desirable to grant the application in order to secure the adequate provision of pharmaceutical services in the neighbourhood to which the application relates. The issue of what is a neighbourhood was considered in the cases of *Re an Application by Boots*, unreported, NI High Court, 4 February 1994, *R v Yorkshire Health Authority, ex parte Baker* (1996) 35 BMLR 118, and *R v Family Health Services Appeal Authority, ex parte Boots the Chemists Ltd* (1996) 33 BMLR 1.

The principles which emerge from these cases suggest that there is no distinction to be drawn between a vicinity and neighbourhood. Further a neighbourhood may be described as an area defined by physical and social factors, and need not include a residential element; it may be a shopping centre, for example. Careful consideration must be given to the needs and interests of all of the people expected to be in the neighbourhood in the course of their daily lives, and the likelihood that they may require pharmaceutical services while there.

An application to a health authority may be granted either in respect of all, or in respect of some only, of the services specified in it. Any question whether an application should or should not be granted is determined by the health authority in accordance with the procedure set out in regs. 5, 6, 7 and 8 of the 1992 Regulations.

Where an application is granted by the health authority, the applicant must notify the health authority, in the form set out in Part II of sch. 3 to the 1992 Regulations, that provision of services will be commenced at the premises to which the application related. Notification of commencement must be made within six months of the date of notification of the original grant. That time limit might be extended up to twenty four months, if good cause can be shown, on appeal to the Secretary of State.

3.5.2 Consideration of application by a health authority

On receipt of an application, a health authority must, as soon as is practicable, give notice of it in writing, to:

(a)   the local pharmaceutical committee;

(b)   the local medical committee;

(c)   any person who is included in a pharmaceutical list and whose interests might, in the opinion of the health authority, be significantly affected if the application were granted;

(d)   any health authority any part of whose locality is within two kilometres of the premises; and

(e)   any community health council serving the locality of the health authority.

A local pharmaceutical committee (LPC) is provided for by s. 44, NHS Act 1977. An LPC will have nine or fifteen members, all of whom must be involved in the provision of pharmaceutical services as either contractors or employees. Two thirds of the membership of such committees must be made up of representatives elected by the chemists in the local area. Members hold office for a term of four years and provision is made for the co-option of members, and the ending of a representative's membership.

The functions of such committees are provided for in s. 45, NHS Act 1977. The main function is consultation with health authorities on a wide range of matters. In addition, the LPC is involved in liaison, appointment of members to other committees and tribunals, advising individual chemists, appointing representatives, considering complaints and making representations.

Any person notified of an application may, within 30 days from the date on which the notification was sent, make representations in writing to the health authority.

A health authority which is notified under paragraph (d) above must, in turn and as soon as is practicable, give further notice of the application in writing to the LPC for its locality, the local medical committee for its locality, and any person whose name is included in a pharmaceutical list and whose interests might, in the opinion of the health authority, be significantly affected if the application were granted. In turn, any person so notified may, within 30 days from the date on which the notification was sent, make representations in writing to the health authority to which the application was made.

In considering any application a health authority must have regard in particular to the following factors:

(a)   whether or not any of the pharmaceutical services specified in the application are already provided by persons included in a pharmaceutical list in the neighbourhood in which the premises named in the application are located;

(b)   any information available to the health authority which, in its opinion, is relevant to the consideration of the application; and

(c)   any representations received by the health authority.

The health authority may determine an application in such manner as it thinks fit and may, if it considers that oral representations are unnecessary, determine the application without hearing any oral representations. In any case where the health authority decides to hear oral representations, it must give the applicant and any person from whom it has received representations not less than 14 days' notice of the time and place at which the oral representations are to be heard.

The applicant may be assisted at any such hearing in the presentation of representations by some other person, but may not be represented in this regard by a solicitor or barrister. The procedure by which representations are heard is such as the health authority may determine.

No person who provides or assists in providing general medical services or pharmaceutical services is permitted to take part in any decision. The health authority may, where it thinks fit, consider two or more applications together in relation to each other and, where it proposes to do so, it must give notice in writing to the applicants and any persons to whom copies of the application were sent.

A health authority must, as soon as practicable, give notice in writing of its decision on an application, to the applicant, any person who is included in a pharmaceutical list and whose interests might, in the opinion of the health authority, be significantly affected by the decision, the LPC, the local medical committee, any health authority any part of whose locality is within two kilometres of the premises, and any community health council serving the locality of the health authority or of any other notified health authority.

Any other health authority which is notified must, in turn and as soon as practicable, give notice in writing of the decision and reasons to the LPC for its locality, the local medical committee for its locality, and any person whose name is included in the pharmaceutical list and whose interests might in the opinion of that authority be significantly affected by the decision, and must notify them of any rights of appeal.

3.5.3   Appeals against health authority decisions

Where a health authority has determined an application or made a decision whether or not to amend the premises named in the original application, the applicant and any person who has been notified of the decision may appeal to the Secretary of State. Any appeal must be made by sending to the Secretary of State a notice of appeal in writing within 30 days from the date on which the health authority sent its decision to the appellant, and must contain a concise statement of the grounds of appeal.

The Secretary of State, after considering the notice of appeal, may dismiss an appeal where he or she is of the opinion that it discloses no reasonable grounds of appeal or that the appeal is otherwise vexatious or frivolous. Otherwise, the Secretary of State must send a copy of the notice of appeal to the health authority whose determination is appealed against and to all other relevant parties. Any person to whom a copy of the notice of appeal is sent may, within 30 days from the date on which the notice was sent, make representations in writing to the Secretary of State on the appeal.

The Secretary of State may require an oral hearing before determining the appeal. The Secretary of State must, where an oral hearing is required, appoint one or more persons to hear the appeal and to report on it. The procedure of any oral hearing is determined by the person or persons hearing the appeal. An oral hearing takes place at such time and place as the Secretary of State may direct, and notice of the hearing must be sent, not less than 14 days before the date fixed for the hearing, to the appellant and to any person to whom a copy of the notice of appeal was sent. The appellant and any person to whom a notice of the hearing is sent may attend the hearing and be heard in person or by a solicitor, barrister or other representative, and the health authority may be represented at the hearing by any duly authorised officer or member, or by a solicitor or barrister.

The Secretary of State must either allow the appeal or confirm the decision of the health authority. The Secretary of State must, as soon as practicable, send to the appellant and to any person to whom a copy of the notice of appeal was sent and who made representations, notice in writing of the decision on the appeal and must include in the notice a statement of the reasons for the decision and of the findings of fact.

3.5.4 Applications for preliminary consent

A preliminary consent procedure is available to anyone considering a full application for inclusion in the pharmaceutical list at some time in the future. An application for preliminary consent must be in writing and must specify the location of the premises at which it is proposed to provide pharmaceutical services and the pharmaceutical services which it is proposed to provide. Where any application for preliminary consent relates to a controlled locality, it will be determined in accordance with the regulations relating to a controlled locality, which are discussed in detail below.

An application for preliminary consent is determined as if it were an application for full consent and the procedures applicable to a full consent, as described above, will apply. A preliminary consent shall have effect for a period of twelve months from its final grant. Before the end of that twelve month period, the health authority may allow an extension of the preliminary consent for such further period as it considers reasonable in the circumstances.

Where the applicant has been finally granted preliminary consent, the health authority must grant an application for full consent provided that the date specified for inclusion in the pharmaceutical list falls within twelve months from the date of the grant of preliminary consent. In addition, the pharmaceutical services which it is proposed to provide must be the same as those specified in the application for preliminary consent, and the premises specified in the application must have the same location as that in respect of which the preliminary consent was granted. Where the premises specified in the application have a different location from that in respect of which preliminary consent was granted, the health authority will treat the application as though it were an application to change the location of the premises.

3.5.5 Controlled localities

Special procedures apply to applications for inclusion in a pharmaceutical list in a controlled locality. A 'controlled locality' is an area which a health authority or, on appeal, the Secretary of State has determined is rural in character. Any area determined to be a controlled locality, before the coming into force of the 1992 regulations, continues to remain as such.

A health authority may at any time consider and determine whether or not an area is rural in character. Alternatively a local medical committee or an LPC may apply in writing to a health authority to consider and determine whether or not an area specified in the application is rural in character. On receiving an application, the health authority must, before making a determination, give notice in writing to the local medical committee, the LPC and any doctor or chemist who, in the opinion of the health authority, may be affected by the determination. The health authority must also inform them that they may make representations in writing within 30 days from the date on which the notice was sent.

Where the health authority determines that any area or part of an area is or is not rural in character, it must consider whether the provision of general medical services by any doctor, or pharmaceutical services by any chemist, is likely to be adversely affected in consequence of that determination. The health authority must determine the boundaries of any area or part of an area referred to in the application which it determines to be rural in character, and any area so determined will become a controlled locality. The health authority must delineate precisely the boundaries of any controlled locality on a map.

Where it has been determined that an area is, or is not, rural in character, the issue will not be considered again for a period of five years, except where the health authority is satisfied, whether on an application or otherwise, that there has been a substantial change of circumstances in relation to the area in question, or the relevant part of it, since the question was last determined.

The health authority must give notice in writing of its determination and of the reasons for it, and must inform the local medical committee and LPC that they may appeal to the Secretary of State. The procedures for an appeal in these circumstances are similar to those for appeal against health authority decisions, described above.

On determining an appeal, the Secretary of State must, where an appeal against a refusal is allowed, also determine the question whether or not the relevant area is rural in character and may, in certain circumstances, remit the question to the health authority for further determination. The Secretary of State must give notice of the decision in writing, together with reasons for it, to all the persons to whom the notice of appeal was sent.

3.5.6 Applications for inclusion in pharmaceutical lists in respect of controlled localities

Where the premises specified in an application for inclusion in the pharmaceutical list are in a controlled locality, that application must be determined in accordance with reg. 12 of the 1992 Regulations. An exception exists where the applicant is seeking only to change within that controlled locality the premises at which he or she provides pharmaceutical services, and the granting of the application would not, in the view of the health authority, result in a significant change in the arrangements for the provision of pharmaceutical services in any part of a controlled locality.

Special rules apply to applications where the premises specified are within one mile of any part of any controlled locality, in which patients reside for whom a doctor provides pharmaceutical services, and where the premises are within one mile of the locality of another health authority.

The provisions for the determination of an application for inclusion in a pharmaceutical list in a controlled locality are similar to those for other applications to health authorities, noted above. The health authority shall refuse an application to the extent that it is of the opinion that to grant it would prejudice the proper provision of general medical services or pharmaceutical services in any locality. Otherwise, the health authority shall grant every application and shall consider whether the provision of general medical services by any doctor or pharmaceutical services by any chemist is likely to be adversely affected in consequence of that grant.

Where a health authority has determined an application or made a decision, the applicant, health authority or other notified health authority, may appeal to the Secretary of State. Any appeal must be made by sending to the Secretary of State a notice of appeal in writing within 30 days from the date on which the health authority sent its decision to the appellant, and must contain a concise statement of the grounds of appeal. Again, the procedures for the determination of the appeal are similar to those for appeals against other decisions of a health authority, noted above.

On determining an appeal, the Secretary of State must either allow the appeal or impose such conditions as thought fit, remit the case to the health authority or dismiss it. The Secretary of State must, as soon as practicable, send to the appellant and to any person to whom a copy of the notice of appeal was sent and who made representations, notice in writing of his decision on the appeal and must include in the notice a statement of the reasons for the decision and of the findings of fact.

3.5.7 Removal from pharmaceutical lists

Where a health authority determines that a chemist has died or is no longer a chemist, the health authority must remove that chemist's name from the list. The name of any chemist whose business is carried on by representatives in accordance with the provisions of the Pharmacy Act 1954 shall not be removed from the pharmaceutical list so long as the business is carried on by them, and the representatives agree to be bound by the terms of service.

The name of a chemist who has not been providing pharmaceutical services for a period of six months may be removed from the list. Before making that determination, the health authority must give the chemist 28 days' notice of its intention, afford the chemist an opportunity of making representations to the health authority in writing or, if the chemist so desires, in person, and consult the LPC.

Where the health authority decides to remove a chemist's name from its pharmaceutical list, it must give notice in writing of its decision to the chemist. A chemist to whom a notice has been given may, within 30 days of receiving the notice, appeal to the Secretary of State against the decision of the health authority. The health authority must not remove the chemist's name from the pharmaceutical list until the appeal is determined, or until the expiry of the 30 days' notice period. An appeal must be in writing and must set out the relevant grounds. Where the Secretary of State allows the appeal, he must direct the health authority not to remove the chemist's name from the pharmaceutical list.

3.6 ARRANGEMENTS FOR PROVISION OF PHARMACEUTICAL SERVICES BY DOCTORS

A doctor must provide to a patient any appliance or drug, not being a scheduled drug, where it is needed for the immediate treatment of that patient before it can otherwise be obtained. Otherwise, where a patient satisfies a health authority that he or she would have serious difficulty in obtaining any necessary drugs or appliances from a pharmacy by reason of distance or inadequacy of means of communication, or is resident in a controlled locality, at a distance of more than one mile from any pharmacy, he or she may request in writing, that the doctor on whose list he or she is included is to provide pharmaceutical services.

For this request to be permitted, there must be in effect an outline consent granted to that doctor or to his partner or to any previous doctor in his practice in respect of the area in which the patient resides. Alternatively pharmaceutical services may continue to be provided if prior arrangements or requirements were in effect for that doctor or his partner or any previous doctor in his practice to provide drugs or appliances to patients, and no change of circumstances has occurred.

A doctor requested by a patient to provide pharmaceutical services, may then apply to the health authority to make arrangements for the provision of those services by sending the patient's request in writing, to the health authority. Where the doctor does not apply within 30 days, the health authority may require the doctor to undertake such provision and shall give him notice in writing to that effect.

An arrangement made by a health authority, requiring the doctor to provide the services, has effect from the date of the patient's request in writing, and enables that doctor, any partner of his or any doctor who subsequently joins his practice to provide pharmaceutical services for the patient so long as the arrangement remains in effect.

A health authority must not require a doctor to provide pharmaceutical services to a person on his list if that doctor satisfies the health authority or, on appeal, the Secretary of State that he does not normally provide pharmaceutical services, or that the person would not have serious difficulty, by reason of distance or inadequacy of means of communication, in obtaining drugs and appliances from a pharmacy. Equally a health authority must give a doctor reasonable notice that it requires him to provide, or to discontinue to provide pharmaceutical services to any person.

Any appeal to the Secretary of State must be made in writing within 30 days from the date on which notice of the decision was sent to the doctor and shall contain a concise statement of the grounds of appeal. The Secretary of State must, on receipt of any notice of appeal under this regulation, send a copy of that notice to the health authority and the health authority may, within 30 days, make representations in writing. The Secretary of State may determine an appeal in such manner as thought fit and must give notice of the decision in writing, together with the reasons for it, to the appellant and to the health authority.

3.6.1 Outline consent

A doctor wishing to be granted the right to provide pharmaceutical services by arrangement with a health authority to patients residing in an area, may apply to the health authority in writing for consent ('outline consent') specifying the area in relation to which the outline consent is to be granted. An application for outline consent is determined in accordance with the provisions, described above, for the determination of applications in respect of controlled localities.

An outline consent has effect from its final grant but will cease to have effect where either no arrangement has been made pursuant to it within 12 months from its final grant, or more than 12 months elapse after the last provision of drugs and appliances under an arrangement made pursuant to it.

3.7 ADVICE ON THE PROVISION OF PHARMACEUTICAL SERVICES

Under s. 6(3), NHS Act 1977, as amended, the Secretary of State is given power to constitute standing advisory committees for the purpose of giving advice on the services to be provided under the Act. That power has been exercised through the National Health Service (Standing Advisory Committees) Order 1981. Under the provisions of this Order, a Standing Pharmaceutical Advisory Committee is constituted for the purpose of advising the Secretary of State on the provision of pharmaceutical services.

The current Standing Pharmaceutical Advisory Committee has 12 members, chosen for their knowledge and experience in pharmacy. Each member serves for a four year term. The President of the Royal Pharmaceutical Society of Great Britain is an *ex officio* member of this committee.

3.8 TERMS OF SERVICE FOR CHEMISTS

Inclusion on the pharmaceutical list does not give an automatic right to provide pharmaceutical services. Further rigorous controls are exercised on the manner in which such services are to be provided. The terms of service for chemists are to be found in Part II of sch. II to the National Health Service (Pharmaceutical Services) Regulations 1992, as amended. The terms of service also incorporate the Regulations under which they are made, the Drug Tariff and parts of the National Health Service (Service Committees and Tribunal) Regulations 1992 (S.I. 1992/664), as amended, (to be discussed in more detail in chapter twelve below).

The Pharmaceutical Services Negotiating Committee (PSNC) is officially recognised as the organisation representative of the general body of chemists. It consists of 25 members representing a wide range of interests of persons engaged in the provision of pharmaceutical services. The PSNC is responsible for negotiating the terms and conditions of service for chemists and for payment for those services.

3.8.1   General terms of service

Under paragraph 3 of schedule II of the National Health Service (Pharmaceutical Services) Regulations, as amended, where any person presents on a prescription form:

   (a) an order for drugs, not being scheduled drugs or appliances, signed by a doctor; or

   (b) an order for a drug specified in sch. 11 to the National Health Service (General Medical Services) Regulations 1992, signed by, and endorsed on its face with the reference 'SLS' [Selected List Scheme], signed by a doctor; or

   (c) an order for listed drugs or medicines, signed by a dentist or a dentist's deputy or assistant; or

   (d) an order for listed drugs or medicines, or listed appliances, signed by a nurse prescriber,

a chemist must, with reasonable promptness, provide the drugs so ordered, and such of the appliances so ordered, as are supplied in the normal course of business.

A 'prescription form' is defined under reg. 2 of the National Health Service (Pharmaceutical Services) Regulations 1992 as a form provided by a health authority or trust and issued by a doctor or dentist to enable a person to obtain pharmaceutical services. Schedule 11 to the National Health Service (General Medical Services) Regulations 1992 (S.I. 1992/635), as amended, contains a list of medicines which may only be prescribed for certain listed conditions, and only when the prescription form is endorsed by the doctor with the initials 'SLS'.

Under paragraph 1A, which was inserted by the National Health Service (Pharmaceutical Services) Amendment Regulations 1996 (S.I. 1996/698), if the person presenting the prescription form asks the chemist to do so, the chemist must give an estimate of the time when the drugs, medicines or appliances will be ready, and if they are not ready by then, must give a revised estimate.

Any drug which is provided as part of pharmaceutical services and included in the Drug Tariff, the British National Formulary, the Dental Practitioner's Formulary, the European Pharmacopoeia or the British Pharmaceutical Codex, must comply with the standards or formulae specified in those documents.

Where an order, which is issued by a doctor, a dentist or nurse prescriber, on a prescription form for drugs, does not prescribe their quantity, strength or dosage, a chemist may provide the drugs in such strength and dosage as in the exercise of his or her professional skill, knowledge and care, he or she considers to be appropriate. The chemist may also provide the drugs in such quantity as he or she considers to be appropriate for a course of treatment, for the patient for a five-day period. This discretion does not apply to an order to which the

Poisons Rules 1982, as amended, or the Misuse of Drugs Regulations 1985, as amended, apply.

Where an order is for:

(a)   an oral contraceptive service; or

(b)   a drug, which is available for supply as part of pharmaceutical services only with one or more drugs; or

(c)   an antibiotic in a liquid form for oral administration in respect of which pharmaceutical considerations require its provision in an unopened package,

and is only available for supply in a package with a minimum quantity appropriate to a course of treatment for a patient for a period of more than five days, the chemist may provide that minimum available package.

Where any drug, ordered by a doctor, dentist or nurse prescriber on a prescription form, is available for provision by a chemist in a pack in a quantity which is different from the quantity which has been ordered, and that drug is:

(a)   sterile;

(b)   effervescent or hygroscopic;

(c)   a liquid preparation for addition to bath water;

(d)   a coal tar preparation;

(e)   a viscous preparation; or

(f)   packed at the time of its manufacture in a calendar pack or special container,

the chemist must provide the drug in the pack whose quantity is nearest to the quantity which has been ordered. 'Special container' means any container with an integral means of application or from which it is not practicable to dispense an exact quantity. This discretion does not apply to any drug to which the Misuse of Drugs Regulations 1985 apply.

A chemist must not provide a drug in a calendar pack where, in the opinion of the chemist, it was the intention of the doctor or dentist who ordered the drug that it should be provided only in the exact quantity ordered. 'Calendar pack' means a blister or strip pack showing the days of the week or month against each of the several units in the pack.

Where in an urgent case, a doctor personally known to a chemist, requests the chemist to provide a drug, the chemist may provide the drug before receiving the prescription form, provided that:

(a)   the drug is not a scheduled drug;

(b)   the drug is not a controlled drug other than a sch. 4 and 5 controlled drug; and

(c)   the doctor undertakes to give the chemist a prescription form within 72 hours.

A scheduled drug, as mentioned in paragraph (a), is one which is contained in sch. 10 to the National Health Service (General Medical Services) Regulations 1992 (S.I. 1992/635) as amended. These Regulations implemented a governmental scheme, the 'Selected List Scheme', designed to reduce National Health Service disbursement, by prohibiting the prescription and dispensing of certain medicines in various categories, thereby restricting the availability of certain medicines on the National Health Service.

The select list originally included the categories of indigestion remedies, laxatives, analgesics for mild to moderate pain, bitters and tonics, vitamins and the benzodiazepine tranquillisers and sedatives, all of which were included in sch. 10 to the 1992 Regulations. Those categories are added to, or otherwise amended, on a regular basis, through amendments to the original Regulations. As a result, the categories of hypnotics, and anxiolytics, anti-diarrhoeals, drugs for allergic disorders, appetite suppressants, drugs for vaginal and vulval conditions, contraceptives, drugs used in anaemia, topical anti-rheumatics, drugs acting on the ear and nose, drugs acting on the skin, and Temazepam capsules have been added to the original list.

A chemist must not provide a scheduled drug in response to an order by name, formula or other description on a prescription form. However, where a drug has an appropriate non-proprietary name, and it is ordered on a prescription either by that name or by its formula, a chemist may provide a drug which has the same specification notwithstanding that it is a scheduled drug. Where a scheduled drug is a pack which consists of a drug in more than one strength, part only of the pack must not be supplied.

A chemist is under an obligation to provide any drug which he or she is obliged to provide in a suitable container. Finally, a chemist must not give, promise or offer to any person any gift or reward (whether by way of a share of or dividend on the profits of the business or by way of discount or rebate or otherwise) as an inducement to, or in consideration of presenting an order for drugs or appliances on a prescription form.

3.8.2 Premises and hours

Pharmaceutical services must be provided in each premises at such times as, following an application in writing from the chemist, will have been approved by the health authority or, on appeal, the Secretary of State.

The health authority will not approve any application submitted by a chemist in relation to the times at which pharmaceutical services are to be provided unless it is satisfied that the times are such that a pharmacist will normally be available for no less than 30 hours in any week, and on five days in any week. Further the health authority must be satisfied that the hours when any pharmacist will normally be available in any week are to be allocated in such a manner as is likely to meet the needs of persons in the neighbourhood for pharmaceutical services, on working days between the hours of 9.00 and 17.30 (or 13.00 on an early closing day).

'Available' means available to provide pharmaceutical services of the kind undertaken to be provided and 'availability' is construed accordingly. 'Working day' means Monday to Saturday excluding a Good Friday, Christmas Day, 28 December if 26 December is a Saturday, or a bank holiday which falls on any such day. An 'early closing day' means any working day when most shops in the neighbourhood are habitually closed after the hour of 13.00.

The health authority may approve an application to provide pharmaceutical services for less than 30 hours in any week provided that it is satisfied that the provision of pharmaceutical services in the neighbourhood is likely to be adequate to meet the need for such services on working days between the hours of 9.00 and 17.30 (or 13.00 on an early closing day), at times when the pharmacist is not available.

The procedure for the determination of applications relating to the times for the provision of pharmaceutical services, and for appeals against determinations, is provided for in paras. 4(5)–(12) of Part II of sch. II to the National Health Service (Pharmaceutical Services) Regulations 1992, as amended.

At each of the premises at which a chemist provides pharmaceutical services, the following notices must be exhibited:

(a)   a notice provided by the health authority specifying the time when the premises are open for the provision of drugs and appliances; and

(b)   at times when the premises are not open, a notice, where practicable legible from outside the premises, to be provided by the health authority in a prescribed form, specifying the addresses of other chemists included in the pharmaceutical list and the times at which drugs and appliances may be obtained from those addresses.

For the purposes of the second notice, the health authority must notify the chemist in writing of the names and addresses of other chemists included in the pharmaceutical list whose premises are situated in the neighbourhood for the provision of pharmaceutical services during that time.

Where a chemist is prevented by illness or other reasonable cause from complying with obligations regarding premises and hours, that chemist must, where practicable, make arrangements with one or more chemists, whose premises are situated in the neighbourhood, for the provision of pharmaceutical services during that time.

A chemist may apply for a variation in the times at which pharmaceutical services are required to be provided. The provisions of paras. 4(16) and 4(17) of Part II of sch. II to the National Health Service (Pharmaceutical Services) Regulations 1992, as amended, relate to the determination of such an application. Similarly paras. 4(18)–(31) relate to the procedures to be adopted by the health authority in reviewing the needs of a neighbourhood for the provision of pharmaceutical services.

Significant amendments to these procedures were introduced by the National Health Service (Pharmaceutical Services) Amendment Regulations 1995 (S.I. 1995/644). The LPC must be consulted, and individual chemists must be notified. There is a significant and detailed appeal process against directions made by the health authority.

3.8.3 Supervision, professional standards and withdrawal from the pharmaceutical list

Drugs must be provided either by or under the direct supervision of a pharmacist. Where the pharmacist is employed by a chemist, that pharmacist must not be disqualified under the appropriate legislation from being included in the pharmaceutical list of a health authority, nor be an individual who is suspended by a tribunal. A chemist must give the health authority, if it so requires, the name of any pharmacist employed for the provision of drugs to persons from whom orders for the provision of pharmaceutical services have been accepted.

The National Health Service (Pharmaceutical Services) Amendment Regulations 1996 (S.I. 1996/698), introduced significant changes to the terms of service of chemists by outlining new requirements relating to professional standards. Under these new provisions, a pharmacist whose name is on the pharmaceutical list must provide pharmaceutical services and exercise any professional judgment in connection with the provision of such services in conformity with the standards generally accepted in the pharmaceutical profession. A chemist who employs a pharmacist in connection with the provision of pharmaceutical services must ensure that the pharmacist complies with the professional standards requirements.

Paragraph 10 of Schedule II of the National Health Service (Pharmaceutical Services) Regulations, as amended, allows for the withdrawal of names from the pharmaceutical list. At any time a chemist may give notice in writing to the health authority of a desire to withdraw from the pharmaceutical list. That chemist's name must be removed from the list at the expiry of three months from the date of receipt of such a notice or at such earlier time as the health authority might agree.

3.8.4 Complaints procedure and supplemental services

The National Health Service (Pharmaceutical Services) Amendment Regulations 1996 introduced significant changes to the terms of service of chemists by inserting new provisions, relating to complaints. Chemists are under a duty to establish, and operate, a procedure to deal with any complaints made by or on behalf of any person to whom the chemist has provided pharmaceutical services. Details of the new complaints procedure are provided in chapter twelve below.

Under reg. 16 of the National Health Service (Pharmaceutical Services) Regulations 1992, as amended, a chemist may undertake the following supplemental services:

(1)   in relation to homes registered under the Registered Homes Act 1984,

(i)   giving advice in connection with the safe keeping and correct administration of those drugs provided to persons resident in such a home, to the person appearing to the chemist to be in charge of the home, or to the person authorised by that person to control such safe keeping and correct administration; and

(ii)   keeping records of visits to those homes.

The records to be maintained include the name and address of the home, the date of each visit by the pharmacist, and the nature of any advice given during the visit.

(2)   the keeping of records in connection with drugs supplied to anyone in circumstances where the nature of the drug is such that, in the opinion of the pharmacist providing it, the same or a similar dug is likely to be prescribed for that person regularly on future occasions.

The records to be maintained include the name and address of the person to whom the drug is supplied, the name, quantity and dosage of the drug provided, and the date on which it was provided.

The range of supplemental services which a pharmacist may undertake was added to by the National Health Service (Pharmaceutical Services) Amendment Regulations 1993 (S.I. 1993/2451). These Regulations insert a new reg. 16A into the 1992 Regulations. Under this new provision a chemist may, in addition, undertake to provide additional professional services. 'Additional professional services' means:

(a)   publishing a leaflet (practice leaflet) which must include:

(i)   a list of the pharmaceutical services which the chemist has undertaken to provide and in respect of which his name is included in a pharmaceutical list of the health authority;

(ii)   the name, address and telephone number of the pharmacy from which he provides those services and the hours in each day of the week during which he provides those services from those premises;

(iii)   the arrangements made by the chemist to provide, or such arrangements as the chemist has made with other chemists to provide, pharmaceutical services to any person who needs those services in an emergency or outside of the normal hours during which the chemist provides pharmaceutical services;

(iv)   the procedure by which any person may comment upon the provision of pharmaceutical services undertaken by the chemist;

(b)   displaying such health promotion leaflets as the health authority may, in consultation with the LPC, approve.

A chemist who has undertaken to provide supplemental services must, on request, make available to the health authority all records kept. Equally a chemist who has undertaken to provide additional professional services must, on request, permit the health authority or another person on its behalf at any reasonable time to inspect the premises from which those services are provided, for the purposes of satisfying itself that those services are being provided in accordance with the undertaking.

3.9 NATIONAL HEALTH SERVICE CHARGES

Section 1(2) of the National Health Service Act 1977, as amended, makes it clear that a general principle behind the provision of services in the National Health Service is that such services should be free of charge. The general principle is qualified by allowing for the making and recovery of charges by express provision in subsequent primary and secondary legislation. The general principle that pharmaceutical services, as part of the variety of services offered within the National Health Service, should be provided for free of charge is reinforced in the terms of service of chemists. Paragraph 7 of the terms of service, as outlined in sch. 2 to the National Health Service (Pharmaceutical Services) Regulations 1992, as amended, makes it clear that all drugs, containers and appliances must be provided free of charge. Again, however, the general principle is qualified by the provision for further regulations.

Section 77, National Health Service Act 1977, as amended, makes specific provision for charges for drugs, medicines or appliances, or pharmaceutical services. It states:

(1) Regulations may provide for the making and recovery in such manner as may be prescribed of such charges as may be prescribed in respect of—

(a) the supply under this Act ... of drugs, medicines or appliances (including the replacement and repair of those appliances),

(b) such of the pharmaceutical services ... as may be prescribed, ...

Sub-section (2) of s. 77 provides for the possibility of exemption from any charges in respect of pharmaceutical services or in respect of drugs, medicines and appliances.

The principal regulations made under the power given by s. 77 are the National Health Service (Charges for Drugs and Appliances) Regulations 1989 (S.I. 1989/419). These Regulations are the subject of annual amendment to include revised charges for drugs, medicines and appliances. The latest are the National Health Service (Charges for Drugs and Appliances) Amendment Regulations 1998 (S.I. 1998/491).

In the 1989 Regulations, 'appliance' means a listed appliance within the meaning of s. 41, National Health Service Act 1977 but does not include a contraceptive appliance, 'chemist' includes any person, other than a doctor, providing pharmaceutical services, 'drugs' includes medicines, but does not include contraceptive substances and 'patient' means:

(a) any person for whose treatment a doctor is responsible under his terms of service;

(b) any person who applies to a chemist for the provision of pharmaceutical services including a person who applies on behalf of another person; or

(c) a person who pays or undertakes to pay on behalf of another person a charge.

For the purposes of the Regulations the supply against an order, on one prescription form, of quantities of the same drug in more than one container, is treated as the supply of only one quantity of a drug. Similarly the supply of more than one appliance of the same type, except in the case of elastic hosiery and tights, or of two or more component parts of the same appliance is treated as the supply of only one appliance.

Under reg. 3(1) a chemist who provides pharmaceutical services to a patient must make and recover a specified charge from that patient in respect of the supply of each appliance and of each quantity of a drug. Under reg. 3(2) no charge is to be made and recovered where there is an exemption and a declaration of entitlement to exemption on the prescription form is duly completed by or on behalf of the patient. A chemist, notwithstanding the provisions of the terms of service, is under no obligation to provide pharmaceutical services in respect of an order on a prescription form unless first paid by the patient any charge required to be made and recovered in respect of that order.

A chemist who makes and recovers a charge must, if so required by the patient, give a receipt for the amount received on a form provided for the purpose. A doctor who provides pharmaceutical services to a patient is under similar obligations with respect to the making and recovery of charges.

Exemptions are provided for in reg. 6. No charge is payable by:

(a) a person who is under 16 years of age;

(b) a person who is under 19 years of age and is receiving qualifying full-time education;

(c) persons aged 60 or over;

(d) a woman with a valid exemption certificate on the ground that she is an expectant mother or has within the last 12 months given birth to a live child or a child registrable as still-born;

(e) a person with a valid exemption certificate issued on the ground that he is suffering from one or more of the following conditions, namely permanent fistula (including cecostomy, colostomy, laryngostomy or ileostomy) requiring continuous surgical dressing or an appliance or the following disorders for which specific substitution therapy is essential, namely Addison's disease and other forms of hypoadrenalism, diabetes insipidus and other forms of hypopituitarism, diabetes mellitus, hypoparathyroidism, myasthenia gravis, myxoedema, epilepsy requiring continuous anti-convulsive therapy;

(f) a person with a continuing physical disability which prevents the patient from leaving his residence without the help of another person;

(g) a person with a valid exemption certificate issued by the Secretary of State in respect of the supply of drugs and appliances for the treatment of accepted disablement, but only in respect of those supplies to which the certificate relates;

(h) a person with a valid pre-payment certificate.

A pre-payment certificate, supplied by the health authority on payment of the specified sum, is valid for a period of either four months or twelve months.

Under the provisions of the National Health Service (Travelling Expenses and Remission of Charges) Regulations 1988 (S.I. 1988/551), as amended, certain persons on low income are also exempted from the requirement to pay charges for drugs, medicines and appliances. Low income is defined in terms of entitlement to, and receipt of certain categories of social security benefits including income support, family credit, disability working allowance, and income-based jobseeker's allowance.

3.10 PAYMENT FOR PHARMACEUTICAL SERVICES

The procedures for payments to pharmacists for pharmaceutical services are also subject to legal control and regulation. Under para. 8(2) of the terms of service, as outlined in sch. 2 to the National Health Service (Pharmaceutical Services) Regulations 1992, as amended, the health authority is under a duty to make payments, calculated in the manner provided by the Drug Tariff, to chemists in respect of drugs and appliances, containers, medicines measures and dispensing fees. The health authority is also under a duty to make such payments, if any, as are provided for by the Drug Tariff to chemists who provide additional services within the meaning of reg. 16A.

Provision for the Drug Tariff is made under reg. 18 of the 1992 Regulations, as amended. The Secretary of State is under a duty, for the purpose of enabling arrangements to be made for the provision of pharmaceutical services, to compile and publish a statement, to be referred to as the Drug Tariff, which may be further amended from time to time. The Drug Tariff includes:

(a) the list of appliances for the time being approved by the Secretary of State for the purposes of s. 41 of the National Health Service Act 1977, as amended;

(b) the list of chemical reagents for the time being approved by the Secretary of State for the purposes of s. 41 of the National Health Service Act 1977, as amended;

(c)   the list of drugs for the time being approved by the Secretary of State for the purposes of s. 41 of the National Health Service Act 1977, as amended;

(d)   the prices on the basis of which the payment for drugs and appliances ordinarily supplied is to be calculated;

(e)   the method of calculating the payment for drugs not mentioned in the Drug Tariff;

(f)   the method of calculating the payment for containers and medicine measures;

(g)   the dispensing or other fees payable in respect of the supply of drugs and appliances and of supplemental services and additional professional services;

(h)   arrangements for claiming fees, allowances and other remuneration for the provision of pharmaceutical services;

(i)   the method by which a claim may be made for compensation for financial loss in respect of oxygen equipment.

The prices referred to in (d) above may be fixed prices or may be subject to monthly or other periodical variations to be determined by reference to fluctuations in the cost of drugs and appliances.

A chemist must supply, in response to a request from the Secretary of State, within 30 days of the notification of the request, any information which the Secretary of State may require for the purpose of conducting any inquiry into the prices, payments, fees, allowances and remuneration specified in (d) to (i) above.

The calculation of payments is carried out by the Prescription Pricing Authority (PPA). The PPA is a special health authority within the National Health Service Executive. It is established under s. 11 and sch. 5 of the National Health Service Act 1977. Its constitution and functions are now provided for under the Prescription Pricing Authority Constitution Order 1990 (S.I. 1990/1718), and the Prescription Pricing Authority Regulations 1990 (S.I. 1990/1719).

The PPA consists of eight members, of whom one must be a registered pharmacist providing pharmaceutical services. The remaining members are made up of the chairman, representatives of the medical profession, the health authorities and lay members. The Secretary of State appoints all members who hold their term of office for three years.

The PPA perform such functions as the Secretary of State may direct it to perform on his or her behalf or on behalf of health authorities. Those legislative functions include examining, checking and pricing of prescriptions for drugs, listed drugs, medicines and listed appliances supplied as part of pharmaceutical services. The PPA also deals with payment to contractors who dispense NHS prescriptions, provide prescribing and dispensing information to the NHS, and prevent prescribing and dispensing fraud within the NHS.

3.11 CONCLUSION

The practical nature of the relationship between the pharmacist and the NHS often disguises its distinct legal reality. The analysis in this chapter has shown that this reality is manifested through the comprehensive and detailed rules governing all aspects of that relationship, including the important terms of service for pharmacists. Pharmacists should pay close attention to the details of these rules and regulations.

The maintenance of the association with the NHS is vital for the pharmacy profession, as it is for the NHS itself. The structure of the NHS is currently subject to important changes which will have important implications for all of those who provide health care services to it. Pharmacists, and other health care professionals, will have to monitor the legislative provisions which implement those structural changes, in order that the important and vital relationship with the NHS can continue and flourish.

FOUR

The licensing of medicinal products

4.1 INTRODUCTION

A number of factors have influenced the development of the legal controls over
the licensing of medicinal products. In the post-war period, those responsible
for the development of the NHS were concerned to establish mechanisms and
procedures for the specification of certain medicines. This initiative took on a
greater importance with the occurrence of the tragedy surrounding the drug
thalidomide in the early 1960s. A number of committees were established to
recommend the introduction of new laws relating to the safety and efficacy of
medicines, and the implementation of procedures to ensure that proper and
effective manufacturing processes would be introduced.

Many of the recommendations of these committees became governmental
policy resulting, after the publication of relevant white papers, in the passing of
the Medicines Act 1968 (MA 1968). The provisions of this vital piece of
legislation still form the basis of the regulation and control of the licensing of
medicines. However the initial provisions have been subject to significant
amendment as a result of the implementation of European Union Directives.

The EEC had commenced the process of introducing new controls on
medicines prior to the United Kingdom joining in 1973. The EU's initiative
has been subject to greater momentum since then, resulting in the implementation of significant legislative provisions which now form the basis of the
domestic law of all member states. These provisions have the twofold purpose
of harmonising the laws of all members states and strengthening the existing
provisions relating to safety, quality and efficacy.

The current EU system of control is based around a centralised procedure
relating mainly to biotechnology and other high technology products, and a

mutual recognition or decentralised procedure applicable to all other human medicines. The new system is co-ordinated and supported by a newly established European Medicines Evaluation Agency, advised by the Committee for Proprietary Medicinal Products.

The EU legislative provisions have resulted in substantial amendments to the UK domestic legislative provisions. Most of the EU system of control has now been introduced and the text of this chapter analyses the current legislative provision. The detailed structure has been introduced by the Medicines for Human Use (Authorisations Etc.) Regulations 1994 (S.I. 1994/3144) (MAR 1994). The new system allows for a variety of different types of licences for medicinal products which are clearly defined in the new secondary legislation. They include marketing authorisations, registration certificates for homeopathic medicines, manufacturers' licences, wholesale dealers' licences, and clinical trial certificates. The relevent legislative provisions are backed up by a series of criminal offences. The control is not absolute, however, and specific exemptions are also permitted in certain circumstances.

Licences are also required for a process called 'parallel importing'. This is where forms of medicinal products, with existing United Kingdom marketing authorisations, are imported for sale from another member state of the European Union. The licensing authority issues a revised form of licence for this purpose. As the conditions for issue represent a variation form of a full application, no separate legislative provisions have been made for this type of licence.

In essence, the conditions for issue are that the product must be licensed in an EU member state, have no difference in therapeutic effect from an equivalent product licensed in the UK, be manufactured by the same group of companies, or by another company under licence, as the UK product, and be labelled in English.

The advertising of medicinal products is also subject to strict control and regulation. The process of controlling advertisements commenced with the introduction of the MA 1968. While these legislative provisions still form the basis of the regulation in the United Kingdom, the influence of the European Union has also been strong in this area. A series of EU Directives has been implemented to amend the domestic legislation. The relevant provisions create specific criminal offences to back up the legislative requirements.

Advertising regulation takes three main forms — control over the form and content of advertisements, control over the directing of those advertisements to both health care professionals and the public and further monitoring of advertisements already satisfying the first two criteria. The legislative provisions relating to the regulation of advertising complement the provisions relating to safety, quality and efficacy. The ideology behind these joint policies is to ensure that medicinal products which arrive in the hands of those with further responsibilities for their distribution have been subject to rigorous control.

Pharmacists need to know how medicinal products are licensed, understand the detailed procedures which exist to control the safety, quality and efficacy of medicinal products, and comprehend how such products may be lawfully marketed to health care professionals and to the public. That knowledge and comprehension will form the basis for the further analysis of the rules and regulations relating to the classification of medicinal products and the distribution of those products as part of the provision of health care.

Part ① Administration

4.2 ADVICE ON LICENSING — THE MEDICINES COMMISSION

Section 2, MA 1968 establishes the Medicines Commission ('the Commission'). The Commission, which has the legal classification of being a body corporate with perpetual succession, is required to have at least eight members, appointed by the Health and Agriculture Ministers (classified as 'the Ministers' under s. 1(1), MA 1968), after consultation with appropriate organisations. The Commission must include at least one person who has wide and recent experience, and has shown capacity, in each of the following areas: (a) the practice of medicine (other than veterinary medicine); (b) the practice of veterinary medicine; (c) the practice of pharmacy; (d) chemistry other than pharmaceutical chemistry; and (e) the pharmaceutical industry. One of the members is appointed as chairman by the Ministers.

Under s. 3, MA 1968, the general function of the Commission is to advise the Ministers on any matter relating to the administration of the MA 1968 or on any matters relating to medicinal products. More specifically, the Commission has a duty to make recommendations to the Ministers about the number, constitution, functions, and review of other committees required to be established under s. 4, MA 1968. Further the Commission is under a duty to undertake any of the functions, statutorily empowered to other committees, which have not been assigned to those committees.

The Commission reports to the licensing authority which, in certain circumstances, is under a duty, or may elect, to take account of the Commission's advice in determining an application for licences relating to medicinal products. The Commission is also under a duty to submit an annual report on the performance of its functions, and the functions of any committee appointed by it to the Ministers. The annual report is laid before Parliament.

4.3 MEDICINES ACT COMMITTEES

Other committees may be established by the Ministers for any purpose in connection with the MA 1968, or in connection with any power conferred by it. In particular, s. 4, MA 1968 allows for the establishment of committees for the purpose of:

(a)   giving advice with respect to safety, quality and efficacy;

(b)   promoting the collection and investigation of information relating to adverse reactions; and

(c)   the formulation, editing and publication of British Pharmacopoeia.

Committees established under s. 4 are obliged to make an annual report on the performance of their functions, to the Commission and to the Ministers.

Committees which have been established under s. 4, MA 1968 include the important Committee on the Safety of Medicines, established under the Medicines (Committee on Safety of Medicines) Order 1970 (S.I. 1970/1257); the Veterinary Products Committee, established under the Medicines (Veterinary Products Committee) Order 1970 (S.I. 1970/1304); the British Pharmacopoeia Committee, established under the Medicines (British Pharmacopoeia Commission) Order 1970 (S.I. 1970/1256, and 1982/1335; and the Advisory Board on the Registration of Homeopathic Products, established under the Medicines (Advisory Board on the Registration of Homeopathic Products) Order 1995 (S.I. 1995/309).

The administrative functions of the Commission and the other committees are provided for in sch. 1 to MA 1968 and in the provisions of the Medicines Commission and Committees Regulations 1970 (S.I. 1970/746). The Ministers, after consultation with the Commission, may add to, vary or revoke any of the Commission's functions, subject to the approval of a resolution to do so by both Houses of Parliament.

4.4   LICENSING AUTHORITY

Under s. 6, MA 1968, and the provisions of the MAR 1994 the authority responsible for the grant, renewal, variation, suspension and revocation of licences, marketing authorisations and certificates is a body of Ministers to be known as the licensing authority. The body of Ministers is made up of the relevant Health and Agriculture Ministers of England, Scotland, Wales and Northern Ireland. In reality the functions of the licensing authority are carried out through the Medicines Control Agency (MCA), an executive arm of government which regulates the pharmaceutical sector and which implements policy in this area, and the European Medicines Evaluation Agency (EMEA).

4.5   MARKETING AUTHORISATIONS

Regulation 3(1) of the MAR 1994 makes it clear that, except in accordance with any exception or exemption, no relevant medicinal product may be placed on the market, nor distributed by way of wholesale dealing, unless a marketing authorisation in respect of that product has been granted and is in force. Subject to the appropriate exemptions, it is an offence to place on the market, or sell, supply, manufacture, import or export relevant medicinal products, without an appropriate marketing authorisation. Several other major offences are also created by the legislation.

A relevant medicinal product is a medicinal product for human use to which Chapters II to V of Council Directive 65/65/EEC apply. In Council Directive 65/65/EEC, a medicinal product is defined as:

(a)   any substance or combination of substances presented for treating or preventing disease in human beings or animals;

(b)   any substance or combination of substances which may be administered to human beings or animals with a view to making a diagnosis or to restoring, correcting, or modifying physiological functions in human beings or animals.

The term 'medicinal product for human use to which Chapters II to V of Council Directive 65/65/EEC apply' has its own definition. It refers to all medicinal products for human use except those prepared on the basis of a magistral or official formula, medicinal products intended for research, or intermediate products intended for further processing by an authorised manufacturer.

In reality, the majority of commercially produced medicinal products are covered by the definitions contained in the European legislation, and inserted into the United Kingdom domestic legislation. We shall see, however, that a limited number of medicinal products remain outside the definitional scope of the European Union legislative provisions. Existing licensing requirements will continue to apply to such products. These requirements are discussed below in 4.12.

4.6   APPLICATIONS FOR MARKETING AUTHORISATIONS

Applications for the grant, renewal or variation of a marketing authorisation are made to the licensing authority, must be made in a prescribed form and manner, and must contain, or be accompanied by, certain prescribed information, documents, samples and other material.

Under reg. 4 of the MAR 1994, every application, which must also be made in accordance with relevant European Union provisions, must be in writing, must be signed by or on behalf of the applicant and be accompanied by the requisite fee. In the case of an application for a grant of a marketing authorisation, 26 copies of the application and accompanying material must be supplied to the licensing authority. In the case of an application for the renewal of a marketing authorisation, three copies of the application and accompanying information are required. An application for the renewal of a marketing authorisation must be made not later than three months before the date on which the existing authorisation expires.

An application for the grant of a marketing authorisation must include a statement indicating whether the relevant medicinal product is one which should be available on prescription, or only from a pharmacy or on general sale, and details of what provisions of the authorisation are proposed concerning the method of sale or supply of the product, including any proposed restrictions affecting the circumstances of the use or promotion of the product.

Details of the accompanying material for an application for a marketing authorisation are outlined in a series of EC directives including Council Directive 65/65/EEC, Council Directive 75/319/EEC and Council Directive 75/318/EEC. The accompanying material must include the important summary of product characteristics. The summary of product characteristics includes the data sheet, if there is one, or if there is no data sheet, (as these are no longer required for relevant medicinal products), certain required basic information.

In addition, the accompanying material must include certain specific information, too detailed to be described here, e.g., the name and address of the person responsible for placing the product on the market, and, where applicable, the name and address of the manufacturer; details of the brand, scientific or common name of the medicinal product, trade mark or name of the manufacturer; qualitative and quantitative particulars of all of the constituents of the product; description of the method of preparation.

Other information includes particulars of the therapeutic indications, contra-indications and side-effects; posology, pharmaceutical form, method and route of administration, expected shelf life and precaution and safety measures; control methods and tests employed by the manufacturer; results of clinical tests and trials; mock ups of the sales presentation of the product together with a package leaflet; authorisation to produce medicinal products and copies of any authorisation obtained in another member state or other country. There are further detailed requirements for applications concerning immunologicals, radiopharmaceuticals and blood products.

4.7 DETERMINING AN APPLICATION

In dealing with an application for a marketing authorisation, the licensing authority is required, under s. 19, MA 1968, to give particular consideration to the safety, efficacy, and quality of the medicinal products of each description to which the application relates. In taking into consideration the efficacy of a medicinal product for particular purposes, the licensing authority must leave out of account any question whether medicinal products of another description would or might be equally efficacious for that purpose. Under s. 20(2), MA 1968, the licensing authority must not refuse to grant a marketing authorisation on any grounds relating to the price of the product.

Under s. 132(2), MA 1968, considerations of safety are taken to include consideration of the extent to which the substance or article:

(a)   if used without proper safeguards, is capable of causing danger to the health of the community; or

(b)   may interfere with the treatment, prevention or diagnosis of disease; or

(c)   may be harmful to the person administering it or (in the case of an instrument, apparatus or appliance) the person operating it.

Where the application relates to imported products, the licensing authority must take into consideration the methods, standards and conditions of manufacture of the products. The licensing authority may require the applicant to produce any one or more of the following:

(a)   an undertaking, given by the manufacturer, to permit the inspection of the premises and manufacturing operations;

(b)   an undertaking, given by or on behalf of the manufacturer, to comply with any prescribed conditions;

(c)   a declaration, given by or on behalf of the manufacturer, that any requirements imposed by or under the law of the country in which they are or are to be manufactured have been or will be complied with.

The prescribed conditions mentioned in (b) have been outlined in the schedule to the Medicines (Manufacturer's Undertakings for Imported Products) Regulations 1977 (S.I. 1977/1038 as amended by The Medicines (Manufacturers Undertakings for Imported Products) Amendment Regulations 1992 (S.I. 1992/2845)). Again, they are too specific to be described in detail here.

Schedule 2 of the Medicines Act (MA) 1968, outlines detailed procedural provisions relating to the grant, renewal, variation, revocation, and suspension of a marketing authorisation. The licensing authority must consult with the appropriate committee or the Medicines Commission, before refusing to grant, renew, revoke, vary or suspend an application on any ground other than those relating to the accuracy or completeness of the application.

The appropriate committee or the Commission may form a provisional opinion that, on grounds relating to safety, quality or efficacy, they may be unable to advise the licensing authority to grant or renew an authorisation, or that it may be granted but subject to conditions, or that an authorisation ought to be revoked, varied or suspended. In such circumstances, the applicant must be notified. The applicant may make oral or written representations to the appropriate committee or the Commission which is under a duty to take these into account. The committee or Commission must then make a report of its findings, advice and reasons for advice to the licensing authority.

After making its decision regarding grant, renewal, suspension, variation or revocation, the licensing authority must notify the applicant accordingly and also give notice of the advice given by the appropriate committee or the Commission. Applicants who are dissatisfied with the decision of the licensing authority may then, if they have not already done so, make oral or written representations to the Commission. Dissatisfied applicants may also be heard by the Commission which must then report its findings and advice to the licensing authority. Such findings and advice must then be notified to the applicant.

Special rules exist for the situation where the licensing authority determines an application in a way which differs from the advice of the Commission or the appropriate committee. If it proposes to act against such advice, it must notify the applicant accordingly. The applicant must also be notified where the licensing authority proposes not to alter its decision following further representations to, or a hearing before the Commission, or proposes not to grant or renew or vary, suspend or revoke a licence, on grounds other than safety, quality or efficacy. Such notification must include, where relevant, the advice of the appropriate committee and the reasons of the Commission, and, as appropriate, include a statement of the proposals of the licensing authority and its reasons.

A person given a notification, as described in the previous paragraph, may apply to be heard by a person appointed for the purpose by the licensing authority or make written representations with regard to the decision or proposal. The person appointed under these provisions must not be an officer or servant of the Ministers, and any hearing may be in public. The licensing authority must forward a copy of the report of the person appointed to hear the case, and must take that report into account in determining whether to grant, renew, vary, suspend or revoke an authorisation, or confirm or alter its original decision.

Any marketing authorisation granted under these provisions will include a set of standard stipulations and requirements imposed by the appropriate European Union legislation, and to be found, in part, in the MAR 1994. An applicant for a marketing authorisation may seek to have such standard conditions and obligations omitted from the final marketing authorisation. These conditions and obligations are too detailed to be outlined here. A marketing authorisation, unless previously renewed or revoked, is valid for a period of five years beginning with the date on which it was granted.

4.8 HOMEOPATHIC MEDICINAL PRODUCTS

Under the Medicines (Homeopathic Medicinal Products for Human Use) Regulations 1994 (S.I. 1994/105) as amended, a homeopathic medicinal product means any product (which may contain a number of principles) prepared from products, substances, or compositions called homeopathic stocks in accordance with a homeopathic manufacturing procedure described by the European Pharmacopeia or by any pharmacopeia used officially in a member state of the European Union.

Under reg. 3 of the Medicines Act 1968 (Amendment) (No. 2) Regulations 1994 (S.I. 1994/276), the requirement to have a marketing authorisation does not apply to homeopathic medicinal products in respect of which a certificate of registration has been granted. Certificates of registration for homeopathic medicinal products are provided for by the Medicines (Homeopathic Medicinal Products for Human Use) Regulations 1994 (S.I. 1994/105).

Applications must be in writing to the licensing authority, and must be accompanied by certain specified material and information. The specifics of the accompanying materials, which are provided for in Council Directive 92/73/EEC, are too detailed to be described here, but may be found in sch. 1 to the Medicines (Homeopathic Medicinal Products for Human Use) Regulations.

In dealing with an application for a certificate of registration, the licensing authority must take into account any registration granted by another member state in accordance with Council Directive 92/73/EEC. The licensing authority may grant a certificate on an application to do so but must refuse to grant where:

(a) the product is not for oral or external administration;

(b) a specific therapeutic indication appears on the labelling of the product or in any information relating to the product;

(c) the product does not have a sufficient degree of dilution to guarantee its safety;

(d) after verification of the material and information submitted with the application, the product proves to be harmful in the normal conditions of use, or the qualitative or quantitative composition of the product is not as declared; or

(e) the application does not comply with the specific requirements for registration.

Further to condition (c), products are not considered to have a sufficient degree of dilution to guarantee their safety where they contain more than one part per 10,000 of the mother tincture. In addition there is not a sufficient degree of dilution where there is more than one hundredth of the smallest dose used in allothapy with regard to active principles whose presence in an allopathic medicinal product would require it to be sold or supplied in accordance with a prescription given by a doctor.

Certificates of registration shall, unless previously revoked, last for five years, and may be renewed by the licensing authority on application by the holder. Renewal procedures are the same as those for initial grant. A certificate of registration may be suspended or revoked by the licensing authority where the product to which it relates proves to be harmful in the normal conditions of use, the qualitative or quantitative composition of such a product is not as declared or certain of the required registration information proves to be incorrect.

In such circumstances, products to which that certificate relates may be withdrawn from the market. The licensing authority may also vary the provisions of a certificate of registration, on an application from the holder, where the variation relates to a change which does not require medical, scientific or pharmaceutical assessment.

4.9 MANUFACTURER'S LICENCE

Under s. 8, MA 1968, and subject to other exemptions, no person, in the course of a business is permitted to manufacture or assemble any medicinal product except in accordance with a licence granted for these purposes. Under s. 132, MA 1968, 'manufacture' includes any process carried out in the course of making the product, but does not include dissolving or dispersing the product in, or diluting or mixing it with, some other substance used as a vehicle for the purpose of administering it.

'Assemble' means enclosing the product (with or without other medicinal products of the same description) in a container which is labelled before the product is sold or supplied, or, where the product (with or without other medicinal products of the same description) is already enclosed in the container in which it is to be sold or supplied, labelling the container before the product is sold or supplied. 'Assembly' is given a corresponding meaning.

Applications for the grant of a manufacturer's licence are made to the licensing authority, must be in a prescribed form and manner, and must contain, or be accompanied by, prescribed information, documents, samples and other material. Any such application must indicate the descriptions of medicinal products in respect of which the licence is required, either by specifying the descriptions of medicinal products in question or by way of an appropriate general classification.

Under s. 19(5), MA 1968, the licensing authority must, in dealing with an application for a manufacturer's licence, in particular, take into consideration:

(a) the operations proposed to be carried out in pursuance of the licence;

(b) the premises in which those operations are to be carried out;

(c) the equipment which is or will be available on those premises for carrying out those operations;

(d) the qualifications of the persons under whose supervision those operations will be carried out; and

(e) the arrangements made or to be made for ensuring the safe-keeping of, and the maintenance of records in respect of, medicinal products manufactured or assembled in pursuance of the licence.

The prescribed form for applications for a manufacturer's licence is provided for in the Medicines (Applications for Manufacturer's and Wholesale Dealer's Licences) Regulations 1971 (S.I. 1971/974) as amended by the Medicines (Applications for Manufacturer's and Wholesale Dealer's Licences) Amendment Regulations 1977 (S.I. 1977/1052). Every application for the grant of a manufacturer's licence must contain or be accompanied by particular materials and information. These particulars are too specific to be detailed here but may be found in sch. 1 to the 1971 Regulations.

Six copies of the application, together with the accompanying materials, and signed by the applicant, must be supplied to the licensing authority. In turn, the licensing authority may decide to grant or refuse a licence. As with a marketing authorisation, the licensing authority must consult with the appropriate committee or the Medicines Commission, before refusing to grant an application on any ground relating to the price of the product. In addition, the licensing authority must not refuse to grant a licence on grounds relating to safety, quality or efficacy except after consultation with the appropriate committee or with the Commission. Where the licensing authority grants a licence, it must send a copy of the licence to every appropriate committee or to the Commission.

The process for the consideration of an application for a manufacturer's licence, for notification of decisions to the applicant, for the making of representations, and for the making of appeals is the same as that for a marketing authorisation, described in 4.6 and 4.7.

Any manufacturer's licence granted under these provisions will include a set of standard stipulations and requirements imposed under s. 47, MA 1968, and the relevant European Union legislation, and to be found, in part, in the Medicines (Standard Provisions for Licences and Certificates) Regulations 1971 (S.I. 1971/972), as amended. An applicant for a manufacturer's licence may seek to have such standard conditions and obligations omitted from the final manufacturer's licence. These conditions and obligations are too detailed to be outlined here.

A manufacturer's licence granted under these provisions, unless previously renewed or revoked, will last for a period of five years from the date on which it was granted. The power to revoke a licence, or to suspend or vary its terms, is vested in the licensing authority under s. 28, MA 1968. A suspension may be total or may be limited to particular medicinal products or to medicinal products manufactured, assembled or stored on particular premises.

The power to suspend, revoke or vary a manufacturer's licence is exercisable only on one of a number of limited grounds outlined in s. 28(4) and (5). The detailed procedure where the licensing authority proposes to exercise any power to suspend, vary or revoke a licence under s. 28 is outlined in sch. 2, MA 1968. The procedure includes consultation with the appropriate committee or the Commission and the right for the holder of the licence to be heard and to make representations. Further detailed procedures are provided for urgent cases.

Renewal applications for a manufacturer's licence are provided for in the Medicines (Renewal Applications for Licences and Certificates) Regulations 1974 (S.I. 1974/832), as amended. Renewal applications must be in writing, in an approved form and may specify which of the standard provisions, if any, are to be excluded in the licence. Six copies of the application, together with

specified accompanying material, and any relevant samples must be supplied
to the licensing authority. The particulars to be included in the accompanying
material are provided for in the schedules to the Regulations. Further provision
is made for early and late renewal applications.

 ### 4.10   WHOLESALE DEALER'S LICENCE

Under s. 8(3), MA 1968, and subject to other exemptions, no person, in the
course of a business is permitted to:

(a)   sell, or offer for sale, any medicinal product by way of wholesale
dealing, or
(b)   distribute, otherwise than by way of sale, any medicinal product which
has been imported, but was not consigned from a member state of the
European Union.

except in accordance with a licence granted for these purposes.

Under the provisions of the Medicines Act 1968 (Amendment) Regulations
1993 (S.I. 1993/834), no person may, in the course of business, distribute by
way of wholesale dealing a product to which Chapters II to V of Directive
65/65/EEC apply, except in accordance with a wholesale dealer's licence.
Under reg. 6 of the same Regulations, a licence is also required for the
exportation of such a product to a member state of the European Union.

There are a number of exemptions from the requirement to hold a wholesale
dealer's licence. Under s. 131, MA 1968, sales by the manufacturer of the
product are excluded from the definition of wholesale dealing. Equally, under
the provisions of the Medicines (Exemption from Licences) (Wholesale
Dealing) Order 1990 (S.I. 1990/566), as amended, a licence is not required by
the holder of a marketing authorisation or by the person who assembled the
medicinal product to the order of the holder of the marketing authorisation,
where the product has not left the premises of the manufacturer or assembler
until its sale.

A licence is also not required by the person who handles the medicinal
product in the course of the provision of facilities solely for the transport of the
medicinal product, or who, in the course of a business carried on as an import
agent, imports the medicinal product solely to the order of another person who
intends to offer the product for sale by way of wholesale dealing or in any other
way distribute it.

Otherwise, under s. 8(7), MA 1968, as inserted by the Medicines Act 1968
(Amendment) Regulations 1993, distribution by way of wholesale dealing
means selling or supplying it, or procuring, holding or exporting it for the
purposes of sale or supply to a person who receives it for the purposes of selling
or supplying it, or administering it, or causing it to be administered to one or
more human beings in the course of business.

Under s. 132, MA 1968, 'business' includes a professional practice and includes any activity carried on by a body of persons, whether corporate or unincorporate. Further under s. 131(5) the provision of services under the National Health Service is treated as the carrying on of a business by the appropriate Minister, Secretary of State or Ministry.

Applications for the grant of a wholesale dealer's licence are made to the licensing authority, and must be made in a prescribed form and manner, and must contain, or be accompanied by, prescribed information, documents, samples and other material. Any such application must indicate the descriptions of medicinal products in respect of which the licence is required, either by specifying the descriptions of medicinal products in question or by way of an appropriate general classification.

Under s. 19(6), MA 1968, in dealing with an application for a wholesale dealer's licence, the licensing authority must, in particular, take into consideration:

(a)   the premises on which medicinal products of the descriptions to which the application relates will be stored;

(b)   the equipment which is or will be available for storing medicinal products on those premises;

(c)   the equipment and facilities which are or will be available for distributing products from those premises;

(d)   the arrangements made or to be made for ensuring the safe-keeping of, and the maintenance of records in respect of, medicinal products stored on or distributed from those premises.

The prescribed form for applications for a wholesale dealer's licence is provided for in the Medicines (Applications for Manufacturer's and Wholesale Dealer's Licences) Regulations 1971 (S.I. 1971/974) as amended by the Medicines (Applications for Manufacturer's and Wholesale Dealer's Licences) Amendment Regulations 1977 (S.I. 1977/1052). Every application for the grant of a wholesale dealer's licence must contain or be accompanied by particular materials and information. These particulars are too specific to be detailed here but may be found in sch. 2 to the 1971 Regulations.

Six copies of the application, together with the accompanying materials, signed by the applicant, must be supplied to the licensing authority. In turn, the licensing authority may decide to grant or refuse a licence. As with a marketing authorisation, and a manufacturer's licence, there are particular consultation requirements and representation requirements on the part of the licensing authority. These have been described in detail above.

Any wholesale dealer's licence granted under these provisions will include a set of standard stipulations and requirements imposed under s. 47, MA 1968, and the relevant European Union legislation, and to be found, in part, in the Medicines (Standard Provisions for Licences and Certificates) Regulations

1971 (S.I. 1971/972), as amended. An applicant for a wholesale dealer's licence may seek to have such standard conditions and obligations omitted from the final licence. These conditions and obligations are too detailed to be outlined here.

A wholesale dealer's licence granted under these provisions, unless previously renewed or revoked, will last for a period of five years from the date on which it was granted. The power to revoke a licence, or to suspend or vary its terms, is vested in the licensing authority under s. 28, MA 1968. A suspension may be total or may be limited to particular medicinal products or to medicinal products manufactured, assembled or stored on particular premises.

The power to suspend, revoke or vary a wholesale dealer's licence is exercisable only on one of a number of limited grounds outlined in s. 28(4) and (6). The detailed procedure where the licensing authority proposes to exercise any power to suspend, vary or revoke a licence under s. 28 is outlined in sch. 2, MA 1968. The procedure includes consultation with the appropriate committee or the Commission and the right for the holder of the licence to be heard and to make representations. Further detailed procedures are provided for urgent cases.

Renewal applications for a wholesale dealer's licence are provided for in the Medicines (Renewal Applications for Licences and Certificates) Regulations 1974 (S.I. 1974/832), as amended. Renewal applications must be in writing, in an approved form and may specify which of the standard provisions, if any, are to be excluded in the licence. Six copies of the application, together with specified accompanying material, and any relevant samples must be supplied to the licensing authority. The particulars to be included in the accompanying material are provided for in the schedules to the Regulations. Further provision is made for early and late renewal applications.

4.11 CLINICAL TRIAL CERTIFICATES

Under s. 31(1), MA 1968, 'clinical trial' means an investigation or series of investigations consisting of the administration of one or more medicinal products, by or under the direction of one or more doctors or dentists, to one or more patients of theirs, where there is evidence that:

(a)   medicinal products of that type have effects which may be beneficial to the patient or patients in question; and
(b)   the administration of the product is for the purpose of ascertaining whether, or to what extent, the products have, beneficial or harmful effects.

Under s. 31(2) no person may, in the course of a business:

(a)   sell or supply any medicinal product for the purposes of a clinical trial; or

(b)   procure the sale or supply of any medicinal product for the purposes of a clinical trial; or

(c)   procure the manufacture or assembly of any medicinal product for sale or supply for the purposes of a clinical trial; or

(d)   import any medicinal product for the purposes of a clinical trial;

unless;

(a)   that person holds a marketing authorisation which permits the clinical trial, or acts to the order of the holder of a marketing authorisation, in conformity with the terms of the marketing authorisation; or

(b)   a current certificate has been issued warranting that the licensing authority has consented to the clinical trial and the trial is to be carried out in accordance with that certificate.

Under s. 35, MA 1968, a marketing authorisation or manufacturer's licence is not required in relation to the manufacture or assembly of a medicinal product for the sole purpose of being administered, or sold, supplied or exported for the sole purpose of being administered, by way of a clinical trial.

Applications for the grant of a clinical trial certificate are made to the licensing authority, and must be made in a prescribed form and manner, and must contain, or be accompanied by, certain prescribed information, documents, samples and other material. In dealing with any such application, the licensing authority must have regard to any available evidence as to any risks involved in the proposed clinical trial.

The prescribed form for applications for a clinical trial certificate is provided for in the Medicines (Applications for Product Licences and Clinical Trial and Animal Test Certificates) Regulations 1971 (S.I. 1971/973) as amended. Every application for the grant of a clinical trial certificate must contain or be accompanied by particular materials and information. These particulars are too specific to be detailed here but may be found in sch. 2 to the 1971 Regulations.

Six copies of the application, together with the accompanying materials, signed by the applicant, must be supplied to the licensing authority. In turn, the licensing authority may decide to grant or refuse a certificate. As with a marketing authorisation, a manufacturer's licence, and a wholesale dealer's licence, there are particular consultation requirements and representation requirements on the part of the licensing authority. These have been described in detail above.

A clinical trial certificate granted under these provisions, unless previously renewed or revoked, will last for a period of two years from the date on which it was issued. The power to revoke a clinical trial certificate, or to suspend or vary its terms, is vested in the licensing authority under s. 39, MA 1968. The power to suspend, revoke or vary a clinical trial certificate is exercisable only on one of a number of limited grounds outlined in s. 39(2).

The detailed procedure where the licensing authority proposes to exercise any power to suspend, vary or revoke a certificate under s. 39 is outlined in sch. 2, MA 1968. The procedure includes consultation with the appropriate committee or the Commission and the right for the holder of the certificate to be heard and to make representations. Further detailed procedures are provided for urgent cases.

Any clinical trial certificate granted under these provisions will include a set of standard stipulations and requirements imposed under s. 47, MA 1968, and the relevant European Union legislation, and to be found, in part, in the Medicines (Standard Provisions for Licences and Certificates) Regulations 1971 (S.I. 1971/972), as amended. These conditions and obligations are too detailed to be outlined here. An applicant for a clinical trial certificate may seek to have such standard conditions and obligations omitted from the certificate.

Renewal applications for a clinical trial certificate are provided for in s. 38(2), MA 1968, and the Medicines (Renewal Applications for Licences and Certificates) Regulations 1974 (S.I. 1974/832), as amended. Renewal applications must be in writing, in an approved form and may specify which, standard provisions, if any, are to be excluded in the certificate. Six copies, application, together with specified accompanying material, and any relevant samples must be supplied to the licensing authority. The particulars to be included in the accompanying material are provided for in the schedules to the Regulations. Further provision is made for early and late renewal applications.

4.12   OTHER MEDICINAL PRODUCTS

As noted above, the majority of commercially produced medicinal products are covered by the definitions contained in the European legislation, and inserted into the United Kingdom domestic legislation. A limited number of medicinal products remain outside the definitional scope, European Union legislative provisions. Existing licensing requirements will continue to apply to such products.

Under s. 7, MA, and subject to other exemptions, no person, in the course of a business is permitted to:

(a)   sell, supply or export any medicinal product; or

(b)   procure the sale, supply or exportation of any medicinal product; or

(c)   procure the manufacture or assembly of any medicinal product for sale, supply or exportation; or

(d)   import any medicinal product;

except in accordance with a marketing authorisation granted for these purposes. The legislative requirements relating to applications, grant, renewal, suspension, revocation and variation of such an authorisation are the same as for a manufacturer's and wholesale dealer's licence, described above.

4.13   EXEMPTIONS

The regulation of the licensing of medicinal products is not absolute. Both the primary and secondary legislation allow for a series of exemptions, relating to particular circumstances, practitioners, other health care professionals, products, ingredients, and clinical trials. Some of these have a direct connection with the practice of pharmacy. The others continue to be worthy of analysis.

4.13.1   Exemption for imports and exports

Under s. 13(1), MA 1968, the prohibition against the import of medicinal products except in accordance with a marketing authorisation does not apply to the importation of a medicinal product by any person for self-administration or for administration to members of that person's household.

Under s. 48(1), MA 1968, the operation of the earlier provisions relating to licensing, as they apply to exports, is postponed until a 'special appointed day'. Under the provisions of the Medicines (Exportation of Specified Products for Human Use) Order 1971 (S.I. 1971/1198), the Health Ministers have decided that this exemption should not apply to medicinal products consisting wholly or partly of substances the purity or potency of which cannot, in their opinion, be adequately tested. The medicinal products specified as such under the Order include antigens, antitoxins, sera, antisera, toxins and vaccines.

Under the provisions of the Medicines (Importation of Medicinal Products for Re-exportation) Order 1971 (S.I. 1971/1326), as amended, the prohibition, importation, except in accordance with a marketing authorisation, of medicinal products, does not apply to medicinal products which are to be exported in the form in which they were imported, and:

(a)   without being assembled in a way different from the way in which they were assembled on being imported; or

(b)   assembled in a way different from the way they were assembled on being imported but the assembler, being the holder of a manufacturer's licence and having supplied the licensing authority with required information, has been told that the product may be imported.

4.13.2   Exemptions for practitioners

Under the provisions of sch. 1 to the MAR 1994, the prohibition against the placing on the market of a medicinal product except in accordance with a marketing authorisation, does not apply to the supply of a medicinal product in response to the bona fide solicited order of a doctor or dentist, for use by the doctor or dentist's patients under their direct responsibility. This exemption is subject to a number of conditions. The medicinal product must be supplied to a doctor or dentist for use in a registered pharmacy, hospital or health centre under the supervision of a pharmacist. No advertisement or representation relating to the medicinal product may be issued.

Further, the manufacture or assembly of the medicinal product must be carried out under the supervision of such staff and such precautions must be taken as are adequate to ensure that the product is, character required by and meets the specifications, doctor or dentist who requires it. Written records as to the manufacture or assembly must be made and maintained and be available for inspection by the licensing authority. The medicinal product must be manufactured, assembled or imported by the holder of a marketing authorisation. Finally the medicinal product must be distributed by way of wholesale dealing by the holder of a wholesale dealer's licence.

An exemption from the requirement to have a marketing authorisation is also provided in circumstances where a doctor or dentist is a member of a group of practitioners working together to provide general medical or dental services to one or more patients, and where the group wishes to procure a stock, product. For this exemption to apply, the amount, procured stock must not exceed a total of five litres of fluids or 2.5 kilogrammes of solids of all medicinal products. The products to which this exemption applies must have been manufactured by the holder of a manufacturer's licence relating to those products.

Under s. 9, MA 1968, the requirement to hold an appropriate licence does not apply to a doctor or a dentist in relation to a medicinal product specially prepared, or imported to the order of that practitioner, for administration to a patient. A similar exemption will be applied to the circumstances where the medicinal product is specially prepared or imported at the request of another doctor or dentist for administration to a particular patient of theirs.

All of the exemptions in relation to practitioners are subject to the further requirement that they maintain appropriate records and undertake requisite notifications under the provisions of sch. 1 to the MAR 1994.

4.13.3 Exemptions for nurses, midwives and pharmacists
Under s. 11, MA 1968, the restrictions relating to the holding of a manufacturer's licence do not apply to the assembly of a medicinal product by registered nurses or registered midwives in the course of their profession.

Under s. 10, MA 1968, as amended by the Medicines (Retail Pharmacists — Exemptions from Licensing Requirements) Order 1971 (S.I. 1971/1445), the legislative requirements for the holding of marketing authorisations, and manufacturer's and wholesale dealer's licences do not apply to any of the following activities carried out in a registered pharmacy, hospital or health centre under the supervision of a pharmacist:

(a) preparing or dispensing a medicinal product in accordance with a prescription given by a practitioner, or preparing a stock of medicinal products with a view to dispensing them;

(b) assembling a medicinal product;

(c) preparing or dispensing a medicinal product in accordance with a specification furnished by the person to whom the product is, or is to be, sold or supplied for administration to that person or a person under their care, or preparing a stock of medicinal products for these purposes;

(d)   preparing or dispensing a medicinal product for administration to a person where the pharmacist is requested by or on behalf of that person to do so in accordance with the pharmacist's own judgment as to the treatment required, and that person is present in the pharmacy at the time of the request in pursuance of which that product is prepared or dispensed (preparing a stock of medicinal products for this purpose is also permitted);

(e)   preparing or dispensing a medicinal product otherwise than in pursuance of an order from any other person, provided that the product is prepared with a view to retail sale or supply in circumstances corresponding to retail sale at the registered pharmacy at which it is prepared, and that the product has not been the subject of an advertisement; and

(f)   wholesale dealing, where such dealing constitutes no more than an inconsiderable part of the business carried on by the pharmacist at that pharmacy.

For the exemption in (b) to apply, the assembling must take place in a registered pharmacy where the business in medicinal products is restricted to retail sale. The assembling must also be done with a view to the sale or supply of it either at the registered pharmacy where it was assembled or at any other such registered pharmacy forming part of the same retail pharmacy business. Finally, the medicinal product must not have been subject of an advertisement.

4.13.4   Exemptions for certain practitioners
Under the provisions of the Medicines (Exemption from Licences) (Assembly) Order 1979 (S.I. 1979/1114), certain exemptions from the legislative requirements relating to manufacturers' licences apply to members of registering bodies or to persons who customarily administer medicinal products to human beings in the course of a business in the field of osteopathy, chiropody, naturopathy or other similar field. For the exemption to apply, the medicinal product must be for human use and may lawfully be sold by retail otherwise than by or under the supervision of a pharmacist. Further the product must be for administration to a particular person who has requested the practitioner to use their own judgment as to the treatment required.

The person seeking exemption under these provisions must notify the licensing authority in writing, giving details of their name and the address at which the assembly is proposed to be carried out. Any exemption granted will have effect from the date of a direction in writing from the licensing authority and will continue in force for five years, subject to renewal. The licensing authority may also terminate the exemption in certain specified circumstances.

4.13.5   Exemptions in respect of herbal remedies
The legislative requirements relating to marketing authorisations and manufacturer's and wholesale dealer's licences do not apply to the sale, supply,

manufacture or assembly of any herbal remedy in the course of a business in certain circumstances. A herbal remedy is a medicinal product consisting of a substance produced by subjecting a plant or plants to drying, crushing or any other process, or of a mixture whose sole ingredients are two or more substances so produced, or of a mixture whose sole ingredients are one or more substances so produced and water or some other inert substances. The circumstances relevant to the applicability of the exemption are that:

(a)   the remedy is manufactured or assembled on premises of which the person carrying on the business is the occupier and which are able to be closed so as to exclude the public; and

(b)   the person carrying on the business sells or supplies the remedy for administration to a particular person after being requested by or on behalf of that person and in that person's presence to use their own judgment as to the treatment required.

Further an exemption will apply where the process to which the plant or plants are subjected consists only of drying, crushing or comminuting, and the herbal remedy is, or is to be, sold or supplied:

(a)   under a designation which only specifies the plant or plants and the process does not apply any other name to the remedy; and

(b)   without any written recommendation (whether by means of a labelled container or package or a leaflet or in any other way) as to the use of the remedy.

4.13.6   Exemptions for wholesale dealing in confectionery
Under the provisions of the Medicines (Exemption from Licences) (Wholesale Dealing in Confectionery) Order 1975 (S.I. 1975/762), the legislative requirements relating to wholesale dealing do not apply to the sale or offer for sale by way of wholesale dealing of a medicinal product, other than a veterinary drug, which is for sale as confectionery, under certain specified conditions. The first condition is that the marketing authorisation in respect of the medicinal product must provide that the product may be sold or offered for sale by way of wholesale dealing by persons exempt from the need to hold a wholesale dealer's licence.

In addition the medicinal product must not be sold or supplied accompanied by, or having in relation to it, any particulars in writing specifying that product's curative or remedial function in relation to a disease other than in relation to the relief of symptoms of coughs, colds or nasal congestion. Finally the medicinal product must be lawfully sold by retail otherwise than in accordance with a prescription given by a doctor or dentist or from premises other than a registered pharmacy.

4.13.7   Exemptions for food and cosmetics
Under the provisions of the Medicines (Exemption from Licences) (Foods and Cosmetics) Order 1971 (S.I. 1971/1410), as amended by the Medicines

(Exemption from Licences) (Foods and Cosmetics) Amendment Order 1973 (S.I. 1973/2079), the legislative requirements relating to marketing authorisations, manufacturer's and wholesale dealer's licences do not apply to anything done in relation to a medicinal product which is wholly or mainly for use by being administered to one or more human beings and which is or is to be for sale either for oral administration as a food or for external use as a cosmetic.

Under these legislative provisions 'food' includes beverages, confectionery and articles and substances as ingredients in the preparation of food and includes any manufactured substances to which there has been added any vitamin and which is advertised for sale to the general public as a dietary supplement. 'Vitamins' means any of the following vitamins: A, B1, B2, B6, C, D and E, biotin, nicinamide, nicotinic acid, pantothenic acid and its salts, biflavonoids, inositol, choline, para-eminobenzoic acid, cyanocobalamin, or folic acid. 'Vitamin preparation' means any medicinal product the active ingredients of which consist only of vitamins or vitamins and mineral salts. In turn, 'mineral salts' means salts of any one or more of the following: iron, iodine, calcium, phosphorous, fluorine, copper, potassium, manganese, magnesium or zinc.

'Cosmetic' means any substance or preparation intended to be applied to the various surfaces of the human body including epidermis, pilary system and hair, nails, lips and external genital organs, or the teeth and buccal mucosa wholly or mainly for the purpose of perfuming them, cleansing them, protecting them, caring for them or keeping them in condition, modifying their appearance (whether for aesthetic purposes or otherwise) or combating body odours or normal body perspiration.

The exemption conferred by these legislative provisions does not apply to:

(a)   a medicinal product which is, or is to be, sold as with, accompanied by, or having in relation to it, any particulars in writing, specifying that product's curative or remedial function in relation to a disease specified or the use of that product for such curative or remedial purposes;

(b)   any vitamin preparation for oral administration as a food in relation to which there are no written particulars or directions as to dosage;

(c)   any vitamin preparation for oral administration as a food in relation to which there are written particulars or directions as to dosage specifying a recommended daily dosage for adults which involves a daily intake in excess of the equivalent of 2,500 units of vitamin A activity, 250 units of antirachitic activity, 25 micrograms of folic acid, 5 micrograms of cyanocobalamin;

(d)   any medicinal product, not being a vitamin preparation, to which one or more of the ingredients vitamin A or D, folic acid or cyanocobalamin has been added and in relation to which there are written particulars or directions as to recommended use of that substance which involves a daily intake in excess of the quantities and ingredients specified in (c);

(e)   any medicinal product which is neither a vitamin preparation not a substance coming within the description in (d), which is or is to be sold with, accompanied by or having in relation to it any particulars in writing specifying the dosage relevant to that product's medicinal purpose;

(f)   a product for external use as a cosmetic which contains any antibiotic, or hexachlorophane, or any hormone in a proportion in excess of 0.004 per cent, or resorcinol in a proportion in excess of 1 per cent.

4.13.8   Exemptions for ingredients

Under s. 130(1)(b), MA 1968, a medicinal product means, amongst other things, any substance or article which is manufactured, sold, supplied, imported or exported for use wholly or mainly as an ingredient in the preparation of a substance or article which is to be administered to one or more human beings for a medicinal purpose. By virtue of the Medicines (Exemption from Licences) (Ingredients) Order 1974 (S.I. 1974/1150), the legislative requirements relating to marketing authorisations, manufacturer's and whole-sale dealer's licences do not apply to ingredients provided that certain conditions are satisfied.

The conditions are that anyone proposing to carry on the activity of using ingredients must notify the licensing authority of their intention and furnish any necessary particulars. The exemption will not apply where the licensing authority is of the opinion that, in the interests of safety, the exemption should not apply, or where the holder of the exemption fails to comply with further administrative requirements.

Under the provisions of the Medicines (Control of Substances for Manufacture) Order 1971 (S.I. 1971/1200) and the Medicines (Control of Substances for Manufacture) Order 1985 (S.I. 1985/1403, certain substances, which are not in themselves medicinal products, but are used as ingredients in medicinal products, are specified as being subject to, amongst other things, the licensing requirements of the MA 1968.

4.13.9   Exemptions for clinical trials

By virtue of the Medicines (Exemption from Licences) (Clinical Trials) Order 1995 (S.I. 1995/2808), and the Medicines (Exemption from Licences and Certificates) (Clinical Trials) Order 1995 (S.I. 1995/2809) the legislative requirements relating to marketing authorisations and clinical trial certificates do not apply to the sale, supply, or the procuring of the sale or supply, manufacture or assembly of a medicinal product for the purposes of a clinical trial, provided that certain conditions are satisfied.

The conditions are that anyone proposing to carry on such activity must notify the licensing authority of their intention and furnish a set of specified particulars. These particulars, which are too detailed to be described here, are outlined in sch. 1 to S.I. 1995/2808. The notification must also include a further certificate of verification and a usage guideline. The information to be contained in the usage guideline is set out in sch. 2 to S.I. 1995/2808. For the exemption to apply, the supplier must also give an undertaking to supply further information to the licensing authority relating to the clinical trial including serious unexpected adverse reactions.

Any granted exemption will take effect for a period of three years unless terminated. Termination by the licensing authority is on grounds of safety, failure to meet specifications or standards, or failure to make required notifications or supply information, or failure to comply with administrative arrangements.

Under the provisions of the Medicines (Exemption from Licences) (Clinical Trials) Order 1974 (S.I. 1974/498), the legislative requirements relating to the holding of a clinical trial certificate do not apply to the sale, supply, or the procuring of the sale or supply, import, or the manufacture or assembly of certain medicinal products and control products for the purposes of a clinical trial, if certain conditions are satisfied. The particular medicinal products affected by these provisions include those in respect of which there is in force a marketing authorisation including such products enclosed in or surrounded by inert substances.

They also include medicinal products that do not correspond with the relevant marketing authorisation because of a change in a manufacturing process or in the shape or colour of the product or because of the omission of distinctive markings. The conditions applicable to the exemption for these medicinal products relate to the proper administration of the product, the proper conduct of the clinical trial, and further notification of information relating to the clinical trial to the licensing authority.

'Control products', in relation to a clinical trial mean substances or articles that are administered by way of such a trial, in order that the effects, if any, of those substances or articles may be compared with the effects, if any, of those medicinal products. For an exemption in relation to this type of product to apply, conditions relating to the content of the clinical trial certificate, the active composition of the medicinal product, and notification of certain information to the licensing authority, must be satisfied.

Under the provisions of art. 4 of the Medicines (Exemption from Licences) (Special Cases and Miscellaneous Provisions) Order 1972 (S.I. 1972/1200), exemptions from the requirement to hold a clinical trial certificate are given to certain medicinal products for the purposes of a clinical trial. For this exemption to apply, the product must be sold, supplied or imported exclusively for the purposes of the clinical trial, and must be for administration under the direction of a doctor or dentist.

4.14   FEES

The Medicines (Products for Human Use — Fees) Regulations 1995 (S.I. 1995/1116) as amended, make provision for the fees payable in respect of marketing authorisations, licences and certificates relating to medicinal products for human use. Capital fees are payable in connection with applications for, or variations to, marketing authorisations, manufacturer's licences, whole-sale dealer's licences, clinical trial certificates and certificates permitting the export of medicinal products and for associated inspections. Periodic fees are payable in connection with the holding of marketing authorisations, manufac-turer's licences and wholesale dealer's licences. Administrative provisions deal with time of payment and waiver or refund of both capital and periodic fees in specified circumstances.

The Medicines (Homeopathic Medicinal Products for Human Use) Amendment Regulations 1996 (S.I. 1996/482) make similar provisions in relation to registration certificates for homeopathic medicines.

4.15   OFFENCES IN RELATION TO LICENSING OF MEDICINAL PRODUCTS

Schedule 3 to the Medicines for Human Use (Marketing Authorisations Etc.) Regulations 1994 (S.I. 1994/3144), creates a series of criminal offences in relation to marketing authorisations. The first relates to the placing of a relevant medicinal product on the market without an EU or UK marketing authorisation, in breach of relevant EU provisions or UK domestic legislation. The second offence relates to sale, supply, manufacture, assembly, possession, or the procurement of any of these, of a relevant medicinal product, by a person in the course of a business, where that person knows or has reasonable cause to believe that there is no marketing authorisation in respect of it.

A third offence relates to contravention of any condition attached to a marketing authorisation. A fourth relates to the sale, supply or marketing of a relevant medicinal product where such activities have been suspended in line with relevant EU provisions. A fifth offence relates to the failure by the holder of a marekting authorisation to comply with relevant notices relating to revocation and suspension. There are detailed offences relating to provision and updating of information relating to the marketing authorisation, including failure to record and report adverse reactions to the licensing authority. Finally there are specific offences relating to the sale or supply of relevant medicinal products by the holders of marketing authorisations without the required labels or the provision of information leaflets.

The penalties imposed for the above offences include scale fines for summary conviction or a term of imprisonment for conviction on indictment. Further provisions allow for the conviction of an employer where the act is that of an employee and for limited defences for the holders of marketing authorisations.

Under the provisions of s. 45, MA 1968, any person found guilty of any contravention of the provisions relating to manufacturing, wholesale dealing, and clinical test certificates is guilty of an offence liable on summary conviction to a scale fine, or on indictment to a term of imprisonment. The offences relate to all aspects of the provisions relating to manufacture, wholesale dealing and clinical trials. Certain limited defences are provided for in s. 46, MA 1968.

4.16 ADVERTISING MEDICINAL PRODUCTS

The advertising of medicinal products is strictly controlled under the relevant legislative provisions.

Under s. 92, MA 1968, 'advertisement' includes every form of advertising, whether in a publication, or by the display of any notice, or by means of any catalogue, price list, letter (whether circular or addressed to a particular person) or other document, or by words inscribed on any article, or by the exhibition of a photograph or a cinematograph film, or by way of sound recording, sound broadcasting or television, or by inclusion in a cable programme service, or in any other way. For the purposes of the MA 1968, advertisement does not include spoken words except words forming part of a sound recording, embodied in a sound-track associated with a cinematograph film, or broadcast by way of sound broadcasting or television or included in a cable programme service.

In addition, the sale or supply, or offer or exposure for sale or supply, of a medicinal product in a labelled container or package, or the supply, with a medicinal product of any description, of a leaflet relating solely to medicinal products of that description, does not constitute the issue of an advertisement. 'Representation' means any statement or undertaking (whether constituting a condition or a warranty or not) which consists of spoken words other than words forming part of a sound recording, embodied in a sound-track associated with a cinematograph film, or broadcast by way of sound broadcasting or television or included in a cable programme service.

'Sound recording' has the meaning assigned to it by s. 12, Copyright Act 1956 which is 'the aggregate of the sounds embodied in, and capable of being reproduced by means of, a record of any description, other than a soundtrack associated with a cinematograph film'.

Under s. 95, MA 1968, the appropriate Ministers are given the power to make regulations prohibiting any one or more of the following:

(a)   the issue of advertisements relating to medicinal products of a specified description, or falling within a specified class;

(b)   the issue of advertisements likely to lead to the use of any medicinal product, or any other substance or article, for the purpose of treating or preventing a specified disease or for the purpose of diagnosing such a disease or of ascertaining the existence, degree or extent of a physiological condition or of permanently or temporarily preventing or otherwise interfering with the normal operation of a physiological function or for the purpose of artificially inducing a condition of body or mind;

(c)   the issue of advertisements likely to lead to the use of medicinal products of a particular description or falling within a particular class, or the use of any other substance or article of a specified description or class, for any purpose outlined in (b);

(d)   the issue of advertisements relating to medicinal products and containing a specified word or phrase, as being a word or phrase which, in the opinion of the appropriate Ministers, is likely to mislead the public as to the nature or effects of the products or as to any condition of body or mind in connection with which the products might be used.

Any regulations made in accordance with (b), (c) and (d), may also prohibit the making of any representation, if the representation:

(a)   is made in connection with the sale or supply, or offer for sale or supply, of a medicinal product or other substance or article to which the regulations apply; or

(b)   is made to a person for the purpose of inducing that person to purchase such a medicinal product, substance or article from a person selling medicinal products by retail; or

(c)   is made to a practitioner for the purpose of inducing that practitioner to prescribe or supply medicinal products, or made to a patient or client of a practitioner for the purpose of inducing the patient to request the practitioner to prescribe the medicinal product.

The appropriate Ministers are also empowered to make regulations, imposing requirements for certain specified purposes, which they consider necessary or expedient, with respect to the form, particulars and duration of advertisement, and the regulations may prohibit the use of any such advertisement. The specified purposes are:

(a)   securing that adequate information is given with respect to medicinal products;

(b)   preventing the giving of misleading information with respect to such products;

(c)   promoting safety in relation to such products.

Prohibitions ordered under any regulations made under these provisions may be total or may be subject to specified exemptions.

4.16.1   The advertising regulations
The principal regulations made under these powers are the Medicines (Advertising) Regulations 1994 (S.I. 1994/1932) (the Advertising Regulations 1994). Under reg. 2(2) the term 'advertisement' is given the meaning assigned to it by s. 92, MA 1968, except that, in relation to a relevant medicinal product:

(a)   provided that it makes no product claim, reference material, a factual, informative statement or announcement, a trade catalogue or a price list shall not be taken to be an advertisement; and

(b)   an advertisement includes a representation.

In turn, 'representation' is given the meaning assigned to it by s. 92, MA 1968, except that it does not include the making of a factual, informative statement or announcement which includes no product claim.

Under reg. 3 of the Advertising Regulations, no person may issue an advertisement for a relevant medicinal product in respect of which no marketing authorisation is in force. This general prohibition does not apply to any advertisement relating to a registered homeopathic medicinal product. Under reg. 3A, no person may issue an advertisement relating to a relevant medicinal product unless the advertisement complies with the particulars listed in the summary of product characteristics.

Regulation 3A, which was inserted into the Advertising Regulations by the Medicines (Advertising and Monitoring of Advertising) Amendment Regulations 1999 (S.I. 1999/267), also prohibits advertisements which do not encourage the rational use of a medicinal product by presenting it objectively and without exaggerating its properties. Finally the new reg. 3A prohibits the issue of misleading advertisements.

Under reg. 4 of the Advertising Regulations, any person holding a marketing authorisation relating to a relevant medicinal product is under a duty to:

(a)   establish a scientific service to compile and collate all information, whether received from employed medical sales representatives or from any other source, relating to that product;

(b)   ensure that, in relation to any such product which medical sales representatives promote, those medical sales representatives are given adequate training and have sufficient technical knowledge to enable them to provide information which is precise and as complete as possible about that product;

(c)   keep available for the Health Ministers, or communicate to them, a sample of any advertisement, together with a statement indicating the persons to whom the advertisement is addressed, the method of dissemination and the date of first dissemination; and

(d)   supply any information and assistance requested by the Health Ministers in order to carry out their functions under the relevant advertising legislation.

These latter two duties were inserted by the Medicines (Advertising and Monitoring of Advertising) Amendment Regulations 1999.

Under reg. 14 of the Advertising Regulations, no person may issue an advertisement relating to a relevant medicinal product and wholly or mainly directed at persons qualified to prescribe or supply relevant medicinal products, unless such an advertisement contains essential information compatible with the summary of product characteristics and contains certain particulars set out in sch. 2 to the Advertising Regulations. These particulars are:

(a)   the licence number of the product;

(b)   the name and address of the holder of the marketing authorisation which relates to the medicinal product or the business name and address of the part of the business that is responsible for the sale or supply;

(c)   the supply classification of the medicinal product, specifying whether the product is a medicinal product for supply by prescription only, a medicinal product on a general sale list, or a pharmacy medicinal product;

(d)   the name of the product, and a list of the active ingredients using the common name placed immediately adjacent to the most prominent display of the name of the product;

(e)   one or more of the indications for the product consistent with the terms of the licence;

(f)   a succinct statement (where relevant) of the entries in the summary of product characteristics or, if there is no summary of product characteristics, the data sheet, relating to side-effects, precautions and relevant contra-indications;

(g)   a succinct statement of the entries in the summary of product characteristics or, if there is no summary of product characteristics, the data sheet, relating to dosage and method of use relevant to the indications shown together with the method of administration where this is not obvious;

(h)   a warning issued by the licensing authority under Part II, MA 1968 which is required to be included in advertisements;

(i)   the cost (excluding value added tax) of either a specified package of the medicinal product to which the advertisement relates, or a specified quantity or recommended daily dose, calculated by reference to any specified package of the product, except that such cost may be omitted in the case of an advertisement inserted in a publication which is printed in the United Kingdom but with a circulation outside the United Kingdom of more than 15 per cent of its total circulation.

The particulars contained in (f), (g) and (h) above must be printed in a clear and legible manner and be placed in such a position in the advertisement that their relationship to the claims and indications for the product can readily be appreciated by the reader.

4.16.2   Abbreviated advertisements

An 'abbreviated advertisement' means an advertisement, other than a loose insert, which does not exceed in size an area of 420 square centimetres, in a publication sent or delivered wholly or mainly to persons qualified to prescribe or supply relevant medicinal products. Under reg. 16 of the Advertising Regulations, no person may issue an abbreviated advertisement unless such an advertisement contains essential information compatible with the summary of product characteristics and contains certain particulars set out in sch. 2 to the Advertising Regulations. These particulars are:

(a)   the name and address of the holder of the marketing authorisation which relates to the medicinal product, or the business name and address of the part of the business that is responsible for its sale or supply;

(b)   the supply classification of the medicinal product, specifying whether the product is a medicinal product for supply by prescription only, a medicinal product on a general sale list, or a pharmacy medicinal product;

(c)   the name of the product, and a list of the active ingredients using the common name placed immediately adjacent to the most prominent display of the name of the product;

(d)   a form of words which clearly indicates that further information is available on request to the licence holder or in the summary of product characteristics, or, if there is no summary of product characteristics, the data sheet, relating to the product.

The advertisement must also contain any warning which the licensing authority has required in exercise of powers under Part II, MA 1968.

4.16.3   Audio-visual advertisements

Under reg. 15 of the Advertising Regulations, no person may issue, in a programme service or video recording, an advertisement relating to a relevant medicinal product and wholly or mainly directed at persons qualified to prescribe or supply relevant medicinal products, which includes or shows any words, unless such an advertisement contains essential information compatible with the summary of product characteristics and contains certain particulars set out in sch. 2 to the Advertising Regulations. These particulars are:

(a)   the licence number of the product;

(b)   the name and address of the holder of the marketing authorisation which relates to the medicinal product or the business name and address of the part of the business that is responsible for the sale or supply;

(c)   the supply classification of the medicinal product, specifying whether the product is a medicinal product for supply by prescription only, a medicinal product on a general sale list, or a pharmacy medicinal product;

(d)   the name of the product, and a list of the active ingredients using the common name placed immediately adjacent to the most prominent display of the name of the product;

(e)   one or more of the indications for the product consistent with the terms of the licence;

(f)   a succinct statement (where relevant) of the entries in the summary of product characteristics or, if there is no summary of product characteristics, the data sheet, relating to side-effects, precautions and relevant contra-indications;

(g)   a succinct statement of the entries in the summary of product characteristics or, if there is no summary of product characteristics, the data sheet, relating to dosage and method of use relevant to the indications shown together with the method of administration where this is not obvious;

(h)   a warning issued by the licensing authority under Part II, MA 1968 which is required to be included in advertisements;

These particulars may be supplied by way of written material made available to all persons to whom the advertisement is shown or sent as an alternative to being referred to in the advertisement.

Under reg. 17 of the Advertising Regulations, the prohibitions and requirements imposed in relation to advertisements to health professionals, audio-visual advertisements, and abbreviated advertisements do not apply to an advertisement relating to a relevant medicinal product which is on a promotional aid. This exception is subject to the further requirement that the advertisement must consist solely of the name of the product and be intended solely as a reminder.

4.16.4   Written materials

Under reg. 18 of the Advertising Regulations, no person may send or deliver to persons qualified to prescribe or supply relevant medicinal products, as part of the promotion of the relevant medicinal product, any written material relating to that product unless it contains essential information compatible with the summary of product characteristics, gives the supply classification of the medicinal product, specifying whether the product is a medicinal product for supply by prescription only, a medicinal product on a general sale list, or a pharmacy medicinal product, and states the date on which it was drawn up or last revised.

Information contained in written material must also be accurate, up-to-date, verifiable or sufficiently complete to enable the recipient to form an opinion of the therapeutic value of the product to which the documentation relates. It must not include any quotation, table or other illustrative matter taken from a medical journal or other scientific work unless it is accurately reproduced and the precise sources of the information indicated.

4.16.5   Free samples

Under reg. 19 of the Advertising Regulations, a person may supply a free sample of a relevant medicinal product only under certain limited circumstances. The supply must be to a person qualified to prescribe relevant medicinal products, the medicinal product must not be a narcotic or psychotropic drug and the sample must correspond with the requirements of sch. 4 to the Advertising Regulations. These requirements are:

(a)   samples shall be supplied on an exceptional basis only;

(b)   a limited number only of samples of each product may be supplied in any one year and to any one recipient;

(c)   samples shall be supplied only in response to a written request, signed and dated, from the recipient;

(d)   suppliers of samples shall maintain an adequate system of control and accountability;

(e)   every sample shall be no larger than the smallest presentation available for sale in the United Kingdom;

(f)   every sample shall be marked 'free medical sample — not for resale' or shall bear a similar description;

(g)   every sample shall be accompanied by a copy of the summary of product characteristics (or, if there is no summary of product characteristics, a copy of the data sheet) for each such product.

4.16.6   Medical sales representatives and inducements

Under reg. 20 of the Advertising Regulations, medical sales representatives, in relation to any medicinal product which they promote, must during each visit, give to all persons whom they visit or have available for them a copy of the summary of product characteristics (or, if there is no summary of product characteristics, a copy of the data sheet) for each such product. Medical sales representatives must also report all information which they receive from persons whom they visit, including reports of any adverse reactions, to the scientific service established as part of the duties of holders of marketing authorisations, described above.

Under reg. 21, where relevant medicinal products are being promoted to persons qualified to prescribe or supply relevant medicinal products, no person shall supply, offer or promise to such person any gift, pecuniary advantage or benefit in kind, unless it is inexpensive and relevant to the practice of medicine or pharmacy. This prohibition against inducements does not prevent the offering of hospitality (including the payment of travelling or accommodation expenses) at events for purely professional or scientific purposes, or at a meeting or event held for the promotion of relevant medicinal products, to persons qualified to prescribe or supply relevant medicinal products. In turn, such hospitality must be reasonable in level, be subordinate to the main scientific objective of the meeting and be offered to a health professional.

Under reg. 21(5), no person qualified to prescribe or supply relevant medicinal products may solicit or accept any gift, pecuniary advantage, benefit in kind, hospitality or sponsorship prohibited by reg. 21.

4.16.7   Advertising to the public

Under reg. 6 of the Advertising Regulations, no person may issue an advertisement, wholly or mainly directed at members of the public, which is likely to lead to the use of a relevant medicinal product for the purpose of the treatment, prevention or diagnosis of a series of specified diseases. The diseases, which are listed in sch. 1 to the Advertising Regulations, are bone diseases, cardiovascular diseases, chronic insomnia, diabetes and other metabolic diseases, diseases of the liver, biliary system and pancreas, endocrine diseases, genetic disorders, malignant diseases, psychiatric diseases, serious disorders of the eye and ear, serious gastrointestinal diseases, serious infectious diseases including HIV related diseases and tuberculosis, serious neurological and muscular diseases, serious renal diseases, serious respiratory diseases, serious skin disorders, and sexually transmitted diseases.

This general and all encompassing prohibition does not apply to an advertisement which is likely to lead to the use of a relevant medicinal product for the purpose of the prevention of neural tube defects, or of the treatment of the symptoms of rheumatic or non-serious arthritic conditions. This latter exemption was introduced to the Advertising Regulations by the Medicines (Advertising) Amendment Regulations 1996 (S.I. 1996/1552).

4.16.8　Other advertising controls

It is also not permissible, under reg. 6(3), for any person to issue an advertisement which is likely to lead to the use of a relevant medicinal product, or any other substance or article for the purpose of inducing an abortion in women.

Under reg. 7 of the Advertising Regulations, no person may issue an advertisement for a medicinal product which is a prescription only medicine for human use. Under reg. 8, no person may issue an advertisement for a medicinal product which contains a substance listed in any of schedules I, II or IV to the Narcotics Drugs Convention or schedules I to IV of the Psychotropic Substances Convention.

Under reg. 9 of the Advertising Regulations, no person shall issue an advertisement relating to any relevant medicinal product which contains any material which:

(a)　gives the impression that a medical consultation or surgical operation is unnecessary, in particular by offering a diagnosis or by suggesting treatment by post, FAX or telephone;

(b)　suggests that the effects of taking the medicinal product are guaranteed, are unaccompanied by side effects or are better than, or equivalent to, those of other identifiable treatment or medicinal products;

(c)　suggests that health care can be enhanced by not taking the medicinal product;

(d)　is directed exclusively or principally at children;

(e)　refers to a recommendation by scientists, health professionals or persons who are neither of the foregoing but who, because of their celebrity, could encourage the consumption of medicinal products;

(f)　suggests that the medicinal product is a foodstuff, cosmetic or other consumer product;

(g)　suggests that the safety or efficacy of the medicinal product is due to the fact that it is natural;

(h)   might, by a description or detailed representation of a case history, lead to erroneous self-diagnosis;

(i)   refers, in improper, alarming or misleading terms, to claims of recovery;

(j)   uses, in improper, alarming or misleading terms, pictorial representations of changes in the human body caused by the disease or injury, or of the action of a medicinal product on the human body, or parts thereof; or

(k)   mentions that the medicinal product has been granted a marketing authorisation.

Under reg. 11 of the Advertising Regulations, the regulations relating to advertising medicinal products to the public do not apply to any advertisement as part of a vaccination campaign relating to a relevant medicinal product which is a vaccine or serum, provided that such a campaign has been approved by the Health Ministers.

Under reg. 12, no person who is the holder of a marketing authorisation or is in the manufacturing or wholesale dealing business, may sell or supply, for a promotional purpose, any unsolicited relevant medicinal product to any member of the general public.

4.16.9   Form and content of advertisements

Under reg. 10 of the Advertising Regulations, no person may issue an advertisement relating to a relevant medicinal product unless that advertisement:

(a)   is set out in such a way that it is clear that the message is an advertisement and so that the product is clearly identified as a medicinal product;

(b)   includes the following:

(i)   the name of the medicinal product;

(ii)   if it contains only one active ingredient, the common name of the medicinal product;

(iii)   the information necessary for correct use of the medicinal product; and

(iv)   an express and legible invitation to read carefully the instructions on the leaflet contained within the package or on the label, as the case may be.

These requirements do not apply to an advertisement relating to a relevant medicinal product which is on promotional aid if the advertisement consists solely of the name of the product (or, in the case of a registered homeopathic medicinal product, the scientific name of the stock or stocks) and the advertisement is intended solely as a reminder.

4.16.10   Advertisements for homeopathic products

Under reg. 22 of the Advertising Regulations, no person may issue an advertisement relating to a registered homeopathic medicinal product which mentions any specific therapeutic indications and which does not contain the following particulars, outlined in sch. 5.

(a)   the scientific name of the stock or stocks followed by the degree of dilution, making use of the symbols of the pharmacopoeia used in relation to the homeopathic manufacturing procedure described therein for that stock or stocks;

(b)   the name and address of the holder of the certificate of registration and, where different, the name and address of the manufacturer;

(c)   the method of administration and, if necessary, route;

(d)   the expiry date of the product in clear terms (stating the month and year);

(e)   the pharmaceutical form;

(f)   the contents of the sales presentation;

(g)   any special storage precautions;

(h)   any special warning necessary for the product concerned;

(i)   the manufacturer's batch number;

(j)   the registration number allocated by the licensing authority preceded by the letters 'HR' in capital letters;

(k)   the words 'homeopathic medicinal product without approved therapeutic indications';

(l)   a warning advising the user to consult a doctor if the symptoms persist during the use of the product.

4.17   MONITORING ADVERTISEMENTS

The Medicines (Monitoring of Advertising) Regulations 1994 (S.I. 1994/1933), give powers to monitor the form and content of advertisements. Regulation 4 provides that it is the duty of the Health Ministers under the MA 1968 to consider complaints about advertisements for medicinal products for human use, except those complaints which appear to be frivolous or vexatious.

Under reg. 5, where a complaint is made either that an advertisement is in breach of Part IV of the Advertising Regulations (advertising to health professionals), or that a non-broadcast advertisement is in breach of reg. 9 of those Regulations (prohibition of certain material in advertisements to the public), a self-regulatory body which deals with complaints about such advertisements, selected by the Health Ministers, may consider such complaint, if the complainant and the Health Ministers agree.

Regulation 6 provides that the Health Ministers may apply to the court for an injunction about a particular advertisement, to prevent its publication or further publication. Regulations 7 and 8 give details in relation to the granting of an injunction. Before granting an injunction the court must have regard to all the interests involved and in particular the public interest. An injunction may relate not only to a particular advertisement but to any advertisement in similar terms or likely to convey a similar impression, and may prohibit the publication or further publication of an advertisement.

In considering an application for an injunction the court may require any person appearing to the court to be responsible for the publication of the advertisement to which the application relates to furnish the court with evidence as to the accuracy of any factual claim made in the advertisement. If such evidence is not furnished to it, the court may consider the factual claim inaccurate.

Where the court grants an injunction it must give reasons in detail, and the Health Ministers must communicate those reasons in writing to the person against whom the injunction has been granted, referring to any remedy available in the court and any time limit which must be met in order for any such remedy to be available. If a final injunction is granted, the Health Ministers have power to require the publication of the decision and a corrective statement.

Regulations 9 and 10 provide that the Independent Television Commission, the Radio Authority or the Welsh Authority, as appropriate (statutory bodies given powers over advertisements by the Broadcasting Act 1990), have a duty to consider complaints that a broadcast advertisement may be in breach of reg. 9 of the Advertising Regulations. Those bodies also have power under the Broadcasting Act 1990 to prevent transmission or further transmission of an advertisement.

Regulation 13 of the Medicines (Advertising and Monitoring of Advertising) Amendment Regulations 1999 inserts a new schedule into the the Medicines (Monitoring of Advertising) Regulations 1994. The schedule contains a new notices procedure relating to the scrutiny of published or proposed advertisements for relevant medicinal products. This procedure is to be used by the Health Ministers for determining whether or not the advertisements, if published, would be in breach of advertising regulations. The new procedures allow for written representations to be made to the Health Ministers before they reach their decision or determination. Breach of the notices will, in certain circumstances, be offences.

4.18   OFFENCES RELATING TO ADVERTISEMENTS

Regulation 23 of the Advertising Regulations states that any contravention of the Regulations is a criminal offence punishable on summary conviction with a scale fine, or on indictment to a term of imprisonment.

4.19   CONCLUSION

The extensive detail of the rules and regulations relating to the licensing of medicinal products, and the complementary provisions relating to the advertising of drug products, is evidence of the desire of the regulators to ensure that medicinal products are manufactured to the highest quality, and that safety and efficacy is not misrepresented to both health care professionals and members of the public. The influence of EU directives on UK domestic legislation has ensured that the current controls are comprehensive in meeting their desired purpose.

Knowledge of the legal control of the licensing of medicinal products is essential for those health care professionals, including pharmacists, who are charged with their further distribution. That distribution is subject to yet more control and regulation which is discussed in subsequent chapters below.

An understanding of the legal regulation of the advertising of medicinal products is also essential for pharmacists. Many doctors formulate a therapeutic plan, involving drug therapy, based on information which they receive about medicinal products from manufacturers. Individual patients devise their own therapeutic plan based on what they hear and learn about drug therapy and individual medicinal products. That therapeutic plan in either case may involve the request for the sale or supply of those products from the pharmacy. Knowledge of the methods by which representations are made, and information provided, equips pharmacists with certain of the skills necessary to implement the required therapy.

FIVE

The regulation of medicinal drug products — prescription only medicines

5.1 INTRODUCTION

It is important to have a specific structure for the designation of certain drug products as falling into a class or description which are available on prescription only. In outlining such a structure, the regulators have to seek to achieve a balance between permitting the therapeutic value of such products to be exploited in the provision of health care, and restricting their use for specific treatments for individual patients.

The first task in describing the law on prescription only medicines is to outline the procedures and systems underlying the specification of such products. The regulation of the classification of prescription only drug products is principally to be found in specific United Kingdom primary and secondary legislation. The content of these rules has been heavily influenced by European Union provisions, designed to strengthen control over the distribution of such products, and to harmonise such provisions throughout the European Union.

The power to distribute those classes of drug products, designated as prescription only, is restricted to a small number of health care professionals. Those granted such rights are known as 'appropriate practitioners'. However, recent legislative changes and amendments have extended distribution rights to others involved in health care and particular attention should be paid to the legal structures for the acquisition of such rights.

The prerogative over the dispensing of prescription only medicines, and their actual distribution to the patient, remains with the pharmacist, as part of the more generalised licence to provide pharmaceutical services. The granting of exclusive distribution rights is contingent on the parallel assumption of duties and obligations relating to the methods by which sales and supplies are undertaken. There are specific legislative provisions outlining requirements for the form of valid prescriptions, reinforcing the underlying philosophy of control and regulation.

These requirements are strictly adhered to. For the most part, failure to follow the required procedures has specific legal consequences. Those responsible for the distribution of such products are also under strict duties to maintain records of any sales and supplies. Further specific rules relate to the supply of prescription only medicines in emergency situations. The relevant legislative provisions create specific criminal offences.

Control over the sale and supply of prescription only medicines is not absolute. The legal requirements for the sale, supply and administration of such products are relaxed in certain limited circumstances. Some of these exemptions apply specifically to pharmacists and require close analysis for that reason. Other exemptions are not linked directly to the practice of pharmacy. However it is important for pharmacists to know what others, both within and outside health care, are permitted to do with prescription only medicines.

Finally, it is important to remember that under s. 67(2), MA 1968, any contravention of the requirements for the sale or supply of prescription only medicines, as contained in provisions of the Act itself or secondary legislation made under it, amounts to a criminal offence, punishable on summary conviction by a fine or on indictment by a fine or imprisonment or both. That fact alone merits close examination of the relevant rules and regulations.

5.2   THE CLASSIFICATION OF PRESCRIPTION ONLY MEDICINES

Under s. 58(1), MA 1968, the appropriate Ministers may by order specify descriptions or classes of medicinal products which are to be prescription only. Council Directive 92/26/EEC (OJ L113/5) laid down the criteria to be applied by member states in specifying which medicinal products for human use are to be supplied only upon medical prescription. This Directive (and Council Directive 81/851/EEC (OJ L317/1), as amended by Council Directive 90/676/EEC (OJ L373/15)) have been implemented by the Medicines Act 1968 (Amendment) (No. 2) Regulations 1992 (S.I. 1992/3271).

These Regulations have inserted a new s. 58A into the MA 1968, which now sets out the criteria to be applied by the appropriate Ministers in determining, under the power given by s. 58(1), which descriptions or classes of medicinal products are to be prescription only. Section 58A specifies that a product is to classified as prescription only if it:

(a)   is likely to present a direct or indirect danger to human health, even when used correctly, if used without supervision;

(b)   is frequently and to a very wide extent used incorrectly, and as a result is likely to present a direct or indirect danger to human health;

(c)   contains substances or preparations of substances of which the activity requires, or the side effects require, further investigation; and

(d)   is normally prescribed for parenteral administration.

In considering whether the above criteria apply to a particular product, the appropriate Ministers are further charged to take into account other factors. These include whether it falls into a specified category of narcotic or psychotropic substance, or is likely to, or unknowingly may, present a substantial risk of medicinal abuse, addiction or illegal use if used incorrectly. Finally they must consider whether it is by its nature reserved for hospital treatments or other special diagnostic facilities, or is intended for outpatients' use and would require special supervision.

Section 58A allows the appropriate Ministers to determine that a product should not be classified as prescription only, having regard to the maximum single or daily dose, the strength of the product, its pharmaceutical form or packaging or any other specific circumstances.

5.3   APPROPRIATE PRACTITIONERS

Section 58, MA 1968 also empowers the appropriate Ministers to determine, by order, who should be appropriate practitioners for the purpose of the sale and supply of prescription only medicines. Article 2(a) of the Prescription Only Medicines (Human Use) Order 1997 (S.I. 1997/1830) designates doctors, dentists, veterinary surgeons, and veterinary practitioners as appropriate practitioners for the sale and supply of most prescription only medicines.

Article 2(b) designates appropriate nurse practitioners as appropriate practitioners for the sale and supply of certain medicinal products, specified in sch. 3 to the Order. The list of medicinal products was added to by art. 4 of the Prescription Only Medicines (Human Use) Amendment Order 1998 (S.I. 1998/108). The legal process of adding nurses to the traditional list of doctors, dentists and vets, as appropriate practitioners authorised to regulate the sale and supply of prescription only medicines commenced in 1992, is a reflection of developing trends in health care practice.

The Medicinal Products: Prescription by Nurses etc. Act 1992 had amended the MA 1968 and allowed for the making of further secondary legislation to designate certain nurse practitioners as appropriate practitioners for the sale and supply of prescription only medicines. Appropriate secondary legislation was introduced in The Medicines (Product Other than Veterinary Drugs) (Prescription Only) Amendment Order 1994 (S.I. 1994/3050). Article 2(b) of the Prescription Only Medicines (Human Use) Order 1997 (which revokes S.I. 1994/3050) consolidates the position of certain nurse practitioners as appropriate practitioners for the purpose of the sale and supply by directly placing them beside the traditional list. For the purposes of the 1997 Order, an appropriate nurse practitioner means:

(a)   a person who:

(i)   is registered in Part 1 or 12 of the Register maintained by the United Kingdom Central Council for Nursing, Midwifery and Health Visiting under section 10 of the Nurses, Midwives and Health Visitors Act 1979 (the professional register); and
(ii)   has a district nursing qualification additionally recorded in the professional register under rule 11 of the Nurses, Midwives and Health Visitors Rules 1983; or

(b)   a person who is registered in the professional register as a health visitor.

Further amendments to the descriptions and classes of prescription only medicines which appropriate nurse practitioners may sell or supply were introduced by the Prescription Only Medicines (Human Use) Amendment Order 1998 (S.I. 1998/108).

5.4   DESIGNATION OF PRESCRIPTION ONLY MEDICINES

Section 58(2)(a), MA 1968 states that no person shall sell by retail, or supply in circumstances corresponding to retail sale, a medicinal product specified by order as falling into the class or description of prescription only, except in accordance with a prescription given by an appropriate practitioner. A series of pieces of secondary legislation have sought to specify the classes and descriptions of medicinal products for human use to be categorised as prescription only.

The first, and principal of these was the Medicines (Products Other Than Veterinary Drugs) (Prescription Only) Order 1983 (S.I. 1983/1212). With advances in medical science, this Order had to be amended on numerous occasions. The resultant plethora of legislative provisions, and interpretative confusion, led to the introduction of consolidated legislation in 1997. As a result the principal legislative provisions, for the designation of classes and descriptions of medicinal products for human use as prescription only, are now the Prescription Only Medicines (Human Use) Order 1997 (S.I. 1997/1830).

Article 3 of the 1997 Order specifies certain descriptions and classes of medicinal products for human use as prescription only.

The first of these classes are medicinal products consisting of or containing a substance listed in column 1 of sch. 1 to the 1997 Order. Exemptions from this category exist in relation to certain substances with a published maximum strength. 'Maximum strength' means:

(a)   the maximum quantity of a substance by weight or volume contained in a dosage unit of a medicinal product;
(b)   the maximum percentage of a substance contained in a medicinal product calculated in terms of:

(i)   weight in weight,
(ii)   weight in volume,
(iii)   volume in weight, or
(iv)   volume in volume

and if the maximum percentage calculated in those ways differs, the higher or highest such percentage.

Maximum strengths for certain substances listed in column 1 of sch. 1 are published in column 2 of the same schedule. A medicinal product which consists of or contains a substance with a published maximum strength is exempt from the restrictions on sale or supply by prescription only, where the maximum strength of the substance in the product does not exceed the specified maximum.

Specific routes of administration, uses, in terms of purposes and classes of persons, and pharmaceutical form, for certain substances listed in column 1 of sch. 1, are published in column 3 of the same schedule. Where a route of administration is so specified, a medicinal product which consists of or contains that substance, is exempt from the restrictions on sale or supply by prescription only where it is sold or supplied for administration only by that route, use or in that particular pharmaceutical form.

Maximum doses, maximum daily doses, maximum periods of use, maximum frequencies of use, and maximum quantities for certain substances listed in column 1 of sch. 1 are published in column 4 of the same schedule. Maximum dose or 'MD' means the maximum quantity of a substance contained in the amount of a medicinal product which it is recommended should be taken or administered at any one time. Maximum daily dose or 'MDD' means the maximum quantity of a substance contained in the amount of a medicinal product which it is recommended should be taken or administered in a period of 24 hours.

A medicinal product which consists of or contains a substance with a published MD, MDD, maximum period of use, maximum frequency of use or maximum quantity, is exempt from the restrictions on sale or supply by prescription only, where it is sold or supplied for use at a maximum dose, maximum daily dose, maximum quantity, maximum period or frequency which does not exceed the specified maximum.

Article 8 of the Prescription Only Medicines (Human Use) Order 1997 specifies that a medicinal product which contains one or more of a range of atropine, hyoscine and hyoscyamine based substances, is exempt from the restrictions on sale or supply by prescription only where it is sold or supplied for use at a maximum daily dose which does not exceed 1 milligram in total of the alkaloids derived from belladonna, hyoscyamus, stramonium or other solanaceous plant which are contained in that medicinal product.

The second class of medicinal products specified for human use as prescription only by the Prescription Only Medicines (Human Use) Order

1997, are medicinal products that are controlled drugs. Exemption from the requirement for prescription only classification exists in relation to certain controlled drugs, although subject to strict conditions.

Where a medicinal product contains not more than one of the substances listed in column 1 of sch. 2 to the 1997 Order and no other controlled drug, at a strength which does not exceed the maximum strength specified in column 2, and is sold or supplied in the particular pharmaceutical form specified in column 3, and for use at a maximum dose which does not exceed that specified in column 4, it will be exempt from the prescription only requirements.

The third class of medicinal products, specified for human use as prescription only, are those medicinal products that are for parenteral administration, other than preparations of insulin. Parenteral administration, for the purposes of the Order, means administration by breach of the skin or mucous membrane. In essence all medicinal products for injection, except for insulin preparations are prescription only medicines.

Cyanogenetic substances, other than preparations for external use and medicinal products that on administration emit radiation, or contain or generate any substance which emits radiation, in order that radiation may be used, make up the fourth class of medicinal products specified for human use as prescription only.

The fifth class are medicinal products for human use which are classified as subject to medical prescription in marketing authorisations granted under Council Regulation 2309/93. Included as prescription only medicines are those medicines in respect of which such an authorisation has been granted and which classifies a medicine as being subject to medical prescription. An exemption exists in relation to a medicine with a marketing authorisation which does not classify the medicinal product as subject to medical prescription.

Medicinal products which are not of a description and do not fall within any of the classes mentioned above, but which do fall into an MA 1968 category of 'new medicinal products', are also specified as medicinal products for human use as prescription only. These products must also have been granted a marketing authorisation which contains a provision to the effect that the method of sale or supply of the medicinal product is to be only in accordance with a prescription given by an appropriate practitioner. Where a product licence or marketing authorisation has been granted for a new medicinal product which restricts its classification to prescription only, the duration of the restriction, under Article 4 of the Prescription Only Medicines (Human Use) Order 1997, is five years.

Section 58(2)(b), MA 1968 indicates that no person shall administer (otherwise than to themselves) a medicinal product on prescription only unless they are appropriate practitioners or are acting in accordance with the directions of an appropriate practitioner. Article 7 of the Prescription Only Medicines (Human Use) Order 1997 provides for certain exemptions from this requirement. The restriction does not apply to a series of medicinal products, outlined in the Article, for parenteral administration, where the administration is for the purpose of saving life in an emergency.

5.5 PRESCRIPTIONS

As has already been indicated, s. 58(2)(a), MA 1968 provides that the sale and supply of prescription only drug products must be in accordance with a prescription given by an appropriate practitioner. Article 15 of the Prescription Only Medicines (Human Use) Order 1997 outlines the conditions applicable to a valid prescription.

The prescription must be signed in ink with their own name by the appropriate practitioner giving it. Without prejudice to the signature requirement, the prescription must be written in ink, or otherwise, so as to be indelible. This requirement does not apply to a health prescription which is not for a controlled drug specified in schs. 1, 2 or 3 to the Misuse of Drugs Regulations, in which case it may be written by means of carbon paper or similar material. The Royal Pharmaceutical Society, in its detailed guidance contained in its publication *Medicines, Ethics and Practice*, has given advice to its members relating to the 'fax' of a prescription. That advice is discussed further below in 5.11.

Article 15 of the Prescription Only Medicines (Human Use) Order 1997 outlines further particulars which a prescription must have. They include the address of the appropriate practitioner giving it, the appropriate date, particulars which give an indication of the status of the appropriate practitioner, and the name, address and, if aged under twelve, age of the person for whose treatment the prescription has been issued.

Restrictions are also imposed on the duration of a prescription. A prescription must not be dispensed after a period of six months from the appropriate date. If the prescription is a repeatable prescription (to be discussed below), it must not be dispensed for the first time after the end of a period of six months nor otherwise than in accordance with the directions contained in the repeatable prescription.

The appropriate date is different in relation to different types of prescription. In the case of a prescription issued by doctor, dentist or nurse prescriber under the appropriate national health service conditions (a health prescription), it means the date on which it was signed by the appropriate practitioner, or the date indicated as the date before which it must not be dispensed. Where the health prescription bears both dates, those of signature and optimal dispensing date, the appropriate date is the later of these. In the case of any other prescription, the appropriate date means the date on which it was signed by the appropriate practitioner.

A repeatable prescription is a prescription which contains a direction that it may be dispensed more than once. Where the prescription does not specify how many times it may be dispensed, Article 15(2)(e) of the 1997 Order provides that it must not be dispensed on more than two occasions. That restriction will not apply to a prescription for oral contraceptives in which case it may be dispensed six times before the end of the period of six months from the appropriate date.

5.6   FURTHER CONDITIONS FOR PRESCRIPTIONS FOR CONTROLLED DRUGS

The sale or supply of a medicinal product against a prescription which does not fulfil the legislative requirements will not necessarily be rendered unlawful. Article 15(3) of the 1997 Order allows for an exemption where the person selling or supplying the prescription only medicine, having exercised all due diligence, believes on reasonable grounds that the prescription is otherwise valid. Further exemptions exist in relation to cases involving another's default and to forged prescriptions.

Article 13 allows for the sale or supply of a prescription only medicine, without a valid prescription, by a person who, having exercised all due diligence, believes on reasonable grounds that the product sold or supplied is not a prescription only medicine. Article 14 provides a conditional exemption for a pharmacist who sells or supplies a prescription only medicine in accordance with a forged prescription. The conditions are that, having exercised all due diligence, the pharmacist believes that the prescription is genuine.

The introduction of the 'due diligence' provisions in relation to forged prescriptions, has certainly improved the position of pharmacists. Prior to this, pharmacists dispensing a prescription only medicine, pursuant to a forged prescription, could find themselves in distinct difficulties, and unable to rely on a general due diligence defence. Such was the case in *Pharmaceutical Society of Great Britain* v *Storkwain Ltd* [1985] 3 All ER 4, [1986] 2 All ER 635. The facts were that Storkwain Ltd, a pharmacy, had supplied prescription only medicines, on the strength of two prescriptions which were offered to them. Both prescriptions were proved to be forgeries. Relevant charges under the MA 1968 and the relevant secondary legislation were brought by the Pharmaceutical Society.

The magistrate who heard the original charges dismissed them on the basis that the sections under which the charges had been brought required proof of *mens rea*, or guilty intent, which had not been shown. He did, however, state a case for the Queen's Bench Division. The Divisional Court decided that the offences created by the relevant provisions of the MA 1968 were offences of strict liability where proof of intent or *mens rea* was not necessary. The Divisional Court also found that the existing general due diligence defence was inapplicable to the present case even though the facts showed that the prescription was a forgery and that there was no evidence to suggest that the pharmacy had acted negligently, improperly or dishonestly.

The Divisional Court found that the secondary legislation in which the exemption was contained related to the conditions applicable to a genuine prescription which is defective in that it has not fulfilled one of the conditions applicable to a valid prescription. In this case the court was not concerned with a genuine prescription, whether defective or not, but with a forged prescription. Accordingly the exemption did not apply.

The court therefore held that the offence of selling or supplying prescription only medicines except in accordance with a prescription was an absolute offence on its construction in the MA 1968 and that it was no defence for a pharmacist to argue that the prescription was a forgery and that he had not been negligent or dishonest, despite the wording of the exemptions offered in the appropriate regulations. Leave was granted to appeal to the House of Lords.

There, Lord Goff was clear that the offence was one of strict liability. He offered two main justifications for this view. First, he pointed to the fact that the MA 1968 made it clear that *mens rea* was to be an ingredient of certain offences under the Act, by providing a general defence to those offences. The offence of selling or supplying prescription only medicines without a prescription was not included in that list of offences.

Secondly, the Act provided the power to confer further exemptions from the requirements of the Act subject to certain conditions or limitations. The exemptions which were conferred on pharmacists under this power through the relevant secondary legislation were not capable of a wide interpretation. The use of the phrase 'due diligence' created a narrow exemption and so the offence was one of strict liability.

As noted above, the introduction of the due diligence defence in relation to the dispensing of prescription only medicines pursuant to a forged prescription has negated aspects of the effect of the Storkwain case. However, it is clear that the courts are interpreting the meaning of 'due diligence' in a narrow manner, balancing the need to take account of the propriety of an individual pharmacist's conduct against the need to protect the public from the dangers of unlawful drugs. As we shall see below, in chapter ten, the case reinforces the high standard of care which is expected of pharmacists in their professional pharmacy role.

The Standards of Good Professional Practice section of the Royal Pharmaceutical Society of Great Britain's *Medicines, Ethics and Practice*, gives detailed advice on the issue of forged prescriptions. The advice, which would be indicative of whether an individual pharmacist has exercised due diligence, is discussed in detail below in 5.11.

5.7 PHARMACY RECORDS

Under the provisions of reg. 6 of the Medicines (Sale or Supply) (Miscellaneous Provisions) Regulations 1980 (S.I. 1980/1923) every person lawfully conducting a retail pharmacy business must make an entry, in a written or computerised record kept for the purpose, in respect of every sale or supply of a prescription only medicine. Each entry must include the following particulars:

(a)   the date on which the prescription only medicine was sold or supplied;

(b)   the name, quantity and, except where it is apparent from the name, the pharmaceutical form and strength of the prescription only medicine sold or supplied;

(c)   the name and address of the practitioner giving the prescription;

(d)   the name and address of the person for whom the prescription only medicine was prescribed; and

(e)   the date on the prescription.

Where the sale or supply is the second or further sale or supply pursuant to a repeatable prescription, the entry should include, as a minimum, the date on which the prescription only medicine is sold or supplied, and a reference to the other particulars, described above, entered in relation to the first supply. Entries must be made on the day the sale or supply takes place, or if that is not reasonably practicable, on the next following day. The potential for entries to be made in a written or computerised format was introduced through the provisions of the Medicines (Sale or Supply) (Miscellaneous Provisions) Amendment Regulations 1997 (S.I. 1997/1831).

Every person lawfully conducting a retail pharmacy business must preserve the record for a period of two years from the date on which the last entry was made. Prescriptions, and orders or invoices relating to the sale or supply of controlled drugs, must also be preserved for a period of two years from the date on which the prescription only medicine was sold or supplied. In the case of a repeatable prescription, the preservation period is two years from the date of the final sale or supply pursuant to that prescription.

The record keeping requirement does not apply where the sale or supply is in pursuance of a health prescription or a prescription for oral contraceptives. In addition, the requirement does not apply where a separate record of the sale or supply is made in accordance with the legislative requirements relating to controlled drugs. These requirements are described in detail in chapter six below. Further exemptions are provided for the sale and supply to persons involved in quality testing schemes and for certain other schemes in Scotland and Northern Ireland.

The Royal Pharmaceutical Society of Great Britain has given further detailed guidance to its members on keeping records of sales or supplies of prescription only medicines. This guidance is discussed in greater detail in 5.11 below.

5.8   EMERGENCY SUPPLIES

Article 8 of the Prescription Only Medicines (Human Use) Order 1997 provides exemptions from the restrictions relating to the sale and supply of prescription only medicines in circumstances where the sale or supply is made in an emergency. Specific conditions are applied to the emergency sale or supply of prescription only medicines, which must adhered to if the exemption is to bite. The conditions envisage two different types of emergency sale or supply of prescription only medicines — those instigated at the request of a doctor and those instigated at the request of an individual patient. In relation to each, the sale or supply must be eventually made by a person lawfully conducting a retail pharmacy business, who will be usually be an individual pharmacist.

For an emergency sale or supply of a prescription only medicine, instigated at the request of a doctor, to be exempt, the pharmacist must be satisfied that the request is valid and has been made by a doctor who by reason of an emergency is unable to furnish a prescription immediately. Further the pharmacist must be satisfied that the doctor has undertaken to furnish the pharmacist with a prescription within 72 hours of the sale or supply and that the prescription only medicine is eventually sold or supplied in accordance with the requesting doctor's directions.

Importantly, a controlled drug, specified in schs. 1, 2 or 3 to the Misuse of Drugs Regulations 1985 (S.I. 1985/2066, as amended) may not be supplied under an emergency doctor request. Finally, an entry of the sale or supply of the prescription only medicine must be made in the register, stating the following particulars:

(a)   the date on which the medicine was sold or supplied;

(b)   the name, quantity, and except where it is apparent from the name, the pharmaceutical form and strength of the medicine;

(c)   the name and address of the person for whom the prescription only medicine has been supplied;

(d)   the date on which the prescription was received and the name and address of the practitioner giving it;

(e)   the date on the prescription.

For an emergency sale or supply of a prescription only medicine, instigated at the request of a patient, to be exempt, several important conditions must be satisfied, as follows:

(a)   The pharmacist must interview the person requesting the prescription only medicine, and be satisfied that there is an immediate need for the prescription only medicine requested to be sold or supplied, and that it is impracticable in the circumstances to obtain a prescription without undue delay. Further, the pharmacist must be satisfied that treatment with the requested prescription only medicine has been prescribed by a doctor for the person requesting it on a previous occasion, and also be satisfied as to the dose which in the circumstances it would be appropriate for the person to take.

(b)   The quantity of the prescription only medicine sold or supplied to the patient must not be greater than what will provide five days' treatment. There are certain exceptions to this requirement. First, where the prescription only medicine is an aerosol for the relief of asthma, an ointment or a cream, and has been made up for sale in a container elsewhere than the pharmacy, the smallest pack that the pharmacist has for sale or supply may be sold or supplied. Secondly, where the prescription only medicine is an oral contraceptive, a quantity sufficient for a full treatment cycle may be sold or supplied. Finally, where the prescription only medicine is an antibiotic for oral administration in liquid form, the smallest quantity that will provide a full course of treatment may be sold or supplied.

(c)   An entry of the sale or supply of the prescription only medicine must be made in the register, stating the following particulars:

(i)   the date on which the medicine was sold or supplied;

(ii)   the name, quantity, and except where it is apparent from the name, the pharmaceutical form and strength of the medicine;

(iii)   the name of the person requesting the prescription only medicine;

(iv)   the name and address of the registered pharmacy from which the prescription only medicine is sold or supplied;

(v)   the words 'Emergency Supply'.

(d)   Finally, no prescription only medicine which consists of or contains one of the substances specified in sch. 4 to the Prescription Only Medicines (Human Use) Order 1997 or is a controlled drug specified in schs. 1, 2 or 3 of the Misuse of Drugs Regulations 1985, may be sold or supplied.

This final requirement, and the equivalent constraint in relation to the emergency sale or supply at the instigation of a doctor, will not apply where the prescription only medicine consists of or contains phenobarbitone or phenobarbitone calcium, but no other substance specified in sch. 4 to the Prescription Only Medicines (Human Use) Order 1997 or is a controlled drug specified in schs. 1, 2 or 3 of the Misuse of Drugs Regulations 1985, and is sold or supplied for use in the treatment of epilepsy.

The Royal Pharmaceutical Society of Great Britain has given further detailed guidance to its members on the issue of the emergency supply of prescription only medicines. This guidance is discussed in greater detail in 5.11 below.

5.9   EXEMPTIONS

The legislative provisions allow for a series of exemptions from the otherwise strict requirements relating to the distribution of prescription only medicines. Exemptions are permitted for three methods of distribution — sale and supply, supply and administration. Some of the exemptions relate specifically to the practice of pharmacy, and are detailed below.

Other exemptions have a less tenuous connection. Many pharmacists might argue that they have no direct interest in the permitted distribution rights of qualified first-aid personnel on off-shore installations. However it is important to be aware that the law recognises that certain circumstances may arise necessitating the immediate sale, supply, or administration of prescription only medicines in situations where the normal legislative requirements cannot, or need not, be met. Some of these further situations are also described below.

5.9.1   Sale and supply exemptions for pharmacists
Pharmacists are exempt from the general restrictions relating to the sale and supply of prescription only medicines, in relation to the sale and supply of amyl nitrate. This exemption is subject to the restriction that the sale or supply must be to persons to whom cyanide salts may be sold by virtue of ss. 3 or 4, Poisons Act 1972, or arts. 5 or 6 of the Poisons (Northern Ireland) Order 1976, and the sale or supply must only be so far as is reasonably necessary to enable an antidote to be available to persons at risk of cyanide poisoning.

5.9.2   Sale and supply exemptions for drugs at high dilutions
Article 10 of the Prescription Only Medicines (Human Use) Order 1997 provides exemptions from the restrictions relating to the sale and supply of prescription only medicines at high dilutions. The conditions applicable to this exemption are that the medicinal product is not for parenteral administration, and consists of, or contains, any of the substances listed in column 1 of schs. 1 or 2 to the Order, only one or more unit preparation of such substances, if:

(a)   each such unit preparation has been diluted to at least one part in a million (6x), and the person selling, supplying or administering the medicinal product has been requested by or on behalf of a particular person and in that person's presence to use judgment as to the treatment required; or
(b)   each such unit preparation has been diluted to at least one part in a million million (6c).

5.9.3   Sale and supply exemptions for hospitals
Article 12 of the Prescription Only Medicines (Human Use) Order 1997 provides exemptions from the restrictions relating to the sale and supply of prescription only medicines in hospitals. Prescription only medicines may be sold or supplied in the business of a hospital in accordance with the written directions of a doctor or dentist. Those written directions do not have to be in the same form, nor satisfy the same conditions, applicable to all other prescriptions, as outlined in art.15(2) of the Order, as discussed in 5.5 above.

5.9.4   Sale and supply exemptions for certain persons
Under s. 58(3), MA 1968, the restrictions relating to the sale and supply of prescription only medicines do not apply to the sale and supply of any

medicinal product to patients under their care by doctors or dentists who are appropriate practitioners.

Article 11(1)(a) and Part I of sch. 5 of the Prescription Only Medicines (Human Use) Order 1997 provides exemptions from the restrictions relating to the sale and supply of prescription only medicines for certain categories of persons, subject to certain defined conditions.

5.9.4.1   *Sale and supply exemptions for universities*   Persons selling or supplying prescription only medicines to universities, other institutions concerned with higher education or institutions concerned with research, are exempt from the restrictions on condition that:

(a)   the sale or supply is subject to the presentation of an order signed by the principal of the institution concerned with education or research, or the appropriate head of department in charge of a specified course of research, stating:

(i)   the name of the institution for which the prescription only medicine is required;
(ii)   the purpose for which the prescription only medicine is required; and
(iii)   the total quantity required; and

(b)   the sale or supply is for the purposes of the education or research with which the institution is concerned.

5.9.4.2   *Sale and supply exemptions for statutory officers*   Exemptions from the restrictions relating to the sale and supply of prescription only medicines apply to persons selling or supplying prescription only medicines to any of the following:

(a)   a public analyst appointed under s. 27, Food Safety Act 1990, or art. 36 of the Food (Northern Ireland) Order 1989;
(b)   an authorised officer within the meaning of s. 5(6), Food Safety Act 1990;
(c)   a sampling officer within the meaning of art. 38(1) of the Food (Northern Ireland) Order 1989;
(d)   a person duly authorised by an enforcement authority under ss. 111 and 112, MA 1968;
(e)   a sampling officer within the meaning of sch. 3 to the MA 1968.

For the exemption to apply, the sale or supply must be subject to the presentation of an order signed by or on behalf of any of the persons mentioned in (a)–(e), stating the status of the person signing it, the amount of prescription only medicine required and must only be in connection with the exercise by those persons of their statutory functions.

Exemptions from the restrictions relating to the sale and supply of prescription only medicines apply to persons selling or supplying prescription only medicines to any person employed or engaged in connection with a scheme for testing the quality and checking the amount of the drugs and appliances supplied under the National Health Service Act 1977, the National Health Service (Scotland) Act 1978, the Health and Personal Social Services (Northern Ireland) Order 1972, or under any subordinate legislation made under those Acts or that Order. The exemption is subject to the condition that the sale or supply will be subject to the presentation of an order signed by or on behalf of the person so employed or engaged, stating the status of the person signing it, the amount of prescription only medicine required, and must be for the purpose of the relevant testing scheme.

Exemptions from the restrictions relating to the sale and supply of prescription only medicines apply to persons selling or supplying prescription only medicines to the British Standards Institute, in relation to all prescription only medicines. This exemption is subject to the requirement that the sale or supply shall be subject to the presentation of an order signed on behalf of the British Standards Institution, stating the status of the person signing it and the amount of the prescription only medicine required. Further the sale or supply must only be for the purpose of testing containers of medicinal products or determining the standards for such containers.

5.9.4.3   Sale and supply exemptions for registered midwives and opticians   Registered midwives are exempt from the general restrictions relating to the sale and supply of prescription only medicines in relation to certain medicinal products containing chloral hydrate, ergometrine maleate, pentacozine hydrochloride or triclofos sodium. The exemption is subject to the further condition that the sale or supply shall be only in the course of the midwives' professional practice, and, in the case of ergometrine maleate, only when contained in a medicinal product which is not for parenteral administration.

Registered ophthalmic opticians are exempt from the general restrictions relating to the sale and supply of prescription only medicines in relation to certain medicinal products. The products, which are not for parenteral administration, are:

(a)   eye drops and are prescription only medicines by reason that they contain not more than 0.5% Chloramphenicol; or

(b)   eye ointments and are prescription only medicines by reason only that they contain not more than 1% Chloramphenicol; or

(c)   prescription only medicines by reason only that they contain any of the following, namely, stropine sulphate, bethanecol chloride, carbachol, cyclopentolate hydrochloride, homatropine hydrobromide, naphazoline hydrochloride, naphazoline nitrate, physostigmine salicylate, physostigmine sulphate, pilocarpine hydrochloride, pilocarpine nitrate, or tropicamide.

For the exemption to be effective, the sale or supply must only be in the course of the professional practice of the registered ophthalmic optician and must only be in an emergency.

Persons lawfully conducting a retail pharmacy business may sell or supply the ophthalmic products mentioned above, without the normal restriction applicable to prescription only products, to registered ophthalmic opticians on presentation of an order by them to that effect.

5.9.4.4   Sale and supply exemptions for chriopodists   Article 5(1) of the Prescription Only Medicines (Human Use) Amendment Order 1998 (S.I. 1998/108), amends Part 1 of sch. 5 to the Prescription Only Medicines (Human Use) Order 1997, to grant exemptions to certain state registered chiropodists from the general restrictions relating to the sale and supply of certain prescription only medicines. The exemption relates to Co-dydramol 10/500 tablets, Amorolfine hydrochloride cream where the maximum strength of the Amorolfine in the cream does not exceed 0.25 per cent by weight in weight, Amorolfine hydrochloride lacquer where the maximum strength of the Amorofline in the lacquer does not exceed 5 per cent by weight in volume; and topical hydrocortisone where the maximum strength of the hydrocortisone in the medicinal product does not exceed 1 per cent by weight in weight.

The exemption is also subject to the further restrictions that the state registered chiropodists must have a certificate of competence in the use of the above named medicines, the sale and supply must be only in the course of their professional practice, and, in the case of Co-dydramol 10/500 tablets, the quantity sold or supplied to a person at any one time must not exceed the amount sufficient for three days' treatment to a maximum of 24 tablets.

5.9.4.5   Sale and supply exemptions for holders of marketing authorisations   Holders of marketing authorisations, product licences or manufacturers' licences are exempt from the restrictions relating to the sale and supply of prescription only medicines in relation to the medicinal products referred to in the authorisations or licences. This exemption is subject to the conditions that the sale or supply shall be only to a pharmacist so as to enable that pharmacist to prepare an entry relating to the prescription only medicine in a tablet or capsule identification guide or similar publication, and is of no greater quantity than is reasonably necessary for that purpose.

5.9.5   Supply exemptions for certain persons
Article 11(1)(b) and Part II of sch. 5 of the Prescription Only Medicines (Human Use) Order 1997 provide exemptions from the restrictions relating to the supply of prescription only medicines for certain categories of person, subject to certain defined conditions.

The Royal National Lifeboat Institution, and certified first aiders of the Institution are exempt from the general restrictions relating to the supply of prescription only medicines, subject to the condition that the supply shall only be so far as is necessary for the treatment of sick or injured persons in the exercise of the functions of the Institution. The owner or master of a ship which does not carry a doctor on board as part of its compliment is exempt from the general restrictions, subject to the condition that the supply shall only be so far as is necessary for the treatment of persons on the ship.

Persons authorised by licences granted under reg. 5 of the Misuse of Drugs Regulations to supply a controlled drug, are exempt from the general restrictions relating to the supply of prescription only medicines, in relation to the controlled drugs specified in the licence. This exemption is subject to the conditions, circumstances and to such an extent as is specified in the licence.

Persons requiring prescription only medicines for the purpose of enabling them, in the course of their business, to comply with any requirements made by or in pursuance of any enactment with respect to the medical treatment of their employees, are exempt from the general restrictions relating to the supply of prescription only medicines. This exemption is restricted to the prescription only medicines specified in the relevant enactment, and is subject to the condition that the supply must be for the purposes of enabling them to comply with any requirements made by or in pursuance of any such enactment, and be subject to the conditions and circumstances specified in the relevant enactment.

Exemptions extend to persons operating an occupational health scheme, in relation to prescription only medicines supplied to those persons in response to an order in writing signed by a doctor or a registered nurse. For this exemption to apply, the supply must be in the course of the occupational health scheme, and the individual supplying the prescription only medicine, if not a doctor, must be a registered nurse acting in accordance with the written instructions of a doctor as to the circumstances in which the relevant prescription only medicines are to be used in the occupational health scheme.

Exemptions extend to the operator or commander of an aircraft, in relation to prescription only medicines which are not for parenteral administration and which have been sold or supplied to the operator or commander in response to an order in writing signed by a doctor. The exemption is subject to the further condition that the supply must be only so far as is necessary for the immediate treatment of sick or injured persons on the aircraft and be in accordance with the written instruction of a doctor as to the circumstances in which the relevant prescription only medicine are to be used on the aircraft. Persons employed as qualified first-aid personnel on offshore installations are exempt to the extent that the supply is only so far as is necessary for the treatment of persons on the installation.

5.9.6 Administration exemptions for certain persons

Article 11(2) and Part III of sch. 5 to the Prescription Only Medicines (Human Use) Order 1997 provide exemptions from the restrictions relating to the administration of prescription only medicines, as outlined in s. 58(2)(b), MA 1968, for certain categories of person, subject to certain defined conditions.

Exemptions apply to persons who are authorised as members of a group by a group authority granted under regs. 8(3) or 9(3) of the Misuse of Drugs Regulations to supply a controlled drug by way of administration only. The exemption is restricted to prescription only medicines that are specified in the group authority and are subject to the further restriction that the administration shall be subject to the conditions, circumstances and extent as may be specified in the group authority.

Exemptions again apply to the owner or master of a ship which does not carry a doctor on board as part of its compliment, in relation to prescription only medicines which are for parenteral administration. The administration must be only so far as is necessary for the treatment of persons on the ship. Exemptions also extend to persons operating an occupational health scheme, in relation to prescription only medicines sold or supplied to those persons in response to an order in writing signed by a doctor or a registered nurse. For this exemption to apply, the administration must be in the course of the occupational health scheme. Further, the individual administering the prescription only medicine, if neither a doctor, nor acting in accordance with the directions of a doctor, must be a registered nurse acting in accordance with the written instructions of a doctor, as to the circumstances in which the relevant prescription only medicines are to be used in the occupational health scheme.

Exemptions extend to the operator or commander of an aircraft, in relation to prescription only medicines for parenteral administration and which have been sold or supplied to the operator or commander in response to an order in writing signed by a doctor. The exemption is subject to the further condition that the administration must be only so far as is necessary for the immediate treatment of sick or injured persons on the aircraft and must be in accordance with the written instruction of a doctor as to the circumstances in which the relevant prescription only medicine is to be used on the aircraft.

Persons who were at 11 February 1982 customarily administering medicinal products to human beings by parenteral administration in the course of a business in the field of osteopathy, naturopathy, acupuncture or other similar field, except chiropody, are also exempt, in relation to medicinal products which are for parenteral administration. This exemption is subject to the further requirement that the person administering the prescription only medicine shall have been requested by or on behalf of the person to whom it is administered, and in that person's presence, to use judgment as to the treatment required.

Persons employed as qualified first-aid personnel on offshore installations are exempt from the general restrictions relating to the administration of prescription only medicines for parenteral administration to the extent that the administration is only so far as is necessary for the treatment of persons on the installation.

Persons who hold a certificate of proficiency in ambulance paramedic sk issued by, or with the approval of, the Secretary of State, are exempt from th general restrictions relating to the administration of certain prescription only medicines for parenteral administration. These medicines are diazepam 5mg per 5ml for injection, succinylated modified fluid gelatin 4 per cent intravenous infusion, or prescription only medicines containing no active ingredient but one or more of adrenaline acid tartrate, anhydrous glucose, compound sodium lactate intravenous infusion, Hartman's solution, ergometrine maleate, glucose, heparin sodium, lignocaine hydrochloride, nalbuphaine hydrochloride, naloxone hydrochloride, polygeline, sodium bicarbonate, or sodium chloride. The exemption is subject to the requirement that the administration must be only for the immediate, necessary treatment of sick or injured persons, and in the case of a prescription only medicine containing heparin sodium, be only for the purpose of cannula flushing.

State registered chiropodists who hold a certificate of competence in the use of analgesics issued by or with the approval of the Chiropodists Board, are exempt in relation to prescription only medicines for parenteral administration that contain, as the sole active ingredient, not more than one of a number of substances. These are bupivacaine hydrochloride, bupivacaine hydrochloride with adrenalin where the maximum strength of the adrenaline does not exceed 1mg in 200ml of bupivacaine hydrochloride, lignocaine hydrochloride, lignocaine hydrochloride with adrenaline where the maximum strength of the adrenaline does not exceed 1mg in 200ml of lignocaine hydrochloride, or prilocaine hydrochloride.

The administration must only be in the course of the chiropodist's professional practice. The regulations relating to the exemptions for the administration of certain prescription only medicines by state registered chiropodists were introduced by art. 5(2) of the Prescription Only Medicines (Human Use) Amendment Order 1998 (S.I. 1998/108).

Registered midwives are exempt in relation to prescription only medicines for parenteral administration that contain any of a number of substances. These include ergometrine maleate, lignocaine, lignocaine hydrochloride, naloxone hydrochloride, natural and synthetic oxytocins, pentaocine lactate, pethidine hydrochloride, phytomenadione, or promazine hydrochloride. The administration must be only in the course of the professional practice of the registered midwife. In the case of promazine hydrochloride, lignocaine, and lignocaine hydrochloride, the administration must be only while the midwife is attending on a woman in childbirth.

5.10   OFFENCES IN RELATION TO PRESCRIPTION ONLY MEDICINES

Section 67(2), MA 1968 states that any person who contravenes the legislative provisions relating to prescription only medicines will be guilty of an offence,

imary conviction by a scale fine and on indictment by a term
Section 68 allows for the disqualification, by the court, of an
rying on a retail pharmacy business, following conviction for

any proposal to impose such an order must relate to the gravity of the
offence, the unsatisfactory state of the premises and any similar prior
convictions. Further provisions allow for another enforcement authority to
apply for such an order, further convictions for breach of such an order and
applications for early revocation of the order.

5.11 PROFESSIONAL STANDARDS AND PRESCRIPTION ONLY MEDICINES

The principles of the *Code of Ethics* of the Royal Pharmaceutical Society of
Great Britain impose specific obligations on pharmacists relating to the
dispensing of prescriptions. Breach of these principles may form the basis of a
complaint of professional misconduct. These principles are supplemented by
detailed advice, contained in the published *Standards of Good Professional
Practice*. It is important to remember that the *Code of Ethics* also requires that
pharmacists must comply with the obligations in the standards of good
professional practice where applicable. Failure to meet the standards could also
form the basis of a complaint of misconduct.

As part of the principle that a pharmacist's prime concern must be for the
welfare of both the patient and other members of the public, a series of
obligations are imposed which have both general and specific implications for
the supply of prescription only medicines. Generally, the pharmacist is under a
duty to act in a manner which promotes and safeguards the interests of the
public, and justifies public trust in the pharmacist's knowledge, ability and
judgment. Further, the pharmacist has a professional responsibility to exercise
control over all medicinal products which are supplied.

The pharmacist must exercise professional judgment to prevent the supply
of unnecessary and excessive quantities of medicines and other products,
particularly prescription only medicines. Care should be taken over their
supply even when it is legally authorised by prescription or signed order. A
pharmacist must be alert to the possibility of drug dependency in health care
professionals and patients and must be prepared to make inquiries to ensure
that such medicines are to be used responsibly.

In addition, the pharmacist must, on each occasion that a pharmaceutical
service is provided, use professional judgment to decide whether the patient
needs to be seen. Further guidance on this latter obligation indicates that a
face-to-face consultation need not take place on every occasion that a service is
provided. However, a pharmacist has a professional duty to ensure that it
occurs when considered necessary with a medicine for an acute condition or at
appropriate intervals for repeat medication.

Further obligations are more closely related to the supply of prescription only medicines. A pharmacist must not deviate from the prescriber's instructions when dispensing, except when necessary to protect the patient. Further guidance on this obligation indicates that, in cases of uncertainty, the pharmacist should make every effort to contact the prescriber. If it is impossible to contact the prescriber, the pharmacist should use professional judgment and decide, in all of the circumstances, what course of action would be in the best interest of the patient. Where the problem cannot be resolved and if there appears to be a potential risk to the patient, the pharmacist may properly decide not to dispense the prescription even if the prescriber confirms that the product should be dispensed. In taking this decision the pharmacist should assess the relative harm which may result from this refusal and use professional judgment to decide what course of action would be in the best interest of the patient.

Except in an emergency, a pharmacist must not substitute any other product for a specifically named product without the approval of the prescriber. Further guidance on this obligation indicates that unless the prescription bears the British approved (generic) name of the medicinal product, a pharmacist may not dispense a parallel import medicine if the name of that medicine is different from the name appearing on the prescription. The name used on the pharmacy dispensing label must be the name that is given on the prescription. Dispensed medicines should normally be supplied directly to the patient or the patient's carer in the pharmacy, where there is an opportunity for face-to-face contact, and the pharmacist has access to records and references which enable the pharmacist to provide the best pharmaceutical service.

Pharmacists are advised that a 'fax' of a prescription does not fall within the definition of a legally valid prescription because it is not written in indelible ink, and has not been signed by an appropriate practitioner. A fax can, however, confirm that at the time of receipt, a valid prescription is in existence.

Further guidance is given to the effect that any pharmacist who decides to dispense a prescription only medicine against a fax, without sight of the original prescription, must ensure that adequate safeguards exist to ensure that the integrity of the original prescription is maintained, and that the prescription will be in the possession of the pharmacist within a short time. Any doubt as to the content of the original prescription, caused by poor reproduction, must be overcome before the medicine is supplied. Finally, pharmacists are advised that under no circumstances can medicines listed in schs. 2 or 3 of the Misuse of Drugs Regulations 1985 be dispensed against a fax.

Pharmacists are also warned that forged prescriptions are extremely difficult to detect and that every pharmacist should be alert to the possibility that any prescription calling for a misused product could be a forgery. Warning signals of the possibility that a prescription might be forged could include a fundamental written error or an instinctive feeling relating to the behaviour of the individual.

The Royal Pharmaceutical Society of Great Britain advises further scrutiny and checking of the signature on the prescription, where the prescriber is known to the pharmacist, and the patient has not previously visited the pharmacy, or is not known to be suffering from a medical condition which requires the medicinal product prescribed. Large doses or quantities should be checked with the prescriber in order to detect alterations to previously valid prescriptions. Where the prescriber's signature is not known, the prescriber must be contacted and asked to confirm that the prescription is genuine. A further, non-exhaustive, list of matters which should alert a pharmacist and prompt further checking includes an uncharacteristic prescribing or method of writing prescription by a known doctor, peculiar letter heading compilation or 'Dr' written before or after the prescriber's signature.

While close professional co-operation between medical practitioners and pharmacists is encouraged, pharmacists are warned that patients who are issued with a prescription which may be dispensed at any pharmacy have the right to present it to the pharmacy of their choice. The purpose of this warning is to ensure that no undesirable business relationship develops between a medical practitioner and a pharmacist whereby one can excercise undue influence over the other. A pharmacist must not approach a medical practitioner or pharmacy staff to secure direction of prescriptions to a particular pharmacy nor offer inducements for such purposes.

A prescription may be sent directly to a particular pharmacy where the patient has requested such a direction, the patient is in residential care, or the patient is an addict receiving medication by instalments.

The Royal Pharmaceutical Society of Great Britain has also issued more general guidelines on the use of pharmacy computer systems for record keeping. These guidelines specify minimum requirements for hardware and software systems and minimum requirements for the use of such systems in the pharmacy. These further minimum requirements include details relating to patient medication records, and security of information.

Pharmacists are also advised that where they elect to keep records electronically, all the relevant particulars must be recorded, adequate backups must be made and arrangements made so that inspectors can examine the records during visits with minimal disruption to the dispensing process.

Finally the Royal Pharmaceutical Society has issued detailed guidelines on standards for dispensary design and equipment, procurement and sources of materials, manufacturing and quality assurance and dispensing procedures. The latter includes detailed advice on the supervision of dispensing and the furnishing of information, advice and counselling.

Dispensing must be under the direct supervision of a pharmacist. Every prescription must be seen by a pharmacist and judgment made as to what action is required. A pharmacist may be able to delegate to suitably trained staff certain tasks but must be available in the pharmacy to intervene, advise and check the dispensing of any prescription. A pharmacist must ensure that a dispensed product will still be in date at the end of the treatment period, where this is predictable.

Dispensing procedures must ensure that dispensing takes place with reasonable promptness. If, on occasion, a prescription cannot be dispensed promptly, and the supply is required urgently, the patient must be directed to an alternative dispensing source. Where a prescription cannot be dispensed in its entirety when first received in the pharmacy, detailed procedures must be followed in relation to the owed balance. Systems must also be developed to ensure that the distribution of medicines is reliable and secure to the point of delivery.

The Royal Pharmaceutical Society of Great Britain advises that a pharmacist must seek to ensure that the patient understands sufficient information and advice to enable safe and effective use of the medicine. Such advice must be given personally by the pharmacist. Where that is not practicable, and the pharmacist judges that the advice or directions may be given by a dispensing technician or other member of staff, it should also be made clear that the advice of the pharmacist is available if required.

5.12   CONCLUSION

The importance of prescription only medicines to the practice of health care cannot be underestimated. The figures on the use of such products as a major part of drug therapy emphasise the importance of this class of drugs in the provision of health care. A balance has been struck in the legal regulation and control of such drug products, between permitting their continued exploitation for use in drug therapy, and controlling both the range of products to be specified as falling into this class and the range of practitioners authorised to prescribe their use.

The pharmacy profession has negotiated a virtual monopoly over the provision of pharmaceutical services to the National Health Service. In addition it has devised a parallel control over the sale and supply of prescription only drug products. The statistics on the annual number, and cost, of dispensed prescriptions within the NHS, reinforces the significance of the prescription only medicines for the practice of pharmacy.

As noted in the introduction to this chapter, the awarding of exclusive distribution rights is contingent on the parallel assumption of duties and obligations relating to the methods by which sales and supplies are undertaken. The specific legislative provisions outlining requirements for the form of valid prescriptions, and the duties to maintain records of any sales and supplies need to be closely analysed by those involved in the practice of pharmacy.

Any contravention of the requirements for the sale or supply of prescription only medicines, amounts to a criminal offence, punishable on summary conviction by a fine or on indictment by a fine or imprisonment or both. That fact alone reinforces the need for close examination of the relevant rules and regulations outlined in this chapter.

However, the pharmacist's responsibility does not stop with strict adherence to the technical controls and procedures. The analysis of the pharmacist's professional responsibility undertaken in chapters ten to thirteen below, demonstrates that further legal duties and obligations are owed. Failure to carry out such duties and obligations carries its own civil and administrative consequences.

SIX

The regulation of medicinal drug products — controlled drugs

6.1 INTRODUCTION

There are certain drugs which have both a therapeutic value in medicine and a potential for misuse through addiction and abuse. These drugs pose a regulatory dilemma for society. Their therapeutic value means that their use in medicine ought to be permitted, while their potential for abuse means that their distribution must be strictly controlled. These drugs therefore require stringent regulation. The regulators have designated such drugs as 'controlled drugs' and their import, export, production, supply and possession are supervised by specific primary and secondary legislation. The purpose of the legislative provisions is twofold — to control the distribution of such drugs in society and to permit the use of such drugs in medicine.

The legislation allows for the establishment of an advisory body to assist in the process of reviewing those drugs which are or are capable of being misused, particularly where the misuse has harmful effects sufficient to constitute a social problem. In addition to this general duty the advisory body has more specific obligations relating to the giving of advice concerning the restriction of availability of such drugs, the care of those misusing them, education concerning misuse and the potential for addiction, and research aimed at preventing misuse.

The major purpose of the legislation is concerned with the classification of controlled drugs and regulation of import, export, production, possession and supply. Detailed provisions have been enacted in relation to each of these areas, reflecting the importance which the regulators attach to the control of these products. Those provisions are reinforced by the creation of distinctive criminal offences punishable by significant fines and/or terms of imprisonment.

The classification of controlled drugs under the primary legislation, the Misuse of Drugs Act 1971, as amended, is sometimes ignored by pharmacists as being of no practical importance. This is because this classification relates to the imposition of penalties for unlawful possession, supply, manufacture, export and import. Attention is usually focused on the classification of controlled drugs for lawful purposes. Such practical consequences should not disguise the importance of an understanding of how the regulators deal with other aspects of the control of these dangerous substances.

The rules and regulations on controlled drugs also reflect the desire to exploit the therapeutic potential of these products and permit their use in drug therapy. Control is again the key word. There are detailed rules on the possession and supply of scheduled controlled drugs and in relation to prescriptions for these products. The detailed rules on prescriptions supplement the existing rules for prescriptions for prescription only medicines, outlined in the previous chapter. Further provisions outline requirements for record keeping and the maintenance of registers.

The legislative provisions regulate the safe-keeping of controlled drugs and the eventual destruction of any such products no longer required. In addition, there are specific requirements relating to addicts.

6.2   THE ADVISORY COUNCIL ON THE MISUSE OF DRUGS

Section 1 of the Misuse of Drugs Act (MDA) 1971, as amended, allows for the constitution of an Advisory Council on the Misuse of Drugs in accordance with sch. 1 to the Act. Schedule 1 to the MDA 1971 gives specific details of the constitution of the Advisory Council. It should consist of not fewer than 20 members, appointed by the Secretary of State after consultation with appropriate organisations. Members should include at least one person appearing to the Secretary of State to have wide and recent experience of:

(a)   the practice of medicine (other than veterinary medicine);
(b)   the practice of dentistry;
(c)   the practice of veterinary medicine;
(d)   the practice of pharmacy;
(e)   the pharmaceutical industry;
(f)   chemistry other than the pharmaceutical industry.

Membership should also include persons appearing to the Secretary of State to have wide and recent experience of social problems connected with the misuse of drugs.

The Secretary of State appoints one of the members of the Advisory Council to be chairman of the Council. The Advisory Council may appoint committees which may include persons who are not members of the Council. The purpose of the committees is to report to the Advisory Council on any matter referred to them by the Council. Provision is also made in sch. 1 for the conduct of meetings of the Advisory Council, and for remuneration and expenses of individual members.

Under s. 1, MDA 1971, the Advisory Council has a duty to keep under review the situation in the United Kingdom with respect to drugs which are being, or appear likely to be misused, and of which the misuse is having or appears to be capable of having harmful effects sufficient to constitute a social problem.

In addition, the Advisory Council has a duty to give advice to any one or more of the Ministers, (the Secretary of State for the Home Department, and the Secretaries of State responsible for health and education in England, Wales and Northern Ireland), where either the Council thinks it expedient to do so, or after consultation by the Ministers in question, on measures which, in the opinion of the Council, ought to be taken for preventing the misuse of drugs which are being, or appear to be, capable of being misused, or dealing with social problems connected with their misuse.

In particular, the Advisory Council is charged with giving advice on measures which ought to be taken:

(a)   for restricting the availability of such drugs or supervising the arrangements for their supply;

(b)   for enabling persons affected by the misuse of such drugs to obtain proper advice, and for securing the provision of proper facilities and services for the treatment, rehabilitation and after-care of such persons;

(c)   for promoting co-operation between the various professional and community services which in the opinion of the Advisory Council have a part to play in dealing with social problems connected with the misuse of such drugs;

(d)   for educating the public (and in particular the young) in the dangers of misusing such drugs, and for giving publicity to those dangers; and

(e)   for promoting research into, or otherwise obtaining information about, any matter which in the opinion of the Advisory Council is of relevance for the purpose of preventing the misuse of such drugs or dealing with any social problem associated with their misuse. Under s. 32, MDA 1971, the Secretary of State may conduct or assist in conducting research into any matter relating to the misuse of dangerous or otherwise harmful drugs.

The Advisory Council also has the duty to consider any matter, and to advise on any question, relating to drug dependence or the misuse of drugs which may be referred to it by any Minister. In particular, the Advisory Council has a duty to consider and to advise the Secretary of State on any communication, referred by the Council, relating to the control of any dangerous or otherwise harmful drug, made to HM government in the United Kingdom by any organisation or authority established by or under any treaty, convention or other agreement or arrangement to which the government is for the time being a party. Under s. 31(3), MDA 1971, the Advisory Council must also be consulted before the Secretary of State makes any regulations under the Act.

6.3   CLASSIFICATION OF CONTROLLED DRUGS AND REGULATION OF IMPORT, EXPORT, PRODUCTION, POSSESSION AND SUPPLY

Under s. 2, MDA 1971, the expression 'controlled drug' means any substance or product for the time being specified in Parts I, II or III of sch. 2 to the Act. In turn, the substances and products in Parts I, II and III are classified respectively as 'Class A', 'Class B' and 'Class C' drugs. Amendments to sch. 2, and its constituent parts, in terms of the addition or removal of substances from the list of controlled drugs, or individual classification or re-classification within individual parts, may be made by an Order in Council. The Advisory Council must be consulted before any draft of such an amending Order in Council is laid before Parliament. Once laid, the Order requires approval, for enactment, of a resolution of each House of Parliament.

Under Part 1 of sch. 2 to the MDA 1971, poppy straw is classified as a controlled drug. Poppy straw is defined in Part IV of the same schedule as all parts, except the seeds of the opium poppy after sowing.

6.3.1   Import, export, production, possession and supply
Under s. 3(1), MDA 1971, the importation and exportation of a controlled drug is prohibited. This blanket prohibition is subject to two different exemptions offered by s. 3(2). First, the prohibition does not apply to those controlled drugs specifically excepted under regulations made under s. 7, MDA 1971. Secondly, the veto does not apply to the importation or exportation of a controlled drug under and in accordance with the terms and conditions of a licence issued by the Secretary of State.

Subject to any regulations made under s. 7, MDA 1971, it is unlawful, under ss. 4, 5 and 6 of the Act, for a person:

(a)   to produce a controlled drug; or
(b)   to supply or offer to supply a controlled drug to another;
(c)   to possess a controlled drug; or
(d)   to cultivate any plant of the genus *Cannabis*.

Under s. 37, MDA 1971, 'producing' a controlled drug means producing it by manufacture, cultivation or any other method. 'Production' has a similar meaning. 'Supplying' includes distribution. Further, under s. 37, for the purposes of the Act, the things which a person has in their possession includes any thing subject to their control which is in the custody of another person.

As substituted by s. 52, Criminal Law Act 1977, 'cannabis' (except in the expression 'cannabis resin') means any plant of the genus *Cannabis* or any part of such plant (by whatever name designated) except that it does not include cannabis resin or any of the following products after separation from the rest of the plant, namely:

(a)   mature stalk of any such plant;
(b)   fibre produced from mature stalk of any such plant; and
(c)   seed of any such plant.

Under s. 7, MDA 1971, the Secretary of State may, by regulations:

(a)   except from the restrictions relating to the importation, exportation, production, supply, offer to supply, or possession, such controlled drugs as may be specified in regulations;
(b)   to the extent that is thought fit, make it lawful for persons to produce, supply, possess, or cultivate controlled drugs;
(c)   authorise by the terms and conditions of a licence or other authority the production, possession, supply, or cultivation of controlled drugs.

Under the same section, the Secretary of State is under a duty to make regulations to secure that it is not unlawful for a doctor, dentist, veterinary practitioner or veterinary surgeon, acting in their capacities as such, to prescribe, administer, manufacture, compound or supply a controlled drug, or for a pharmacist or a person lawfully conducting a retail pharmacy business, acting in their capacity as such, to manufacture, compound, or supply a controlled drug.

The Secretary of State may further consider it to be in the public interest for it to be unlawful for practitioners, pharmacists or persons lawfully conducting retail pharmacy businesses to prescribe, administer, manufacture, compound or supply a controlled drug except under a licence or other authority. In such a case the Secretary of State will make an order designating the drug to that effect.

The Secretary of State may also be of the opinion that it is in the public interest for the production, supply and possession of a controlled drug to be unlawful except for the purposes of research or other special purposes. Where this is the case, the Secretary of State may also make an order designating the drug to that effect. The Secretary of State must consult or consider the recommendations of the Advisory Council when proposing to make an order under either of these provisions, which in turn is exercisable by a statutory instrument, subject to annulment in pursuance of a resolution of either House of Parliament.

6.3.2   Prevention of misuse

Under s. 10, MDA 1971, the Secretary of State may make regulations as appear necessary or expedient for preventing the misuse of controlled drugs. In particular provision might be made for:

(a)   requiring precautions to be taken for the safe custody of controlled drugs;

(b)   imposing requirements as to the documentation of transactions involving controlled drugs, and for requiring copies of documents relating to such transactions to be furnished to the prescribed authority;

(c)   requiring the keeping of records and the furnishing of information with respect to controlled drugs in such circumstances and in such manner as may be prescribed;

(d)   the inspection of any precautions taken or records kept in pursuance of regulations under this section;

(e)   the packaging and labelling of controlled drugs;

(f)   regulating the transport of controlled drugs and the methods used for destroying or otherwise disposing of such drugs when no longer required;

(g)   regulating the issue of prescriptions containing controlled drugs and the supply of controlled drugs on prescriptions, and for requiring persons issuing or dispensing prescriptions containing such drugs to furnish to the prescribed authority such information relating to such prescriptions as may be prescribed;

(h)   requiring a doctor who attends a person considered, or with reasonable grounds suspected to be addicted (within the meaning of the regulations) to controlled drugs of any description, to furnish to the prescribed authority such information relating to those prescriptions as may be prescribed; and

(i)   prohibiting any doctor from administering, supplying and authorising the administration and supply to persons so addicted, and from prescribing for such persons such controlled drugs as may be prescribed, except under, and in accordance with the terms of a licence issued by the Secretary of State in pursuance of the regulations.

Under s. 11, MDA 1971, the Secretary of State may by notice in writing served on the occupier of any premises on which controlled drugs are or are proposed to be kept, give directions as to the taking of precautions or further precautions for the safe custody of any controlled drugs of a description specified in the notice which are kept on those premises.

6.3.3   Directions

Under s. 12, MDA 1971, where a practitioner or pharmacist has been convicted of an offence under the Act, certain provisions of the Customs and Excise Act 1952, or certain provisions of the Customs and Excise Management Act 1979, the Secretary of State may give a direction in respect of them.

In the case of a practitioner, the direction will prohibit the possession, prescription, administration, manufacture, compounding, supplying and authorising the administration and supply of the controlled drugs specified in the direction. In the case of a pharmacist, the direction will prohibit the possession, prescription, administration, manufacture, compounding, supplying and from supervising and controlling the manufacturing, compounding and supply of the controlled drugs specified in the direction.

The Secretary of State may at any time give a further direction cancelling or suspending any existing direction already given or re-activating a suspended direction. A copy of any such direction must be served on the person to whom it applied and notice of it must be published in the London, Edinburgh and Belfast Gazettes. A direction takes effect when a copy of it is served on the person to whom it applies. It is an offence to contravene any such direction.

Under s. 13, MDA 1971, a contravention, by a doctor, of the regulations made under s. 10, or the terms of a licence, relating to the provision of particulars to the prescribed authority concerning persons addicted to controlled drugs, and the administration, supply and prescription of controlled drugs to addicts, does not amount to an offence. However, the Secretary of State may give a direction, under s. 13(1), in respect of the doctor concerned, prohibiting that doctor from prescribing, administering and supplying and from authorising the administration and supply of such controlled drugs as may be specified in the direction. In turn, any contravention of such a direction amounts to an offence.

Under s. 13(2), MDA 1971, if the Secretary of State is of the opinion that a practitioner is prescribing, administering, supplying, or authorising the administration or supply of any controlled drug in an irresponsible manner, the Secretary of State may give a direction in respect of the practitioner concerned prohibiting the prescription, administration, supply, or authorisation for administration and supply of the controlled drugs specified in the direction.

Under s. 14(1), MDA 1971, where the Secretary of State has grounds for believing that there are grounds for giving a direction prohibiting the prescription, administration or supply of controlled drugs by a doctor, under s. 13(1) and (2), the Secretary of State may refer the case to a tribunal. The composition of the tribunal is provided for under s. 16(1) of and sch. 3 to the MDA 1971. The tribunal consists of five persons made up of a legally qualified chairman and four other persons from among the members of the doctor or practitioner's profession. The procedure of the tribunal is provided for by the Misuse of Drugs Tribunal (England and Wales) Rules 1974 (S.I. 1974/85).

It is the duty of the tribunal to consider any case referred to it and to report to the Secretary of State. Under s. 14(3), MDA 1971, where the tribunal finds that there has been no contravention under s. 13(1) by a doctor, or conduct alleged under s. 13(2) by another practitioner, or there has been a contravention or conduct alleged and is not recommending the giving of a direction, the Secretary of State will serve notice to that effect on the doctor or practitioner.

On the other hand, under s. 14(4), MDA 1971, where the tribunal finds that there has been a contravention and considers that a direction should be given, the tribunal is under a duty to include in its report a recommendation to that effect indicating the controlled drugs which it considers should be included in the recommendation. Under s. 14(5), the doctor or practitioner must be served with a notice, indicating whether or not it is proposed to make a direction. Where it is proposed to make a direction, the notice must also set out the terms of the proposed direction and inform the doctor or practitioner that consideration will be given to any written representations relating to the case made within 28 days of the serving of the notice.

Under s. 14(6), MDA 1971, where the doctor or practitioner does make such written representations, the Secretary of State is under a duty to refer the case to an advisory body. In turn, it is the duty of the advisory body to consider the case and to advise the Secretary of State as to the exercise of powers. As with the tribunal, the composition of the advisory body is provided for under s. 16(1) of and sch. 3 to the MDA 1971. The advisory body consists of three persons, a senior barrister, and two members of the doctor or practitioner's profession, one of whom should also be an officer of a government department. The doctor or practitioner is entitled to appear before the advisory body, either in person or with a legal representative. Otherwise the advisory body is entitled to regulate its own procedure.

After receiving the advice of the advisory body, or where no written representations were received, after the expiry of the period of 28 days, the Secretary of State may either give a direction specifying the controlled drugs indicated in the recommendation of the tribunal, order that the case be referred back to the original tribunal, or a different tribunal, or order that no further proceedings be taken. Where the case is referred back to a tribunal, that tribunal is under a duty to hear the case *de novo*, and all of the above procedures applicable to decisions of a tribunal shall re-apply.

Under s. 15, MDA 1971, where the Secretary of State is of the opinion that there are grounds for giving a direction in respect of a practitioner who is prescribing, administering, supplying, or authorising the administration or supply of any controlled drug in an irresponsible manner, and that the circumstances of the case require that the direction be given with the minimum of delay, then the case must be referred to a professional panel.

As with the tribunal and advisory body above, the composition of the professional panel is provided for under s. 16(1) of and sch. 3 to the MDA 1971. The professional panel consists of a chairman and two other members appointed by the Secretary of State from among the members of the practitioner's profession. The practitioner is entitled to appear before the professional panel, either in person or with a legal representative. Otherwise the professional panel is entitled to regulate its own procedure.

It is the duty of the professional panel, after affording the practitioner the opportunity of appearing and being heard, to consider the case and to report to the Secretary of State whether there are reasonable grounds for thinking that there has been such irresponsible conduct. The Secretary of State is not permitted to issue a direction under these provisions unless the panel reports that such reasonable grounds exist. Where the Secretary of State gives such a direction the case must be referred to a tribunal in accordance with the procedures described above. A direction shall take effect, in the first instance, for a period of six weeks, but may be renewed for further periods of 28 days' by notice in writing, with the consent of the tribunal, pending its determination.

Following determination of the case by the tribunal, or advisory body, the Secretary of State may service a notice of a direction or determine that no further proceedings shall be taken. In each case the temporary direction will cease to have effect.

6.3.4 Offences, penalties, defences and enforcement

The MDA 1971, in line with its overall objective of regulating dangerous or harmful drugs, creates a wide range of offences throughout its provisions. These offences, their enabling provisions, their mode of prosecution and the range of punishments imposed on conviction are conveniently summarised in tabular form in sch. 4 to the Act, under the provisions of s. 25. The punishments for conviction of the series of offences vary in accordance with the class of drug (A, B or C) involved. The main offences, and the enabling provisions of the Act which created them, are summarised as follows:

(a) production, or being concerned in the production of a controlled drug (s. 4(2));

(b) supplying or offering to supply a controlled drug or being concerned in the doing of either activity by another (s. 4(3));

(c) having possession of a controlled drug (s. 5(2));

(d) having possession of a controlled drug with intent to supply it to another (s. 5(3));

(e) cultivation of a cannabis plant (s. 6(2));

(f) being the occupier, or concerned in the management of premises and permitting or suffering certain activities to take place there (s. 8);

(g) offences relating to opium (s. 9);

(h) prohibition of supply etc. of articles for administering or preparing controlled drugs (s. 9A);

(i) contravention of directions relating to safe custody of controlled drugs (s. 11(2));

(j) contravention of direction prohibiting practitioner etc. from possessing, supply etc. controlled drugs (s. 12(6));

(k) contravention of direction prohibiting practitioner etc. from prescribing, supplying etc. controlled drugs (s. 13(3));

(l) failure to comply with notice requiring information relating to prescribing, supply etc. of drugs (s. 17(3));

(m) giving false information in purported compliance with notice requiring information relating to prescribing, supply etc. of drugs (s. 17(4));

(n) contravention of regulations (s. 18(1));

(o) contravention of terms of licence or other authority (s. 18(2));

(p) giving false information in purported compliance with obligation to give information imposed under or by virtue of regulations (s. 18(3));

(q) giving false information, or producing document etc. containing false statement etc. for purposes of obtaining issue or renewal of a licence or other authority (s. 18(4));

(r) assisting in or inducing commission outside United Kingdom of an offence punishable under a corresponding law (s. 20); and

(s) obstructing exercise of powers of search etc. or concealing books, drugs etc. (s. 23(4)).

In relation to the offence (c), unlawful possession of a controlled drug, it will be a defence for an accused to prove:

(a) that, knowing or suspecting the drug to be a controlled drug, the possession was for the purpose of preventing another from committing or continuing to commit an offence in connection with that drug, and that as soon as possible after taking possession of it, all reasonable available steps were taken to destroy the drug or deliver it into the custody of a person lawfully entitled to take custody of it; or

(b) that, knowing or suspecting it to be a controlled drug, the possession was for the purpose of delivering it into the custody of a person lawfully entitled to take custody of it and that as soon as possible after taking possession of it took all such steps as were reasonably open to deliver it into the custody of such a person.

Under s. 28, MDA 1971, it will be a defence to the offences in (a) to (e) above for the accused to prove that he neither knew of nor suspected nor had reason to suspect the existence of some fact alleged by the prosecution which is necessary for the prosecution to prove for a successful conviction. Under the same section, where it is necessary, for a successful conviction, for the prosecution to prove that some substance or product is a controlled drug, and it is proved that the substance was that controlled drug, it will be a defence for the accused to prove that he neither believed nor suspected nor had reason to suspect that the substance or product in question was a controlled drug, or, in certain circumstances, a different controlled drug.

Further, under s. 19, MDA 1971, it is an offence for a person to incite another to commit an offence. Under s. 20 it is an offence to assist in or induce the commission in any place outside the United Kingdom of an offence punishable under the provisions of a corresponding law in force in that place.

Under s. 36(1) 'corresponding law' means a law stated in a certificate purporting to be issued by or on behalf of the government of a country outside the United Kingdom to be a law providing for the control and regulation in that country of the production, supply, use, export, and import of, either:

(a)   drugs and other substances in accordance with the provisions of the Single Convention on Narcotic Drugs signed at New York on 30 March 1961; or

(b)   dangerous or otherwise harmful drugs in pursuance of any treaty, convention or other agreement or arrangement to which the government of that country and HM Government in the United Kingdom are for the time being parties.

Under s. 21, MDA 1971, where any offence committed by a body corporate is proved to have been committed with the consent or connivance of, or to be attributable to any neglect on the part of, any director, manager, secretary, or other similar officer of the body corporate, or any person purporting to act in any such capacity, that person will be guilty of that offence as well as the body corporate and will be proceeded against accordingly.

Under s. 23, MDA 1971, a constable or other person authorised in that behalf by the Secretary of State, has power to enter the premises of a person carrying on business as a producer or supplier of any controlled drug and to demand the production of, and to inspect, any books or documents relating to dealings in any such drugs and to inspect any stocks of such drugs. A constable who has reasonable grounds to suspect that any person is in possession of a controlled drug in contravention of the Act or any regulations made under its provisions, may search that person or detail that person for the purpose of searching, search any vehicle or vessel in which the constable suspects the drug may be found, and for that purpose require the person in control of the vehicle or vessel to stop it, and seize and detain anything found in the course of the search which appears to be evidence of an offence.

A justice of the peace who is satisfied that there is a reasonable ground for suspecting that a person is unlawfully in possession of a controlled drug on premises, or documents directly or indirectly connected to transactions or dealings in controlled drugs, may issue a warrant to a constable allowing the constable to enter, if need be by force, the premises named in the warrant, to search the premises and any persons in them, and to seize and detain any drugs or documents found. As we have seen above, it is an offence intentionally to obstruct a person exercising powers under these provisions.

Under s. 27, MDA 1971, a court which has convicted a person of an offence under the Act may order the forfeiture and destruction of anything shown to the satisfaction of the court to relate to the offence. Such an order is subject to the requirement of allowing any person claiming to be the owner, or having an interest in the property, to show cause why the order should not be made.

6.4   MISUSE OF DRUGS REGULATIONS

Under ss. 7, 10, 22 and 31, MDA 1971, the Secretary of State is given powers to make detailed regulations in relation to the restrictions on controlled drugs, the prevention of misuse of controlled drugs, and the creation and enforcement of offences relating to controlled drugs. The principal regulations made by the Secretary of State under these powers are the Misuse of Drugs Regulations (MDR) 1985 (S.I. 1985/2006). These regulations have been subject to further amendments on a number of occasions.

Regulation 3, MDR 1985 classifies controlled drugs into five schedules, corresponding to different levels of required control. Schedule 1 drugs include the hallucinogenic drugs (for example LSD) and cannabis. Schedule 2 drugs include opiates (such as diamorphine and methadone), the major stimulants (such as the amphetamines) and quinalbarbitone. Schedule 3 drugs include a small number of minor stimulant drugs, such as benzphetamine, and other drugs which are not thought so likely to be misused as the drugs in sch. 2, nor to be so harmful if misused. Schedule 4 is split into two parts. Part I contains most of the anabolic and androgenic steroids, together with clenbutarol (adrenoceptor stimulant) and growth hormones (polypeptide hormones). Part II contains most of the benzodiazepines. Schedule 5 contains preparations of certain controlled drugs, including codeine, pholcodine, cocaine and morphine.

6.4.1   Importation, exportation and production of scheduled controlled drugs

We have already seen that s. 3(1), MDA 1971, the importation and exportation of a controlled drug is, subject to two exceptions, prohibited. Regulation 4(1), MDR 1985, as amended, provides that this prohibition shall not apply to the controlled drugs in Part II of sch. 4 and all of the controlled drugs in sch. 5. Controlled drugs in Part I of sch. 4 may be exported or imported without restriction provided they are in the form of a medicinal product and are exported or imported by a person for self-administration.

In addition, we have already seen that under s. 4, MDA 1971, it is unlawful to produce a controlled drug. Under reg. 8, MDR 1985, as amended, a practitioner, pharmacist or person lawfully conducting a retail pharmacy business, acting in their capacity as such, may manufacture or compound any drug specified in sch. 2 or sch. 5. Under reg. 9 of the same Regulations, a practitioner, pharmacist or person lawfully conducting a retail pharmacy business, acting in their capacity as such, and any person authorised in writing by the Secretary of State, may manufacture or compound any drug specified in sch. 3 or sch. 4.

6.4.2   Possession and supply of scheduled controlled drugs

We have already seen that, under ss. 4 and 5, MDA 1971, the possession and supply of controlled drugs is, subject to exceptions, prohibited. Regulation

4(2), MDR 1985, as amended, provides that the prohibition on possession shall not apply to the drugs specified in sch. 4 when contained in a medicinal product nor to the drugs specified in sch. 5. In addition to this general exemption, under regs. 8, 9 and 10 of the same Regulations, exemption from the prohibition on possession and supply is given to certain classes of persons in relation to certain specified controlled drugs. As a result, a summary of the extent of permitted possession and supply would be as follows:

(a)   a practitioner may lawfully possess or supply any drug specified in schs. 2, 3, 4 and 5;

(b)   a pharmacist may lawfully possess or supply any drug specified in schs. 2, 3, 4 and 5;

(c)   a person lawfully conducting a retail pharmacy business may lawfully possess or supply any drug specified in schs. 2, 3, 4 and 5;

(d)   a person in charge or acting person in charge of a hospital or nursing home which is wholly or mainly maintained by a public authority out of public funds, by a charity or by public subscriptions, may lawfully possess or supply any drug specified in schs. 2, 3, 4 and 5, except where there is a pharmacist responsible for the dispensing and supply of medicines;

(e)   the sister or acting sister for the time being in charge or a ward, theatre or other department in a hospital or nursing home which is wholly or mainly maintained by a public authority out of public funds, by a charity or by public subscriptions, may lawfully possess or supply any drug specified in schs. 2, 3, 4 and 5, in the case of drugs supplied by a person responsible for the dispensing and supply of medicines; the supply must be for administration to a patient in that ward, theatre or department, in accordance with the directions of a doctor or dentist;

(f)   a person who is in charge of a laboratory the recognised activities of which consist of, or include, the conduct of scientific education or research and which is attached to a university, university college or hospital which is wholly or mainly maintained by a public authority out of public funds, by a charity or by public subscriptions or any other institution approved for the purpose by the Secretary of State, may lawfully possess or supply any drug specified in schs. 2, 3, 4 and 5;

(g)   a public analyst appointed under s. 27, Food Safety Act 1990 may lawfully possess or supply any drug specified in schs. 2, 3, 4 and 5;

(h)   a sampling officer within the meaning of sch. 3 to the Medicines Act 1968 may lawfully possess or supply any drug specified in schs. 2, 3, 4 and 5;

(i)   a person employed or engaged in connection with a scheme for testing the quality or amount of the drugs, preparations and appliances supplied under the National Health Service Act 1946 or the National Health Service (Scotland) Act 1947, and any regulations made under these Acts, may lawfully possess or supply any drug specified in schs. 2, 3, 4 and 5;

(j)   a person authorised by the Royal Pharmaceutical Society for Great Britain for the purposes of ss. 108 and 109, Medicines Act 1968, may lawfully possess or supply any drug specified in schs. 2, 3, 4 and 5;

(k)   a person who is authorised as a member of a group may, under and in accordance with the terms of the group authority, lawfully supply any drug specified in schs. 2, 3, 4 and 5 subject to the condition that any controlled drug specified in sch. 4 must be contained in a medicinal product; the same person may also lawfully possess any drug specified in schs. 2, 3 and 5;

(l)   a person who is authorised by a written authority issued by the Secretary of State may, at premises and in compliance with any conditions specified in that authority, lawfully possess any drug specified in sch. 5;

(m)   the owner or master of a ship which does not carry a doctor among the crew employed on it may lawfully supply any drug specified in schs. 2, 3, 4 and 5, for the purposes of complying with the provisions of the Health and Safety at Work Act 1974, the Merchant Shipping Acts and the Mineral Workings (Offshore Installations) Act 1971; the supply may be to any person who may lawfully supply the drug or to any constable for the purpose of the destruction of the drug; the controlled drug specified in sch. 4 must be contained in a medicinal product.

Under reg. 11, MDR 1985, a registered midwife who has, in accordance with the rules made under s. 15(1)(b), Nurses, Midwives and Health Visitors Act 1979, notified to the local supervising authority, an intention to practise, is exempt from certain of the legislative requirements relating to controlled drugs. The midwife may, so far as is necessary for professional practice, possess and administer any controlled drug which, under, and in accordance with the provisions of the Medicines Act 1968, or any secondary legislation made under it, she is entitled to administer. The midwife may only possess such a controlled drug under the authority of a midwife's supply order signed by the appropriate medical officer. This is an order in writing specifying the name and occupation of the midwife obtaining the drug, the purpose for which it is required and the total quantity to be obtained. An appropriate medical officer may be either:

(a)   a doctor who is for the time being authorised in writing for the purpose of the regulations by the local supervising authority for the region or area in which the drug was, or is to be, obtained; or

(b)   a person appointed under and in accordance with s. 16, Nurses, Midwives and Health Visitors Act 1979 by that authority to exercise supervision over registered midwives within their area.

Under reg. 11(1)(c), a registered midwife may surrender to the appropriate medical officer such stocks of controlled drugs which are no longer required.

6.4.3 Requisitions for controlled drugs

Under reg. 14(1), MDR 1985, a supplier, who is not a practitioner, and who supplies a controlled drug otherwise than on a prescription, is under reasonably strict regulation as to the class of person to whom the controlled drug may be supplied. The supplier must not deliver the drug to a person who purports to be sent by or on behalf of the recipient, and who is not authorised to possess the drug, unless that person produces to the supplier a statement in writing signed by the recipient to the effect that the person is empowered by the recipient to receive the drug on behalf of the recipient. Before releasing the drug, the supplier must be satisfied that the document is a genuine one.

Under reg. 14(2), MDR 1985, a supplier, who supplies a controlled drug, otherwise than on a prescription, or by way of administration, to a certain class of recipient, is under strict duties with regard to the documents which must be obtained prior to the supply of the controlled drugs. The class of recipient at which these controls are aimed includes a practitioner, person in charge, or acting person in charge, of a hospital or nursing home, a person in charge of a laboratory, the owner or master of certain ships and the installation manager of an offshore installation. The requirements are that the supplier must not deliver the drug:

(a)   until the supplier has obtained a requisition in writing which:

(i)   is signed by the recipient;
(ii)   states the name, address and profession or occupation of the recipient;
(iii)   specifies the purpose for which the drug supplied is required and the total quantity to be supplied;

(b)   unless the supplier is reasonably satisfied that the signature is that of the person purporting to have signed the requisition and that person is engaged in the profession or occupation specified in the requisition.

Where the requisition is furnished by the person in charge, or acting person in charge, of a hospital or nursing home, there is the further requirement that the requisition must be signed by a doctor or dentist employed or engaged in that hospital or nursing home. Further the person responsible for the dispensing and supply of medicines at any hospital or nursing home, who supplies a controlled drug to the sister or acting sister for the time being in charge of any ward, theatre or other department in the hospital or nursing home, must:

(a)   obtain a requisition in writing, signed by the recipient, which specifies the total quantity of the drug to be supplied; and
(b)   mark the requisition in such a manner as to show that it has been complied with.

Any requisition obtained for these purposes must be retained in the dispensary at which the drug was supplied and a copy of the requisition or a note of it must be retained or kept by the recipient.

Where the requisition is furnished by the master of a foreign ship, it must contain a statement signed by the proper officer of the port health authority or, in appropriate circumstances, a designated medical officer, within whose jurisdiction the ship is, that the quantity of the drug to be supplied is the quantity necessary for the equipment of the ship.

Under reg. 14(2), MDR 1985, where the recipient is a practitioner and represents that the controlled drug is required urgently for professional purposes, the supplier may, if reasonably satisfied that the recipient so requires the drug and is, by reason of some emergency, unable before delivery to furnish to the supplier a requisition in writing duly signed, deliver the drug to the recipient on an undertaking by the recipient to furnish such a requisition within the following 24 hours. Under reg. 14(3) a person who has given such an undertaking must deliver to the person by whom the controlled drug was supplied a signed requisition in accordance with the undertaking.

None of the above requirements relating to requisitions for controlled drugs applies to the supply of schs. 4 and 5 drugs or poppy-straw.

6.4.4   Prescriptions for controlled drugs

Regulation 15, MDR 1985 outlines specific requirements for prescriptions for controlled drugs. Regulation 15(1) provides that a person must not issue a prescription containing a controlled drug, other than schs. 4 and 5 controlled drugs, unless the prescription complies with the following requirements:

(a)   it must be in ink or otherwise so as to be indelible and be signed and dated by the person issuing it with that person's usual signature;

(b)   except in the case of a health prescription, it must specify the address of the person issuing it;

(c)   it must have written thereon, if issued by a dentist, the words 'for dental treatment only' and, if issued by a veterinary surgeon or a veterinary practitioner, a declaration that the controlled drug is prescribed for an animal or herd under his care;

(d)   it must specify, in the handwriting of the person issuing it, the name and address of the person for whose treatment it is issued or, if it is issued by a veterinary surgeon or practitioner, the name and address of the person to whom the controlled drug prescribed is to be delivered; under reg. 15(3) this requirement as to name and address will be satisfied if the prescription is written on the patient's bed card or case sheet, in the case of a prescription issued for the treatment of a patient in a hospital or nursing home;

(e)   it must specify, in the handwriting of the person issuing it, the dose to be taken and—

(i)   in the case of a prescription containing a controlled drug which is a preparation, the form and, where appropriate, the strength of the preparation, and either the total quantity (in both words and figures) of the preparation or the number (in both words and figures) of dosage units, as appropriate, to be supplied;

(ii)   in any other case, the total quantity (in both words and figures) of the controlled drug to be supplied;

(f)   in the case of a prescription for a total quantity to be supplied by instalments, it must contain a direction specifying the amount of the instalments of the total amount which may be supplied and the intervals to be observed when supplying.

Under reg. 15(2), MDR 1985, the requirements in (d) and (e) do not apply to a prescription issued by a person approved, either personally or as a member of a class, by the Secretary of State for this purpose. They do not also apply to a prescription containing no controlled drug other than phenobarbitone, phenobarbitone sodium or a preparation containing either of these drugs. There are no prescription requirements for the drug Temazepam (The Misuse of Drugs (Amendment) Regulations 1995, S.I. 1995/3244).

Regulation 16 of the MDR 1985 imposes additional requirements relating to prescriptions for controlled drugs, other than schs. 4 and 5 controlled drugs. A controlled drug must not be supplied on a prescription:

(a)   unless the address specified in the prescription, as the address of the person issuing it, is an address in the United Kingdom;

(b)   unless the supplier either is acquainted with the signature of the person by whom it purports to be issued and has no reason to suppose that it is not genuine, or has taken reasonably sufficient steps to be satisfied that it is genuine;

(c)   before the date specified in the prescription;

(d)   later than thirteen weeks after the date specified in the prescription.

A person supplying a controlled drug, other than a schs. 4 and 5 controlled drug, on prescription must mark on the prescription the date on which the drug is supplied and, unless it is a health prescription, retain the prescription on the premises from which the drug was supplied.

Where the prescription contains a direction that specified instalments of the total amount may be supplied at stated intervals, it must not be supplied otherwise than in accordance with that direction. The first instalment must be supplied not later than thirteen weeks after the date specified in the prescription. In addition, the prescription must be marked with the date on each occasion on which an instalment is supplied and retained, for two years, on the premises from which the drug was supplied.

Nothing in the prescription requirements, noted above, has any effect in relation to a prescription issued for the purposes of a scheme for testing the quality or amount of the drugs, preparations and appliances supplied under the primary and secondary legislation relating to the National Health Service, or to any prescriptions issued to sampling officers for the purposes of food and drug legislation.

6.4.5 Containers, registers and records for controlled drugs

Under reg. 18, MDR 1985, a controlled drug, other than a preparation, must be supplied in a bottle, package or container which is plainly marked with the amount of the drug contained in it. Controlled drugs, which are preparations, made up into tablets, capsules or other dosage units, must be supplied in a bottle, package or container, plainly marked with the amount of each component (being a controlled drug) of the preparation in each dosage unit and the number of dosage units in the bottle, package or container. All other controlled drugs, which are preparations, must be supplied in a bottle, package or container plainly marked with the total amount of the preparation, and the percentage of each of its components which is a controlled drug.

None of these requirements apply to poppy straw, schs. 4 and 5 controlled drugs, the supply of a controlled drug by or on the prescription of a practitioner, the supply of a controlled drug for administration in a clinical trial or any sch. 3 controlled drug in a preparation used as a buffering agent in chemical analysis, or which has present in it both a substance in sch. 3 and a salt of that substance, or is pre-mixed in a kit.

The MDR 1985 impose specific requirements in respect of the keeping of records and registers relating to the supply of controlled drugs. Every person authorised to supply schs. 1 and 2 controlled drugs is obliged to keep a register and enter into that register, in chronological sequence, and according to specified formats, particulars of every quantity of schs. 1 and 2 drugs obtained and supplied, whether by way of administration or otherwise. There is also an obligation to use a separate register or separate part of the register for entries made in respect of each class of drugs. Each of certain drugs specified in schs. 1 and 2, together with its salts, and any preparation or other product containing it, or any of its salts is treated as a separate class. Any stereoisomeric form of a drug or its salts may be classed with the drug.

Regulation 20, MDR 1985 outlines further requirements relating to the registers. The class of drugs to which the entries on any page of any such register relate must be specified at the head of that page. Every entry required to be made in such a register must be made on the day on which the drug is obtained or supplied, by the person required to make the entry, or if that is not reasonably practicable, on the following day. No cancellation, obliteration or alteration of any such entry may be made, and a correction of such an entry shall be made only by way of a marginal note or footnote which, in turn, must specify the date on which the correction is made.

Every entry and correction of entry must be made in ink or otherwise be indelible. A register must not be used for any purpose other than the purposes of recording dealings in controlled drugs. A register must be kept at the premises to which it relates. Only one register may be kept at any one premises although the Secretary of State may permit the keeping of separate registers in different departments. A separate register must be kept at each different premises of one particular business.

Where a drug specified in sch. 2 is supplied to any person on board a ship, or to a person on an offshore installation, an entry into the official log book of the ship, or a report signed by the master of the ship, or an entry into the installation logbook (all required to be kept under the relevant shipping and off-shore legislation) is a sufficient record of the supply of a controlled drug for the purposes of the regulations.

A midwife, authorised to have possession of a sch. 2 controlled drug, must, on each occasion of obtaining a supply of such a drug, enter into a book kept solely for the purpose, the date, name and address of the person from whom the drug was obtained, the amount obtained and the form in which it was obtained. When administering the controlled drug to a patient, the midwife must also enter into the book as soon as is reasonably practicable, the name and address of the patient, the amount administered and the form in which it was administered.

Under reg. 23, MDR 1985, all registers and books kept for the purposes of these provisions must be preserved for a period of two years from the date of the last entry. Every requisition, order or prescription (other than a health prescription) on which a controlled drug is supplied must be preserved for a period of two years from the date on which the last delivery under it was made.

Under reg. 24, MDR 1985, all producers and wholesale dealers of schs. 3 and 5 controlled drugs, must keep every invoice or other record issued in respect of each quantity of any such drug obtained or supplied. The keeping of a copy of any document required to be kept under these provisions is treated as if it were the keeping of the original document. Every document, or copy of it, must be preserved for a period of two years from the date on which it was issued.

Certain information relating to the production, possession, stock and supply of controlled drugs must be furnished on demand to the Secretary of State or any person authorised in writing by the Secretary of State. The information to be furnished includes particulars in respect of the producing, obtaining or supplying of any controlled drug, or in respect of any stock of such drugs, any register book or document required to be kept under the MDR 1985 relating to dealings in controlled drugs and, if necessary, the production of any drugs in possession. The persons affected by these requirements include any person authorised to produce, import or export any controlled drug, wholesale dealers, retail dealers, practitioners, persons in charge of hospitals, nursing homes or laboratories, and persons authorised to supply any controlled drug. There is an exemption from these requirements for the personal records which any person has acquired or created in the course of professional practice, and which are held in confidence. Personal records mean documentary or other records concerning an individual, living or dead, who can be identified from them, and which relate to that person's physical or mental health.

6.5   DESTRUCTION OF CONTROLLED DRUGS

Under the provisions of reg. 26, MDR 1985, no person who is required to keep records with respect to schs. 1, 2, 3 or 4 controlled drugs, may destroy them except in the presence of a person authorised (whether personally or as a member of a class) for such purposes by the Secretary of State. Such authorised persons may, for the purpose of analysis, take a sample of the controlled drug which is to be destroyed. Particulars of the date of destruction and the quantity of the controlled drug destroyed must be entered into the controlled drug register which must also be signed by the authorised person in whose presence the drug is destroyed.

The master or owner of a ship or installation manager of an offshore installation who has possession of a sch. 2 controlled drug which is no longer required, must not destroy the drug but must dispose of it to a constable or other person who may lawfully supply that drug.

6.6   CONTROLLED DRUGS AND ADDICTS

The provisions of the Misuse of Drugs (Notification of and Supply to Addicts) Regulations 1973 (S.I. 1973/799) regulate the supply of controlled drugs to addicts and outline the requirements for notification of suspicion of addiction. Under reg. 2(2) a person is regarded as being addicted to a drug if, and only if, that person has as a result of repeated administration become so dependent upon the drug that they have an overpowering desire for the administration of it to continue.

Under reg. 3(1) any doctor who attends a person whom he or she considers to be addicted to any drug must, within seven days of the attendance, furnish in writing to the Chief Medical Officer of the Home Office, such of the following particulars with respect to that person as are known to the doctor, that is the name, address, sex, date of birth, national health service number, the date of attendance and the name of the drug or drugs concerned.

Notification is not required if the doctor is of the opinion, formed in good faith, that the continued administration of the drug or drugs concerned is required for the purpose of treating organic disease or injury. No doctor may administer or supply, or authorise the administration or supply, to a person considered to be addicted to any drug, cocaine, diamorphine or their salts except for the purpose of treating organic disease or injury, or under and in accordance with the terms of a licence issued by the Secretary of State. Addicts may receive daily supplies of cocaine or diamorphine on special prescriptions under an administrative arrangement within the National Health Service.

6.7   SAFE CUSTODY OF CONTROLLED DRUGS

The provisions of the Misuse of Drugs (Safe Custody) Regulations 1973 (S.I. 1973/798), as amended, regulate the safe custody of controlled drugs. These provisions apply to all controlled drugs except those specifically exempted under sch. 1 to the Regulations. The provisions apply to the following premises:

(a)   any premises occupied by a retail dealer for the purpose of business;

(b)   any nursing home within the meaning of Part VI of the Public Health Act 1936 or the Nursing Homes Registration (Scotland) Act 1938;

(c)   any residential or other establishment provided for under or by virtue of s. 59, Social Work (Scotland) Act 1968;

(d)   any mental nursing home within the meaning of Part III of the Mental Health Act 1959;

(e)   any private hospital within the meaning of the Mental Health (Scotland) Act 1960.

The occupier and every person concerned in the management of the above premises must ensure that all controlled drugs (other than those exempted under sch. 1) on the premises, are, so far as circumstances permit, kept in a locked safe, cabinet or room which is so constructed and maintained as to prevent unauthorised access to the drugs. The relevant requirements, which are reasonably extensive, apply to every safe, cabinet or room in which controlled drugs are kept, and which must be complied with, are set out in sch. 2 to the Regulations.

The safe custody requirement does not apply, under reg. 3(4), in respect of any controlled drug which is for the time being under the direct personal supervision of:

(a)   in the case of any premises occupied by a retail dealer, a pharmacist; or

(b)   in the case of other premises, the person in charge of the premises or any member of staff designated by the person in charge for the purpose.

Under reg. 4 of the Regulations, an owner of a retail pharmacy business may apply to the chief officer of police for the police area in which the premises are situated, for a certificate relating to safes, cabinets and rooms where controlled drugs are kept. On receiving such an application, which must be in writing, the chief officer may have the premises and any safe, cabinet or room inspected, and, if satisfied that they provide an adequate degree of security, issue a certificate. Each certificate will specify every safe, cabinet or room to which it relates and any security conditions necessary to be observed. An issued certificate will be valid for one year and may be subject to further annual renewal.

When a certificate has been issued, the chief officer may cause the premises to be subject to further inspection at any reasonable time to see if any security conditions have been complied with and whether there are any changes of circumstances warranting the cessation of the certificate. A certificate may be cancelled by the chief officer where it appears that there has been a breach of any condition specified in it, where there has been a change of circumstances leading to the lack of provision of an adequate degree of security warranting such cancellation, or where the occupied has refused entry to any police officer.

Where any controlled drug is kept otherwise than in a locked safe, cabinet or room which is so constructed and maintained as to prevent unauthorised access, any person having possession of the drug must ensure that, so far as circumstances permit, it is kept in a locked receptacle which can only be opened by him or her or by some other person so authorised. This latter requirement does not apply to a person to whom the drug has been supplied by or on the prescription of a practitioner for that person's own treatment or for that of another person. It shall not also apply to a carrier during the course of business nor to a person engaged in the business of the Post Office.

6.8   PROFESSIONAL STANDARDS AND CONTROLLED DRUGS

The principles of the *Code of Ethics* of the Royal Pharmaceutical Society of Great Britain, impose specific obligations on pharmacists relating to controlled drugs. Breach of these principles may form the basis of a complaint of professional misconduct. These principles are supplemented by detailed advice, contained in the published *Standards of Good Professional Practice*. It is important to remember that the *Code of Ethics* also requires that pharmacists must comply with the obligations in the *Standards of Good Professional Practice* where applicable. Failure to meet the standards could also form the basis of a complaint of misconduct.

As part of the principle that a pharmacist's prime concern must be for the welfare of both the patient and other members of the public, a series of obligations are imposed which have both general and specific implications for the supply of controlled drugs. Generally, the pharmacist is under a duty to act in a manner which promotes and safeguards the interests of the public, and justifies public trust in the pharmacist's knowledge, ability and judgment. Further, the pharmacist has a professional responsibility to exercise control over all medicinal products which are supplied.

The pharmacist must exercise professional judgment to prevent the supply of unnecessary and excessive quantities of medicines and other products, particularly controlled drugs. Care should be taken over their supply even when it is legally authorised by prescription or signed order. A pharmacist must be alert to the possibility of drug dependency in health care professionals and patients and must be prepared to make inquiries to ensure that such medicines are to be used responsibly.

In addition, the pharmacist must, on each occasion that a pharmaceutical service is provided, use professional judgment to decide whether the patient needs to be seen. Further guidance on this latter obligation indicates that a face-to-face consultation need not take place on every occasion that a service is provided. However, a pharmacist has a professional duty to ensure that it occurs when considered necessary with a medicine for an acute condition or at appropriate intervals for repeat medication.

More specifically, pharmacists must, if likely to be called upon to supply controlled drugs in the course of their duties, carry sufficient stocks of such drugs to deal with all likely requests for urgent supplies. Finally the Royal Pharmaceutical Society has issued detailed guidelines on standards for dispensary design and equipment, procurement and sources of materials, manufacturing and quality assurance and dispensing procedures. The last includes detailed advice on the supervision of dispensing and the furnishing of information, advice and counselling.

6.9   CONCLUSION

The comprehensive detail of the rules and regulations relating to controlled drugs is evidence of the desire of the regulators to formulate and implement a system of strict control and supervision. All aspects of controlled drugs are regulated, from production, through possession and supply and beyond towards export and import. The philosophy of the regulators is to restrict and limit access to these dangerous products by making most involvement with them unlawful.

Balanced against this is the desire to maximise the therapeutic capacity of controlled drugs in order to permit their use in drug therapy as an integral aspect of the provision of health care. As such, certain controlled drugs may be used for lawful purposes. That use and those purposes are, in turn, subject to rigorous control, evidenced by the specific rules on lawful possession and supply, prescriptions for controlled drugs, records and registers, packaging and labelling, safe custody and destruction. All of the legislative provisions are strictly enforced by the creation of specific criminal offences.

A pattern is beginning to emerge in our analysis of the regulation of medicinal drug products. It is a strategy of strict control and regulation, and limitation and restriction of access. We have seen that medicinal drug products must have the appropriate licence, must be advertised in the correct manner, and may be only available for certain purposes. That system of control continues in the next chapter which looks at other dangerous substances, namely poisons.

SEVEN

The regulation of medicinal drug products — poisons

7.1 INTRODUCTION

A common theme of the analysis of this text has been the strict control and management of medicinal drug products. That theme continues with an examination of the rules and regulations relating to poisons. We have also seen that the systems and procedures for the control and regulation of medicinal drug products are relatively modern, being heavily influenced by recent developments in European Union law. The laws relating to poisons have a longer history, reflecting, in part, the significance which the regulators have attached to the supervision of such dangerous products.

The term 'poison' automatically suggests for most people that such products have little therapeutic value and that is largely the case. The aim of the law, therefore, is to control their supply and possession, and limit their availability for specified, restricted uses. The format of the current laws follows that for prescription only medicines and controlled drugs already examined in previous chapters.

Advisory machinery is established to make recommendations on the substances to be designated as poisons. After that, the detailed rules, contained in both primary and secondary legislation, make provision for the designation of substances as poisons, through the publication of a Poisons List. Local authorities are under specific obligations to keep lists of persons, including details of their names and business premises, who are entitled to sell poisons.

The Royal Pharmaceutical Society of Great Britain, has a distinctive role to play in the enforcement of the rules relating to poisons. The Society has specific powers of inspection of premises and powers of enforcement of the legislative provisions. The requirements outlined in the legislation, both primary and secondary, are backed up with the creation of a series of distinct criminal offences. The punishments associated with these offences are significant.

The regulators have recognised that certain poisonous substances have specific uses. The sale of poisons for those restricted purposes is permitted but subject to strict regulation. Those permitted to sell poisons have specific duties with regard to the storage of poisons in advance of sales and the maintenance of records relating to those sales.

There are specific legislative provisions relating to the sale of certain poisons such as strychnine. Finally, the legislative provisions relating to poisons have recently been strengthened by the implementation of European Union directives. These impose new requirements relating to the labelling and packaging of chemicals and the protection of the health of employees who come into contact with hazardous substances.

7.2   ADVISORY MACHINERY ON POISONS

Section 1, Poisons Act (PA) 1972 states that there shall continue to be an advisory committee called the Poisons Board to be constituted in accordance with the provisions of sch. 1 to the PA 1972. The Board consists of sixteen members although the Secretary of State may from time to time appoint up to three additional members as appropriate. Of the sixteen full members, five must be persons appointed by the Council of the Royal Pharmaceutical Society of Great Britain. One of these five must be a person engaged in the manufacture for sale by way of wholesale dealing of pharmaceutical preparations.

The Secretary of State appoints one of the members of the Board as Chairman and all of the members hold office for three years. Any appointed member ceasing to be a member of the Board may be eligible for reappointment. Vacancies are filled from the constituency of the vacating member. The quorum for the Board is eleven. The Board determines its own procedure through the making of appropriate regulations with the approval of the Secretary of State.

7.3   DESIGNATION OF POISONS

Under s. 11, PA 1972, as amended, a 'non-medicinal poison' is defined as a substance which is included in Part I or Part II of the Poisons List and is neither a medicinal product as defined under s. 130, MA 1968 nor a substance which is subject to an order made under s. 104 or s. 105, MA 1968, and is treated as a medicinal product as such.

Section 2, PA 1972 provides for a list of substances treated as poisons for the purpose of, and to be referred to as the Poisons List. The Secretary of State may from time to time, after consultation with or on the recommendation of the Poisons Board, by order amend or vary the Poisons List. The Poisons List is divided into two Parts. Part I consists of those substances which are prohibited from being sold except by a person lawfully conducting a retail pharmacy business. Part II consists of those substances which are prohibited from being sold except by a person lawfully conducting a retail pharmacy business or by a person whose name is entered in a local authority's list.

7.4 LOCAL AUTHORITY LISTS

Every local authority is obliged to keep, for the purposes of the legislation, a list of persons, including details of their names and business premises, entitled to sell Part II poisons. The local authority list should also include the name of any person who, having premises in the area of the authority, makes an application in the prescribed form to be included in the list. Provision is made for the form of application for entry in a local authority's list in rule 24 and sch. 8 of the Poisons Rules 1982, as amended. A local authority may refuse to enter on, or may remove from, the list the name of any person who fails to pay any required fees, or who in the opinion of the local authority is, for any sufficient reason, not fit to be on the list. Any person aggrieved by a decision to refuse to enter on or remove a name from the list, may appeal the decision to the Crown Court.

A local authority's list shall include particulars of the premises of those named on the list and shall be in such form as may be prescribed. Provision is made for the form of the local authority list in rule 24 and sch. 9 of the Poisons Rules 1982, as amended. It must also be open at all reasonable times to the inspection of any person without fee. Individuals whose name appears on the list must pay to the local authority such reasonable fees as the authority may determine in respect of entry of their name on the list, alteration of particulars relating to premises contained in the list, and annual retention of their name on the list.

If any person whose name is entered on a local authority's list is convicted of any offence which, in the opinion of the court, renders that person unfit to have their name retained on the list, the court may, as part of the sentence, order the removal of that person's name and direct that they should be disqualified, for a specified period, from having their name on the list. It is unlawful for any person whose name is entered on a local authority's list to use in connection with their business any title, emblem or description reasonably calculated to suggest that that person is entitled to sell any poison which they are not entitled to sell. Contravention of this provision amounts to an offence.

7.5 INSPECTION

Under s. 9, PA 1972, it is the duty of the Royal Pharmaceutical of Great Britain to take all reasonable steps by means of inspection and otherwise to enforce, amongst other things, the provisions of the poisons legislation. In order to fulfil this duty, the Royal Pharmaceutical Society is given the power to appoint inspectors. Eligibility for appointment as an inspector is restricted to pharmacists, and appointment is subject to the approval of the Privy Council.

An inspector appointed by the Royal Pharmaceutical Society has power, for the purposes of securing compliance with the provisions of the poisons legislation, at all reasonable times, to enter any registered pharmacy, and to enter any premises where there is reasonable cause to suspect that a breach of the law has been committed. In addition, an inspector has power to make such examination and inquiry, and to do such other things such as the taking of samples, as is necessary to ascertain that the legislative requirements are being complied with.

It is the duty of the local authority, by means of inspection and otherwise, to take all reasonable steps to secure compliance with the legislative provisions relating to pharmacy, by persons not lawfully conducting a retail pharmacy business and by persons lawfully conducting a retail pharmacy business in so far as the business is carried on at premises which are not a registered pharmacy. In order to carry out this duty, the local authority must appoint inspectors. Inspectors appointed by the Royal Pharmaceutical Society, under the inspection provisions noted above, may also, with the consent of the Royal Pharmaceutical Society, serve as local authority inspectors for these provisions.

An inspector appointed by the local authority has power, for the purposes of securing compliance with the provisions of the poisons legislation, at all reasonable times, to enter any registered pharmacy, and to enter any premises where there is reasonable cause to suspect that a breach of the law has been committed. In addition, an inspector has power to make such examination and inquiry, and to do such other things, such as the taking of samples, as is necessary to ascertain that the legislative requirements are being complied with.

An inspector appointed by the local authority has power, with the consent of the local authority, to institute proceedings under the legislation before a court of summary jurisdiction in the name of the authority, and to conduct any proceedings so instituted. Under the provisions of s. 9(8), PA 1972, it is an offence, liable on summary conviction to a fine, for any person wilfully to delay or obstruct inspectors in the exercise of their powers under the legislation, to refuse to allow any sample to be taken, or to fail without reasonable excuse to give any information duly required to be given.

7.6 GENERAL OFFENCES

Any person who contravenes or fails to comply with the provisions of the legislation relating to poisons will be liable, on summary conviction to a scale fine, and in the case of a further offence, to a further fine. In the case of proceedings for or in connection with the sale, exposure for sale or supply of a non-medicinal poison effected by an employee, it shall not be a defence that the employee acted without the authority of the employer and any material fact known to the employee is deemed to have been known to the employer.

Proceedings may be commenced at any time within the period of 12 months after the date of the commission of the offence or within a period of three months after the date on which sufficient evidence to justify a prosecution for the offence comes to the knowledge of the Secretary of State, whichever is the later.

7.7 POISONS RULES

Under s. 7, PA 1972, the Secretary of State, after consultation with or on the recommendation of the Poisons Board, may make rules with respect to any of the following matters or for the following purposes:

(a)   the sale, whether wholesale or retail, or the supply of non-medicinal poisons, by or to any persons or classes of persons and in particular:

(i)   for regulating or restricting the sale or supply of poisons by persons whose names are entered in a local authority's list and for prohibiting the sale of any specified non-medicinal poison or class of non-medicinal poisons by any class of such persons; and

(ii)   for dispensing with or relaxing with respect to non-medicinal poisons any of the provisions of the legislation relating to the sale of non-medicinal poisons;

(b)   the storage and labelling of poisons;

(c)   the containers in which non-medicinal poisons may be sold or supplied;

(d)   the addition to non-medicinal poisons of specified ingredients for the purpose of rendering them readily distinguishable as non-medicinal poisons;

(e)   the compounding of non-medicinal poisons, and the supply of non-medicinal poisons on and in accordance with a prescription duly given by a doctor or dentist;

(f)   the period for which any books required to be kept for the legislation are to be preserved;

(g)   the period for which any certificate is to remain in force;

(h)   the prescribing of any other matter required under the legislation to be prescribed by rules.

The Secretary of State may issue to the Poisons Board a direction that the power to make recommendations for rules under (a)(i), (b), (c) and (d) shall not be exercised except after consultation with a body representative of persons engaged in the manufacture of poisons or preparations containing poisons.

The principal rules which have been made under these provisions are the Poisons Rules 1982 (S.I. 1982/218), as amended.

7.7.1 Regulation of the sale of poisons

Under s. 3, PA 1972, and subject to certain exemptions, it is not lawful for a person to sell any non-medicinal poison which is a substance included in Part I of the Poisons List, unless:

(a) that person is lawfully conducting a retail pharmacy business; and
(b) the sale is effected on premises which are a registered pharmacy; and
(c) the sale is effected by, or under the supervision of, a pharmacist.

The meaning of the word 'supervision', in equivalent 1933 legislation, was considered by the High Court in the case of *Roberts* v *Littlewood Stores* [1943] 1 All ER 1943. An inspector had purchased a poison at a time when the registered pharmacist in charge of the department was upstairs in the stockroom. Caldecote LCJ could not accept the contention that an individual could supervise a sale without being bodily present. Supervision, in the absence of an individual, might be exercised through the medium of a telephone, but there was no such evidence in the present case. Humphreys and Tucker JJ agreed.

It is not lawful for a person to sell any non-medicinal poison which is a substance included in Part II of the Poisons List, unless:

(a) that person is lawfully conducting a retail pharmacy business and the sale is effected on premises which are a registered pharmacy; and

(b) that person's name is entered into a local authority's list in respect of the premises on which the poison is sold.

Under rule 9 of the Poisons Rules 1982, as amended, it is not lawful for any person lawfully conducting a retail pharmacy business to sell any poison included in sch. 1 to the Rules, notwithstanding that it is a poison included in Part II to the Poisons List, unless the sale is effected by, or under the supervision of, a pharmacist.

7.7.2 Listed sellers

Under rule 10 of the Poisons Rules 1982, as amended, listed sellers are restricted in the range of poisons which they may sell. A 'listed seller' is a person whose name is for the time being entered into a local authority's list, under the provisions noted above.

Listed sellers may not sell any poison which has, since being obtained, been subject to any form of manipulation, treatment or processing as a result of which the poison has been exposed. A listed seller may not sell any poison included in sch. 1 to the Rules, unless the sale is effected by the listed seller or a responsible deputy. A 'responsible deputy' means a person nominated as a deputy on the listed seller's form of application, for entry as a listed seller of Part II poisons, or any person substituted, by notice in writing to the local authority, for the person so nominated. Not more than two deputies may be nominated at the same time in respect of one set of premises. Listed sellers are also prevented from selling:

(a)   any poison included in the first column of Part A of sch. 5 to the Poisons List, unless the article or substance is in the form specified in the second column to that Part;
(b)   any poison included in Part B of sch. 5 unless the purchaser is engaged in the trade or business of agriculture, horticulture or forestry and requires the poison for the purpose of that trade or business.

It is not lawful for a non-medicinal poison to be exposed for sale in, or to be offered for sale by means of, an automatic machine.

7.7.3   Selling non-medicinal poisons

Subject to any further exemption, it shall not be lawful, under s. 3, PA 1972, to sell any non-medicinal poison to any person unless that person is either:

(a)   certified in writing in the prescribed manner by a person authorised by the Poisons Rules to give a certificate for this purpose; or
(b)   known by the seller or by a pharmacist in the employment of the seller at the premises where the sale is effected,

to be a person to whom the poison may properly be sold. The provisions of rule 25 of, and sch. 10 to the Poisons Rules 1982, as amended, provide for the form and particulars of a certificate, required under these provisions.

Under the provisions of rule 5 to the Poisons Rules 1982, as amended, the requirement that the seller must have knowledge of the purchaser is deemed to be satisfied, in relation to sales of Part II poisons by listed sellers, if the person to whom the poison is sold is known by the person in charge of the premises on which the poison is sold, or of the department of the business in which the sale is effected, to be a person to whom the poison may properly be sold. A similar relaxation applies, under rule 6 to the Poisons Rules 1982, as amended, to the supply of commercial samples of poisons included in sch. 1, and to sales of poisons exempted under s. 4, PA 1972.

7.7.4   Records

The seller of any poison must not deliver it, unless an entry has been made into a book kept for the purpose, stating in the prescribed form the date of the sale, the name and address of the purchaser and of the person by whom the certificate was given, the date of any such certificate, the name and quantity of the article sold, and the purpose for which it is stated it is required. Any such entry must also be signed by the purchaser. Provision is made for the form for the record of sales in rule 26 of, and sch. 11 to the Poisons Rules 1982, as amended.

Under rule 27 of the Poisons Rules 1982, as amended, all books must be preserved for a period of two years from the date of the last entry.

Under the provisions of rule 6(3) of the Poisons Rules 1982, as amended, the requirement for the purchaser to sign the poisons book is relaxed under certain defined circumstances. The relaxation applies to the sale of a poison to persons for the purpose of their trade, business or profession, and is subject to the following requirements being satisfied:

(a)   the seller must obtain before the completion of the sale an order in writing signed by the purchaser stating their name and address, trade business or profession, the purpose for which the article is required and the total quantity to be purchased;

(b)   the seller must be reasonably satisfied that that signature is that of the person purporting to have signed the order, and that that person carries on the trade, business or profession stated in the order, being one in which the poison to be purchased is used;

(c)   the seller must insert in the entry the words 'signed order' and a reference number by which the order can be identified.

When a person represents that they urgently require a poison for the purpose of their trade, business or profession, the seller may, if reasonably satisfied that the person so requires the poison and is, by reason of some emergency, unable before delivery either to furnish to the seller an order in writing duly signed or to attend and sign the entry in the book, deliver the poison to the purchaser on an undertaking by the purchaser to furnish such an order within the next 72 hours.

There is a relaxation, under rule 6 of the Poisons Rules 1982, as amended, from the legislative requirements relating to knowledge of the purchaser, and entry of signatures or signed orders into the poisons book in relation to sales of poisons to be exported to purchasers outside the United Kingdom. The relaxation also applies to the sale or supply of any article by the manufacturer, or by a person carrying on a business in the course of which poisons are regularly sold by way of wholesale dealing, if:

(a)   the article is sold or supplied to a person carrying on a business in the course of which poisons are regularly sold or are regularly used in the manufacture of other articles; and

(b)   the seller or supplier is reasonably satisfied that the purchaser requires the article for the purposes of that business.

There is a further relaxation, under rule 5, of the knowledge and signature entry rules in relation to the sale of nicotine, its salts or its quaternary compounds, and to sales of agricultural and horticultural insecticides consisting of nicotine dusts containing not more than four per cent, weight in weight, of nicotine. Finally, under rule 7, the requirements do not apply to the sale of articles containing barium carbonate or zinc phosphide and prepared for the destruction of rats or mice.

7.7.5 Storage

Under the provisions of rule 21, it is not lawful to store any poison contained in sch. 1 in any retail shop or premises unless it is stored:

    (a)   in a cupboard or drawer reserved solely for the storage of poisons; or

    (b)   in a part of the premises which is partitioned off or otherwise separated from the remainder of the premises and to which customers are not permitted to have access; or

    (c)   on a shelf reserved solely for the storage of poisons and no food is kept directly under the shelf.

Under the provisions of rule 18(2), it is not lawful to sell or supply any compressed hydrogen cyanide unless the container is labelled with the words 'Warning. This container holds poisonous gas and should only be opened and used by persons having expert knowledge of the precautions to be taken in its use'. This requirement does not apply to the sale or supply of compressed hydrogen cyanide to be exported to purchasers outside the United Kingdom.

7.7.6 Restriction of sale and supply of strychnine and certain other persons

Rule 12 restricts the sale and supply of strychnine and certain other poisons, subject to certain exemptions allowed for in sch. 12. The first three categories of exempted case, described in sch. 12, are general in nature, as follows:

    (1)   the sale of substances to be exported to purchasers outside the United Kingdom;

    (2)   the sale of a substance to a person or institution concerned with scientific education or research or chemical analysis, for the purposes of that education or research or analysis;

    (3)   the sale of a substance by way of wholesale dealing.

Under the provisions of rule 12 and sch. 12, it is not permissible to sell or supply sodium arsenites or potassium arsenites except in each of the circumstances outlined in (1)–(3).

It is also not permissible, under the same rules, to sell strychnine, its salts or its quaternary compounds except in each of the circumstances outlined in (1)–(3) above, or:

    (a)   to a person producing a written authority in the form set out in Part II of sch. 12, issued by the appropriate statutory officer authorising the purchase of the substance for the purpose of the killing of moles; the amount of strychnine to be supplied must not exceed 100 grams and must be supplied within three months of the date of the written authority; or

(b) to an officer of the Ministry of Agriculture, Fisheries and Food, or the equivalent department in Scotland, producing a written authority in the form set out in Part III of sch. 12, authorising the purchase by that officer of the substance for the purpose of killing foxes in an infected area within the meaning of the Rabies (Control) Order 1974 (S.I. 1974/2212).

Under the provisions of rule 12 and sch. 12, it is not permissible to sell fluoroacetic acid, its salts or fluoroacetamide except in each of the circumstances outlined in paragraphs (1)–(3) above, or:

(a) to a person producing a certificate in form 'A' in Part IV to the schedule, issued by a proper officer of a local authority or port health authority certifying that the substance is required for use as a rodenticide by employees of that local authority or port health authority:

(i) in ships or sewers as are identified in the certificate;
(ii) in such drains as are indicated in the certificate, being drains which are situated in restricted areas and wholly enclosed and to which all means of access are, when not in actual use, kept closed; or
(iii) in such warehouses as are identified in the certificate, being warehouses which are situated in restricted dock areas and to which all means of access are, when not in actual use, kept securely locked or barred; or

(b) to a person producing a certificate in form 'B' in Part IV to the schedule, issued by a proper officer of a local authority or port health authority certifying that the substance is required for use as a rodenticide by such person or by the employees of such a person, carrying on the business of pest control, or to a person producing a certificate in form 'B' in Part IV to the schedule, issued by the appropriate statutory officer, certifying that the substance is required for use as a rodenticide by officers of the Ministry of Agriculture, Fisheries and Food, for use:

(i) in ships or sewers as are identified in the certificate;
(ii) in such drains as are indicated in the certificate, being drains which are situated in restricted areas and wholly enclosed and to which all means of access are, when not in actual use, kept closed.

The quantity of fluoroacetic acid, its salts or fluoroacetamide sold or supplied must not exceed that stated in the certificate and must be supplied within three months of the date of the issue of the certificate.

Under the provisions of rule 12 and sch. 12, it is not permissible to sell or supply salts of thallium except in each of the circumstances outlined in paragraphs (1)–(3) above, or:

(a)   to a local authority or a port health authority for the purpose of the exercise of its statutory powers;

(b)   to a government department or an officer of the Crown, for the purposes of the public service;

(c)   to a person producing a written authority, issued by the appropriate statutory officer, authorising the purchase of thallium sulphate for use by that person or employees of that person, for the purpose of killing rats, mice or moles in the course of a business of pest control;

(d)   except in the case of thallium sulphate, to a person carrying on a business in the course of which salts of thallium are regularly used in the manufacture of other articles, for the purposes of that business;

(e)   except in the case of thallium sulphate, as an ingredient in any article, not being an article intended for internal consumption by any person.

Under the provisions of rule 12 and sch. 12, it is not permissible to sell or supply zinc phosphide except in each of the circumstances outlined in paragraphs (1)–(3) above, or:

(a)   to a local authority or a port health authority for the purpose of the exercise of its statutory powers;

(b)   to a government department or an officer of the Crown, for the purposes of the public service;

(c)   to a person, or body of persons, carrying on a trade or business, for the purposes of that trade or business.

Under the provisions of rule 13, it is not permissible to sell or supply calcium cyanide, potassium cyanide or sodium cyanide, except in each of the circumstances outlined in s. 4, PA 1972 (see 7.8).

7.8   EXEMPTIONS UNDER THE ACT

Under s. 4, PA 1972, and except as provided by the Poisons Rules, the following categories of sales are exempt from the legislative requirements relating to the regulation of the sale of poisons:

(a)   the sale of poisons by way of wholesale dealings;

(b)   the sale of poisons to be exported to purchasers outside the United Kingdom;

(c)   the sale of an article to a doctor or dentist for the purpose of their profession;

(d)   the sale of an article for use in connection with any hospital, infirmary or dispensary or similar institution approved by an order of the Secretary of State;

(e)   the sale of an article by a person carrying on a business in the course of which poisons are regularly sold either by way of wholesale dealing or for use by the purchasers in their trade or business to:

(i)   a person who requires the article for the purpose of their trade or business;

(ii)   a person who requires the article for the purpose of enabling them to comply with any requirements made by or in pursuance of any enactment with respect to the medical treatment of persons employed by them in any trade or business carried on;

(iii)   a government department or an officer of the Crown requiring the article for the purposes of the public service, or any local authority requiring the article in connection with the exercise of any statutory powers;

(iv)   a person or institution concerned with scientific education or research, if the article is required for the purposes of that education or research.

Under rule 11 of the Poisons Rules 1982, as amended, it is not lawful to sell any poisons by way of wholesale dealing to a shopkeeper unless one of two conditions apply. The first is that the seller must have reasonable grounds for believing that the purchaser is a person lawfully conducting a retail pharmacy business. The second is that the seller has received a statement signed by the purchaser, or by a person authorised by the purchaser, that the purchaser does not intend to sell the poison on any premises used for or in connection with retail business.

7.9   LABELLING AND PACKAGING OF CHEMICALS

The Chemicals (Hazard Information and Packaging for Supply) Regulations 1994 (S.I. 1994/3247), as amended by the Chemicals (Hazard Information and Packaging for Supply) (Amendment) Regulations 1996 (S.I. 1996/1092), provide for the classification, packaging and labelling of dangerous substances, and implement the provisions of a series of European Union Directives on these matters.

Under reg. 3(1), the regulations apply to any substance or preparation which is dangerous for supply, except:

(a)   a substance or preparation which is dangerous by reason that it is a radioactive substance;

(b)   a substance or preparation which is intended for use as an animal feeding stuff and is in a finished state intended for the final user;

(c)   a cosmetic product;

(d)   a substance or preparation which is intended for use as a medicinal product;

(e)   a substance or preparation which is a controlled drug;

(f)   a substance or preparation which is dangerous by reason that it contains disease producing micro-organisms but is not otherwise dangerous for supply;

(g)   a substance or preparation which is a sample taken for enforcement of any requirement;

(h)   munitions, and preparations which are supplied with a view to producing a practical effect by explosion or a pyrotechnic effect;

(i)   a substance or preparation which is intended for use as a food and which is in a finished state intended for the final user;

(j)   a substance or preparation which is under customs control;

(k)   a substance or preparation which is intended for export to a country which is not a member state of the European Union;

(l)   a pesticide;

(m)   a substance or preparation which is transferred from a factory, warehouse or other place of work and its curtilage to another place of work in the same ownership and in the immediate vicinity;

(n)   a substance to which specified provisions of the Notification of New Substances Regulations 1993 (S.I. 1993/3050) apply which is labelled in accordance with those provisions;

(o)   substances, preparations and mixtures in the form of wastes;

(p)   a plant protection product.

'Dangerous for supply' means that the substance has been listed in Part I of the approved supply list, or any other substance which is in one or more of the categories of danger specified in column 1 of sch. 1 to the regulations. The 'approved supply list' means the list entitled 'Information Approved for the Classification and Labelling of Substances and Preparations Dangerous for Supply' and currently approved by the Health and Safety Commission for these purposes.

Under reg. 5(1), substances or preparations which are dangerous for supply must not be supplied unless they have been classified by the manufacturer. Particular classifications are specified for certain categories of substances. Otherwise, substances must be classified by being placed into one or more specified categories of danger corresponding to the properties of the substance, and by being assigned appropriate risk phrases by the use of the criteria set out in the approved classification and labelling guide.

Under Part I of sch. 2, where the substance has physio-chemical properties, the categories of danger are explosive, oxidizing, extremely flammable, highly flammable, and flammable. Where the substance has health effects, the categories of danger are very toxic, toxic, harmful, corrosive, irritant, sensitizing, carcinogenic, mutagenic, toxic for reproduction and dangerous for the environment.

Under reg. 6, the supplier of a substance or preparation dangerous for supply must provide the recipient with a safety data sheet containing certain information specified under the headings in sch. 5. The purpose of this provision is to enable the recipient to take the necessary measures relating to the protection of health and safety at work and relating to the protection of the environment. Under the provisions of sch. 5, the safety data sheet must contain the following obligatory headings: identification of the substance/preparation and company/undertaking, composition/information on ingredients, hazards identification, first-aid measures, fire-fighting measures, accidental release measures, handling and storage, exposure controls/personal protection, physical and chemical properties, stability and reactivity, toxicological information, ecological information, disposal consideration, transport information, regulatory information and other information.

Suppliers must keep safety data sheets up to date and revise them when new safety information becomes available. Safety data sheets must be provided free of charge when the substance or preparation is first supplied. Revised data sheets must also be supplied to the original recipients. Safety data sheets do not need to be provided with substances or preparations which are sold to the general public, if sufficient safety information is furnished to enable the users to take the necessary measures for the protection of health and safety.

A person who supplies or offers to supply a substance must ensure that the substance is not advertised unless mention is made in the advertisement of the hazard or hazards presented by the substance.

The supplier of a substance or preparation must not supply it unless it is in a package suitable for that purpose. In particular, the receptacle containing the substance or preparation, and any associated packaging must be designed, constructed, maintained and closed so as to prevent any of the contents from escaping when subjected to the stresses and strains of normal handling. This requirement does not prevent the fitting of a suitable handling device. The receptacle and any associated packaging must be made of materials which are not liable to be adversely affected by that substance and not liable, in conjunction with that substance, to form any other substance itself a risk to health or safety. Where the receptacle is fitted with a replaceable closure, the closure must be designed so that the receptacle can be repeatedly re-closed without its contents escaping.

Dangerous substances may not be supplied unless the receptacle or layer of packaging clearly shows the following particulars:

(a)   the name, full address, and telephone number of a person in a member state who is responsible for supplying the substance, whether the manufacturer, importer or distributor;

(b)   the name of the substance;

(c)   the following particulars:

(i)   the indication or indications of danger and the corresponding symbol or symbols;

(ii)   the risk phrases (set out in full);

(iii)   the safety phrases (set out in full);

(iv)   the EEC number (if any), and, in the case of a substance dangerous for supply which is listed in Part I of the approved supply list, either the words 'EEC label' or 'EC label'.

Dangerous preparations may not be supplied unless the receptacle or layer of packaging clearly shows the following particulars:

(a)   the name, full address, and telephone number of a person in a member state who is responsible for supplying the substance, whether the manufacturer, importer or distributor;

(b)   the trade name or other designation of the preparation;

(c)   the following particulars:

(i)   identification of the constituents of the preparation which result in the preparation being classified as dangerous for supply;

(ii)   the indication or indications of danger and the corresponding symbol or symbols;

(iii)   the risk phrases (set out in full);

(iv)   the safety phrases (set out in full);

(v)   in the case of a preparation intended for sale to the general public, the nominal quantity.

Certain substances specified in Part IIIA of sch. 6 classified and labelled as carcinogenic, mutagenic or toxic for reproduction must also be labelled with the phrase 'Restricted to professional users'.

Where the package in which the substance or preparation is supplied does not contain more than 125 millilitres of the substance or preparation, the risk and safety phrases do not need to be shown if the substance or preparation is classified only in one or more of the categories of danger: highly flammable, flammable, oxidising or irritant, or in the case of substances not intended to be supplied to the public, harmful. Provision is made in reg. 9 for other minor exemptions.

Under sch. 2 to the regulations, there are 10 categories of indications of danger, each with its own symbol. They are explosive, oxidising, extremely flammable, highly flammable, very toxic, toxic, harmful, corrosive, irritant and dangerous for the environment.

All of the particulars required to be on the label must be clearly and indelibly marked, and the label itself must be securely fixed to the package with its entire surface in contact with it. The colour and nature of the marking must be such that the symbol (if any) and wording stand out from the background so as to be readily noticeable and the wording must be of such a size and spacing as to be easily read. The package must be labelled so that the particulars can be read horizontally when the package is set down normally.

Specific dimensions for the label are outlined in reg. 5(5). In addition any symbol must be printed in black on an orange-yellow background and its size, including the orange-yellow background must be at least equal to an area of one tenth of that of the label. Where, because of the size of the label, it is not reasonably practicable to provide the required safety phrases on it, the information may be given on a separate label or sheet accompanying the package. Equally if the package is an awkward shape or so small that it is unsuitable to attach a label, the label may be attached in some other way.

Under the provisions of reg. 12, certain substances or preparations may not be supplied in a receptacle fitted with a replaceable closure unless that closure conforms to certain standards applicable to child resistant fastenings. The substances and preparations affected by these provisions include those that are classified as very toxic, toxic, or corrosive and certain other preparations. Packaging must also not have a shape, designation or presentation which attracts children or otherwise misleads the public. Packaging for substances and preparations classified as very toxic, toxic, corrosive, harmful, extremely flammable or highly flammable, must also carry a certified tactile warning of danger.

The regulations are enforced as if they were provisions made under the Health and Safety at Work Act 1974, the main enforcing authority being the Health and Safety Executive. However where a substance or preparation is supplied in or from a registered pharmacy, the enforcing authority will be the Royal Pharmaceutical Society of Great Britain.

Further provision is made under regs. 13 to 15 of the regulations for the retention of classification data for substances and preparations for supply, the notification of the constituents of certain preparations for supply to the poisons advisory centre and for exemption certificates in certain specified circumstances.

7.10 DANGEROUS SUBSTANCES AND EMPLOYEES' HEALTH

The Control of Substances Hazardous to Health Regulations 1994 (S.I. 1994/3246), impose duties on employers to protect employees and other persons who may be exposed to substances hazardous to health and also impose certain duties on employers concerning their own protection from such exposure. The regulations also prohibit the import into the United Kingdom of certain articles and substances from outside the specified European Economic Area. The regulations also implement the provisions of a series of European Union Directives on these matters.

Under reg. 2, a 'substance hazardous to health' is defined any substance (including any preparation) which is:

(a) any substance which is listed in Part 1 of the Chemicals (Hazard Information and Packaging for Supply) Regulations 1994 (S.I. 1994/3247), as

amended, and for which an indication of danger specified for the substance is
very toxic, toxic, harmful, corrosive or irritant;

(b)   a substance listed in sch. 1 to the regulations, which lists substances
assigned maximum exposure limits or for which an occupational exposure
standard has been approved;

(c)   a biological agent;

(d)   dust of any kind;

(e)   any other substance which creates a hazard to the health of any person.

The main provisions of the regulations relate to the protection of persons
against risks to their health, whether immediate or delayed, arising from
exposure to substances hazardous to health. They do not apply where certain
other control of lead and asbestos at work regulations apply, nor where the
substance is hazardous solely by virtue of its radioactive, explosive or flammable
properties, or solely because it is at a high or low temperature or a high pressure.
Exemptions are also provided where the risk is to the health of a person to
whom the substance is administered in the course of medical treatment.

The employer's main obligation is not to carry on any work which is liable to
expose any employees to any substance hazardous to health unless a suitable
and sufficient assessment has been of the risks created by that work to the
health of those employees and of the steps needed to comply with the
regulations. In addition the employer must ensure that the exposure of
employees to substances hazardous to health is either prevented or, where this
is not reasonably practicable, adequately controlled.

The employer is under a duty to implement adequate control measures,
including the provision of personal protective equipment, to prevent or limit
exposure to such substances, and must ensure that all such control measures
are maintained in an efficient state, in efficient working order and in good
repair. Requisite tests to determine the adequacy of control measures must also
be carried out. The employer also has a specific obligation to monitor
continuing exposure in the workplace.

Where it is appropriate for the protection of the health of employees who are,
or who are liable to be exposed to a substance hazardous to health, the
employer must ensure that such employees are under suitable health surveillance. Health surveillance includes the keeping of health records and medical
surveillance under the supervision of an employment medical adviser. Employees must subject themselves to examination by the employment medical
adviser and furnish any such information as may be required. Employees may
be withdrawn from employment which involves exposure to substances
hazardous to health on the certification of an employment medical adviser. The
employment medical adviser may also inspect any part of the workplace.

An employer is under a further duty to provide employees with such
information, instruction and training as is suitable and sufficient for the
employee to know the risks to health created by such exposure and the

precautions which should be taken. Provision is also made in the regulations for fumigation of an employer's premises and for the granting of exemptions from the legislative requirements.

7.11 PROFESSIONAL STANDARDS AND POISONS

The principles of the *Code of Ethics* of the Royal Pharmaceutical Society of Great Britain impose specific obligations on pharmacists relating to the supply of poisons. Breach of these principles may form the basis of a complaint of professional misconduct. These principles are supplemented by detailed advice, contained in the published *Standards of Good Professional Practice*. It is important to remember that the *Code of Ethics* also requires that pharmacists must comply with the obligations in the *Standards of Good Professional Practice* where applicable. Failure to meet the standards could also form the basis of a complaint of misconduct.

As part of the principle that a pharmacist's prime concern must be for the welfare of both the patient and other members of the public, a series of obligations are imposed which have both general and specific implications for the supply of poisons. Generally, the pharmacist is under a duty to act in a manner which promotes and safeguards the interests of the public, and justifies public trust in the pharmacist's knowledge, ability and judgment. Further, the pharmacist has a professional responsibility to exercise control over all medicinal products which are supplied. The pharmacist must exercise professional judgment to prevent the supply of unnecessary and excessive quantities of medicines and other products.

In addition, the pharmacist must, on each occasion that a pharmaceutical service is provided, use professional judgment to decide whether the patient needs to be seen. Further guidance on this latter obligation indicates that a face-to-face consultation need not take place on every occasion that a service is provided. However, a pharmacist has a professional duty to ensure that it occurs when considered necessary with a medicine for an acute condition or at appropriate intervals for repeat medication.

More specifically, pharmacists are warned that they must take steps to ensure that all chemicals supplied will be used for a proper purpose and in appropriate circumstances. Reasonable steps should be taken by the pharmacist to ensure that chemicals are not used for the preparation of explosives or fireworks, and that solvents or other chemicals with the potential for misuse for intoxication, are not sold to those under the age of sixteen. Pharmacists are advised to prohibit the sale of such products by self-selection, to question regular purchasers, to investigate demands for large quantities, and to be particularly vigilant if the demand is from teenagers.

7.12 CONCLUSION

The classification of poisons as dangerous substances and the resultant need for legal control has been recognised by the regulators for some time. The initial system of control has been strengthened by the introduction of further reforming primary and secondary legislation.

The legislative structure recognises that poisons have little or no therapeutic value but do have certain other practical uses. The initial aim, therefore, has been to restrict access to designated poisons by limiting the range of individuals who may possess, and sell or supply them. Possession is subject to strict control relating to storage, and marking and labelling, and sale or supply is restricted to certain individuals for specified purposes.

It is important to remember that the regulation of poisons is treated so seriously that significant criminal offences are created in the relevant legislation, and that the legislative requirements are closely monitored and enforced by the appropriate statutory officers. Close attention should be paid to practices and procedures to ensure that they comply with the rules.

Finally, pharmacists should note that the regulators continue to supplement the requirements relating to poisons. Through the influence of appropriate EU Directives, new duties have been imposed relating to the marking and packaging of poisons which are chemicals. These new duties are added to by further obligations relating to the health of employees.

EIGHT

The regulation of medicinal drug products — general sale list and pharmacy medicines

8.1 INTRODUCTION

So far we have seen that the aims and philosophy of the medicines legislation, to monitor closely and regulate the methods of manufacture, advertising, classification and distribution of certain medicinal drug products, have been successfully implemented. The detailed rules on the licensing of medicinal drug products and the restrictions imposed in relation to prescription only medicines, controlled drugs and poisons, are evidence of an effective realisation of the policy of close control.

In this chapter we will look at two descriptions of medicinal drug products — general sale list medicines and pharmacy medicines — where the controls are often described as being less strict. That is because the perception is that the products are readily available on the shelves of supermarkets or pharmacy shops, and available without the requirement of an order of a health care professional. Once on the shelves they are safe, and there are no further legal or regulatory consequences associated with them.

It is important to be careful about this perception. These medicinal drug products are subject to strict legal regulation. That regulation takes the form of careful attention to the methods of classification. Thereafter certain of the products are deemed to be sufficiently safe to be sold in non-pharmacy premises, or to be subject to the requirement that they be sold only from pharmacy premises. Further legal provisions regulate the methods by which these products may be sold and the persons who are permitted to own, manage and conduct business in pharmacy premises.

There are other aspects of the regulation of general sale list and pharmacy medicines which are also worth considering. As noted above, such products are available for sale without the requirement of an authorising order of a health care professional. An individual decision to purchase such products, as part of a therapeutic plan, may be based on the advice of such a health care professional. Equally the individual patient may be persuaded by the marketing methods of the product's manufacturer. Importantly, the individual patient may rely on the recommendation of the pharmacist from whose premises the product is to be sold. Alternatively, the decision may be self-made or on the suggestion of friends or family.

There are important legal consequences attendant on these other aspects to the regulation of general sale list or pharmacy medicines. This is particularly the case when the medicinal drug product does not have the desired therapeutic effect or where some other aspect of a failure in drug therapy results in harm to the patient. Some of those consequences are discussed below in chapter thirteen.

8.2   GENERAL SALE LIST MEDICINES

Section 51(1), MA 1968 provides that the appropriate Ministers may, by order, specify descriptions or classes of medicinal products as being products which in their opinion can, with reasonable safety, be sold or supplied otherwise than by, or under the supervision of a pharmacist. Such products are usually known as general sale list medicines.

The principal Order, in relation to medicines for human use, made under the power given by s. 51(1) is the Medicines (Products Other Than Veterinary Drugs) (General Sale List) Order 1984 (S.I. 1984/769), which re-enacts, with amendments, the provisions of the Medicines (General Sale List) Order 1980 (S.I. 1980/1922), and its amending instrument, the Medicines (General Sale List) Amendment Order 1982 (S.I. 1982/26).

The 1984 Order has itself has been subject to amendment on a number of occasions, reflecting changes in the relevant list of products. The most recent and important example introduced amendments to the rules relating to the sale and supply of aspirin and paracetamol. The appropriate changes, to restrict available strengths, and pack sizes, were introduced in the Medicines (Products Other Than Veterinary Drugs) (General Sale List) Amendment Order 1997 (S.I. 1997/2043) and the Medicines (Sale or Supply) (Miscellaneous Provisions) Amendment (No. 2) Regulations 1997 (S.I. 1997/2045).

8.2.1   Specification of general sale list medicines
The 1984 Order, through art. 2 and schs. 1 and 2, specifies the classes of medicinal products which can, with reasonable safety, be sold or supplied otherwise than by or under the supervision of a pharmacist — the general sale list. It also specifies the classes of products which can with reasonable safety be

sold by means of automatic machines — the automatic machines section of the general sale list.

Schedule 1 outlines the requirements for the inclusion on the general sale list of a class of medicinal products, other than products the subject of a product licence of right. The schedule is further divided into two Tables, A and B. Table A contains a list of substances for both internal and external use, Table B lists substances for external use only.

Table A has four columns, specifying in turn: a list of substances; maximum strengths, if any; uses, pharmaceutical forms or routes of administration, where appropriate; and maximum doses and maximum daily doses, if any. Table B has three columns specifying in turn: a list of substances; maximum strengths, if any; and uses, pharmaceutical forms or routes of administration, where appropriate.

The sch. 1 requirements for inclusion on the general sale list are that the medicinal product is composed solely of one or more of the following substances, namely:

(a)   a substance listed in column 1 of Table A to the schedule where the maximum strength of the substance in the medicinal product does not exceed the maximum strength, if any, specified in column 2 of the same table;

(b)   if the product is for external use only, a substance listed in column 1 of Table B where the maximum strength of the medicinal product does not exceed the maximum strength, if any, specified in column 2 of Table B;

(c)   an aqueous or alcoholic extract, spirit, syrup or liquid suspension derived from a substance listed in column 1 of Table A, or if the product is for external use only, Table B;

(d)   an excipient, defined in art. 1 of the Order as a substance which does not contribute to the pharmacological action of the medicinal product or which contributes only by regulating the release of the active ingredients.

In addition, where the medicinal product is composed solely of a substance which has a listed (in column 3 of Table A or B) specified pharmaceutical form or route of administration, the product must satisfy that specification, or where the medicinal product is composed solely of a substance which has a listed, specified use, it must be in a container or package labelled to show only such use. Finally, sch. 1 specifies that where the medicinal product is composed solely of a substance which has a listed (in column 4 of Table A) specified maximum dose or maximum daily dose, the product must be in a container or package labelled to show a maximum dose or maximum daily dose not exceeding that specified.

Schedule 2 outlines the requirements for the inclusion on the general sale list, of a class of medicinal products, the subject of a product licence of right. Again, the schedule is further divided into two Tables, A and B, in the same format as for sch. 1. Table A contains a list of substances for both internal and external use, Table B lists substances for external use only. Table A has four columns, specifying in turn: a list of substances; maximum strengths, if any; uses, pharmaceutical forms or routes of administration, where appropriate; and maximum doses and maximum daily doses, if any. Table B has three columns specifying in turn: a list of substances; maximum strengths, if any; and uses, pharmaceutical forms or routes of administration, where appropriate.

The sch. 2 requirements for inclusion on the general sale list are that the medicinal product is composed solely of one or more of the following substances, namely:

(a)   a substance listed in column 1 of Table A to the schedule where the maximum strength of the substance in the medicinal product does not exceed the maximum strength, if any, specified in column 2 of the same table;

(b)   if the product is for external use only, a substance listed in column 1 of Table B where the maximum strength of the medicinal product does not exceed the maximum strength, if any, specified in column 2 of Table B;

(c)   an aqueous or alcoholic extract, spirit, syrup or liquid suspension derived from a substance listed in column 1 of Table A, or if the product is for external use only, Table B;

(d)   an excipient;

(e)   haemoglobin or the following parts of animals, namely, bone, horn, brain, genitals, prostate and spleen, but not an extract from such parts;

(f)   a glycerine extract of bone marrow;

(g)   a bovine blood derivative;

(h)   a substance of vegetable origin or an extract of such a substance used in the United Kingdom as a food.

In addition, as for sch. 1 products, where the medicinal product is composed solely of a substance which has a listed (in column 3 of Table A or B) specified pharmaceutical form or route of administration, the product must satisfy that specification, or where the medicinal product is composed solely of a substance which has a listed, specified use, it must be in a container or package labelled to show only such use. Finally, sch. 2 specifies that where the medicinal product is composed solely of a substance which has a listed (in column 4 of Table A) specified maximum dose or maximum daily dose, the product must be in a container or package labelled to show a maximum dose or maximum daily dose not exceeding that specified.

Article 2 of the Medicines (Products Other Than Veterinary Drugs) (General Sale List) Order 1984, also specifies that medicinal products which are for sale or supply either for oral administration as a food or for external use as a cosmetic, other than products which are eye drops or eye ointments or which contain either:

(a)   Vitamin A, Vitamin A acetate or Vitamin A palmitate with a maximum daily dose equivalent to more than 7,500 international units of Vitamin A or 2,250 micrograms of retinol; or

(b)   Vitamin D with a maximum daily dose of more than 400 units of antirachitic activity,

shall also be classified as general sale list medicinal products.

Under art. 3 of the Medicines (Products Other Than Veterinary Drugs) (General Sale List) Order 1984, all medicinal products on the general sale list are designated as being products which in the opinion of the Ministers can with reasonable safety be sold by means of automatic machines — the automatic machines section of the general sale list.

8.2.2   Products not to be on a general sale list

Schedule 3 of the Medicines (Products Other Than Veterinary Drugs) (General Sale List) Order 1984, as amended, specifies a class of medicinal products which are not to be on the general sale list. These include medicinal products promoted, recommended, or marketed:

(a)   for use as anthelmintics;
(b)   for paranteral administration;
(c)   for use as eye drops;
(d)   for use as eye ointments;
(e)   for use as enemas;
(f)   for use wholly or mainly for irrigation of wounds of the bladder, vagina or rectum; or
(g)   for administration wholly or mainly to children being a preparation of Aloxipirin or Aspirin.

8.2.3   Sale of general sale list medicines

Under s. 53, MA 1968, no person, in the course of business, may sell by retail, offer or expose for sale by retail, or supply in circumstances corresponding to retail sale, any medicinal product on a general sale list elsewhere than at a registered pharmacy, unless the following conditions are satisfied:

(a)   the place at which the product is sold, offered, exposed or supplied, must be premises of which the person carrying on the business in question is the occupier and which are capable of being closed so as to exclude the public, unless either:

(i)   the product is sold, offered, exposed for sale or supplied by means of an automatic machine and the product is a medicinal product in the automatic machines section of a general sale list, or
(ii)   the product is a veterinary drug;

(b)   the medicinal product must have been made up for sale in a container elsewhere than at the place at which it is sold, offered, exposed for sale or supplied and the container must not have been opened since the product was made up for sale in it; and

(c)   the business, so far as it concerns the sale or supply of medicinal products, must be carried on in accordance with prescribed conditions.

Under reg. 7 of the Medicines (Pharmacy and General Seal — Exemption) Order1980 (S.I. 1980/1924), the premises requirements in (a) do not apply to the sale, offer or exposure for sale or supply of any medicinal product on a general sale list which is for sale either for oral administration as a food or for external use as a cosmetic.

Section 55(1), MA 1968 states that the restrictions imposed by s. 53 do not apply to the sale, offer for sale, or supply of a medicinal product:

(a)   by a doctor or dentist to a patient under person under the care of a doctor or dentist; or

(b)   in the course of the business of a hospital or health centre, where the product is sold, offered for sale, or supplied for the purpose of being administered (whether in the hospital or health centre or elsewhere) in accordance with the directions of a doctor or dentist.

We have already seen in section 5.9, that similar exemptions exist in relation to prescription only medicines.

Under s. 55(2), MA 1968, the restrictions do not also apply to the sale or supply of a medicinal product by a registered nurse or certified midwife, in the course of their professional practice, or in the case of the midwife, where they are delivered or administered by them in certain other defined circumstances. For this exemption to apply, the medicinal product must be of a description, or falling within a class, specified in an order made by the Health Ministers.

The power to make an order conferring such an exemption on registered nurses has never been exercised. In relation to certified midwives, the power to make an order imposing exemptions from the normal restrictions on the sale or supply of medicinal products on a general sale list, has been exercised through the Medicines (Pharmacy and General Sale-Exemption) Order 1980 (S.I. 1980/1923). Article 4 of this Order specifies all medicinal products that are not prescription only medicines as forming a class of medicinal products attracting exemption from the restrictions imposed by s. 53, MA 1968.

The restrictions on the sale or supply of medicinal products on a general sale list do not apply to their supply or sale by registered midwives, in the course of their professional practice or during delivery or administration by them on being supplied in pursuance of arrangements made by the Secretary of State or the Ministry of Health and Social Services for Northern Ireland. Similar exemptions exist in relation to certain prescription only medicines, as outlined in section 5.9.

8.2.4   Other general sale list exemptions

Under art. 5(2) of the Medicines (Pharmacy and General Sale-Exemption) Order 1980, the restrictions imposed by s. 53, on the sale or supply of medicinal products on the general sale list, do not apply to the sale, offer or exposure for sale, or supply by a number of persons, of certain specified general sale list medicinal products, subject to further stipulated conditions. The designated persons, specified medicines and stipulated conditions are further outlined in sch. 1 of the Order. In summary the exemptions are as follows.

Persons selling or supplying medicinal products to universities, other institutions concerned with higher education or institutions concerned with research, are exempt from the restrictions on condition that:

(a)   the sale or supply is subject to the presentation of an order signed by the principal of the institution concerned with education or research, or the appropriate head of department in charge of a specified course of research, stating:

(i)   the name of the institution for which the medicinal product is required;

(ii)   the purpose for which the medicinal product is required; and

(iii)   the total quantity required; and

(b)   the sale or supply is for the purposes of the education or research with which the institution is concerned.

Exemptions from the restrictions relating to the sale and supply of medicinal products apply to persons selling or supplying medicinal products to any of the following:

(a)   a public analyst appointed under s. 27, Food Safety Act 1990, or art. 36 of the Food (Northern Ireland) Order 1989;

(b)   an authorised officer within the meaning of s. 5(6), Food Safety Act 1990;

(c)   a sampling officer within the meaning of art. 38(1) of the Food (Northern Ireland) Order 1989;

(d)   a person duly authorised by an enforcement authority under ss. 111 and 112, MA 1968;

(e)   a sampling officer within the meaning of sch. 3 to the MA 1968.

For the exemption to apply, the sale or supply must be subject to the presentation of an order signed by or on behalf of any of the persons mentioned in (a)–(e), stating the status of the person signing it, the amount of the medicinal product required and must only be in connection with the exercise by those persons of their statutory functions.

Exemptions also apply to persons selling or supplying prescription only medicines to any person employed or engaged in connection with a scheme for testing the quality and checking the amount of the drugs and appliances supplied under the National Health Service Act 1977, the National Health Service (Scotland) Act 1978, the Health and Personal Social Services (Northern Ireland) Order 1972, or under any subordinate legislation made under those Acts or that Order. The exemption is subject to the condition that the sale or supply will be subject to the presentation of an order signed by or on behalf of the person so employed or engaged, stating the status of the person signing it, the amount of medicinal product required, and must be for the purpose of the relevant testing scheme.

Registered ophthalmic opticians are also exempt from the general restrictions in certain defined circumstances. For the exemption to be effective, the sale or supply must only be in the course of the professional practice of the registered ophthalmic optician and must only be in an emergency. Exemptions also apply to persons selling or supplying general sale list products to the British Standards Institute. This exemption is subject to the requirement that the sale or supply shall be subject to the presentation of an order signed on behalf of the British Standards Institution, stating the status of the person signing it, and the amount of the medicinal product required. Further the sale or supply must only be for the purpose of testing containers of medicinal products or determining the standards for such containers.

Holders of marketing authorisations, product licences or manufacturer's licences are exempt in relation to the medicinal products referred to in the authorisations or licences. This exemption is subject to the conditions that the sale or supply shall be only to a pharmacist so as to enable that pharmacist to prepare an entry relating to the medicinal product in a tablet or capsule identification guide or similar publication, and is of no greater quantity than is reasonably necessary for that purpose.

The holders of certain manufacturer's licences are also exempt from the general restrictions. For this exemption to apply, the licence in question must contain a provision that the licence holder will manufacture the medicinal product for a particular person after being requested by or on behalf of that person and in that person's presence to use professional judgment as to the treatment required. Further, the exemption, as it applies to general sale list medicinal products, is restricted to those products which are for external use, and the eventual sale or supply must be to a particular person following a request made under the circumstances described above.

The Royal National Lifeboat Institution, the British Red Cross Society, St John's Ambulance Association and Brigade, St Andrew's Ambulance Association, Order of Malta Ambulance Corps, and certified first aiders of these bodies are all exempt from the general restrictions relating to the supply of general sale list medicinal products subject to the condition that the supply shall only be so far as is necessary for the treatment of sick or injured persons.

The owner or master of a ship which does not carry a doctor on board as part of its complement is exempt subject to the condition that the supply shall only be so far as is necessary for the treatment of persons on the ship.

Persons requiring general sale list medicinal products for the purpose of enabling them, in the course of their business, to comply with any requirements made by or in pursuance of any enactment with respect to the medical treatment of their employees, are exempt from the general restrictions relating to the supply of general sale list medicinal products. This exemption is subject to the condition that the supply must be for the purposes of enabling them to comply with any requirements made by or in pursuance of any such enactment, and be subject to the conditions and circumstances specified in the relevant enactment. Exemptions extend to persons operating an occupational health scheme. For this exemption to apply, the supply must be in the course of the occupational health scheme, and the individual supplying the medicinal product, if not a doctor, must be a registered nurse.

Certain exemptions extend to the operator or commander of an aircraft. The exemption is subject to the further condition that the supply must be only so far as is necessary for the immediate treatment of sick or injured persons on the aircraft. State registered chiropodists are also exempt from the restrictions relating to the sale and supply of general sale list medicinal products for external use where the sale and supply is in course of their professional practice, and the product has been made up for sale or supply in a container elsewhere than at the place at which it is sold or supplied.

8.2.5   Sales from automatic machines

Under s. 54, MA 1968, no person may sell, or offer or expose for sale, any medicinal product by means of an automatic machine unless it is a medicinal product in the automatic machines section of a general sale list. Further, under s. 66, MA 1968, and reg. 4 of the Medicines (Sale or Supply) (Miscellaneous Provisions) Regulations 1980 (S.I. 1980/1923), every automatic machine which is for use for the sale of any medicinal product in the automatic machines section of a general sale list shall be located in premises which the occupier is able to close to exclude the public.

8.2.6   Offences and enforcement

Under s. 67(5), MA 1968, any contravention of the provisions relating to the sale or supply of medicines on a general sale list is a criminal offence, punishable on summary conviction with a scale fine and on indictment by a term of imprisonment. Section 68 allows for the disqualification, by the court, of an individual from carrying on a retail pharmacy business, following conviction for certain offences.

Any proposal to impose such an order must relate to the gravity of the offence, the unsatisfactory state of the premises and any similar prior convictions. Further provisions allow for another enforcement authority to apply for such an order, further convictions for breach of such an order and applications for early revocation of the order.

The power and duty to enforce ss. 53, 54 and 66, MA 1968, in respect of registered pharmacies has been given to the Royal Pharmaceutical Society, under art. 2 of the Medicines (Sale or Supply) (Miscellaneous Provisions) Regulations 1980. Under the same provisions, the power and duty to enforce ss. 53, 54 and 66, MA 1968 in respect of all other premises, rests with food and drugs authorities, or local authorities.

8.3   PHARMACY MEDICINES

Section 52, MA 1968 states that, subject to any further exemption, no person shall, in the course of a business carried on, sell by retail, offer, or expose for sale by retail, or supply in circumstances corresponding to retail sale, any medicinal product which is not a medicinal product on a general sale list, unless:

(a)   that person is, in respect of that business, a person lawfully conducting a retail pharmacy business;

(b)   the product is sold, offered or exposed for sale, or supplied, on premises which are a registered pharmacy; and

(c)   that person, or if the transaction is carried out on behalf of that person, then that other person, is or acts, under the supervision of, a pharmacist.

Under s. 131(1) and (2), MA 1968, selling by way of 'wholesale dealing' means selling to a person who buys it for the purpose of selling or supplying it, or administering it or causing it to be administered to one or more human beings in the course of a business. Under s. 131(3), MA 1968, 'selling by retail' or 'retail sale' is defined by default as selling to a person who buys otherwise than for the purpose of wholesale selling.

Under ss. 70–72, MA 1968, a retail pharmacy business must be under the personal control of a pharmacist so far as it concerns the sale of medicinal products including products on the general sale list.

As we have already seen, s. 58(2), MA 1968 states that no person shall sell by retail, or supply in circumstances corresponding to retail sale, a medicinal product specified by order as falling into the class or description of prescription only, except in accordance with a prescription given by an appropriate practitioner.

Pharmacy medicines could therefore be categorised as falling into a default category, i.e., any medicinal product which is not a prescription only medicine or which is not a medicinal product on a general sale list is a pharmacy medicine.

Certain medicinal products will only fall into the category of general sale list medicines where they are sold in certain pack sizes or in specified quantities.

Such products include aloxiprin, paracetamol, salicylamide, aspirin, bisacodyl, ibuprofen and clotrimazole. Specific legislative provisions apply to each of the relevant products. Where the products are sold outside the limits imposed by these legislative provisions, the products are classified as pharmacy medicines.

8.3.1   Retail pharmacy business, registered pharmacy and pharmacists

Section 52, MA 1968 restricts the sale and supply of pharmacy medicines to persons lawfully conducting a retail pharmacy business, on premises which are a registered pharmacy; and under the supervision of a pharmacist. We have already seen in 7.7.1 that the High Court has considered the meaning of the term 'supervision' in the case of *Roberts* v *Littlewoods Mail Order Stores Ltd* [1943] 1 All ER 271.

In s. 132, MA 1968, a 'retail pharmacy business' is defined as a business (not being a professional practice carried on by a practitioner) which consists of or includes the retail sale of medicinal products other than medicinal products on a general sale list (whether medicinal products on such a list are sold in the course of that business or not). Professional practice of practitioner is further defined by the same section as meaning a doctor, dentist or vet.

The business qualifies if it consists of, or includes, the retail sale of prescription only medicines or pharmacy medicines and is not an integral part of the professional practice of a doctor, dentist or vet. It does not seem to matter whether the business also includes the retail sale of medicinal products on the general sale list.

By s. 69, MA 1968, a retail pharmacy business may be lawfully conducted by a number of different persons, subject to a series of qualifying conditions. The persons are: a pharmacist, or a partnership; a 'body corporate'; a 'representative' of a deceased, bankrupt, or mentally ill pharmacist.

Under s. 70, MA 1968, the further qualifying conditions for an individual pharmacist are that, at all premises where the business is carried on and medicinal products, other than products on a general sale list, are sold by retail, the business, so far as concerns the retail sale at those premises of medicinal products, whether they are medicinal products on a general sale list or not, is under the personal control of the pharmacist. These convoluted provisions mean that a pharmacist must exercise personal control over the sale and supply of all medicinal products. Further, the name and certificate of registration of the pharmacist must be conspicuously exhibited.

The meaning of the term 'personal control' was considered by the High Court in the case of *Hygienic Stores Ltd* v *Coombes* [1938] 1 All ER 63, in relation to the inclusion of that phrase in equivalent poisons legislation. The appellants carried on business at 16 different shops. At three of the shops the business included the sale of drugs and poisons, and the appellants employed registered pharmacists to manage these premises. At the remaining 13 shops, the business comprised the sale of medicines in various forms under proprietary or trade names. No pharmacists were employed at these premises.

The appellants were prosecuted in respect of the sale of poisons at two of the pharmacies, one of the sales taking place when the employed registered pharmacist was not there. The trial judge found that the appellants' business was not under the personal control of a registered pharmacist, and that the appellants should be convicted accordingly. The convictions were upheld on appeal to the High Court where Hewart LCJ found that the trial judge was correct in finding that the requisite degree of control had not been exhibited.

Under s. 70, MA 1968, the further qualifying conditions for partnerships are that, in England, Wales and Northern Ireland, each person must be a pharmacist. In Scotland, a partnership may lawfully conduct a pharmacy business where one or more of the partners is a pharmacist. At least one must be a pharmacist, the rest need not be. The qualifications regarding the exercise of personal control, and the display of name and certificate of registration, noted above, apply equally to partnerships, except that the personal control must be exercised by a pharmacist partner or other pharmacist.

Under s. 71, MA 1968, the further qualifying conditions for a retail pharmacy business conducted by a body corporate are that the business of keeping, preparing and dispensing prescription only medicines and pharmacy medicines must be under the management of a superintendent. The superintendent must be a pharmacist, who must not act in a similar capacity for any other body corporate. A statement in writing, signed by the superintendent and signed on behalf of the body corporate, specifying the name of the superintendent and stating whether the superintendent is a member of the board of the body corporate, must be sent to the registrar of the Royal Pharmaceutical Society of Great Britain.

In turn, the retail supply of medicinal products at a retail pharmacy business conducted by a body corporate, must be under the personal control of the superintendent or under the personal control of a manager or assistant pharmacist, subject to the directions of the superintendent. The name and certificate of registration of the person (superintendent or other pharmacist subject to the superintendent's directions) must also be conspicuously displayed.

Special rules apply to the lawful conduct of a retail pharmacy business by the representative of a deceased, bankrupt or mentally ill pharmacist, under s. 71, MA 1968. Where the pharmacist has died, the representative is the deceased's executor or administrator, or if the deceased has left no executor who is entitled and willing to carry on the business, for the first three months from the date of the death, any person beneficially interested in the estate.

The representative of a deceased pharmacist may carry on the business for a period of up to five years from the date of death, provided that the name and address of the representative is notified to the registrar of the Royal Pharmaceutical Society of Great Britain; that the premises where there is a retail supply of medicinal products are under the control of a pharmacist; and that the name and certificate of registration of the pharmacist exercising personal control are conspicuously displayed.

Where a pharmacist is adjudged bankrupt, or enters into a composition or scheme or deed of arrangement with creditors, or in Scotland, sequestration of estate is awarded, or the pharmacist makes a trust deed for the advantage of creditors or a composition contract, the representative is the trustee in bankruptcy or in the sequestration, or person appointed under the composition scheme, deed of arrangement, trust deed or composition contract. Such a representative may carry on the business for a period of three years from date of bankruptcy, award of sequestration, or appointment under a composition, deed or scheme, subject to the same further conditions applying to the representative of a deceased pharmacist noted above.

A receiver, or other individual, appointed for a pharmacist under a variety of different pieces of mental health legislation, may be a pharmacist's representative. Again, such a representative may carry on the business for a period of three years from date of appointment, subject to the same further conditions applying to the representative of a deceased pharmacist noted above.

A person, lawfully conducting a retail pharmacy business as a representative of a pharmacist under any of the circumstances outlined above may, under s. 78(8), MA 1968, take or use in connection with that business any title, description or emblem (see 8.3.1.2) which the pharmacist could have used.

Finally, under s. 73, MA 1968, the Health Ministers may by order add to, revoke or vary any of the provisions in the MA 1968 relating to the lawful conduct of a retail pharmacy business. Such an order might modify or provide new conditions or provide alternative conditions for the lawful conduct of a retail pharmacy business but would be subject to laying before Parliament and approval by resolution of each House of Parliament.

8.3.1.1   The registrar and the register   The registrar, under s. 69, MA 1968, is the Registrar of the Royal Pharmaceutical Society of Great Britain, or the Registrar of the Pharmaceutical Society for Northern Ireland. The registrar is required, under s. 75(1), MA 1968, to keep a register of premises. Section 71(1), MA 1968 defines a registered pharmacy as premises for the time being entered into the register.

The registrar has a duty to enter in the register, on payment of the prescribed fee, any premises for which an application for registration is made. Applications for registration of premises should be made in the prescribed manner, must be in writing and be given or sent to the registrar with the prescribed fee. The application must be made and signed by or on behalf of the person carrying on, or intending to carry on, a retail pharmacy business at the premises to which the application relates. A separate application must be made in respect of each premises and each application must contain the following particulars:

(a)   the name of the person carrying on, or intending to carry on a retail pharmacy business and their private residential address. In the case of a partnership, the names and addresses of all of the partners must be given. In the case of a body corporate, the registered name and address of the registered office of the body must be given. Where a business is being carried on by a representative of a pharmacist and the business is under the personal control of a pharmacist, the name of the pharmacist and their certificate of registration must be given;

(b)   the business name, where a person or a partnership or a body corporate is carrying on or intends to carry on such a business under a business name which is different from the name of the person or of the partners or of the corporate body;

(c)   the name of the pharmacist or, if more than one, the names of all of the pharmacists under whose personal control the business is, or is to be, carried on at all the premises to which the application relates, and in the case of a body corporate the name of the superintendent under whose management the business is, or is to be, carried on, and the number of the certificate of each such pharmacist and, as the case may be, superintendent;

(d)   the full postal address of the premises to which the application relates;

(e)   where the application for registration relates to premises in respect of which there has been a change of ownership of the business, the name and address of the immediate former owner of that business and the date of such change of ownership;

(f)   the date or intended date of the commencement of the business;

(g)   a brief description of the premises, including the internal layout of the premises, as regards the areas where medicinal products are or are intended to be sold or supplied, prepared, dispensed or stored together with:

(i)   a statement showing whether or not there are arrangements so as to enable supervision to be exercised by a pharmacist of any dispensing and sale of medicinal products at one and the same time; and

(ii)   a sketch plan, drawn to scale showing these areas and the layouts.

Under s. 75(3), MA 1968, the registrar must notify the appropriate Ministers (depending on jurisdiction) whenever an application is made, specifying the premises to which the application relates and the date on which the application was made. The registrar must not enter the premises in the register until two months from the date of application unless, before the expiry of that time, the appropriate Minister consents to an earlier entry to the register. In addition, under s. 75(7), MA 1968, the registrar must not enter any premises into the register unless reasonably satisfied that, at the time of the application, the applicant is a person lawfully conducting a retail pharmacy business, or will be a person lawfully conducting a retail pharmacy business if and when the premises are entered into the register and business is commenced.

Under s. 75(4), MA 1968, if it appears to the Minister that in a material respect the premises do not comply with the requirements of regulations made under s. 66, MA 1968 (see 8.3.3) relating to the nature of premises, and accordingly the Minister proposes to certify that they are unsuitable for registration, the Minister must, within the two month waiting period mentioned in the previous paragraph, serve a notice on the applicant, stating the Minister's proposals and the reasons for them.

A copy of the same notice will be served on the registrar. Under s. 75(5), any applicant served with such a Minister's notice may, within a specified period, give notice of a desire to be heard with respect to the proposals or make representations in writing. The Minister must then give the applicant an opportunity to be heard or consider any written representation. Following this, the Minister must determine the application by either:

(a)   notifying the applicant and the registrar that the determination is not to issue a certificate that the premises are unsuitable; or

(b)   sending a certificate to the registrar that the premises are unsuitable for registration, notifying the applicant that this has been done and informing the applicant of the reasons for the decision.

In the former case, the registrar must immediately enter the premises in the register.

Under s. 76(1), MA 1968, an annual retention fee in respect of any premises entered in the register in respect of each year subsequent to the year in which the premises were first entered in the register, is payable by the person carrying on a retail pharmacy business at those premises. Under s. 77, MA 1968, each person who carries on a retail pharmacy business must send to the registrar, in January each year, a list of all premises at which business, so far as it consists of the retail sale of medicinal products, is carried on. Further, in the case of any premises where prescription only medicines and pharmacy medicines are sold by retail, or supplied in circumstances corresponding to retail sale, details of the name of the pharmacist, under whose personal control the business is being carried on, must also be supplied.

Under s. 75(2) the Council of the Royal Pharmaceutical Society of Great Britain (or as appropriate, the Minister for Health and Social Services for Northern Ireland) may direct the registrar to remove from the register any premises where the retention fees, payable by the person carrying on the retail pharmacy business, have not been paid within two months from the date on which a demand for payment has been made. This power of removal is subject to the qualification that the premises may be restored to the register, with retrospective effect to the date of removal, where the retention fee is paid, together with an additional sum by way of penalty, either before the end of the year in which the fee fell due, or any such longer period as the Council (or Minister) may allow.

Under s. 76(3), MA 1968, where a change occurs in the ownership of pharmacy premises, the registration becomes void at the end of the period of 28 days from the date on which the change occurs. If the change occurs on the death of the person carrying on the business or, in the case of a partnership, on the death of one of the partners, registration of the premises becomes void at the end of the period of three months from the date of the death. Under s. 76(5), MA 1968, where the registration of the premises becomes void under either of these circumstances, an application for the premises to be restored to the register may be made by the new owner of the premises.

Where such an application is made, and the registrar is reasonably satisfied that either the new applicant is, at the time of the application, a person lawfully conducting a retail pharmacy business, or will be such a person, if the premises are restored to the register and business commences, then the premises must be restored to the register, subject to the payment of the equivalent of any due retention fee.

Fees payable to the registrar, under any of these provisions, are by s. 76(8) to be applied for the purposes of the Royal Pharmaceutical Society of Great Britain.

8.3.1.2   *Titles*   Under s. 78(2) and (3), MA 1968, no person may take or use the title of chemist and druggist, druggist, dispensing chemist, and dispensing druggist, unless that person is lawfully conducting a retail pharmacy business. Further, the titles may not be taken or used in connection with any premises at which any goods are sold by retail or supplied in circumstances corresponding to retail sale, unless those premises are a registered pharmacy. In the case where the person conducting the retail pharmacy business is a body corporate, the titles may only be taken or used where, in the case of premises at which any goods are sold by retail or supplied in circumstances corresponding to retail sale, the premises are a registered pharmacy, and where the managing superintendent pharmacist is a member of the board of the body corporate.

Under the same sections, no person may take or use the title 'chemist' in connection with the sale of any goods by retail or the supply of any goods in circumstances corresponding to retail sale, unless the conditions outlined in the preceding paragraph are satisfied.

Under s. 78(4), MA 1968, no person may, in connection with any business which consists of the retail sale of medicinal products or the supply of any goods in circumstances corresponding to retail sale, use the description 'pharmacy' except in respect of a registered pharmacy or the pharmaceutical department of a hospital or health centre. Under s. 78(7), the use of the title 'pharmacy', in connection with a business carried on at any premises, is taken to suggest that the person carrying on the business (where that person is not a body corporate) is a pharmacist, and that any other person under whose personal control the business, so far as it concerns the retail sale of medicinal products or the supply of such products in circumstances corresponding to retail sale), is carried on at those premises, is also a pharmacist.

Under s. 78(5), MA 1968, no person who is not a pharmacist shall take or use the titles of pharmaceutical chemist, pharmaceutist, pharmacist, member of the Pharmaceutical Society, or Fellow of the Pharmaceutical Society, and these titles may not be taken or used by anyone in connection with a business which includes the retail sale of any goods or the supply of any goods in circumstances corresponding to retail sale, unless those premises are a registered pharmacy or a hospital or health centre.

Under s. 79, MA 1968, the Health Ministers may, by order, after consultation with the Council of the Pharmaceutical Society, provide that the restrictions on the use of titles, descriptions and emblems shall cease to have effect, or impose such further restrictions or other requirements as may be specified. Any such amendments would require to be laid before Parliament and approval by a resolution of each House of Parliament.

Contravention of the requirements relating to the annual return of premises to the registrar and the restrictions on the use of titles, descriptions and emblems, amounts to an offence, and on summary conviction, renders the offender liable to a fine.

8.3.2   Regulatory powers

Under s. 66, MA 1968, the appropriate Ministers are given powers to make regulations to prescribe such requirements as they may consider necessary with respect to any of the following matters:

(a)   the manner in which, or persons under whose supervision, medicinal products may be prepared or may be dispensed;

(b)   the amount of space to be provided in any premises for preparing or dispensing medicinal products, the separation of such space from the remainder of the premises, and the facilities to be provided in any premises for such persons;

(c)   the amount of space to be provided in any premises for the sale and supply of medicinal products;

(d)   the accommodation (including the amount of space) to be provided in any premises for members of the public to whom medicinal products are sold or supplied or for whom medicinal products are being prepared or assembled;

(e)   the amount of space to be provided in any premises for the storage of medicinal products;

(f)   the safekeeping of medicinal products;

(g)   the disposal of medicinal products which have become unusable or otherwise unwanted;

(h)   precautions to be observed before medicinal products are supplied;

(i)   the keeping of records relating to the sale and supply of medicinal products;

(j)   the supply of medicinal products as samples;

(k)   sanitation, cleanliness, temperature, humidity, or other factors relating to the risks of deterioration or contamination in connection with the manufacture, storage, transportation, sale or supply of medicinal products;

(l)   the construction, location and the use of automatic machines for the sale of medicinal products.

The Ministers, under the same section, may also prescribe requirements in respect of:

(a)   the construction, lay-out, drainage, equipment, maintenance, ventilation, lighting and water supply of premises at or from which medicinal products are manufactured, stored transported, sold or supplied;

(b)   the disposal of refuse at or from any such premises; and

(c)   any apparatus, equipment, furnishings or utensils used at any such premises.

Under s. 67, MA 1968, it is an offence to contravene any regulations made under s. 66, and an offender may be liable on summary conviction to a fine. In addition, under s. 68, any person convicted of such an offence may be disqualified from using the premises for a period not exceeding two years, by order of the same court which dealt with the conviction of the offence.

The Royal Pharmaceutical Society of Great Britain, in the Standards of Good Professional Practice section of *Medicines, Ethics and Practice*, has given detailed advice to the members of the profession on the standards for pharmacy premises including appearance, safety, condition, tidiness, environment, size and hygiene. This advice is discussed in detail in 8.4.

8.3.3   Pharmacy medicines exemptions

Section 52, MA 1968 allows for exemptions from the requirements for the sale and supply of pharmacy medicines conferred either under the Act itself or under Order made by the Ministers for the purposes of s. 52.

Under art. 2 of the Medicines (Pharmacy and General Sale-Exemption) Order 1980 (S.I. 1980/1924), the restrictions imposed by s. 52 shall not apply, during a limited period, to certain medicinal products. If a product licence has been granted containing a provision to the effect that the method of sale or supply of the product may be otherwise than by or under the supervision of a pharmacist, then it may be sold as a general sale list medicine, even though it may not yet have been included in the general sale list. The exemption is subject to the further stipulation that the other conditions relating to the sale and supply of medicinal products on the general sale list are fulfilled. The restriction will be limited to two years in the case of a grant of a product licence, or one year in the case of a variation to a product licence.

Under art. 3 of the Medicines (Pharmacy and General Sale-Exemption) Order 1980, the restrictions imposed by s. 52 shall not apply to the sale, offer or exposure for sale or supply of a medicinal product by a person who, having exercised all due diligence, believes on reasonable grounds that the product is a medicinal product:

(a)   on a general sale list; or

(b)   which might be lawfully sold, offered or exposed for sale or supplied, as the case may be, free from restrictions imposed by s. 52 by reason of any exemption conferred under art. 2, as described in the previous paragraph,

where due to the act or default of another person, that product is not such a medicinal product. This exemption will only take effect if and so long as the conditions relating to the sale and supply of medicinal products on the general sale list are fulfilled.

As noted in 5.6, the introduction of the due diligence defence in relation to the dispensing of prescription only medicines pursuant to a forged prescription has negated aspects of the effect of the *Storkwain* case. However, it is clear that the courts are interpreting the meaning of 'due diligence' in a narrow manner, balancing the need to take account of the propriety of an individual pharmacist's conduct against the need to protect the public from the dangers of unlawful drugs. As we shall see below in section 8.4 and chapter 10, the case reinforces the high standard of care which is expected of pharmacists in their professional pharmacy role.

8.3.4   Exemptions for certain persons

Under art. 5(1) of the Medicines (Pharmacy and General Sale-Exemption) Order 1980, the restrictions imposed by s. 52, MA 1968, on the sale or supply of pharmacy medicinal products, do not apply to the sale, offer or exposure for sale, or supply by a number of persons, of certain specified general sale list medicinal products, subject to further stipulated conditions. The designated persons, specified medicines and stipulated conditions are further outlined in sch. 1 to the Order.

Many of the exemptions offered in relation to pharmacy medicines are identical to those offered for general sale list medicines described in 8.2.4. Similar rules and conditions apply to: persons selling or supplying medicinal products to universities, or other institutions concerned with higher education or institutions concerned with research; statutory officers; those involved with testing and quality schemes; registered ophthalmic opticians; the British Standards Institute; holders of marketing authorisations; the Royal National Lifeboat Institution, the British Red Cross Society, St John's Ambulance Association and Brigade, St Andrew's Ambulance Association, Order of Malta Ambulance Corps, and certified first aiders of these bodies; the owner or master of a ship; persons operating an occupational health scheme; those complying with certain enactments relating to the health of employees; and the operator or commander of an aircraft.

The holders of certain manufacturer's licences are also exempt from the restrictions relating to the sale and supply of pharmacy medicines. For this exemption to apply, the licence in question must contain a provision that the licence holder will manufacture the medicinal product for a particular person after being requested by or on behalf of that person and in that person's presence to use professional judgment as to the treatment required. Further, the exemption, as it applies to pharmacy medicines, is restricted to those products which are for external use in the treatment of hair and scalp conditions and which contain any of the following:

(a)   not more than 5.0 per cent of boric acid;
(b)   isopropyl myristrate or lauryl sulphate;
(c)   not more than 0.004 per cent of resorcinol;
(d)   not more than 3.0 per cent of salicylic acid;
(e)   not more than 0.2   per cent of sodium pyrithione or zinc prithione.

The eventual sale or supply must also be to a particular person following a request made under the circumstances described above.

State registered chiropodists are exempt from the restrictions relating to the sale and supply of certain pharmacy medicines, as follows:

(a)   paint containing not more than 9.0 per cent borotannic complex;
(b)   ointment, tincture or dusting powder containing not more than 5.0 per cent diamthazole hydrochloride;
(c)   ointment or lotion containing not more than 10.0 per cent buclosamide or not more than 10.0 per cent crotamiton;
(d)   cream, jelly or powder containing not more than 1.0 per cent fenticlor;
(e)   pastes containing not more than 70.0 per cent salicylic acid or not more than 70 per cent pyrogallol;
(f)   powder or cream containing not more than 2.0 per cent 1-phenoxy-propan-2-ol;
(g)   dusting powder or jelly or tincture containing not more than 0.4 per cent hydrargaphen;
(h)   potassium permanganate crystals or solutions;
(i)   cream, powder or solution containing not more than 1.0 per cent clotrimazole;
(j)   ointment containing not more than 3.0 per cent chlorquinaldol;
(k)   solution containing not more than 10.0 per cent glutaraldehyde;
(l)   ointment containing hyaluronidase and a herarinoid;
(m)   cream containing not more than 2.0 per cent mepyramine maleate;
(n)   cream containing not more than 2.0 per cent miconazole nitrate;
(o)   cream, jelly or powder containing not more than 10.0 per cent polynoxylin;

(p)   salicylic acid lotion BPC;

(q)   cream or tincture containing not more than 0.1 per cent thiomersal.

The sale and supply must also be in the course of the professional practice of the state registered chiropodist, and the product must have been made up for sale or supply in a container elsewhere than at the place at which it is sold or supplied.

Persons authorised by licences granted under reg. 5 of the Misuse of Drugs Regulations 1973 (S.I. 1973/797), or reg. 5 of the Misuse of Drugs (Northern Ireland) 1974 (SR (N.I.) 1974/272) to supply a controlled drug, are exempt from the general restrictions relating to the sale and supply of pharmacy medicines, in relation to any pharmacy medicine specified in the licence. For this exemption to apply, the supply is subject to such conditions, in such circumstances, and to such an extent as may be specified in the licence.

Persons carrying on the business of a school providing full-time education and health authorities are exempt from the general restrictions relating to the sale and supply of pharmacy medicines that are for use in the prevention of dental caries and consist of or contain sodium fluoride. The exemption, as it applies to persons carrying on the business of a school providing full-time education, is subject to the further requirement that the supply must be in the course of a school dental scheme, and if to a child under 16, must only be where the parent or guardian of the child has consented to the supply.

Similarly, the exemption, as it applied to health authorities, is subject to the further condition that the supply must be either in the course of a pre-school dental scheme, and the individual supplying the medicinal product must be a registered or enrolled nurse, or in the course of a school dental scheme, and if to a child under 16, only where the parent or guardian of that child has consented to the supply.

A school dental scheme is a scheme supervised by a doctor or dentist in which medicinal products are supplied at a school to pupils of that school for the purpose of preventing dental caries. A pre-school dental scheme is a scheme supervised by a doctor or dentist in which medicinal products are supplied to parents or guardians of children under five for use by such children for the purpose of preventing dental caries.

8.3.5   Collection and delivery schemes

Under art. 2 of the Medicines (Collection and Delivery Arrangements — Exemption) Order 1978 (S.I. 1978/1421), the restrictions imposed by s. 52, MA 1968 on the sale and supply of pharmacy medicines do not apply to the supply of any medicinal product for human use on premises which are not a registered pharmacy and where such supply is in accordance with a prescription given by doctor or dentist and forms part of a collection and delivery arrangement used by a person who lawfully conducts a retail pharmacy business. A 'collection and delivery arrangement' is any arrangement whereby a person is enabled to take or send a prescription given by a doctor or dentist to premises other than a registered pharmacy and to collect or have collected from such premises a medicinal product prepared or dispensed in accordance with such prescription at a registered pharmacy by or under the supervision of a pharmacist if such premises at which the medicinal product is supplied are capable of being closed by the occupier so as to exclude the public.

8.4   PROFESSIONAL STANDARDS AND GENERAL SALE LIST AND PHARMACY MEDICINES

The principles of the *Code of Ethics* of the Royal Pharmaceutical Society of Great Britain impose specific obligations on pharmacists relating to the supply of general sale list and pharmacy medicines. Breach of these principles may form the basis of a complaint of professional misconduct. These principles are supplemented by detailed advice, contained in the published *Standards of Good Professional Practice*. It is important to remember that the *Code of Ethics* also requires that pharmacists must comply with the obligations in the *Standards of Good Professional Practice* where applicable. Failure to meet the standards could also form the basis of a complaint of misconduct.

As of the principle that a pharmacist's prime concern must be for the welfare of both the patient and other members of the public, a series of obligations are imposed which have both general and specific implications for the supply of general sale list and pharmacy medicines. Generally, the pharmacist is under a duty to act in a manner which promotes and safeguards the interests of the public, and justifies public trust in the pharmacist's knowledge, ability and judgment. Further, the pharmacist has a professional responsibility to exercise control over all medicinal products which are supplied.

The pharmacist must exercise professional judgment to prevent the supply of unnecessary and excessive quantities of medicines and other products. Requests for certain general sale list and pharmacy medicines, with the potential for misuse, should be dealt with personally by the pharmacist and sale should be refused if it is apparent that the sale is not for a genuine medicinal purpose or if the frequency of purchase suggests overuse.

A pharmacist must not give the impression to a potential purchaser that any product associated with the maintenance of health or a food supplement is efficacious when there is no evidence of efficacy. A pharmacist must also ensure that medicines restricted to sale from a pharmacy are not accessible to the public for self-selection or self-service and that general sale list medicines are displayed in such a way as to reduce to an absolute minimum the possibility that the sale is effected by a pharmacist or other suitably trained person.

As part of this latter obligation, further advice is given that medicines known to have a potential for misuse should never be available for self-service. In addition, displays of general sale list medicines for self-selection should be arranged so as to create a professional area in which the customer is guided to a designated service point manned by a suitably trained assistant. Arrangements should be made to ensure that prominent notices tell would-be purchasers of self-selected general sale list medicines to pay at a designated point within the professional area.

There is now a requirement that there should be a written protocol in each pharmacy covering the procedure to be followed in that pharmacy when a medicine is supplied or advice on treatment of a medical condition is sought. In addition, each member of staff whose work in a pharmacy includes the sale of medicines should have completed a course at NVQ level in retail operations.

Further, it is suggested that medicines sales protocols should comply with certain standards outlined in the *Standards of Good Professional Practice* which supplement the obligations contained in the *Code of Ethics*. Pharmacists must obtain sufficient information to allow an assessment to be made that the symptoms indicate that self-medication is appropriate, and to enable a suitable product to be recommended, or other advice given. This will include information about the use of other medications with potential interactions.

Pharmacists must also ensure that the procedures for sales of medicines in the pharmacy provide for professional advice and information whenever this can assist in the safe and effective use of non-prescribed medicines. A pharmacist must be personally involved whenever this is necessary to provide a good standard of pharmaceutical care. Assistants must also be trained to know when the pharmacist should be consulted. Particular care should be provided when supplying products for or to special purchasers such as children or the elderly.

Finally the pharmacists must ensure that they are involved in the decision to supply any medicine which requires special care to be taken. This might be because the medicine has recently become available without prescription, that it may be subject to abuse or misuse, or that the marketing authorisation for non-prescription use is restricted to only selected conditions.

In addition, the pharmacist must, on each occasion that a pharmaceutical service is provided, use professional judgment to decide whether the patient needs to be seen. Further guidance on this latter obligation indicates that a face-to-face consultation need not take place on every occasion that a service is provided. However, a pharmacist has a professional duty to ensure that it occurs when considered necessary with a medicine for an acute condition or at appropriate intervals for repeat medication.

Pharmacists are under a further obligation to ensure that their premises reflect the professional character of pharmacy. A pharmacist must ensure that the external appearance of a community pharmacy premises inspires confidence in the nature of the health care that is to be provided. Further guidance is given on the nature and form of directional signs to be displayed on pharmacy premises. The wording should comprise only the name of the owner of the business and identification of the business as a chemist or pharmacy. Detailed standards for pharmacy premises are also included in the *Standards of Good Professional Practice* which supplement these obligations. These include standards on the appearance of premises, their safety, condition and tidiness, the pharmacy environment, the size of the dispensary and hygiene.

8.5   OFFENCES IN RELATION TO PHARMACY MEDICINES

Under s. 67(2), MA 1968, any contravention of the provision relating to pharmacy medicines amounts to a criminal offence, punishable on summary conviction by the imposition of a scale fine, or on indictment to imprisonment. Section 68 allows for the disqualification, by the court, of an individual from carrying on a retail pharmacy business, following conviction for certain offences.

Any proposal to impose such an order must relate to the gravity of the offence, the unsatisfactory state of the premises and any similar prior convictions. Further provisions allow for another enforcement authority to apply for such an order, further convictions for breach of such an order and applications for early revocation of the order.

8.6   CONCLUSION

The analysis of the legal regulation of general sale list and pharmacy medicines, outlined in this chapter, should dispel any myth that the level of control is any less than that expected for prescription only medicines, controlled drugs or poisons. The key to an understanding of the legal control lies in an understanding of the significance attached to the classification of these products, the regulation of the methods by which they may be sold, and the restriction of the types of persons permitted to own, manage and conduct business in pharmacies, with the parallel exclusive right to distribute those medicines limited to sale in those premises.

The classification of medicinal drug products might be described as hierarchical, depending on the level of control exercised over their availability. Controlled drugs and poisons are subject to the strictest control, prescription only medicines follow, then pharmacy medicines, and finally general sale list medicines. It is important to be careful about language here. All medicinal drug products are subject to the highest levels of legal regulation, general sale list products included.

Our analysis of the regulation of medicinal drug products shows that pharmacists have reasonably exclusive rights to distribute certain of those products, prescription only and pharmacy medicines in particular, and a virtual monopoly over the sale of others. Those absolute privileges and monopolies have resulted from the many years of negotiation undertaken by the pharmacy profession.

The pharmacy profession should be proud of the role which its members play in the distribution of medicinal drug products as part of its important contribution to drug therapy and health care. However, those roles carry parallel duties and obligations, with distinct legal, ethical and administrative realities. Some of those realities will be discussed in chapters ten to thirteen below.

NINE

Identification of medicinal products

9.1 INTRODUCTION

We have already seen that the production, licensing, advertisement and supply of medicinal products are closely regulated by the law with the objective of ensuring that those products are safe for their intended use. Primary regulation of medicinal products is vital but does not necessarily mean that the medicinal products will be used safely. Although the introduction of patient information programmes and the increase in pharmacist counselling are changing the situation, users of medicinal products may be confused about what has been supplied to them, be unable to distinguish between those products or may not have sufficient information about their use. The net result may be that they use those products incorrectly or for the wrong purpose. It is therefore vitally important that medicinal products which are sold or supplied to members of the public are correctly identified and easily distinguishable and that appropriate information about their safe use is provided.

The identification of medicinal products has been closely regulated since the passing of the MA 1968 through that legislation and a number of statutory instruments passed under its provisions. 'Identification' includes the labelling and marking of containers and packages together with the provision of user leaflets in original packs of medicinal products. The law on the identification of medicinal products has taken on a greater significance following the adoption and implementation of a number of European Community directives. That has resulted in a series of important recent amendments to both the primary and secondary legislation particularly in relation to the provision of patient information leaflets. These amendments are designed to revise and consolidate the law in relation to the identification of medicinal products.

The new legislative requirements will apply to most medicinal products by the beginning of 1999. A limited number of medicinal products remain outside the definitions of the new legislative provisions. Certain existing rules will continue to apply to these products. These rules are similar, but not identical to the amendments. An amount of replication is therefore inevitable.

9.2   EUROPEAN COMMUNITY LEGISLATION ON THE IDENTIFICATION OF MEDICINAL PRODUCTS

We shall see below that much of the current secondary legislation on the identification of medicinal products was enacted to implement European Community directives. The European Community legislation has the two-fold purpose of defining medicinal products and outlining a series of standards and requirements appropriate to those products. It is therefore useful to begin by examining the content of some of those directives.

Council Directive 65/65/EEC [1965] OJ 22/369 began the process of the approximation of laws, regulations and administrative action relating to proprietary medicinal products. The directive outlines the common principles which should be adhered to by each member state with regard to the conditions for granting a marketing authorisation for medicinal products, manufacture and quality control procedures, labelling and information leaflets, and detailed guidance on data requirements. Council Directive 65/65/EEC defines 'medicinal products' as:

Any substance or combination of substances presented for treating or preventing disease in human beings or animals or any substance or combination of substances which may be administered to human beings with a view to making a medical diagnosis or to restoring, correcting or modifying physiological functions in human beings or animals.

Article 3 of the directive indicates that medicinal products may not be placed on the market without an authorisation obtained from a competent authority of a member state and art. 4 sets out a number of particulars and documents which must be supplied before such an authorisation will be given. Chapter IV of the directive specifies a detailed list of particulars which must be set out on containers and packages of medicinal products.

At the time of the adoption of this directive, the United Kingdom was not a member of the European Economic Community. However the underlying philosophy of the directive is implicit in the provisions of the Medicines Act 1968. Council Directive 75/319/EEC [1975] OJ L147/13, which did apply to the United Kingdom, continued the process of approximation of the laws relating to medicinal products. Article 6 of the directive indicates that the information contained in a leaflet enclosed with the packaging of a proprietary medicinal product should be in accordance with the particulars and documents supplied pursuant to art. 4 of Directive 65/65/EEC.

Article 6 of Council Directive 75/319/EEC makes the supply of a leaflet with the packaging an optional requirement. In relation to the definition of medicinal products, art. 34 makes it clear that the directive is only intended to apply to proprietary medicinal products for human use and that neither Directive 75/319/EEC nor Directive 65/65/EEC apply to medicinal products consisting of vaccines, toxins or serums, to proprietary medicinal products based on human blood or blood constituents or radioactive isotopes, or to homeopathic medicinal products.

Council Directive 83/570/EEC [1983] OJ L332/1 *inter alia* inserted a new art. 4A into Council Directive 65/65/EEC outlining the information to be contained in the summary of product characteristics supporting an application for authorisation for a medicinal product.

Council Directive 89/341/EEC [1989] OJ L142/11 replaced the phrase 'proprietary medicinal product' in Directive 65/65/EEC with the phrase 'medicinal product'. It also amended Council Directive 75/319/EEC by replacing the optional requirement for the inclusion of a leaflet with the packaging of a medicinal product with a requirement that such a leaflet should be included unless the information is directly conveyed on the container itself and the outer packaging. Council Directive 89/342/EEC [1989] OJ L142/14 derogated from art. 34 of Council Directive 75/319 to indicate that Directives 65/65/EEC and 75/319/EEC should apply to immunological medicinal products for human use consisting of vaccines, toxins or serums and allergen products.

In a similar way Council Directive 89/343/EEC [1989] OJ L142/16 also derogated from art. 34 of Council Directive 75/319 to indicate that Directives 65/65/EEC and 75/319/EEC should apply to radiopharmaceuticals for human use. Finally, Council Directive 89/381/EEC [1989] OJ L181/44 derogated from art. 34 of Council Directive 75/319 to indicate that Directives 65/65/EEC and 75/319/EEC should apply to medicinal products based on blood constituents.

Council Directive 92/27/EEC [1992] OJ L113/8 is the most important of the recent Council directives on the identification of medicinal products. This major piece of European Community legislation was designed to consolidate and revise the EC laws on the labelling of medicinal products for human use and on package leaflets. In relation to labelling, Chapter II of the directive sets out a detailed list of particulars which must be included on the outer or immediate packaging of medicinal products. In relation to leaflets, Chapter III of the directive makes it obligatory to include a package leaflet containing detailed particulars for the information of users in the packaging of all medicinal products unless those particulars are set out on the outer or immediate packaging of the medicinal product itself. Articles 7, 8 and 9 set out a detailed list of particulars which must be included.

These required particulars replace those contained in Chapter IV of Directive 65/65/EEC (noted above) which is repealed by the later dir Articles 6 and 7 of Council Directive 75/319/EEC which had added to ⎓⎓ requirements imposed by Chapter IV of Council Directive 65/65/EEC are also repealed. Articles 10, 11 and 12 of Council Directive 92/27/EEC state that authorisations for placing medicinal products on the market should be refused if the labelling or leaflet requirements are not fulfilled, allow for the suspension of authorisation pending compliance, outline requirements for the approval of changes to labels and leaflets, permit certain exemptions from the requirements and allow for the issue of guidelines on special warnings and information.

Council Directive 92/73/EEC [1992] OJ L297/8 continues the process of the approximation of the laws and regulations relating to medicinal products by laying down additional provisions on the labelling of homeopathic medicinal products for human use.

9.3 LABELLING

Part V of the Medicines Act 1968 outlines the general regulatory background for the identification of medicinal products. Section 85 gives power to the Health Ministers of the United Kingdom to make regulations imposing such requirements as they consider necessary or expedient with respect to the labelling of containers and packages of medicinal products or the display of distinctive marks on such containers or packages. The purposes of any regulations made under this power are to ensure that medicinal products are correctly described and clearly identifiable, that appropriate warnings, information and instructions are given and, conversely, that false or misleading information is not given and that general safety in relation to medicinal products is promoted.

The power to make detailed regulations with respect to the labelling of containers and packages of medicinal products or the display of distinctive marks on such containers or packages was exercised primarily through the Medicines (Labelling) Regulations 1976 (S.I. 1976/1726). These Regulations have been subject to a number of amendments on a number of occasions. The amendments introduced by the Medicines (Labelling) Amendment Regulations 1992 (S.I. 1992/3273), designed to implement in part Council Directive 92/27/EEC, are substantial.

The 1976 Regulations have general effect in relation to medicinal products licensed or relicensed after 22 November 1976. The 1992 amendments apply to certain medicinal products for human use for which a product licence is granted or renewed on or after 1 January 1994. The 1976 Regulations will continue to apply to certain medicinal products outside the definitional scope of the 1992 amendments. By 1 January 1999, all major, commercially produced medicinal products had been subject to licence renewal, and so by that date were subject to the 1992 amendments.

9.4 LABELLING OF 'RELEVANT MEDICINAL PRODUCTS'

Regulation 4 of the 1976 Regulations indicates that the general requirements imposed by the Regulations apply to medicinal products which, in the course of a business carried on, are sold, supplied or are in the possession of a person for the purpose of sale or supply. Regulation 4 was substantially altered by the Medicines (Labelling) Amendment Regulations 1992 (S.I. 1992/3273). New regs. 4A, 4B, 4C, 4D and 4E were inserted into the 1976 Regulations. A further new regulation, reg. 4F, was introduced by the Medicines (Labelling and Leaflets) Amendment Regulations 1994 (S.I. 1994/104).

A new definition of 'relevant medicinal product' is also inserted into reg. 3, the interpretation regulation of the 1976 Regulations. 'Relevant medicinal product', for the purposes of the amendments, means a product to which Chapters II to V of the 1965 Directive applies in respect of which a product licence is granted or renewed on or after 1 January 1994.

In turn 'product to which Chapters II to V of the 1965 Directive applies' means a medicinal product to which, in accordance with art. 2 of Council Directive 65/65/ EEC as amended, art. 34 of Council Directive 75/319/EEC, art. 1 of Council Directive 89/342/EEC, art. 1 of Council Directive 89/343/ EEC and art. 1 of Council Directive 89/381/EEC apply. This definition appears convoluted but legally, can be understood by reference to the developments in European Community legislation referred to above. Practically it covers all major, commercially produced medicinal products.

Regulation 4A states that, with minor exceptions, containers and packages of relevant medicinal products shall be labelled to show the particulars set out in sch. 7 to the Regulations. The source of the new standards is Council Directive 92/27/EEC (noted above).

Schedule 7 sets out a list of standard labelling requirements for containers and packages of medicinal products for human use. Those requirements follow the wording of art. 2 of Council Directive 92/27/EEC:

(a)   the name of the product, followed, where the product contains one active ingredient and its name is an invented name, by the common name;

(b)   a statement of the active ingredients of the product expressed qualitatively and quantitatively per dosage unit or according to the form of administration for a given volume or weight, using the common names of the ingredients;

(c)   the pharmaceutical form of the product;

(d)   the contents of the product by weight, by volume or by number of doses of the product;

(e)   a list of excipients known to have a recognised action or effect. In relation to products which are injectable or are topical or eye preparations, all excipients;

(f)   the method and, if necessary, the route of administration of the product;

(g)   a special warning that the product must be stored out of reach of children;

(h)   any special warning required by the product licence for the product concerned;

(i)   the expiry date of the product (stating the month and year) in clear terms;

(j)   any special storage precautions for the product;

(k)   any special precautions for the disposal of any unused products or waste materials derived from such products;

(l)   the name of the holder of the marketing authorisation;

(m)   the address of the holder of the marketing authorisation;

(n)   the marketing authorisation number;

(o)   the manufacturer's batch reference;

(p)   where a product is intended for self-medication, any instruction on the use of the product.

Regulation 4A(2) indicates that where the container of a relevant medicinal product is not a blister pack and is too small to be labelled to show all of the particulars set out in sch. 7, it has, as a minimum, to be labelled to show the particulars set out in (a), (i), (l) and (o). Regulation 4A(3) states that where the container is a blister pack and is enclosed within a package which complies with the regulation, then it should be labelled to show the particulars set out in (a), (i), (l) and (o).

Regulation 4A(4) indicates that containers and packages of relevant medicinal products may be labelled to show a symbol or pictogram designed to clarify the particulars set out in sch. 7 or contain other information compatible with the summary of product characteristics which is useful for health education. 'Summary of product characteristics' means the information required to accompany any application for a product licence by virtue of art. 4a of Directive 65/65/EEC, which was inserted by art. 1(2) of Directive 83/570/EEC [1983] OJ L332/1), and amended by art. 1(1) and (4) of Directive 89/341/EEC, and can include the data sheet, if there is one.

Regulation 4B outlines the requirements for containers and packages of radiopharmaceuticals for human use. Containers and packages of products which are radiopharmaceuticals should be labelled to show the particulars set out in sch. 8 to the Regulations together with any particulars required by any other provision of the Regulations. Schedule 8, which is new, indicates the following standard labelling requirements for radiopharmaceuticals:

(1)   the container and the package shall be labelled in accordance with the 1985 Edition (as amended in 1990) of the Regulations for the Safe Transport of Radioactive Materials recommended by the International Atomic Energy Agency;

(2)   the labelling on the shielding shall explain in full the codings used on the vial and shall indicate, where necessary, for a given time and date, the

amount of radioactivity per dose or per vial and the number of capsules, or for liquids, the number of millilitres in the container;

(3) the vial shall be labelled to show:

(a) the name or code of the medicinal product, including the name or chemical symbol of the radionuclide;

(b) the international symbol for radioactivity;

(c) the name of the manufacturer; and

(d) the amount of radioactivity as specified in paragraph 2 above.

Regulation 4C states that all labelling of containers and packages of relevant medicinal products shall be legible and indelible, comprehensible and in English (or in English with another language). The Regulation, as amended, also states that, where holders of a marketing authorisation propose to alter the labelling relating to it in any respect relating to the new standard labelling requirements, they must notify the licensing authority of such proposed alteration. In the absence of specific notification of disapproval of the proposed alteration, the holder of the marketing authorisation may, after 90 days, supply the product with the altered labelling.

Regulation 4D outlines certain special requirements for the labelling of particular medicinal products. Where a relevant medicinal product is available in more than one pharmaceutical form or in more than one strength and the name of that product does not include the pharmaceutical form or the strength, then a statement of the pharmaceutical form or strength of that product, including the suitability of the product for a baby, child or adult, should be added after the name of the product, in the same style and size of letters as the name. This regulation also states that the requirement for a container or package of a relevant medicinal product to be labelled to show its name will not be met by a label showing an invented name liable to be confused by the common name.

Regulation 4E indicates that regs. 5 to 8, 11, 12, 14D and E, 15 to 17, 18(2) and 19 of the principal Regulations shall not apply to relevant medicinal products. While the new definition of 'relevant medicinal products' covers most of the commercially produced medicinal products today, which will be covered by this exemption, those Regulations will be relevant to all other medicinal products, as noted below.

9.4.1 Labelling of relevant dispensed medicinal products

Special rules apply to the labelling of relevant dispensed medicinal products. These rules were introduced by sch. 5 of the Medicines for Human Use (Marketing Authorisations Etc.) Regulations 1994 (S.I. 1994/3144). A relevant dispensed medicinal product is a relevant medicinal product prepared or dispensed in accordance with a prescription given by a practitioner. The container of a dispensed medical product must be labelled to show the following particulars:

(a)　the name of the person to whom the medicine is to be administered;

(b)　the name and address of the person who sells or supplies the medicinal product;

(c)　the date on which the medicinal product is dispensed;

(d)　where the relevant dispensed medicinal product has been prescribed by a practitioner, such of the following particulars as may be requested:

(i)　the name of the relevant medicinal product or its common name;

(ii)　directions for use of the relevant medicinal product; and

(iii)　precautions relating to the use of the relevant medicinal product;

or where a pharmacist, in the exercise of professional skill and judgment, is of the opinion that any of such particulars are inappropriate, and is unable to contact the medical practitioner after having made reasonably practicable efforts to do so, may exchange them for other particulars of the same kind;

(e)　a number of warning phrases as follows:

(i)　'Keep out of the reach of children' or words of direction of a similar meaning;

(ii)　'For external use only' within a rectangle if the product is not on the general sale list and is an embrocation, liniment, lotion, liquid antiseptic or other liquid preparation or gel and is for external use only.

Generally a container of a dispensed medicinal product does not have to be labelled with all of the above particulars as long as it is enclosed within a package which is labelled with the required particulars.

9.4.2　Labelling of relevant general sale list products

Special rules apply to relevant medicinal products on a general sale list. Again these rules were introduced by sch. 5 of the Medicines for Human Use (Marketing Authorisations Etc.) Regulations 1994. The rules are as follows:

(a)　if the product contains aloxiprin, aspirin or paracetamol, the words 'If symptoms persist consult your doctor' and, except where the product is for external use only, the recommended dosage;

(b)　if the product contains aloxiprin, the words 'Contains an aspirin derivative';

(c)　if the product contains aspirin, the words 'Contains aspirin' unless the product is for external use only or where the name of the product appears on the container or package and includes the word 'aspirin';

(d)　if the product contains paracetamol, the words 'Contains paracetamol' unless the name of the product appears on the container or package and includes the word 'paracetamol';

(e)   if the product contains paracetamol, the words 'Do not exceed the recommended dose'.

The phrases in (b), (c) and (d) may be combined where more than one of them apply to a particular general sale list product. The phrases must be in a prominent position within a rectangle in which there is no other matter.

9.4.3   Labelling of relevant medicinal products for pharmacy sale only
Special rules apply to relevant medicinal products for pharmacy sale only. Again these rules were introduced by sch. 5 of the Medicines for Human Use (Marketing Authorisations Etc.) Regulations 1994. Where a medicinal product for pharmacy sale only, is sold or supplied by retail, its container or package must be labelled to show the following particulars:

(a)   if the medicinal products contain aspirin, aloxiprin or paracetamol, then the particulars described above in relation to general sale list products;

(b)   The letter 'P' in a rectangle containing no other matter. This requirement also applies to wholesale dealings;

(c)   if the product is exempt from prescription only control by reason of the proportion or level in the product of any substance, the words 'Warning. Do not exceed the stated dose.' except where the product is for external use only or contains antihistaminic or other similar substances;

(d)   if the product is for the treatment of asthma or other conditions associated with bronchial spasm or contains ephedrine or any of its salts, the words 'Warning. Asthmatics should consult their doctor before using this product.' except where the product is for external use only;

(e)   if the product contains antihistaminic or similar substances or any of their salts or molecular compounds, the words 'Warning. May cause drowsiness. If affected do not drive or operate machinery. Avoid alcoholic drink.' except where the product is for external use only;

(f)   if the product is an embrocation, liniment, lotion, liquid antiseptic or other liquid preparation or gel and is for external use only, the words 'For external use only';

(g)   if the product contains hexachlorophane, either with the words 'Not to be used for babies' or a warning that the product is not to be administered to a child under two years except on medical advice.

The relevant words or phrases of warning must be in a rectangle within which there is no other matter. The phrases may be combined where more than one of them apply to a particular product for pharmacy sale only.

9.4.4   Labelling of relevant medicinal products for prescription only medicines
Special rules apply to relevant medicinal products in a prescription only list. Again these rules were introduced by sch. 5 of the Medicines for Human Use

(Marketing Authorisations Etc.) Regulations 1994. The container or package of a prescription only medicine must be labelled to show the following particulars:

(a)   except in the case of dispensed medicines, the letters 'POM' in capital letters within a rectangle within which there is no other matter of any kind;

(b)   if the product is an embrocation, liniment, lotion, liquid antiseptic or other liquid preparation or gel and is for external use only, the words 'For external use only';

(c)   if the product contains hexachlorophane, either with the words 'Not to be used for babies' or a warning that the product is not to be administered to a child under two years except on medical advice.

9.5   LABELLING OF HOMEOPATHIC PRODUCTS

Regulation 4F, and the related sch. 9, were inserted in the 1976 Regulations by the Medicines (Labelling and Leaflets) Amendment Regulations 1994 (S.I. 1994/104) and are designed to implement, in part, Council Directive 92/73/EEC (noted at 9.2). The regulation is designed to impose standard labelling requirements in respect of homeopathic products. Regulation 4F(1) indicates that containers and packages of homeopathic products should be labelled in a clear and legible manner to show a reference to their homeopathic nature, in particular by clear mention of the words 'homeopathic medicinal product'.

Regulation 4F(2) indicates that containers and packages of homeopathic medicinal products which are placed on the market must be labelled to show the particulars set out in sch. 9 and no other particulars. Those particulars, which follow the wording of Council Directive 92/73/EEC are as follows:

(a)   the scientific name of the stock or stocks followed by the degree of dilution, making use of the symbols of the pharmacopoeia used in relation to the homeopathic manufacturing procedure described therein for that stock or stocks;

(b)   the name and address of the holder of the certificate of registration and, where different, the name and address of the manufacturer;

(c)   the method of administration and, if necessary, route;

(d)   the expiry date of the product in clear terms, stating the month and year;

(e)   the pharmaceutical form;

(f)   the contents of the sales presentation;

(g)   any special storage precautions;

(h)   any special warning necessary for the product concerned;

(i)   the manufacturer's batch number;

(j)   the registration number allocated by the licensing authority followed by the letters 'HR' in capital letters;

(k)   the words 'homeopathic medicinal product without approved therapeutic indications';

(l)   a warning advising the user to consult a doctor if the symptoms persist during the use of the product.

9.6   LABELLING OF OTHER MEDICINAL PRODUCTS

As noted in 9.3, the 1992 amendments to the 1976 Regulations apply to certain medicinal products for human use for which a product licence is granted or renewed on or after 1 January 1994. By 1999 the vast majority of commercially produced medicinal products had fallen within the scope of these amendments. However, the 1976 Regulations will continue to apply to a minority of medicinal products outside the definitional scope of the 1992 amendments.

Many of the requirements imposed by the 1976 regulations are similar to those introduced for 'relevant medicinal products', and described above in section 9.4. In addition, the 1976 regulations had adopted the analogous approach of imposing general labelling requirements for all medicinal products, and more specific rules for dispensed medicinal products, general sale list products, products for pharmacy sale only and products for prescription only.

9.7   OFFENCES RELATING TO LABELS

Section 85(3), Medicines Act 1968 makes it clear that no person should, in the course of a business carried on, sell or supply, or possess for the purposes of sale or supply, any medicinal product in such circumstances as to contravene any requirements imposed by regulations made under s. 85. That warning is reinforced in s. 91(2) which makes it clear that any contravention of s. 85(3), or any general regulations made under this part of the Act, a summary or indicatable offence punishable by a fine or imprisonment or both.

Section 85(5) strengthens the general labelling and marking requirements. It indicates that no person should, in the course of a business carried on, sell or supply, or possess for the purposes of sale or supply, any medicinal product which is labelled or marked in such a way so as to describe the product falsely, or to be likely to mislead as to the nature or quality of the product, or as to the uses or effects of medicinal products of that description.

Again, the legislation contains further warnings about the consequences of breach of these legislative provisions. Section 91(1) indicates that any person who contravenes the provisions of s. 85(5) shall be guilty of an offence punishable on summary conviction by a fine, or on conviction on indictment by a fine or imprisonment or both.

The legislators are distinguishing between two types of offences in relation to the possession and sale or supply of medicinal products which have been wrongly labelled or marked. Marking a label in such a way as to describe the product falsely or to mislead the public as to its nature or quality or uses and effects, is a direct contravention of the primary legislation and is punishable as such as a criminal offence. Any other incorrect labelling or marking will amount to an offence under regulations made under the primary legislation. Although contravention of the regulations will also amount to a criminal offence and will be punishable as such, the discrete categorisation of the category, purpose and effect of the incorrect labelling or marking displays the legislators' intent in ensuring that medicinal products can be clearly identified by their users.

Regulation 20 of the 1976 Regulations makes it clear that contravention of ss. 85(3) or 86(2) of the Medicines Act 1968 or the Regulations themselves amounts to a criminal offence punishable on indictment by a fine or imprisonment or both or on summary conviction by a fine. This regulation reinforces the provisions of the 1968 Act which themselves indicate that breach of the enabling provisions amounts to a criminal offence.

9.8 THE LABELLING REQUIREMENTS AND COMMUNITY PHARMACISTS

The importance of the laws relating to the labelling of medicinal products should not be under-emphasised by community pharmacists. Close attention should be paid to the general requirements for all medicinal products and to the particular regulations applicable to specific types of medicinal product.

Undoubtedly the labelling requirements for medicinal products will be most readily fulfilled by the manufacturers of those products. Indeed manufacturers have been quick to accept their responsibilities and detailed guidance about the implementation of the legislative requirements and their implications has been published for the pharmaceutical industry by the Medicines Control Agency. The assumption of duty by manufacturers should not, however, lead to complacency on the part of community pharmacists for a number of reasons.

The primary reason for the need for caution is the fact that the legislation does not discriminate in apportioning liability for breach of its provisions. A pharmacist who sells or supplies medicinal products which do not conform to the detailed requirements may be found guilty of serious criminal offences.

The second reason for vigilance is the importance attached to the labelling requirements by the Royal Pharmaceutical Society of Great Britain. In its *Medicines, Ethics and Practice*, the Royal Pharmaceutical Society of Great Britain has stressed the importance of adherence to the general and specific standards. That guidance re-emphasises the particular rules in relation to dispensed medicinal products which are the type of medicinal products most relevant to the everyday work of community pharmacists. The advice also emphasises the regulations relating to prescription only medicines, products for pharmacy sale only and general sale list products, all of which are familiar to the practising community pharmacist.

In addition to the annotation of the legislation relating to the labelling of medicinal products, the advice offered by the Royal Pharmaceutical Society of

Great Britain is extended later in the Guide. The *Standards of Good Professional Practice* is published as an appendix to the Royal Society's *Code of Ethics*. Obligation 1.14 of the *Code of Ethics* requires that pharmacists must comply with the obligations in the *Standards of Good Professional Practice* where applicable. Failure to meet the *Standards* could form the basis of a complaint of misconduct.

In the published *Standards of Good Professional Practice*, pharmacists are advised, as part of the standards for dispensing procedures in community pharmacies, that labels of dispensed products must be clear and legible and that lettering must be mechanically printed. In addition, the Royal Pharmaceutical Society of Great Britain counsels that dispensed medicines must bear the additional cautionary and advisory labelling recommended in the *British National Formulary* where appropriate. Finally, in this section, the Royal Pharmaceutical Society of Great Britain indicates that the label must indicate the total quantity of the product dispensed in the container to which the label refers. If the total quantity is dispensed in more than one container, the quantity given on the label must be the amount in the container which bears that label and not the total amount. The requirement that simple, direct language should be used on labels for dispensed medicines is repeated later in the *Standards*.

One particular aspect of the practical implications of the labelling legislation for community pharmacists is particularly highlighted by the Royal Pharmaceutical Society for Great Britain. In its minimum requirements for pharmacy computer systems, the Royal Pharmaceutical Society for Great Britain advises on the relationship between pharmacy computer systems and the labelling requirements. The minimum requirements are supplementary to the *Code of Ethics*.

The minimum requirements begin by indicating that a community pharmacy computer system must be capable of producing labels for dispensed medicines, repackaged medicines and medicines prepared for sale in the pharmacy in accordance with the relevant regulation under the Medicines Act 1968 and the *Code of Ethics*. The recommended label size is 70mm by 36mm which is the size communicated to manufacturers and incorporated into package design. Labels must be clearly legible and lettering and numbering conventions must not cause ambiguity. The inadvertent carry over of patient details from one prescription to the next must be prevented. Finally, all warnings should be reproduced in such a manner that the sense of messages stated in the *British National Formulary* is retained. All warnings must be displayed in full, continuing on a second label if necessary.

9.9 LEAFLETS

Section 86, Medicines Act 1968 is concerned with leaflets. That section gives power to the Health Ministers of the United Kingdom to make regulations imposing such requirements as they consider necessary or expedient with respect to leaflets relating to medicinal products which are supplied, or intended to be supplied, with the products. The regulations are to apply to leaflets which are either enclosed in the containers or packages of the products or otherwise supplied to the user of the medicinal products. As with the labelling and marking requirements under s. 85, the legislation makes it clear that the general purpose behind the 'leaflet' regulations is to ensure that medicinal products are correctly described and clearly identifiable; that appropriate warnings, information and instructions are given and, conversely, that false or misleading information is not given and that general safety in relation to medicinal products is promoted.

Section 86, Medicines Act 1968 was substantially amended in 1994 by the Medicines Act 1968 (Amendment) Regulations 1994 (S.I. 1994/101). These Regulations implemented, *inter alia*, parts of Council Directive 92/27/EEC (see 9.2) and inserted a new subsection (4) into s. 86, Medicines Act 1968.

The new subsection requires that no medicinal product to which Chapters II to V of Council Directive 65/65/EEC apply (defined in 9.2) is to be supplied unless a leaflet containing specified information is enclosed in, or supplied with, the package, or the package itself carries that information. The specified information derives from regulations made under s. 86(1) which will be examined below. The amendment applies to products for which product licences are granted or renewed after 14 February 1994.

9.9.1 Leaflet requirements for relevant medicinal products

The power to make detailed regulations with respect to leaflets which are either enclosed in the containers or packages of the products or otherwise supplied to the user of the medicinal products, was exercised primarily through the Medicines (Leaflets) Regulations 1977 (S.I. 1977/1055). These principal regulations were substantially amended by the Medicines (Leaflets) Amendment Regulations 1992 (S.I. 1992/3274) and the Medicines Act 1968 (Amendment) Regulations 1994 (S.I. 1994/101).

The 1992 Amendment Regulations introduce a new reg. 3 into the 1977 Regulations. The new reg. 3, and the related sch. 2, outlines the standard requirements relating to leaflets to be included in the packages and containers of relevant medicinal products which are newly defined in the same manner as for the labelling regulations described above.

The net effect of the amendment to the 1977 Regulations (and to s. 86, Medicines Act 1968 noted above) is that all major, commercially produced medicinal products, for which product licences are granted or renewed after 14 February 1994, may not be supplied unless a leaflet containing specified information, is enclosed in, or supplied with, the package. By 1999 these requirements had applied to most medicinal products.

Regulation 3(2) indicates that all leaflets included in the package or container of any relevant medicinal product shall contain the particulars set out in sch. 2 in the order shown in the schedule. Those requirements follow the wording of art. 7 of Council Directive 92/27/EEC. Schedule 2 sets out the following particulars in the following order.

(1)   For identification of the medicinal product:

(a)   the name of the medicinal product followed where the product contains only one active ingredient and its name is an invented name, by the common name;
(b)   a full statement of the active ingredients and excipients expressed qualitatively and a statement of the active ingredients expressed quantitatively, using their common names, in the case of each presentation of the medicinal product;
(c)   the pharmaceutical form and the contents by weight, by volume or by number of doses of the product, in the case of each presentation of the product;
(d)   the pharmaco-therapeutic group or type of activity in terms easily comprehensible for the patient;
(e)   the name and address of the holder of the marketing authorisation and of the manufacturer.

(2)   The therapeutic indications.
(3)   A list of information which is necessary before taking the medicinal product, as follows:

(a)   contra-indications;
(b)   appropriate precautions for use;
(c)   forms of interaction with other medicinal products, with alcohol, tobacco and food and any other form of interaction which may affect the action of the medicinal product;
(d)   special warnings which:

(i)   take into account the particular condition of certain categories of users;
(ii)   mention, if appropriate, potential effects on the ability to drive vehicles or to operate machinery;
(iii)   give details of those excipients, knowledge of which is important for the safe and effective use of the product.

(4)   The necessary and usual instructions for proper use of the medicinal product which shall include:

(a)   the dosage;
(b)   the method and, if necessary, route of administration;

(c) the frequency of administration, specifying if necessary the time at which the medicinal product may or must be administered;

and where the nature of the product makes it appropriate, shall also include:

(d) the duration of treatment where it should be limited;
(e) the action to be taken in the case of an overdose;
(f) the course of action to be taken when one or more doses have not been taken;
(g) indication, if necessary, of the risk of withdrawal effects.

(5) A description of the undesirable effects which can occur with normal use of the medicinal product and if necessary, the action to be take in such a case, together with an express invitation to the patient to communicate any undesirable effect which is not mentioned in the leaflet to his doctor or pharmacist.
(6) A reference to the expiry date indicated on the label with:

(a) a warning against using the product after this date;
(b) where appropriate, special storage precautions;
(c) if necessary, a warning against certain visible signs of deterioration.

(7) The date upon which the leaflet was last revised.

All of the above particulars contained in such a leaflet shall be drawn up in accordance with the summary of the product characteristics or the data sheet with the information required to accompany an application for a product licence. The particulars must be in the English language, symbols and pictograms may be used to clarify the information and may also include other information useful for health education provided that it excludes information of a promotional nature.

Therapeutic indications need not be included in a leaflet where the product licence indicates that it need not be included. Where the leaflet relates to a relevant medicinal product which is available in more than one pharmaceutical form or in more than one strength and the name of the product does not include its pharmaceutical form or an indication of its strength, then a statement of the pharmaceutical form, and an indication of the strength shall be included immediately after, and in the same form, as the product name.

9.9.2 Leaflet requirements for other medicinal products

As noted above, the 1992 amendments apply to certain medicinal products for human use for which a product licence is granted or renewed on or after 1 January 1994. By 1999 the vast majority of commercially produced medicinal products had fallen under the scope of these amendments. However, the 1977

Regulations will continue to apply to certain medicinal products outside the definitional scope of the 1992 amendments.

Regulation 3(1) of the 1977 Regulations indicates that all leaflets included in the package or container of any proprietary medicinal product other than a relevant medicinal product shall contain the particulars set out in sch. 1. Schedule 1 sets out the following particulars:

(a)   the appropriate non-proprietary name of the proprietary medicinal product (if any) and a proprietary designation;

(b)   a statement of the appropriate quantitative particulars of the proprietary medicinal product together with relevant details of active and non-active ingredients;

(c)   the international non-proprietary name where there is one;

(d)   directions for use;

(e)   therapeutic indications;

(f)   contra-indications, warnings and precautions including any contraindications, warnings and precautions required to be given by the provisions of the product licence;

(g)   any special requirements for the handling and storage of the proprietary medicinal product;

(h)   the name and address of the holder of the product licence or the name and address of the person supplying or selling the product where it has been assembled under the supervision of a pharmacist under s. 10(1)(b), Medicines Act 1968;

(i)   the name and address of the manufacturer of the product or the name and address of the packer of the product.

All of the above particulars should be consistent with the product licence of the product, shall be written in English, in clear and understandable terms for the patient, and be clearly legible. The leaflet must not refer to any other proprietary medicinal product except in relation to instructions, contraindications, warnings or particulars that would be applicable to other products. Directions for use and therapeutic indications are not required for products whose product licences require the product to be sold or supplied in accordance with a prescription or where the product licence indicates that those particulars need not be included.

9.9.3   Offences relating to leaflets

Section 86(2), Medicines Act 1968 makes it clear that no person should, in the course of a business carried on, supply with any medicinal product, or possess for the purposes of supply, a leaflet which contravenes any requirements imposed by regulations made under s. 86. That caution is strengthened by s. 91(2) which makes it clear that any contravention of s. 86(2), or any general regulations made under this part of the Act, is a summary or indictable offence punishable by a fine or imprisonment or both.

Section 86(3) reinforces the general 'leaflet' rules by indicating that no person should, in the course of a business carried on, supply with a medicinal product, or possess for the purposes of supply, a leaflet which falsely describes the product, or is likely to mislead as to the nature or quality of the product, or as to the uses or effects of medicinal products of that description. Again, the legislation contains further warnings about the consequences of breach of these legislative provisions. Section 91(1) indicates that any person who contravenes the provisions of s. 86(3), shall be guilty of an offence punishable on summary conviction by a fine, or on conviction on indictment by a fine or imprisonment or both.

This last direction, that supply or possession for the purposes of supply, of a leaflet which falsely describes or is likely to mislead, is a direct contravention of the primary legislative provisions and will be directly punished as a criminal offence, reinforces the view that the legislators will not tolerate explicit or deliberate deception of the users of medicinal products and will promptly punish the supply of misinformation.

The Medicines Act 1968 (Amendment) Regulations 1994 amended s. 91(1), Medicines Act 1968 so that that any person who contravenes the provisions of the new s. 86(4), shall be guilty of an offence punishable on summary conviction by a fine, or on conviction on indictment by a fine or imprisonment or both.

9.9.4 The leaflet requirements and community pharmacists

As with the laws relating to the labelling of medicinal products, community pharmacists should pay close attention to the requirements concerning the provision of patient information leaflets for all major, commercially produced medicinal products, for which product licences are granted or renewed after 14 February 1994.

Again the emphasis will be on the manufacturer but that should not detract from the community pharmacist's obligations and responsibilities. In parallel with the labelling provisions, the legislation in relation to the provisions of leaflets is non-discriminatory in its application. The community pharmacist may face the same criminal consequences for non-compliance with the legislative provisions as the manufacturer or other supplier of medicinal products.

Members of the pharmacy profession have welcomed the availability of patient information leaflets and view them as a valuable resource to assist patients in improving their understanding of their medicines. (See further Furnell et al, 'Patient Information Leaflets' (1994) 252 Pharm J 7.) However the profession is also concerned at a number of other implications for community pharmacists of the implementation of the legislative requirements. Those implications include the adequate provision of patient information leaflets to pharmacists by pharmaceutical manufacturers, the notification of changes in those leaflets by manufacturers, the legal right to copy original pack information leaflets and, importantly, the potential consequences under civil law of a failure to provide a patient information leaflet or to provide one in specific circumstances.

The civil law consequences are dealt with below in the chapters on professional responsibility. As the detailed rules on the provisions of patient information leaflets are implemented, the remaining questions will be resolved. In the meantime, community pharmacists should note the detail of the regulations and remain alert to the consequences of their breach.

9.10   CONTAINERS

Section 87, Medicines Act 1968 outlines the primary legislative requirements relating to containers for medicinal products. The section gives power to the Health Ministers of the United Kingdom to make regulations prohibiting the sale or supply of medicinal products otherwise than in containers which comply with such requirements as they consider expedient. As with the labelling and marking and 'leaflet' requirements under ss. 85 and 86, the legislation makes it clear that the general purpose behind the 'container' regulations is to ensure that medicinal products are correctly described and clearly identifiable; that appropriate warnings, information and instructions are given and, conversely, that false or misleading information is not given and that general safety in relation to medicinal products is promoted. Section 87(1) also adds that the regulations should have the further purposes of preserving the quality of medicinal products and may require the containers to be of such strength or to be made of such materials, and to be of such shape and patterns, as may be prescribed.

The power to make detailed regulations with respect to containers for medicinal products was exercised primarily through the Medicines (Child Safety) Regulations 1975 (S.I. 1975/2000). These regulations have been amended on a number of occasions. The purpose behind the 1975 Regulations is to ensure that the sale and supply of certain medicinal products is prohibited unless they are contained in child resistant containers.

Regulation 2(1) of the 1975 Regulations, as amended, applies to medicinal products consisting of or containing aspirin or paracetamol in dosage form of tablets, capsules, pills, lozenges, pastilles, cachets, or suppositories for administration to human beings except effervescent tablets containing less than 25 per cent of aspirin or paracetamol by weight. Regulation 2, as originally drafted, applied only to the sale and supply of such products to children. The Medicines (Child Safety) Amendment Regulations 1976 (S.I. 1976/1643) extended the coverage to adults as well.

Regulation 2(2) of the 1975 Regulations states that, subject to a number of exceptions, the sale or supply of the medicinal products named in reg. 2(1), shall be prohibited unless enclosed in a child resistant container. A child resistant container is defined by reg. 2(3), as amended by reg. 2 of the Medicines (Child Safety) Amendment Regulations 1994 (S.I. 1994/1402) as an opaque or dark-tinted reclosable container which complies with British Standard 6652 or opaque or dark-tinted unit packages in the form of bubbles, blisters or other sealed units made of a variety of materials or containers possessing child resistant qualities required to be used for a particular medicinal product by virtue of its product licence. Regulation 2(4) indicates that where the medicinal product is for administration to children, the container must not contain more than 25 unit doses.

The exceptions referred to in reg. 2(1) are detailed in reg. 2(5) and (6). The requirement for child resistant containers does not apply where the sale and supply of the medicinal product is from a pharmacy in accordance with a prescription or where a person, not being a child, requests that the product is not supplied in a child resistant container. In addition, the requirement will not apply to sale or supply by a doctor or dentist to a patient or another doctor or dentist for a patient, a sale or supply in the course of business of a hospital for administration in accordance with the directions of a doctor or dentist, supply in situations not amounting to retail sale or where the medicinal product is for export only.

Special rules apply to certain liquid medicinal products for external use. The Medicines (Fluted Bottles) Regulations 1978 (S.I. 1978/40), made under ss. 87(1), 91(2), 91(3) and 129(5), Medicines Act 1968, set out the detailed rules in relation to such products. Regulation 1 of the 1978 Regulations indicates that 'external use', in relation to human beings, means:

> Application to the skin, teeth, mucosa of the mouth, throat, nose, ear, eye, vagina or anal canal but does not include the use of throat sprays, nasal drops, nasal sprays, nasal inhalations, teething preparations or dental gels.

Regulation 2 states that, for the purposes of promoting safety in relation to medicinal products and securing that medicinal products are readily identifiable, the sale or supply of liquid medicinal products for external use which contain any of the substances set out in the schedule to the regulations, shall be prohibited unless such products are contained in a ribbed or fluted bottle. A ribbed or fluted bottle is one the outer surface of which is fluted vertically with ribs or grooves recognisable by touch. The schedule lists some 34 different substances to which the requirements apply.

Regulation 3 outlines a number of exceptions to the fluted bottle requirement. The requirement does not apply to bottles with a capacity greater than 1.14 litres, to those substances with specific exceptions mentioned in the schedule, to certain medicinal products on prescription only, to medicinal products packed for export use only outside the United Kingdom, to medicinal products sold or supplied solely for the purpose of scientific education, research or analysis, to eye or ear drops sold or supplied in a plastic container or where the product licence certifies otherwise.

9.10.1   Labelling of containers for controlled drugs

Special rules apply to the labelling of containers for certain controlled drugs. These rules are to be found in reg. 18, Misuse of Drugs Regulations (S.I. 1985/2066) made under ss. 7, 10, 22 and 31, Misuse of Drugs Act 1971. Regulation 18(1) applies specifically to sch. 2 and sch. 3 controlled drugs. These drugs, other than as a preparation, must be supplied in a container plainly marked with the amount of the drug contained in it. If the drug is a preparation made up into tablets, capsules or other dosage units, the container must be marked with the amount of the controlled drug or drugs in each dosage unit and the number of dosage units in it. Where the controlled drug is a preparation but is not made up as a tablet, capsule or other dosage unit, the container must be marked with the total amount of preparation in it and the percentage of controlled drugs in the preparation.

These requirements as a whole do not apply to other scheduled controlled drugs, to poppy straw and, importantly, to controlled drugs supplied on prescription.

9.10.2   Offences relating to containers

Section 87(2), Medicines Act 1968 states that no person should, in the course of a business carried on, supply with any medicinal product, or possess for the purposes of supply, any medicinal product which contravenes any requirements imposed by regulations made under s. 87. Section 91(2) indicates that any contravention of s. 87(2), or any general regulations made under that part of the 1968 Act, a summary or indictable offence punishable by a fine or imprisonment or both.

Regulation 4, Medicines (Child Safety) Regulations 1975 states that contravention of s. 87(2), Medicines Act 1968, the enabling provision for the Regulations, or the Regulations themselves, amounts to a criminal offence punishable on indictment to a fine or imprisonment or both or on summary conviction to a fine.

Regulation 4, Medicines (Fluted Bottles) Regulations 1978 makes it clear that contravention of s. 87(2), Medicines Act 1968 or the Regulations themselves amounts to a criminal offence punishable on indictment to a fine or imprisonment or both or on summary conviction to a fine. Section 18, Misuse of Drugs Act 1971 states that it is an offence to contravene any regulations made under the Act.

9.10.3   Containers and community pharmacists

As with the rules on labelling and leaflets, community pharmacists should note carefully the regulations relating to containers for medicinal products. The placing of medicinal products into containers is an important activity in the work of community pharmacists and this importance is reflected in the close management of the activity by the detailed regulations.

The Royal Pharmaceutical Society of Great Britain has also recognised the significance of the rules relating to containers. In its published *Standards of Good Professional Practice*, the Royal Pharmaceutical Society of Great Britain gives specific advice on dispensing containers, as part of its list of standards for dispensing procedures in community pharmacies.

The direction indicates that the container must be appropriate for the product dispensed and the user. All containers intended for medicinal products must be protected and free from contamination. All solid dose and all oral liquid preparations must be dispensed in a reclosable child resistant container unless:

(a)   the medicine is in an original pack or patient pack which makes this inadvisable;

(b)   the patient will have difficulty in opening a child resistant container;

(c)   a specific request is made that the product shall not be dispensed in a child resistant container; or

(d)   no suitable child resistant container exists for a particular liquid preparation.

In cases (a) to (d) advice must be given to keep all medicines out of the reach of children.

The Royal Pharmaceutical Society of Great Britain's advice continues that plastic jars, bottles and caps for solid or liquid dose preparations must not be reused as satisfactory cleaning cannot be ensured. It warns that under no circumstances may reclosable child resistant closures be used more than once, as continued use affects the child resistant properties of the closure. Finally, it advises that glass containers are capable of being reused only after satisfactory cleaning and drying. High standards must be maintained, which may make reuse uneconomical.

It is important to remember that Obligation 1.14 of the *Code of Ethics* requires that pharmacists must comply with the obligations in the standards of good professional practice where applicable. Failure to meet the standards could form the basis of a complaint of misconduct.

Finally, and most importantly, the container regulations make it clear that contravention of the provisions amounts to a criminal offence and community pharmacists should note that this liability may attach directly to them.

9.11   OTHER IDENTIFICATION MEASURES

Section 88, MA 1968 is concerned with the colours, shapes and markings of medicinal products. The section gives power to the Health Ministers of the

United Kingdom to make regulations imposing such requirements as they consider expedient with respect to the colour, shape and distinctive marks to be displayed on medicinal products. As with the labelling and marking, 'leaflet' and 'container' requirements under ss. 85, 86 and 87, the legislation makes it clear that the general purpose behind the 'container' regulations is to ensure that medicinal products are correctly described and clearly identifiable; that appropriate warnings, information and instructions are given and, conversely, that false or misleading information is not given and that general safety in relation to medicinal products is promoted.

Regulations made under s. 88 may control and regulate the colour, shape and distinctive marks on specified classes of medicinal products. Section 88(3) indicates that no person should, in the course of a business carried on, sell or supply, or possess for the purposes of sale or supply, any medicinal product which contravenes any requirements imposed by regulations made under s. 88. Section 91(2) indicates that any contravention of any general regulations made under this part of the 1968 Act, is a summary or indictable offence punishable by a fine or imprisonment or both.

The power to make detailed regulations with respect to colours of medicinal products was exercised primarily through the Medicines (Child Safety) Regulations 1975 (S.I. 1975/2000) Regulation 3(1) indicates that medicinal products consisting of or containing aspirin or paracetamol in dosage form of tablets, capsules, pills, lozenges, pastilles, cachets, or suppositories for administration to children except effervescent tablets containing less than 25 per cent of aspirin or paracetamol by weight must be white in colour. Regulation 4 makes it clear that contravention of the regulations amounts to a criminal offence punishable on indictment to a fine or imprisonment or both or on summary conviction to a fine.

Section 89, MA 1968 gives power to the Health Ministers of the United Kingdom to make regulations imposing such requirements as they consider necessary or expedient with respect to the display of automatic machines, on information relating to medicinal products offered or exposed for sale by means of such machines. Section 89(2) indicates that no person should offer or expose for sale any medicinal product by means of an automatic machine in such circumstances as to contravene any requirements imposed by regulations made under s. 89. Section 91(2) indicates that any contravention of any general regulations made under this part of the 1968 Act, a summary or indictable offence punishable by a fine or imprisonment or both. To date, no regulations have been made under this section.

9.12 DEFENCES

Anyone charged with any of the offences relating to the identification of medicinal products under the provisions discussed above, is provided with two limited but important defences under ss. 121 and 122, Medicines Act 1968.

Section 121 states that where anyone charged with an offence in respect of a contravention of ss. 85–90 can prove to the satisfaction of the court that they acted with all due diligence to ensure that the legislative provision would not be contravened, and that the eventual contravention was due to the act or default of another person, then they should be acquitted of the offence. Notification of reliance on the due diligence defence must be served on the prosecutor. Section 121 also indicates that where the contravention of any of the provisions of ss. 85–90 constitutes an offence and is due to the act or default of another person, then that other person may also be charged with and convicted of that same offence, and shall be liable on conviction to the same punishment.

The meaning of a number of phrases within s. 121 has been discussed in other contexts. 'Act or default' has been interpreted to mean wrongful act or default at the time of the carrying out of the act by the other person (*Noss Farm Products Ltd* v *Lilico* [1945] 2 All ER 609 and *Lamb* v *Sunderland and District Creamery Ltd* [1951] 1 All ER 923). Proof of the act or default of the other person is required although mens rea or negligence need not be proved (*Lindley* v *W G Horner & Co. Ltd* [1950] 1 All ER 234, *Lamb* v *Sunderland and District Creamery Ltd* [1951] 1 All ER 923, *Lester* v *Balfour Williamson Merchant Shippers Ltd* [1953] 2 QB 168, *Fisher* v *Barrett & Pomeroy (Bakers) Ltd* [1954] 1 All ER 249 and *Moore* v *Ray* [1950] 2 All ER 561).

Whether an individual has exercised all due diligence is a question of fact. The due diligence requirement has again been discussed in a number of other contexts (*Pearce* v *Cullen* (1952) 96 Sol Jo 132, *Tesco Supermarkets Ltd* v *Nattras* [1972] AC 153, *Riverstone Meat Co. Pty Ltd* v *Lancashire Shipping Co. Ltd* [1960] 1 All ER 193). Acquittal of an individual under this defence does not depend on the conviction of the other party (*RC Hammett Ltd* v *Crabb* [1931] All ER Rep 70, *Malcolm* v *Cheek* [1947] 2 All ER 881 and *R* v *Epsom Justices, ex parte Dawnier Motors Ltd* [1960] 3 All ER 635).

A second limited defence is provided for by s. 122, Medicines Act 1968. In any proceedings for an offence in respect of a contravention of ss. 85–90, it shall be a defence for the defendant to prove that the substance or article was one which could be lawfully sold or supplied, or offered for sale or supply, in the United Kingdom, under the name or purpose for which it was eventually sold or supplied or offered for sale or supply and has a written warranty to that effect. The defendant will also have to show that no reason existed to believe that it was otherwise and that, at the time it was sold or supplied, or offered for sale, it was in the same state as when it was purchased. The defence can also be relied on by an employee of the person who purchased the article or substance.

Notification of this defence will also have to be served on the prosecutor together with a copy of the warranty relied upon. By s. 122(6), names or descriptions entered into invoices supplied with the article or substance are deemed to amount to a written warranty that the article or substance can be sold, supplied or offered for sale, under that name or description without contravening any of the provisions of ss. 85–88, Medicines Act 1968.

Section 123, Medicines Act 1968 makes it clear that the wilful application of a false warranty to an article or substance by an individual relying on the warranty defence, or the supply of a false warranty by the individual supplying the article or substance in question, will themselves become criminal offences under the 1968 Act punishable on summary conviction by a fine or on indictment by a fine or a term of imprisonment or both.

9.13   CONCLUSION

The objectives of the detailed regulations on the identification of medicinal products are to ensure that medicinal products are correctly described and clearly identifiable, that appropriate warnings, information and instructions are given and, conversely, that false or misleading information is not given and that general safety in relation to medicinal products is promoted. The detail of those regulations and the extent of the legislative management reflect the importance that the legislators attach to this issue. Criminal liability attaches to those who sell or supply medicinal products in circumstances which contravene the provisions of the legislation. The significance of the issue of the identification of medicinal products is reinforced by the importance attached to it by the Royal Pharmaceutical Society of Great Britain in its detailed guidance on appropriate standards and in the consequences of a failure to meet those standards.

The rules on the identification of medicinal products are complex, made so by the requirement to implement EC Council Directives. The directives and the amendments to the legislative provisions are designed to revise and consolidate the law on identification. In the longer term that purpose will be achieved. In the short term, community pharmacists will need to be aware of the content of the rules and the implications for their practice.

TEN

Professional responsibility — liability in negligence

10.1 INTRODUCTION

The pharmacist undertakes a variety of roles in relation to the provision of health care. Pharmacists are expected to carry out their various professional roles, and the duties and obligations which arise from them, in a careful and reliable manner. This is what we refer to as professional responsibility. Pharmacists are under a duty to act professionally and responsibly.

Many writers argue that the issue of professional responsibility only arises when professionals have failed to fulfil their obligations by performing their roles carelessly and irresponsibly. The extent of a professional's responsibility can only be measured by analysing the implications of an omission to carry out professional roles. So, for example, the scope of a professional's duty is often gauged by examining the extent to which the civil law holds the professional liable in negligence. Consequential advice is usually to guarantee adequate professional indemnity insurance.

It cannot be denied that specific sanctions flow from a failure to carry out professional roles. Such sanctions might be criminal, civil or administrative in nature. However, to take the view that professional responsibility is restricted to the analysis of the situations where a professional has failed to act is to take a narrow view. Professional responsibility is an integral aspect of being a professional. Acting responsibly is not only about considering the possibilities of being criminally prosecuted, civilly liable in damages or censured by an administrative tribunal. Careful and conscientious practice results in no criminal, civil or administrative liability. Having a knowledge of the attributes of responsibility, and implementing these into professional practice by acting carefully and responsibly improves healthcare and improves the professions, including pharmacy, which make up the health care team.

The pharmacist's professional role has necessarily changed and altered in recent years. The practice of pharmaceutical care is now obliging the pharmacist to share responsibility for the design, implementation and monitoring of a therapeutic plan which seeks to achieve a set of desired therapeutic objectives. This new role has been enthusiastically accepted and implemented by the pharmacy profession.

However, it is important to remember that the change of role has a direct parallel impact on the scope and extent of a pharmacist's professional responsibility. Adopting a new professional role necessitates performing the functions associated with that role in a careful and conscientious manner. The corollary is that careless and inadvertent implementation of the role attracts the potential for liability in negligence, a potential which will not go unnoticed by those charged with advising claimants.

Acting professionally is not limited to the obligation to conform to the requirements of the law. It includes an obligation to comply with the administrative and organisational requirements of the National Health Service within which the pharmacist is a crucial team member. Acting professionally also involves compliance with the requirements of the pharmacy profession. Specific censure arises from a failure to act professionally within the National Health Service and within the pharmacy profession. The nature, breadth and implications of those sanctions will be explored in chapter twelve. Acting professionally also includes an understanding of ethics and the place of ethics in the professional setting. The ethical aspects of professional responsibility will be explored in the next chapter.

Finally, it is important to remember that the scope of professional responsibility described in this chapter also complements the range of duties and obligations which the pharmacist undertakes in relation to the sale and supply of medicinal drug products, as outlined in chapters five to nine.

10.2   A BRIEF NOTE ON THE LAW OF TORT

The civil law recognises that every individual has certain rights, both personal and in respect of property, which it will protect by compelling anyone who infringes that right to pay damages (or occasionally some other remedy) to the injured party. Infringement of one of these rights is called a tort. The word tort comes from the French word *tort* meaning wrong. Examples of torts are negligence, defamation, nuisance and trespass.

It is important to stress that there does not have to have been a prior relationship between the claimant and the defendant for liability in tort to arise. For example, it is well established that a road user owes a duty of care (in the tort of negligence) to other road users. Breach of that duty, by way of an accident, may result in the payment of substantial damages. The careless driver may not know nor have ever met the accident victim. This fact does not prevent the law of tort from recognising the legal relationship, and allowing the claimant victim to recover compensation. In this regard, the law of tort differs from other aspects of the civil law. There can be no liability in contract, for example, without a pre-arranged, agreed contractual relationship between the parties.

Liability in tort usually requires an element of fault on the part of the wrongdoer. However, there are some torts of strict liability where the wrongdoer will be automatically liable even in the absence of fault. In a similar way, an essential element of a tort is usually that the injured party has suffered some sort of harm or loss as a result of the wrongdoer's conduct; but there are some torts where the claimant does not have to prove loss. These torts are said to be actionable *per se*.

Sometimes one person may be held to be liable for torts committed by others, even though that person was in no way to blame for the wrong and may not have been present when the wrong took place. This principle is known as vicarious liability. The most important example of vicarious liability is the liability of an employer for the wrongful acts of an employee. Liability in this situation depends on two conditions. The first is that the employee was acting under a contract of service or employment, at the time the wrongful act was carried out. Normally this will be fairly straightforward. However, it is important to note the distinction between contracts *of service* involving employees and contracts *for the provision of services* involving independent contractors.

The second condition is that the wrongful act must have been committed during the course of employment. There has been a considerable amount of case law on the meaning of the phrase 'course of employment'. Generally speaking, if an employee is doing what he or she is employed to do even if he or she is doing it carelessly then the employer will be liable.

The justification for holding employers liable for the wrongful acts of their employees is both that the employer exerts some sort of control over the activities of the employee and also that the employer holds insurance cover for the consequences of the employee's wrongful acts. The first justification does not have as much plausibility as it once did. For example, Boots plc as an employer would have no direct control over the individual activities of the pharmacists who work in its shops.

The vicarious liability of an individual employer does not negate the individual liability of an employee. It is in addition to the individual liability of the employee. The consequences of this are that the individual employee might still be joined as a party to the claim or that the employer will expect an indemnity from the employee towards the cost of the claim and any damages paid as a result, or some other form of legal retribution. Liability for damages and actual payment of damages are two separate matters, however. A successful claimant may not claim two sets of damages. Damages will be awarded against one defendant only.

As noted above, the primary remedy in tort is the award of damages by the court to the claimant for infringement of a legally recognised right by the defendant. It is important to note that, potentially, there is no limit to the award of damages in tort. Although there are strict rules on the causation, remoteness of loss, and the assessment of damages, awards in tort can be significant, and in personal injury cases have run into millions of pounds. Again, this is in contrast to other areas of the civil law. In contract, for example, the rules on the assessment of damages are less complex, with the claimant generally receiving what was lost.

Occasionally, the court may be persuaded to award an alternative remedy to damages. For example, a more appropriate remedy in trespass might be an injunction, which is an order of a court preventing the person affected by it from carrying out certain activities. In the case of trespass, an injunction would prevent the defendant trespasser from coming back onto the claimant's property. Remedies, such as an injunction, are only given out at the discretion of the court, and are not available as of right.

10.3   THE TORT OF NEGLIGENCE

Negligence has become the most important of all of the torts, although its development really only started some 70 years ago. This importance is mainly due to the fact that most claims for compensation, either for personal injury or property damage, are based on the tort of negligence. In addition, there appears to be no limit to the number of negligent situations which can arise. Negligence can arise as a result of careless acts, omissions to act or careless statements.

The onus of proof in a negligence claim lies with the claimant. In order to prove that a defendant is liable for the tort of negligence, the claimant must establish that the following three elements are present:

(a)   the defendant owed the claimant a legal duty of care;
(b)   the defendant was in breach of that duty of care;
(c)   the claimant suffered loss as a result of the defendant's breach.

All three elements of the tort of negligence must be proved together. So even where there has been obvious negligent conduct, there can be no liability in the tort of negligence if the court holds that the defendant does not owe a duty of care to the claimant. Even where a duty of care can be established, if there has been no breach the defendant will not be liable. Further, although the claimant may prove that the defendant acted negligently, if that negligence has not caused the claimant's loss or that loss, is too remote, the defendant will not be liable. Finally, even though the defendant has acted negligently, and has caused the claimant's loss, liability may be avoided if an appropriate defence can be proved.

10.3.1 The duty of care

The question of whether a duty of care exists within any particular relationship is a question of law. It is often the most difficult aspect of the negligence action for the lay person to understand. It is a commonly held belief that where a person has suffered loss or damage as a result of the carelessness of another, damages will be payable as a matter of course. That an action in negligence is dismissed by a court, without an order to pay damages, because of a failure to establish a legal duty of care is often difficult for the claimant to comprehend. The claimant sees that carelessness causing harm has occurred and wonders why those elements alone cannot establish liability.

Even where the careless conduct is not so obvious, the claimant often believes that the only significant element of the claim will be measuring the standard of care expected of that person in those particular circumstances against what actually happened. Such considerations are also often to the forefront of the person being sued. Claimants and defendants concentrate on the facts of their own actual case: for example, 'why did the pharmacist recommend that particular treatment?', or, 'should I have checked the prescription with the dispensing doctor?'

The claimant is attempting to show that each defendant (pharmacist, doctor, manufacturer) owes each claimant (patient, consumer) a duty of care in this type of situation. The specific facts of the individual's case are irrelevant to whether a legal duty of care arises in a particular situation. Those facts will have a more important bearing on the issue of whether the duty of care has been broken. A claimant must be able to persuade a court to rule that, as a matter of law, a duty of care is owed in a particular relationship. This is usually done by the claimant pointing to precedents establishing such a duty, either by factual equivalent, or by analogy.

There are some relationships where the courts have already ruled that a legal duty of care does arise. As we shall see below, these include the pharmacist/ patient relationship. They also include the manufacturer/consumer relationship and the doctor/patient relationship. The fact that there are some well-established 'duty' relationships, recognised in law, does not mean that the issue of the existence of the duty of care has no significance.

New duty situations arise on a regular basis. When they do, the courts address them on the basis of particular principles and rules. The approach of the courts to the issue of the existence of a duty of care in novel situations has varied over a period of time. At present, the strategy of the courts is to limit the existence of a duty of care in new situations, but the approach may change again over time.

10.3.2 Breach of the duty of care

If a duty of care is established (and indeed in many situations it is often conceded) the claimant must then prove that the defendant was in breach of the duty. This is a question of fact not law. Two main questions arise under this heading. First, the court will seek to establish the standard of care which is expected of the defendant. Secondly, the court will ascertain whether, as a fact, the defendant has reached that standard of care. If not, a breach has occurred, and the court will go on to determine the issue of whether the breach has caused the claimant's loss. If the defendant has reached the appropriate standard, then the duty of care has not been broken and the claim must fail.

What is the standard of care which is expected or required of the defendant? The standard of care required is that of the ordinary reasonable defendant. This standard has been established over a considerable period of time by the courts. Such a standard could be said to be advantageous to the defendant. The test means that the defendant need not be perfect. While the defendant has to take care, he or she need only take reasonable care; and taking reasonable care can, and does, allow for mistakes.

An objective test is applied. To determine whether a defendant has come up to the reasonable defendant standard the question asked is 'did the defendant come up to the standard which would have been achieved by a prudent and reasonable person acting in the same circumstances?'. For the most part, the defendant will be judged against the standards expected of ordinary members of the public. For example, the standard expected of a driver is measured against a reasonable driver. However, where a person professes to have a particular skill or expertise, the standard of care is measured against the standard expected of a reasonable person having the same skill or expertise.

If the defendant is a pharmacist, and the alleged careless conduct arose in the pharmacy, the standard of care expected is that of the ordinary reasonable pharmacist. The ordinary reasonable pharmacist is not perfect, does not have to agree with other pharmacists, nor be the best pharmacist in the country (*Bolam* v *Friern Hospital Management Committee* [1957] 1 All ER 118).

The claimant has the onus of proof in a negligence action. In many cases, the task of proving that a defendant did not reach the appropriate standard may be a difficult one for the claimant. It is difficult as it involves a detailed investigation of the defendant's procedures and conduct, a comparison with existing standards, and a contrast with procedures adopted by others in the same field. The claimant will need to employ an expert witness who can analyse these processes and procedures and pinpoint any lack of care which may have caused the careless conduct and therefore caused the injury. A claimant who is unable to prove a breach of duty may have to bear the loss without compensation, unless there is another available legal basis for the claim.

Sometimes the court may be prepared to apply the doctrine of *res ipsa loquitur* (the thing speaks for itself). This doctrine has the effect of relieving the claimant of the burden of proving negligence. It may be applied where the defendant's conduct is clearly negligent in that the claimant's injury would not have happened in the ordinary course of events without negligence and there is no satisfactory alternative explanation for the injury other than negligence by the defendant. The effect of the rule is that the onus of proof is shifted to the defendant. The court will infer negligence on the part of the defendant without the need for the claimant to identify the cause of the injury or explain how the defendant failed to take reasonable care. In turn, the defendant will be liable unless evidence can be adduced to show that negligence did not cause the claimant's loss.

10.3.3 Proving damage in negligence

Once it has been established that the defendant is in breach of the duty of care, the claimant must show that he or she has suffered loss. Again, a non-lawyer may find this difficult to understand, because non-lawyers usually view the issue of damages in terms of monetary compensation. Monetary compensation will only be payable where the claimant can show that the defendant's breach of the duty has caused loss. In law this involves two separate issues — the issue of causation and the issue of remoteness of damage.

The causation issue is concerned with the question of cause and effect: did the defendant's breach of duty cause the claimant's loss? The claim will fail if this link cannot be proved. More practically, the claimant must show that if it was not for the carelessness of the defendant there would have been no loss.

It is clear, however, that the losses suffered by a claimant may be immense, even unlimited. The courts have developed a number of rules which limit the extent of the losses for which the defendant must compensate the claimant. These rules are concerned with remoteness of loss or damage. The main rule is that the defendant is only liable to compensate a claimant for the type of damage which was reasonably foreseeable as a result of the wrongful act (*The Wagon Mound* [1961] AC 388 and *The Wagon Mound (No. 2)* [1966] 2 All ER 709).

10.3.4 Defences to a negligence claim

Where the claimant has successfully established all of the elements of the negligence claim against the defendant, but has in some way contributed to the injuries, the defendant may raise the defence of contributory negligence. As a result the claimant's damages may be reduced in direct proportion to the extent to which he or she is to blame for the injuries. The most common example of contributory negligence is when a road traffic accident victim's injuries, otherwise caused by a negligent driver, have been exacerbated by a failure to wear a seat belt.

Further the defendant might argue that the operative cause of the claimant's injuries was some act occurring after the negligent conduct, or that the claimant voluntarily assumed the risks associated with a course of action, after having been given an adequate warning of them. This defence — *volenti non fit injuria* — which has the effect of completely defeating the claimant's claim other than in exceptional circumstances, is rarely applied by the courts. The reason for this is that the type of behaviour which would come within the defence would also usually amount to contributory negligence and a more appropriate and equitable outcome could be achieved by applying the rules relating to contributory negligence.

Under the Limitation Act 1980, as amended, actions in tort, which involve personal injury, must be commenced within three years of the date when the cause of action accrued. Amendments to the limitation legislation mean that the three year period begins with the date when the claimant became possessed of full knowledge about the case. Full knowledge means knowledge of the facts that the injury is significant; the injury is attributable in whole or in part to the acts or omissions complained of; and the identity of the defendant.

A further discretion is given by the limitation legislation to allow claims after the three year period, even if the delay is not attributable to lack of knowledge concerning a material fact. Guidelines have been produced to assist a court in its decision to exercise this discretion:

(a)   the length of time and reasons for the claimant's delay;

(b)   the extent to which the cogency of evidence adduced by either party may be affected by the delay;

(c)   the defendant's conduct after the cause of action arose, including his or her response to requests by the claimant for information or inspection for the purpose of ascertaining relevant facts;

(d)   duration of any disability of the claimant after the cause of action arose;

(e)   the promptness and reasonableness of the claimant's conduct once he or she knew that there might be a cause of action; and

(f)   the steps taken by the claimant to obtain expert advice and the nature of the advice received.

A defendant, anticipating being sued for compensation in a negligence claim, might attempt to limit liability, by issuing, for example, an appropriately worded exclusion clause. Under s. 2(1), Unfair Contract Terms Act 1977, it is not possible for a person who acts in the course of a business to exclude or restrict liability for negligence where this results in personal injury or death.

It is important to note that a claimant, who is injured as a result of careless conduct and behaviour, and who is able to overcome the legal hurdles outlined above, may receive substantial compensation, including damages for physical injury, psychological injury, and economic loss, including loss of earnings.

10.4   THE PHARMACIST AND THE TORT OF NEGLIGENCE

It is well-established in United Kingdom law that the relationship between the pharmacist and the patient is one which gives rise to a duty of care in certain circumstances. In *Collins* v *Hertfordshire County Council* [1947] 1 KB 633, a patient in a hospital, while undergoing an operation, was killed by an injection of cocaine which was given by the operating surgeon in the mistaken belief that it was procaine. The operating surgeon had ordered procaine on the telephone, but the resident house surgeon has misheard procaine as cocaine. The resident house surgeon had orally asked the pharmacist to make up a cocaine with adrenaline mixture, described by Hilbery J, the trial judge, as a dosage and mixture that 'nobody has ever heard of injecting . . . into anybody'.

It was shown, on the facts, that the pharmacist was without doubt aware that the solution was for injection as part of the operative procedure on the patient. Significantly, it was also shown that the hospital's procedures relating to orders for dangerous drugs had been totally ignored. These procedures included the requirements that oral instructions for the ordering of drugs was not permitted and that all prescriptions for dangerous drugs had to be initialled by a medical officer and the number of doses specified. Those requirements had not been complied with, resulting in a dangerous and negligent system. Both the resident house surgeon and the hospital pharmacist had contributed to the danger and the negligence.

As a brief aside, the hospital which employed the resident house surgeon and the pharmacist in this case, was eventually held to be liable to pay the compensation to the deceased patient's wife. This was by virtue of the application of the doctrine of vicarious liability (see 10.2).

In *Dwyer* v *Roderick* (1983) 80 Law Society Gazette 3003, Dr Ian Roderick wrote a prescription for Mrs Joan Dwyer, who had complained to him of severe headaches, for a painkilling drug which was successful in the treatment of migraine. The drug, ergotamine tartrate (Migril), is extremely dangerous if not taken in proper doses. It can produce gangrene. Dr Roderick did not prescribe the drug in the proper doses. Mrs Dwyer took the prescription to the pharmacy of Cross Chemists (Banbury) Ltd. There she was given ergotamine tartrate in a container displaying the exact dosage as recommended and prescribed by Dr Roderick.

Mrs Dwyer began to take the drug as directed and rapidly became very ill. During this time she was seen by a partner of Dr Roderick, Dr Jackson, who called to see Mrs Dwyer from his own home and therefore did not have her medical notes with him. He gave evidence that he was unaware that Mrs Dwyer was taking ergotamine tartrate. He stated that he had examined drugs that were on her bedside but had not seen ergotamine tartrate. By the time the mistake was discovered Mrs Dwyer was suffering from gangrene and her toes had to be amputated. As a result she became permanently crippled.

In the High Court, Stuart-Smith J noted that negligence was admitted by Dr Roderick who had written the prescription and by the pharmacy which had dispensed it. There were therefore two main issues to be decided. First, the judge had to decide whether any further liability lay with Dr Jackson. In an attempt to limit its liability the pharmacy had joined Dr Jackson as another defendant. The judge held that the overwhelming likelihood was that on Dr Jackson's first visit to Mrs Dwyer a bottle containing ergotamine tartrate was by her bedside. Dr Jackson had persuaded himself, during the eight years which it took for the case to come to trial, that he could not have known that the plaintiff was taking the drug.

Having decided that Dr Jackson had also been negligent, the judge had to decide what the proper apportionment of liability should be. Accordingly the judge awarded damages of £100,000 against Dr Roderick, Dr Jackson and the pharmacy to be apportioned as to 45 per cent to Dr Roderick, 15 per cent to Dr Jackson and 40 per cent to the pharmacy.

On appeal, the Court of Appeal reversed the decision of the High Court in relation to the liability of Dr Jackson. May LJ took the view that after the passage of eight years it was inevitable that however truthful a witness might be trying to be, at least part of his evidence would be inaccurate. By agreement, the pharmacy accepted liability for the 15 per cent liability which had rested on Dr Jackson. In the end, therefore, Dr Roderick's initial gross negligence only cost him 45 per cent of the blame with the pharmacy accepting the remaining 55 per cent.

In *Prendergast* v *Sam & Dee Ltd* (1989) 1 MLR 36, Dr Stuart Miller wrote a prescription for Mr Prendergast, who was asthmatic with a chest infection, prescribing three Ventolin (salbutamol) inhalers, 250 Phyllocontin (aminophylline) tablets, and 21 Amoxil (amoxcyllin) tablets. It was accepted to be a commonplace combination of drugs for a patient with asthma and a chest infection.

Mr Prendergast took the prescription to the pharmacy of Sam & Dee Ltd, where it was dispensed by a pharmacist, Mr Peter Kozary. Mr Kozary dispensed the inhalers and Phyllocontin correctly, but instead of Amoxil he had dispensed Daonil (glibenclamide), a drug used for diabetes to reduce the sugar content in the body. Mr Prendergast was not a diabetic and as a result of taking a large dose of Daonil suffered permanent brain damage and symptoms of hypoglycaemia.

In the High Court, Auld J dealt first with the position of the pharmacist, Mr Kozary. Mr Kozary had argued in his defence that the word Amoxil on the prescription was unclear and was capable of being read as Daonil. The 'A' could be mistaken for a lower case 'd' and the 'x' for 'n'. The judge therefore found it necessary to consider Dr Miller's handwriting. While the question would always be one of general impression, in his view, the word Amoxil on the prescription was capable of being read as Daonil.

Assuming, however, that the writing was not clear, the judge was of the opinion that there were sufficient other indications to put Mr Kozary on enquiry that something was wrong. More particularly, it was known that Daonil was made only in 5mg strengths, while the word Amoxil was always followed by '250'. Mr Kozary's defence that he thought that Dr Miller had mixed Daonil up with another diabetic drug which was taken in 250mg doses was confirmation of the need for the prescription to be checked with the doctor.

Secondly, the dosage of 250mg was normal for Amoxil, but unusually high for Daonil. This fact combined with the assumed knowledge that the taking of Daonil was dangerous for non-diabetics should have put Mr Kozary on his guard. Finally, Mr Prendergast had paid for the drugs on collection when it might have been expected that a diabetic would have been entitled to free drugs.

Accordingly, the judge concluded that had Mr Kozary been paying attention when he dispensed the drugs he should have known that something was amiss with the contents of the prescription and should have checked these with the doctor. He had not been paying attention and therefore fell below the standard of care and skill expected of a professional pharmacist and had been negligent. There had been sufficient information on the prescription as a whole and in his dealings with the patient to put him on enquiry.

Auld J then turned to the position of Dr Miller. He first made it clear that if Dr Miller owed a legal duty of care to his patient and had been in breach of that duty it would be no defence to his liability to rely on the already established liability of Mr Kozary. The judge indicated forcefully that a doctor did owe a duty to his patient to write a prescription clearly and sufficiently legibly to allow for possible mistakes by a busy pharmacist who might be distracted by other customers. Having already established that in his opinion the word Amoxil on the prescription could have been read as Daonil, the judge held that Dr Miller had been in breach of his duty to write clearly and had been negligent. Such liability could not be excused by the argument that there had been sufficient information on the prescription to put Mr Kozary on his guard. Dr Miller's negligence had contributed to the negligence of Mr Kozary, although the greater proportion of the responsibility lay with Mr Kozary.

Accordingly, Auld J awarded damages of £119,302 plus interest against Mr Kozary and Dr Miller, the proper apportionment of which was that Dr Miller was 25 per cent liable and Mr Kozary 75 per cent liable.

On an appeal by Dr Miller to the Court of Appeal, Dillon LJ was of the view that the chain of causation from Dr Miller's bad writing was not broken and the consequence of his writing a word which could reasonably be read as 'Daonil', even with the other factors, including the reference to the 250mg dosage, was not enough to make it beyond reasonable foreseeability that Daonil would be prescribed. Dillon LJ was also reluctant to interfere with Auld J's apportionment of liability.

Although the implications in the above cases may seem obvious from the facts, their seriousness should not be underestimated by those health care professionals involved. In each of these cases the courts were prepared to hold that pharmacists possess expertise regarding the supply of medicinal products and reliance is placed on them by patients for that expertise. The cases confirm that the relationship between pharmacist and patient is one which gives rise to the imposition of a duty of care.

Although liability was also imposed on the prescribing doctor in each of these cases, they both demonstrate that liability need not stop when the prescription leaves the hands of the doctor, even when the doctor has been grossly negligent. It may extend into and be a cause of the negligent mistakes of others. The net result is that the pharmacist must be aware that he or she should not tacitly accept what they see, or seem to see, on the written prescription before them. They are under a legal duty of care to draw on their skill and knowledge of drugs to inquire into the surrounding circumstances of the case. In this respect the finding of the judge in *Prendergast* that the pharmacist should have noticed that the patient paid for the drugs is noteworthy. If there is any doubt in the pharmacist's mind then the prescription should be checked by the prescribing doctor.

Having established that a pharmacist does owe a duty of care, any patient, harmed as a result of a pharmacist's involvement in their treatment, will have to show that the pharmacist was in breach of that duty, that the injuries were consequent on that breach, and that the action has been commenced in time. These aspects of the tort of negligence are not easy to prove, as the general discussion of the issue, in relation to the tort of negligence, has shown.

The courts, in deciding whether a pharmacist is in breach of the duty of care owed to a patient, will seek to ascertain the standard expected of a reasonable pharmacist, acting in circumstances similar to those arising in the case, and determine whether the pharmacist has reached that standard. In so doing, the courts will be influenced by the expert evidence provided by both the claimant and the defendant.

In addition, the court may also look to the guidance which has been provided by the pharmacy profession concerning the appropriate standards of professional practice and conduct. This will include the interpretation of, and guidance to, the legal requirements provided by the Royal Pharmaceutical Society of Great Britain, in its publication *Medicines, Ethics and Practice*. It is appropriate for pharmacists to consider the content of the Royal Pharmaceutical Society of Great Britain's advice, and implement the relevant standards into their professional practice. In the cases noted above, the courts were prepared to find that the pharmacists had not reached the appropriate standard and had been in breach of the duty of care owed to the patient.

Once it has been established that there has been a breach of an owed duty, the court will have to decide whether the claimant has suffered consequential loss or damage. As noted above, the simple fact of injury is not enough to satisfy this test. The court will have to apply legal tests relating to causation and remoteness. However, if the claimant can show that the injury was caused by the defendant's breach of duty and that the resultant loss is not too remote, the award of compensation, representing the monetary quantum of this loss, can be substantial.

In addition, the monetary damages may reflect different aspects of the claimant's loss. In *Prendergast*, for example, the claimant was awarded general damages for pain, suffering and loss of amenities, damages for loss of earnings, damages for the value of the care given by his family, and their expenses, damages for future loss of earning capacity with agreed annual multipliers, damages for the future care of the claimant by his family, a contingency sum to cover the cost of professional care in the event of his family becoming unable to care for him, interest on those sums to the date of hearing, and his legal costs.

It goes without saying that the implications of careless conduct are significant, and that specific sanctions flow from a failure to carry out professional roles. A good lawyer will advise pharmacists that close attention should be paid to the significance of professional responsibility and the tort of negligence. A good lawyer will also advise a pharmacist, and other professionals, to take out adequate professional indemnity insurance to cover the costs of any negligence action, and resultant award of damages. Specialists businesses offer such professional indemnity insurance for pharmacists.

10.5 NEW TRENDS IN LIABILITY IN NEGLIGENCE — THE PHARMACIST'S DUTY TO WARN

In each of the above cases, the facts show that there was an error on the face of the prescriptions which the pharmacist ought to have detected and rectified by querying the contents of the prescription or by refusing to dispense it. Technical accuracy is what the United Kingdom courts appear to be asking of the pharmacist. Is the pharmacist under any duty to give warnings about drugs which are correctly prescribed and the appropriate therapy for those drugs?

Those precise issues were at the heart of the recent United States' case of *Pittman* v *The Upjohn Company*, 1994 Westlaw 663372 (Tenn. 1994), which will be discussed in more detail in chapter thirteen. In this case the Supreme Court of Tennessee affirmed that the manufacturer, doctor and pharmacist were not liable to the claimant on the particular facts. However it also clearly recognised that each of those defendants had a duty to provide warnings about potential problems with drug therapy.

The court stated that a pharmacist is a professional who has a duty to his or her patients to exercise the standard of care required by the pharmacy profession in the same community or similar communities as that in which the pharmacist practises. The court noted that the increased complexity of pharmacotherapeutics and accompanying adverse drug reactions and drug interactions have resulted in an expanded role for pharmacists as drug therapy counsellors. The court also observed a trend towards patient-oriented clinical pharmacy practice. As for the pharmacy's duty to the patient, the court concluded (1994 Westlaw 663372 (Tenn. 1994), p. 435):

The record shows that the duty owed [the patient] was greater than merely filling the physician's prescription correctly. As indicated by the evidence in the record, [the drug] posed a danger to [the patient] even if taken according to the physician's order. The pharmacy customer was not aware of that danger because she had not been advised by either the physician, who prescribed the unavoidably unsafe drug or the pharmacy which dispensed the drug. A significant factor affecting the pharmacy's duty was the knowledge that no warning had been given by the physician. Under these circumstances, it was reasonably foreseeable that [the patient] was at risk of injury. Consequently the pharmacy, as well as the physician, owed her the duty to warn.

Thus the court rejected the pharmacy's argument that its only duty was to process the prescription correctly. The pharmacy had a duty to warn the patient.

We noted at 10.4 that in the (UK) cases where a pharmacist was held liable in negligence, the facts show that there was an error on the face of the prescriptions which the pharmacist ought to have detected and rectified by querying the contents of the prescription or by refusing to dispense it. The issue was one of technical accuracy. Is the pharmacist in the UK under any duty to give warnings about drugs which are correctly prescribed and about the appropriate therapy for those drugs?

There are a number of compelling reasons why it may be concluded that such a duty would be imposed in this jurisdiction. The imposition of a duty of care in such circumstances would accord with current pharmacy practice. The pharmacy profession in the United Kingdom has been seeking a move away from a mechanistic role in the drug distribution process towards an increased responsibility for patient care through patient counselling, drug therapy and patient education. The practice of pharmaceutical care is now obliging the pharmacist to share responsibility for the design, implementation and monitoring of a therapeutic plan which seeks to achieve a set of desired therapeutic objectives.

This trend is evidenced in recent pronouncements of the Royal Pharmaceutical Society of Great Britain, amendments to the Society's *Code of Ethics*, adoption of particular standards of practice, Council Statements and vigorous debate on the issue through the pages of the professional journals.

It is a necessary and indeed welcome implication of such a move that expanded responsibility implies the potential for expanded liability should the responsibility be exercised in a careless fashion. It is necessary because the current legal standard which states that pharmacists are only liable for careless, mechanistic errors is legally inappropriate to the expanded role. It is welcome because the imposition of legal liability for failure to perform a role gives greater authority to a claim to have that role.

It is our conclusion that the law will consider that a pharmacist, as a professional, has sufficient knowledge, through education and training and supply of information by the manufacturer, to counsel patients about drug therapy, has a duty to provide such counselling and that a failure to do so which results in injury to the patient will result in liability. That was the conclusion of the court in *Pittman* and it is our view that a similar conclusion would be reached by the courts in the United Kingdom.

There is a growing recognition by those members of the legal profession who advise those who have been harmed by drug products that pharmacists have legal and professional responsibilities beyond the careful filling of prescriptions as written towards the adoption of responsibility for drug therapy. In a recent unreported case, the claimant brought a claim, amongst a series of claims, against a pharmacy. Her allegation was that a pharmacist had been negligent in making up and supplying prescriptions for the drugs Mudocren and Priadel at the same time and on the same day, since any competent pharmacist ought to have known that if taken at the same time by the patient they would cause a dangerous rise in the serum lithium level which, on the facts, was the cause of her admission to hospital in a comatose state. Similar claims were made against her general practitioner and others.

The fact that the actions were eventually dismissed on procedural grounds should not disguise the recognition by the claimant's legal advisers that pharmacists have duties and responsibilities beyond the filling of prescriptions and that liability for failure to perform these expanded roles may result in the award of damages. Aside from the procedural issues in this case, the claimant's lawyers were prepared to argue the substantive point before the courts. Argument about the potential expansion of a duty of care before a judge can sometimes persuade a judge to extend liability accordingly.

10.6   CONCLUSION

This chapter aimed to explore some of the legal implications of a failure to act in a professional and responsible manner, by analysing the pharmacist's responsibility in the tort of negligence. We have noted that pharmacists are expected to carry out their various professional roles, and the duties and obligations which arise from them, in a careful and reliable manner.

Specific sanctions may flow from a failure to carry out specific roles. One of these sanctions is that the pharmacist may be held to be legally liable in the tort of negligence. The courts have ruled that a pharmacist owes a duty of care to a claimant, and will be in breach of that duty when appropriate professional standards have not been reached. Compensation will be payable for any resultant loss to the defendant, and may conclude in the payment of substantial sums of money.

The potential for liability in the tort of negligence is likely to increase with the adoption of new roles and responsibilities. The pharmacy profession is to be complimented for the in depth analysis which has taken place on the future role for pharmacists, as integral members of the health care team, providing essential care for patients. Recent legal decisions recognise that role, placing pharmacists' responsibility in the modern context, strengthening the view that the determination of pharmacy standards by the profession itself is appropriate and presenting a carefully considered analysis of arguments for and against pharmacists' liability for failure to warn.

The potential for an expansion of judicial recognition of pharmacists' responsibility for patient care beyond the routine careful filling of prescriptions as written may alarm some within the pharmacy profession. However, it can be argued that it should be seen as a positive development, primarily because it is reflective of the realities of current pharmacy practice. The cautious pharmacist might counter that this is mere speculation or conjecture and that no case has yet been taken against a pharmacist in the United Kingdom in such circumstances. The evidence, however, has shown that legal advisers are bringing claims for failure to warn and this trend may well mean that the issues will soon be discussed and deliberated upon in the higher courts. A prudent and responsible profession does not wait for the negative imposition of liability and the award of damages before thinking about its role, function and purpose in the health care system. All aspects of the pharmacist's expanded role need to be examined, the legal aspects included with the aim of realising that careful and conscientious practice means no liability.

ELEVEN

Professional responsibility — ethical responsibility

11.1 INTRODUCTION

In addition to the fundamental technical decisions which pharmacists have to make, they are often faced with other difficult questions requiring immediate resolution where technical expertise cannot provide the answer. Certain important factors may arise and even conflict with each other so that the pharmacist is faced with a dilemma, having to choose between two courses of action, both of which have valid reasons for being selected. Dilemmas often leave pharmacists asking themselves the question, 'What should I do?'. When pharmacists, and other health care professionals, ask themselves the question, 'What should I do?' and that question has a direct reference to the rights and welfare of other people, then the question is an ethical one.

The systematic addressing of ethical issues, and the resolution of ethical questions and dilemmas form part of the professional responsibility of pharmacists. Because the practice of pharmacy is specifically concerned with the interests and welfare of other people, it necessarily has an ethical reality. Weinstein (*Ethical Issues in Pharmacy* (Washington, Applied Therapeutics Inc 1996)) notes that the fact that pharmacists place the interests of others above their own interests, is one of the defining characteristics of pharmacy as a profession, in particular, and of health care professions, in general. Every encounter between a pharmacist and a patient has implicit ethical implications, because the pharmacist is under a duty to ask questions about suitable methods to promote the interests and welfare of the patient.

In chapter ten we saw that pharmacists have professional legal responsibilities in negligence. Those duties are complemented by professional ethical responsibilities. In many cases what is legally required of pharmacists is also what is ethically required, although this is not always so. Sometimes what is permissible legally is unethical, and sometimes what is required ethically is illegal. An understanding of the concept of ethics, the place of ethics in the professional setting and a structured method for the resolution of ethical questions and dilemmas is therefore essential.

This chapter is designed to provide opportunities for the better integration of ethics into professional practice. It concentrates on helping community pharmacists further develop their knowledge and skills when assessing the appropriate action to be taken in a given situation. The first objective is to define the concept of ethics in general, and pharmacy ethics in particular and to show the significance of ethics in pharmacy. Secondly, using a defined model, the chapter will describe the procedure to address questions and problems which relate to the resolution of ethical dilemmas, Finally, it will encourage community pharmacists to develop their own personal approach, using a suggested framework, to the resolution of problems arising in the professional setting.

11.2   THE NATURE OF ETHICS

Ethics is the systematic study of what is right and good with respect to conduct and character and is concerned with the making of appropriate decisions and with providing good reasons for those decisions. It is important to emphasise that both of these latter elements are equally significant. To act ethically not only involves the process of appropriate decision-making and action; it also requires justification, in the form of the provision of good reasons, for ethical choices. The sources of ethics, ethical rights and associated ethical responsibilities and duties, are the principles of moral philosophy, or religion, or, at times, the law. These sources provide the foundations for what we understand to be the principles of ethics. Whatever the source, ethics and ethical responsibility are essential aspects of being a professional and of acting responsibly.

It is generally accepted that one of the essential attributes of a profession is the development of, and adherence to, a moral or ethical code. This is a necessary requirement because professional responsibility involves commitment to standards of conduct above technical proficiency or skill and mere adherence to the requirements of the law. Other highly skilled technicians, plumbers or carpenters for example, do not advocate or endorse degrees of responsibility above the technical. Such technicians are content to assume legal responsibility based on an action for breach of a contract to provide specialised services. To be a professional, therefore, requires the assumption of duties and obligations not expected of other members of society.

The usual method by which a profession demonstrates its commitment to ethics or morality, and to ethical or moral responsibility, is the publication of a code of ethics. The pharmacy profession, in the United Kingdom and elsewhere, has shown such a commitment by having a written code of ethics, outlining the range of principles reflecting the profession's ethical standards and a set of obligations reflecting the profession's ethical duties and responsibilities. The codes of ethics of some professions go further than describing ethical standards, duties and responsibilities and attempt to characterise the virtues which are applicable to the practice of that profession and personal qualities expected of individual members.

The development of a moral or ethical code, while an essential characteristic of a profession, is not enough. A profession is also expected to enforce its own code as a method of internal control. This aspect of a profession's ethics is slightly more problematic. Some professions adhere rigidly to the rule that violation of their published code of ethics amounts to misconduct and is therefore subject to internal disciplinary procedures and censure. Other professions take a less strict approach, using the published code as a guide to what is acceptable and unacceptable conduct and behaviour. This latter approach is used by the pharmacy profession in the United Kingdom. Conduct which violates the Royal Pharmaceutical Society of Great Britain's *Code of Ethics* may also amount to misconduct, worthy of censure before the Statutory Committee.

As noted in section 1.2, ethics and the law are closely linked. Many laws have their basis in the reflection of current or past ethical trends. Equally, though, there are many more laws which are ethically ambivalent. The development of law is influenced by a number of factors and morality or ethics is one of them, but it is not the only one. It is entirely possible for a course of action to be perceived to be unethical without being illegal. For example, many pharmacists would find it to be unethical to be involved in the sale and distribution of post-coital contraception but such activities are not unlawful. Equally it is possible for some conduct to be unlawful but to have a sound ethical basis. For example, it would be unlawful for a pharmacist to refuse to disclose specific information about a patient in a court after being served with a witness summons to do so. However the pharmacist can justifiably claim that such conduct is ethically rational in protecting a patient's confidentiality.

Pharmacy ethics involves the application of ethical rules and principles to pharmacy practice. At times those rules and principles will be the same as those which apply to all individuals. For example, all individuals are under an ethical duty to protect confidential information that is entrusted to them. The pharmacist's ethical obligation to protect patient confidentiality is simply an application of this general rule. However, pharmacists (like all health care providers) are often asked to make and justify professional judgments and decisions beyond those expected of individuals. For example, pharmacists have a direct responsibility for the care, welfare and health of ordinary individuals.

As noted above, principles of pharmacy ethics may be found in the profession's published *Code of Ethics*, or in the standards of conduct defined by the law. They may, however, also be found in the principles of moral philosophy, or individual reasoning, or religious belief. As we shall see below, it is appropriate for the pharmacy profession to extend its understanding of the nature of ethics, the source of ethical reasoning, and the methods for the resolution of ethical questions and dilemmas.

11.3   RESOLVING ETHICAL QUESTIONS AND DILEMMAS

We often ask ourselves the question, 'What should I do?'. For example, at lunch we might ask ourselves, 'What should I do — should I have the pasta or the salad?'. This question is a matter of individual aesthetics and taste and does not involve the rights and welfare of others. When the question, 'What should I do?' (and the parallel question, 'Why should I do it?') has a direct reference to the welfare of other people, then the question is an ethical one. So if we ask ourselves the question, 'What should I do — should I keep this £20 note which I found in the hall or should I make an effort to return it?', this is an ethical question because the person who lost the money is almost invariably entitled to its return. Ethics is the attempt to answer the question, 'What should I do?' when that question has a direct reference to the rights and welfare of other people.

An ethical question becomes an ethical dilemma when there are a number of choices which are ethically justifiable but not all can be acted upon at a particular time. Take for instance a university lecturer who learns from one of his students, for whom he acts as studies adviser, that she is suffering emotional difficulties which concern a relationship with another member of the university staff. Despite the fact that those difficulties are impinging on her academic performance, she wishes the lecturer to keep them confidential and to mention them to no one else. Later he learns that she has failed her end of year examinations. There are a number of choices which he could make which are ethically justifiable but not all can be acted upon at a particular time. He is faced with an ethical dilemma.

All of the questions posed so far are questions related to what we should do as individuals and have nothing to do with the profession of pharmacy. We often ask ourselves the question, 'What should I do as a pharmacist?'. Because the practice of pharmacy is specifically concerned with the interests and welfare of other people, such a question is necessarily an ethical question. Every pharmacist who is asked to dispense a prescription only medicine is faced with an ethical question because they must consider the interests and welfare of the patient presenting the prescription.

Ethical questions in pharmacy may also (but not necessarily always) become ethical dilemmas. At times pharmacists have to decide whether to protect their patients by refusing to fill certain prescriptions, because they disagree with the proposed therapeutic plan, or complying with their professional and legal responsibility to fill all validly written prescriptions. At other times pharmacists have to balance their responsibility to their patients against their responsibility to fellow members of the health care team with whom they have come into conflict. In such situations, pharmacists are faced with a number of choices which are all ethically justifiable but not all of which can be acted upon at a particular time.

Pharmacists will often look to the profession's *Code of Ethics* for guidance to the answer of, 'What should I do?'. Often the *Code* will be specific and will provide the mechanism for making appropriate decisions and justifying them. Professional codes of ethics are very useful tools to assist in the process of ethical decision-making, and for the resolution of ethical questions and dilemmas. It is appropriate for a pharmacist to consider the profession's *Code of Ethics* when undertaking this difficult process. However professional codes of ethics are necessarily limited in both their application and utility, for a number of reasons.

First, professional codes of ethics must describe the range of principles, duties, obligations and virtues generally and succinctly. Codes of ethics cannot account for, nor give a solution to every ethical question and dilemma which may arise. The result is an identification of very general precepts, designed to be applicable to a whole range of situations. For example, the first principle of the Royal Pharmaceutical Society of Great Britain's *Code of Ethics* is that 'a pharmacist's prime concern must be for the welfare of both the patient and other members of the public'. This principle is ethically justifiable and very appropriate for a profession committed to health care but quite clearly covers a wide realm of activities, issues, duties and obligations.

Secondly, professional codes of ethics rarely address conflicting ethical obligations. For example, the principle, contained in the Royal Pharmaceutical Society of Great Britain's *Code of Ethics*, that 'a pharmacist must respect the confidentiality of information acquired in the course of professional practice' does not help a pharmacist faced with the ethical dilemma of a court order demanding production of patient medication records for the purposes of litigation. The *Code of Ethics* does not assist pharmacists to prioritise conflicting ethical obligations; rather it gives general guidance without balancing the pharmacist's duties and responsibilities.

Finally, professional codes of ethics are silent on some important ethical issues, questions and dilemmas. The generality and concision of professional codes does not allow for significant amendment based on changing social and clinical circumstances. New ethical issues arise in pharmacy on a regular basis, based on the formulation of new medicinal products, the development of innovative medical therapies, and changes and alteration in professional roles. At times, the profession's *Code of Ethics* responds to such changes by the inclusion of specific guidance and advice. However piecemeal additions in this fashion do not assist the systematic addressing of ethical questions and dilemmas. At other times, it is clear that the ethical implications of the new developments are too specific to allow for significant alteration to the *Code*, leaving pharmacists to resort to an analysis of general principles.

Where the answer to an ethical problem, and the settlement of disputes, could be found in the law, that solution is often advocated as the most obvious, rational and intelligible. Strict adherence to the requirements of the law is deemed to be the most appropriate response to the ethical dilemma: the law is seen to encapsulate ethics and to be the best representation of them. That thinking is reinforced by the further ethical obligation to obey the law.

Compliance with legal standards is also often advocated as the best method for the resolution of ethical problems or dilemmas which arise in pharmacy. As will be seen below, the resolution of ethical dilemmas has something to with adherence to the law, something to do with observation of professional standards but much more to do with the development of a systematic procedure for ethical decision making. To adhere unquestioningly to the requirements of the law, involves the unquestioning acceptance of the ethical basis of those laws. That is too narrow a view. The ethical basis for some laws is clearly dubious.

Law is necessarily limited in its effect. That might be because many individuals might question its ethical basis, and having done so, decide that their own ethical standards justify an ignorance of the law's requirements. Unless and until the ignorance of the law, and parallel continued action in conformity with individual morality, results in the disruption of human relationships or the violation of society's code of behaviour, the law will be restricted in its effect. Individuals may therefore continue to act in an unethical fashion without infringing the law or legal requirements. Further, the law is an inappropriate method for the regulation of all human behaviour and disputes which arise in human relationships. Quite clearly, there are aspects of human relationships which are better regulated by those involved in the relationship. Finally, it is not feasible for the law to regulate every minor violation of human behaviour and conduct.

To rely on professional codes of ethics and/or the requirements of the law to answer ethical questions or dilemmas is to take a narrow view. What is required is to take a wider view of ethical decision-making as having something to do with professional codes, something to do with legal requirements but more to do with the development of a systematic procedure for the resolution of all ethical questions and dilemmas. It is possible for pharmacists to develop a structured approach to follow when faced with the question, 'What should I do?'. Certain decisions and actions will be necessary in the event of ethical dilemmas. It is possible to formulate a systematic procedure which addresses those decisions and actions and which balances responsibility to the patient against responsibility to colleagues. That systematic procedure, described below, may then be used constructively and knowledgeably in the professional setting.

11.4   A SYSTEMATIC PROCEDURE FOR ETHICAL DECISION-MAKING

This procedure is one which was formulated, and has been used for many years, by Weinstein (*Ethical Issues in Pharmacy* (Washington, Applied Therapeutics Inc 1996)). Weinstein advocates a five-stage strategy for the systematic resolution of ethical questions.

11.4.1 Identify the ethical questions which are raised by a problematic situation
Any problematic situation is going to raise a number of questions, not all of which will be ethical questions. An ethical question is one which has a direct relation to the rights and welfare of other persons. Only the ethical questions have to be resolved in a problematic ethical situation. The first stage in the process therefore is to identify the relevant ethical questions.

11.4.2 Gather the medical, social and all other clinically relevant facts
Rarely does anyone attempt to resolve a problematic situation without attempting to obtain as much information about it as possible. The same principle applies to ethical decision-making. It is not possible to make an appropriate decision and provide good reasons for that decision, without first gathering all of the medical, social and other clinically relevant facts.

11.4.3 Identify the values which play a role and decide which values are in conflict
Weinstein proposes that facts, while relevant, are not sufficient to resolve an ethical question. Ethical questions require a consideration of values as well as facts. Values give rise to ethical rules or guidelines. Therefore the third stage of the strategy for the resolution of ethical questions is to identify the values which are appropriate to the situation and decide which values are in conflict. If the identified values are not in conflict then there is no ethical dilemma. An ethical dilemma will only arise when there a number of choices, all of which are ethically justifiable but not all of which can be acted upon at a particular time. Conflicting values gives rise to such a dilemma.

11.4.4 Propose options or possible solutions
Weinstein's fourth stage is to propose options or possible solutions. This involves answering the question, 'What could I do?'. It is important to remember that problematic decisions require resolution. This stage allows for the proposition of options and permits the contemplation of a range of possible solutions.

11.4.5 Choose the best solution for this particular situation, justify it and respond to possible criticism
Saying that someone could do something does not necessarily mean that they should do it. The fifth and final stage of the procedure for resolving ethical questions and dilemmas is to choose a solution to the particular pr~~~~ justify it and respond to possible criticism. This involves asking the que 'What should I do?' and 'Why should I do it?'. This final stage all~

individual to resolve a problematic situation in the knowledge that they have acted conscientiously and professionally.

11.5 APPLICATION OF A SYSTEMATIC PROCEDURE FOR ETHICAL DECISION MAKING

The following case study gives a good example of a pharmacist's dilemma.

Case Study 1

Diana Brown has recently qualified as a pharmacist. After about six months working as a locum in a different area, she accepted a job as manager of an independent community pharmacy in her home town as she wanted to live and work close to her elderly parents.

Shortly after Diana started work, the pharmacy is visited by Susan and James Wilson, an elderly couple well known to Diana as close friends and neighbours of her parents. Susan explains that they have come with a repeat prescription from their GP Dr Moss who has been treating James for high blood pressure. Susan tells Diana that this is the first time that her husband has been ill for many years and comments that she supposed that they would have to get used to infirmity as part of the ageing process. She jokes that her husband has recently become more confused, forgetful and hard of hearing. Susan indicates that they have other shops to visit and that they will return for the medication.

Diana takes the prescription to the dispensary and notes that it is for Bumetanide. By consulting the PMR (patient medication record) she sees that this is the third time James has presented a prescription for Bumetanide. Her professional judgment/knowledge tells her that Bumetanide is a loop diuretic. She feels that long-term use of this drug with the elderly could lead to the development of hypokalaemia and is worried that James's forgetfulness and confusion could be symptomatic of a fall in potassium levels. She thinks that there may be a more appropriate treatment.

Diana telephones Dr Moss to discuss her proposals with him. After listening in silence, Dr Moss responds indignantly, 'I have been a doctor for 38 years and do not need a pharmacist, especially one just qualified, to tell me how to treat and care for my patients. I don't know what they are teaching at universities these days, but in my day the pharmacist knew that his job was to dispense prescriptions, not to question the decisions of doctors. Just dispense the prescription as written.'. Diana replaces the telephone and is concerned about what she ought to do next.

Diana is faced with an ethical dilemma. She has to decide whether to protect her patient from further harm by refusing to fill the prescription or complying with her professional responsibility to fill valid prescriptions. She also has to balance her responsibility to her patient with her responsibility to a fellow member of the primary health care team. Diana has a number of choices which are all ethically justifiable but not all of which can be acted upon at the same time.

It might be argued that the solution to Diana's dilemma is to be found in the pharmacy profession's *Code of Ethics*. Diana might note that the first principle of the Royal Pharmaceutical Society of Great Britain's *Code of Ethics* requires that her prime concern must be for the welfare of both the patient and other members of the public. This might provide a justification for deciding that she will not fill the prescription for James.

It might also be argued that the answer to this ethical dilemma is to be found in the requirements of the law, because the law often attempts to codify morality. For example, the prescription which has been presented to Diana is likely to be an NHS prescription. Subject to certain qualifications, the secondary legislation, which determines the rights and duties of pharmacists in relation to the dispensing of NHS prescriptions and the pharmacist's signed contract or terms of service, imposes a duty on the pharmacist to dispense with reasonable promptness any prescription which is presented. A refusal to dispense an NHS prescription may leave Diana in breach of contract or her terms of service which, potentially, has serious, adverse consequences. Diana might argue that she has no right to refuse to dispense the prescription and that satisfaction of this legal requirement is sufficient to dispose of the ethical obligation.

It is clear that the solutions offered to Diana by the *Code of Ethics* and by the law are adequate but not satisfactory. The adoption of either solution is likely to leave Diana feeling that she has not considered all of the facts, weighed up the possible options and chosen and justified the appropriate solution for the problematic situation. Using the facts of this case study, it is possible to show how the adoption of the five-stage strategy leads to a systematic resolution of the ethical questions which arise.

The first task is to identify the ethical questions which arise in this case. The case raises a number of questions but not all of them are ethical. Some of the questions which arise are:

(a) Is James Wilson receiving the correct drug treatment for his medical condition?

(b) Are there potential side-effects when using that particular drug for that particular condition?

(c) Are James's symptoms linked to that drug?

(d) Should Diana tell James that she does not agree with Dr Moss's prescription?

(e) Should Diana tell James about her telephone conversation and disagreement with Dr Moss?

(f) Should Dr Moss have dismissed Diana's suggestion so readily?

(g)   Should Diana refuse to dispense the prescription?

(h)   Should Diana make a fresh attempt to persuade Dr Moss that he may be wrong?

(i)   Should Diana dispense the prescription? What else should she do?

(j)   What difference will it make to James if he continues to take the prescribed medication?

All of these questions arise naturally from this case study but not all these questions are ethical questions i.e., questions which ask, 'What should I do?' with respects to the rights and welfare of others. According to this definition, questions (c)–(i) are probably ethical questions.

The second step in the process is to gather the medical, social and other clinically relevant facts relating to the particular situation, i.e., in this case study:

(a)   James is an elderly patient and is being treated for hypertension with Bumetanide.

(b)   James has symptoms of being confused, forgetful and hard of hearing.

(c)   One of the side effects of Bumetanide is a fall in potassium levels in the blood (hypokalaemia) which can cause weakness and confusion particularly in the elderly.

(d)   There are other drugs which are available which can correct the side effect of potassium loss or imbalance or there are alternative treatments for hypertension.

(e)   Weakness and confusion in the elderly is potentially life-threatening.

Weinstein proposes that facts, while relevant, are not sufficient to resolve an ethical question. Ethical questions require a consideration of values as well as facts. Therefore the *third* stage of the strategy for the resolution of ethical questions is to identify the values which are appropriate to the situation and decide which values are in conflict. In our first case study, there are a number of values which are readily identifiable:

(a)   The obligation to maintain good inter-professional relationships.

(b)   The obligation to promote the welfare and well-being of a patient and to avoid harming a patient.

(c)   The obligation to ensure that the patient has all the available evidence to make an informed decision about his care.

The identification of the appropriate values which play a role in the situation leads to a secondary analysis of the values which are in conflict. When we do this we see that each of the values identified so far conflicts with the others. Once conflict is evident it is necessary to move to the next stage of ethical analysis.

Weinstein's fourth stage is to propose options or possible solutions. This involves answering the question, 'What could I do?'. In relation to our case study, there are a number of possible options. Some of these are:

(a)   Diana could dispense the prescription as written.

(b)   Diana could fill the prescription as written and explain to James the risks associated with the use of the medication.

(c)   Diana could refuse to fill the prescription and say nothing to James and Dr Moss.

(d)   Diana could refuse to fill the prescription and explain the reasons why to James and Dr Moss.

Saying that someone *could* do something does not necessarily mean that they *should* do it. The fifth and final stage of the procedure for resolving ethical questions and dilemmas is to choose a solution to the particular problem, justify it and respond to possible criticism. This involves asking the questions, 'What should I do?' and 'Why should I do it?'. In relation to our case study, Diana might decide that her primary duty and obligation is the welfare of James and her responsibility to the patient outweighs her responsibility to her professional colleague, Dr Moss. The option therefore is to refuse to dispense the prescription and to explain to James and Dr Moss the reasons why.

Modern pharmacy practice must be carried out in co-operation with patients and other professional members of the health care team. However, care is provided for the direct benefit of the patient and the pharmacist must accept direct responsibility for the quality of that care. Diana might therefore conclude that the adverse consequence of direct damage to the inter-professional relationship is necessary if she is to be committed to and be responsible for the quality of the direct care to her patient.

That might be an extreme view of the outcomes of the provision of care. Care is dependent upon co-operation rather than subordination. It must be integrated into other aspects of health care if the patient is to receive its direct benefits. Care is also dependent upon maintaining communication between all of the participants in the process. Diana might conclude that an intervention which necessitates the refusal to fill the prescription does not achieve the purpose of care and is too extreme. She might therefore introduce further options:

(e)   She might seek advice from one or other of her colleagues within pharmacy and use their counsel and experience to re-evaluate an appropriate course of action.

It is important to remember that the provision of care is about teamwork and can and should involve fellow members of the pharmacy team in the resolution of problems. Discussion with sympathetic, experienced colleagues could elicit further, important information and might generate a range of options which Diana has not yet considered.

(f)   Diana might contact the GP again and use her inter-personal skills to persuade him to change his mind about the prescribed medication.

It will be clear to Diana that her initial approach has been soundly dismissed by Dr Moss. She will also feel that she has an important contribution to make to the welfare of James and would wish to make a further effort at establishing a coherent, team approach to her patient's care. A perceptive use of inter-personal skills is vital to this option. Diana will need to be aware that the relationship with Dr Moss is already strained and that he may not be readily persuaded that his judgment should be questioned. Diana will have to use an approach which is supportive of Dr Moss's position and which seeks to convince him that her training allows her to suggest an appropriate choice for this patient. Remember that the development and maintenance of communications between members of the primary health care team is an essential element of the provision of care.

(g)   Diana might wish to discuss the matter further with her patient, James and his wife.

This option will generate more information as much as anything else. It is important to remember that the first stage of ethical decision-making, as advocated by Weinstein, is the assimilation of all of the relevant facts. It is also important to remember that the provision of care demands the maintenance of necessary communications among all participants in the process. This option, of reviewing the matter further with the patient, might lead Diana to reassess the seriousness of the situation and allow her to conclude that there is less of a basis for her concerns than she first thought. Further deliberation and reflection might well assist the decision-making process.

11.6   PRACTICAL IMPLICATIONS OF ETHICAL DECISION-MAKING

An ethical dilemma demands a decision. You must consider the facts, identify and assign values, list options and choose and justify an option. You are faced with a dilemma because the values which you have identified conflict and each of the options, although all equally justified, cannot be implemented at the same time. Ethical decision-making is about respecting and honouring competing values: this means conceding that one option has to be chosen although it is likely to have at least some unfavourable results. Hard choices can still be good choices.

At this stage you might think that ethical decision-making is a difficult, time-consuming task which you would rather not undertake in a busy clinical practice with more important competing demands. Ethical decision-making *is* difficult and time-consuming. However, it is important to remember that pharmacy is a moral practice and that almost every decision which a pharmacist has to make will have an ethical dimension to it. The adoption and constructive use of a systematic procedure for the resolution of ethical questions and dilemmas will ease the difficulty of the task and allow you to fit ethical decision-making into your crowded clinical practice.

It is equally important to remember that the primary health care team is made up of a number of distinct and different individuals who collaborate to achieve the goal of the optimisation of therapeutic outcomes for patients who use medications. Despite this uniform focus on the advancement of the welfare of the patient, there are frequently occasions for disagreement among members of that team on a wide variety of matters.

Diversity of view is a source of strength for any group. The fact that all health care team members do not think the same way is a good thing; it is quite possible to respect another point of view without agreeing with it. Therapeutic differences are regularly accommodated and addressed in a systematic fashion and this enhances the development of the pharmacy profession and its perception in the eyes of the public. In a similar way the systematic addressing of moral issues, through the accommodation and addressing of controversies and disagreements, will also improve the profession. To this extent ethical decision-making should be viewed as an opportunity rather than a problem.

11.7 PHARMACEUTICAL CARE AND FUTURE ETHICAL DILEMMAS

We noted above in section 11.3 that new ethical issues arise in pharmacy on a regular basis, based on a number of factors, including changes and alteration in professional roles. The most significant alteration in the professional role of pharmacists has been the implementation of the concept of pharmaceutical care. The requirement for a pharmacist to address ethical questions and dilemmas systematically is likely to increase with the implementation of pharmaceutical care into primary health care practice.

In section 2.7 we have seen that pharmaceutical care moves the practice of pharmacy beyond the traditional model where the primary function of the community pharmacist is to dispense prescriptions, to a new model where the pharmacist is involved in rational drug therapy. Within this new model pharmacists, in their professional capacity, continue to function as experts in the dispensing of drugs but also collect, find and interpret evidence relating to specific clinical questions and provide information that permits patients to assess risk, enhance their autonomy, and develop their own medication practice.

When patients obtain their medicines they may choose not to take the drug at all or to take it in a certain way based on their own individual social and familial circumstances. The patient has a great deal of autonomy in deciding whether or not to take a drug, is largely unsupervised in making that decision and has no one with the appropriate knowledge of their individual circumstances to assist them in making rational and careful decisions about self-administration and re-administration.

The community pharmacist is well placed to fill this void and assume a client-specific role with respect to decisions about drug taking. Pharmacists are highly trained in the science of drug therapy, are readily available in the community in which they live and are highly regarded and trusted by members of that community. As a result of this, pharmacists often have a greater access to information about the prescription process relating to a particular patient.

The pharmacist in this new role is still concerned with the initial choice of prescription and more concerned with patient outcomes, using patient-specific evidence to monitor and manage the patient's care. This role equates with the current expectations of the profession, applying existing knowledge of drug therapy in original and creative ways to improve patient outcomes. The new role naturally requires co-operation with patients and with other members of the primary health care team. However, the pharmacist's intervention is provided for the direct benefit of the patient and the pharmacist must accept direct professional responsibility for the quality of that intervention. A number of specific issues relating to professional responsibility arise. Among these is the development and maintenance of new professional relationships with patients and with other members of the primary health care team.

Part of that development necessitates the exploration of the decisions and actions that might be necessary in the event of professional disagreement. Disagreement might arise because this new model of pharmaceutical care critically and necessarily upsets the traditional medicines use process. The pharmacist in the pharmaceutical care system is less concerned with initial choice of prescription and more concerned with monitoring, management and patient outcomes. The pharmacist in such a system will use patient-specific evidence to monitor and manage the patient's care. Pharmaceutical care changes episodic drug therapy to coherent, continual care. Responsibility for patient outcomes is spread from the individual (doctor) to the team (all health care providers).

The critical, even though necessary, alteration of a traditional process can lead to tension, disagreement and conflict which will often leave a pharmacist asking, 'What should I do?'. The case study used in this chapter is illustrative of the potential for conflict and disagreement between members of the primary health care team as part of the process of integrating pharmaceutical care into primary health care practice. Answering the question, 'What should I do?' in this type of situation means the resolution of ethical questions and ethical dilemmas and the requirement for the formulation and implementation of a systematic procedure for the resolution of such problematic situations takes on an even greater significance.

Part of that process will involve a pharmacist persuading patients and fellow team members that pharmacists, with their education in the outcomes of drug therapy and ready access to patient-specific evidence, accessibility to patients and location within the medicines use process, have a full role to play in the improvement of the outcomes of drug therapy. By analogy such a model will seek to persuade patients and fellow team members that pharmaceutical care means shared rather than substituted responsibility, harmonisation rather than polarisation and that the true idea of care is based on the idea that professionals are more able to improve the quality of care with co-operation from their patients and fellow patients than without.

11.8   CONCLUSION

The purpose of this chapter has been to discuss the integration of ethics into professional practice and to explore the decisions and actions which might be necessary in the event of dilemmas arising. We have seen that when we ask the question, 'What should I do?' with respect to the rights and welfare of other people, then the question is an ethical one. Ethical questions become ethical dilemmas when there are a number of choices which are ethically justifiable but not all of which can be acted upon at the same time. The practice of pharmacy, as a moral practice, involves the consideration of ethical questions and dilemmas the answers to which will not necessarily be found in the profession's *Code of Ethics* or by considering the requirements of the law.

A systematic procedure for the addressing of ethical questions and dilemmas as they relate to inter- and intra-professional relationships has been proposed by Weinstein. It involves a five-stage process of ethical analysis where an individual will identify the ethical questions which are raised by a problematic situation; gather the medical, social and all other clinically relevant facts; identify and assign the values which play a role; propose options or possible solutions and choose the best solution for this particular situation, justify it and respond to possible criticism.

Although the process of ethical analysis is not easy and is time-consuming for professionals who have competing demands within their clinical practice, that practice is a moral one and requires the professional to be ethically aware and responsible. The requirement for a pharmacist to address ethical questions and dilemmas systematically is likely to increase with the implementation of pharmaceutical care into primary health care practice. A systematic procedure for the resolution of ethical questions and dilemmas produces answers by way of ethically justifiable options. This allows the pharmacist to integrate the process of ethical analysis into clinical health care and team-based practice. The systematic addressing of moral issues, through the accommodation and addressing of controversies and disagreements, improves health care and improves the professions of those who make up the health care team. Ethical decision-making and ethical responsibility should therefore be greeted with anticipation rather than with apprehension.

TWELVE

Professional responsibility — administrative responsibility

12.1 INTRODUCTION

In chapter two we explored in detail how the pharmacist's functions and responsibilities have been shaped by the economic determinant of the growth of the pharmaceutical industry and the health policy determinant of the development of the National Health Service. That chapter also analysed the growth of the pharmacy profession in the United Kingdom, and discussed the pivotal roles of that profession in the provision of health care. In chapter three we continued this theme by examining the practical nature of the relationship between the pharmacist and the National Health Service, concluding that the maintenance of this symbiotic association is vital for both the pharmacy profession, and the National Health Service itself.

In chapters ten and eleven we began to explore aspects of pharmacist responsibility. We have seen that pharmacists are expected to carry out their various professional roles, and the duties and obligations which arise from them, in a careful and reliable manner. We gave this obligation the term 'professional responsibility' and noted that it includes professional legal responsibilities in negligence, and those duties are complemented by professional ethical responsibilities.

The purpose of this chapter is continue the theme of professional responsibility by exploring the duties and obligations which arise from membership of the pharmacy profession and from the significant relationship which the pharmacy profession has with the National Health Service. We have called this aspect of professional duty 'administrative' responsibility. However, the use of that term should not disguise the importance of this aspect of professional obligation, nor make it appear that it is a lesser form of responsibility when compared with the duties owed in the law of negligence or in ethics.

Indeed, this form of responsibility is equally as significant. We shall see below that failure to undertake professional roles and responsibilities, or to accede to the norms of the pharmacy profession may result in disciplinary action which can, in turn, lead to admonishment and expulsion from the profession. In one stage, the exclusive rights and monopolies enjoyed as a result of being a member of the pharmacy profession may disappear. The inadequate performance of functions within the National Health Service may also lead to significant administrative sanction, including the loss of exclusive and financially lucrative privileges.

The organisation of the chapter is designed to examine the current structure of the pharmacy profession, together with its professional bodies, outlining the requirements for membership, and analysing the important disciplinary powers which the profession, over a considerable period of time, has reserved for itself. The chapter will then analyse certain aspects of the administrative structure of the National Health Service, and will examine significant recent reforms of that structure to deal with complaints and discipline.

12.2   THE ROYAL PHARMACEUTICAL SOCIETY OF GREAT BRITAIN

We noted in chapter two that the Royal Pharmaceutical Society for Great Britain was founded in 1841 and received its first royal charter of incorporation in 1843. The first charter incorporated the Society and authorised it to have a common seal and to sue and be sued. The first royal charter was supplemented by a second charter in 1953. The 1953 charter was quickly followed by the Pharmacy Act 1954. These arrangements, together with the remaining parts of the original royal charter of incorporation, and other important legislative provisions, including those contained in the Medicines Act 1968, provide for the structure, organisation, management and organisation of the pharmacy profession today. The 1953 charter sets out the main objects of the Royal Pharmaceutical Society which are:

(a)   to advance chemistry and pharmacy;

(b)   to promote pharmaceutical education and the application of pharmaceutical knowledge;

(c)   to maintain the honour and safeguard and promote the interests of the members in the exercise of the profession of pharmacy; and

(d)   to provide relief for distressed persons being:

(i)   members;

(ii)   persons who at any time have been members or have been registered as pharmaceutical chemists or as chemists and druggists;

(iii)   widows, orphans, or other dependants of deceased persons who were at any time members or registered as aforesaid; and

(iv)   students.

The 1953 charter also allows for the Royal Pharmaceutical Society to have the power to take and hold personal property and from time to time to purchase, acquire, take or hold land. The charter also requires that there shall be a Council of the Royal Pharmaceutical Society, consisting of 21 members, nominated and elected in a manner to be determined, and laid down by the by-laws and a president, vice-president and treasurer of the Royal Pharmaceutical Society, again appointed and to be given such powers as might be determined, and laid down by the by-laws.

Section XII, and the first Schedule, of the Council's by-laws outline the mechanism and procedures for election of the 21 members to the Council. Annually, seven members 'retire' from office and the vacancies are filled, following a nomination procedure, by election by postal single transferable vote. The 'retiring' members are eligible for re-election and all members have the right to vote.

Section 15, Pharmacy Act 1954 allows for the appointment of three further members to the Council, nominated by the Privy Council. Privy Council nominees do not necessarily have to be members of the Royal Pharmaceutical Society.

Power to make by-laws, for all or any of the purposes for which by-laws could, by the express provisions of the charter, be made, and such other by-laws as seem to the Council to be necessary for the management and regulation of the affairs and property of the Royal Pharmaceutical Society, was originally given to the Council of the Royal Pharmaceutical Society under the 1953 charter. In addition, s. 16, Pharmacy Act 1954 gives power to the Council to make by-laws for the purposes of the registers and registration, examination for registration, qualification for registration, certificates of registration, and control of registration by the Statutory Committee.

The Council of the Royal Pharmaceutical Society has made, and continues to make, extensive use of these powers and has formulated by-laws to deal with a whole range of administrative and regulatory matters including members and fellows, including honorary members and fellows students; annual and special general meetings; membership of, elections to, and meetings of the Council; officers of the Royal Pharmaceutical Society; the secretary; auditors; common seal; funds and property; benevolent funds; branches and branch representatives; membership groups; overseas pharmacists; registrar and registrations; the register; certificates of registration; journals and transactions; and by-laws.

Section XXVII of the Council's own by-laws outline the procedures to be adopted for the further making of by-laws. Proposals to make, alter, or revoke a by-law shall be in writing, and after notification to the Council by a Council member, or through a report of a Committee, shall be read. If seconded and approved, notice of that approval and the intention of the Council to make, alter or revoke the by-law, as the case may be, will be given to the members of the Royal Pharmaceutical Society through the *Pharmaceutical Journal*. Members are entitled to have a copy of the proposal.

Any observations on the proposal, made by members to the Secretary, will be reported at the next meeting of the Council held after the expiry of 60 days from the date of notification to the members. Following this, if the Council confirms the proposal, it is sent to the Privy Council for further confirmation and approval. Section 16, Pharmacy Act 1954 confirms that Privy Council approval is required for by-laws made by the Council under the powers given by that section, relating to the purposes of the registers and registration, examination for registration, qualification for registration, certificates of registration, and control of registration by the Statutory Committee. Subsequent confirmation and approval of the Privy Council of the proposal is also published in the *Pharmaceutical Journal*.

12.2.1 Management and organisation of the Society

Section 4, Pharmacy Act 1954, and s. XX of the by-laws make provision for registration as a pharmaceutical chemist. Any person who holds a degree in pharmacy from a university of the United Kingdom, approved by the Council under by-law 5 of s. XX, and has attained the age of 21, may be registered as a pharmaceutical chemist, provided that further evidence is produced to the satisfaction of the registrar concerning identity, age, award of degree, good character, good physical and mental health, and importantly, a declaration of satisfactory completion, of a period of pre-registration training.

Pre-registration training amounts to 52 weeks full-time employment in one (or more) of the following establishments, approved for training purposes by the Council: a community pharmacy, the pharmaceutical department of a hospital or similar institution, a pharmaceutical industrial establishment, a school of pharmacy or a registered pharmacy engaged solely in the supply of animal and agricultural products. Experience in two approved establishments is acceptable provided that at least 26 weeks is spent in a community pharmacy or hospital pharmaceutical department. During any period of pre-registration training, each trainee is required to be under the supervision of a registered pharmacist. On completion of the pre-registration training, there is a further requirement to pass a registration examination.

Exceptionally, the registrar may specify alternative requirements for registration for pre-registration failing, or failing to resit the pre-registration examination. Further details on these requirements, on the requirements for approval of institutions for the conduct of pre-registration training, and on the nature and form of the pre-registration examination procedures are contained in the by-laws.

Under s. 14, Pharmacy Act 1954, and s. II of the by-laws, and subject to certain minor exceptions, no person who is not registered as a pharmacist is entitled to be a member of the Royal Pharmaceutical Society. Registration confers automatic membership, but membership ceases with the ending of registration. Membership is conditional upon the payment of an initial registration fee and an annual retention fee. The level and category of fee are reviewed annually by the Council, and failure to pay the retention fee, following regulatory demand by the registrar, may result in removal of the pharmacist's name from the register, on direction by the Council. The name of a fee payment defaulter will be restored to the register, upon payment of due fees within a stipulated period plus an additional sum by way of penalty.

Certain individuals may be designated to be fellows of the Royal Pharmaceutical Society, under s. III of the by-laws. Fellows include those members registered as pharmaceutical chemists on or before 1 February 1951 and other members falling into particular, pre-1955 categories. In addition, members of not less than five years' standing, who have made outstanding original contributions to the advancement of pharmaceutical knowledge, or who have attained exceptional proficiency in a subject embraced by or related to the practice of pharmacy, may be designated as fellows by the Council.

Individual members may apply to be so designated, and will have their application assessed for these purposes. In addition, a member of not less than 20 years' standing, who has made outstanding original contributions to the advancement of pharmaceutical knowledge or who has attained distinction in the science, practice, profession or history of pharmacy, may be designated as a fellow, on the recommendation of a panel of fellows appointed for that purpose. Members designated as fellows only remain so as long as they remain members of the Royal Pharmaceutical Society.

Under s. IV of the by-laws the Council may, at its discretion, elect as honorary fellows such scientific workers as have distinguished themselves in any of the branches of knowledge embraced in the educational objects of the Society and persons who are eminent in national life. Similarly, the Council may elect as honorary members such persons who have rendered distinguished service to the Society or to pharmacy. Suggestions of names of individuals for election as honorary fellows or members may be made by members of the Society. The three members of the Council, appointed to their positions by the Privy Council under s. 15, Pharmacy Act 1954, will be designated as honorary members for the period while they hold their office, if they are not already registered pharmacists.

Section V of the by-laws recognises the formation of the section of the Royal Pharmaceutical Society called the British Pharmaceutical Students' Association. Membership of the section is open to all students and to members of the Royal Pharmaceutical Society who have been registered initially for not more than 12 months. The Association is regarded by the Council as the representative body for students, is administered by an elected executive in accordance with its constitution and is jointly financed by the Royal Pharmaceutical Society. Annual meetings take place between the Association's executive and the Council and the Association is allowed to participate in and contribute to the branch representatives' meeting. Members of the Association also retain other minor rights.

12.2.2 Further categories of membership

The Pharmaceutical Society (EEC Recognition) Order 1987 (S.I. 1987/2202), as amended, was made to allow for the implementation of Council Directive 85/433/EEC, as amended by Council Directive 85/584/EEC. The purpose of these important European legislative provisions was to allow for the mutual recognition of diplomas, certificates and other evidence of formal qualifications in pharmacy.

The 1987 Order inserts a new s. 4A and sch. 1A into the Pharmacy Act 1954. Any national of a member state who holds an appropriate European qualification, and satisfies any prescribed conditions as to character, physical and mental health, is entitled to have their name registered in the United Kingdom register of pharmaceutical chemists. The categories of recognised European qualifications are set out in the new sch. 1A to the 1954 Act.

Article 3 of the 1987 Order amends s. 70(1) and s. 71(1), Medicines Act 1968 which specify conditions in respect of individual pharmacists, partners and bodies corporate, carrying on a retail pharmacy business. The amendments impose the additional condition that such a business is not, for the purposes of those provisions, under the personal control of a pharmacist registered under the mutual recognition procedures, where the business has been open for less than three years.

Articles 4 and 5 of the 1987 Order amend the appropriate NHS legislative provisions relating to the provision of pharmaceutical services. The statutory bodies who are responsible for the provision of pharmaceutical services are required to ensure that a pharmacist, registered under the mutual recognition procedures, who wishes to provide such services has a sufficient knowledge of English for that purpose.

Section XIX of the by-laws allow the Council, by resolution, to enter into reciprocal agreement with the Pharmaceutical Society for Northern Ireland, for the registration as a pharmaceutical chemist under the Pharmacy Act 1954, of a person registered as a pharmaceutical chemist in Northern Ireland, who is able to satisfy the registrar concerning registration in Northern Ireland after qualifying in pharmacy in the United Kingdom or by virtue of holding an appropriate European diploma. An individual applying for registration pursuant to such a reciprocal agreement must also produce, for the registrar, satisfactory evidence of identity, good character, good physical and mental health and details of registration as a pharmaceutical chemist in Northern Ireland. Subject to the production of such evidence and the payment of the appropriate fee such an individual may be registered as a pharmaceutical chemist.

This section of the by-laws also allows the Council, by resolution, to enter into reciprocal agreements with a pharmacists' registration authority in any country or state outside the United Kingdom (other than a member state of the European Union), for the registration as a pharmaceutical chemist under the Pharmacy Act 1954, of any person who is able to produce, to the registrar, satisfactory evidence of residence in the United Kingdom, identity, good character, good physical and mental health, satisfactory evidence of having passed a qualifying examination, and satisfactory evidence of registration and good standing as a pharmacist in the reciprocal state.

In addition, those persons, from an Australian state or from New Zealand, seeking reciprocal registration must also produce: a certificate from the appropriate registrar of the pharmacists' registration authority that, prior to statutory registration, a period of at least one year's employment in pharmacy had been completed; satisfactory evidence of completion in Great Britain of a period of four weeks' experience in the practice of pharmacy in a pharmacy or pharmacy department under the direct personal control and supervision of a pharmacist registered in Great Britain; and a declaration of study of the laws affecting the practice of pharmacy and the current *Code of Ethics* and *Notes for Guidance*. Subject to the production of such evidence and the payment of the appropriate fee such an individual may be registered as a pharmaceutical chemist.

Outside of the reciprocal agreements schemes mentioned above, the Council may, by resolution, authorise the registration as a pharmaceutical chemist under the Pharmacy Act 1954, of a person who produces, to the registrar, satisfactory evidence of residence in the United Kingdom, identity, good character, good physical and mental health, evidence of holding a pharmaceutical qualification comparable with an approved degree in pharmacy awarded in the United Kingdom, and evidence of registration or qualification for registration as a pharmacist in the jurisdiction awarding the pharmaceutical qualification.

The individual seeking registration under these provisions must satisfy an adjudicating committee, appointed by the Council, as to the content and standard of the course and examination in pharmacy already undertaken, knowledge of the current practice of pharmacy in Great Britain and of proficiency in English. Subsequently the individual must produce evidence of completion of a period of employment in Great Britain in the practice of pharmacy under conditions laid down by the adjudicating committee. Subject to the production of such evidence and the payment of the appropriate fee, such an individual may be registered as a pharmaceutical chemist.

12.2.3 Registrar, the register and certificates of registration

Under s. 1, Pharmacy Act 1954, the Council of the Royal Pharmaceutical Society is obliged to keep 'a fit and proper person' appointed as a registrar. Under s. 2, the registrar is given the duty to maintain the register of pharmaceutical chemists and under s. 75, Medicines Act 1968 is under a duty to maintain the register of premises (registered pharmacies). The registrar is under a further duty to have printed, published and made available for sale each year, an annual register of pharmaceutical chemists. Section XXI of the by-laws gives further details of the requirements and form of the register and the annual register. Each entry in the register should include the name of the person concerned, address, a distinguishing registration number, date of registration, and particulars of qualification for registration, in alphabetical order according to surname. Each entry in the annual register contains certain particulars, and is in a particular form, as set out in the third schedule to the by-laws, in alphabetical order according to surname.

Under s. 5, Pharmacy Act 1954, the Council is under a duty, on the demand of any registered pharmaceutical chemist, to issue without fee a certificate of registration signed by the registrar and countersigned by the president of the Royal Pharmaceutical Society or by two members of the Council. If a registered pharmaceutical chemist is able to satisfy the registrar that an originally issued certificate of registration has been lost or destroyed, then a substitute may be issued upon payment of an appropriate fee. Under s. 6, a certificate of registration is admissible in any proceedings as evidence that the person named therein is a registered pharmaceutical chemist, as is a print-out from the annual register of pharmaceutical chemists for its extant year.

Under s. 13, Pharmacy Act 1954, the registrar has certain duties and powers in relation to corrections of the register. These include the removal of the names of deceased pharmaceutical chemists, any entry which was procured by fraud, and any other alteration deemed necessary by the Council's direction. The registrar may also remove names by default where, after the making of further enquiries, there is evidence of the cessation of practice or change of address without notification.

Under s. 20, any person who fraudulently exhibits any certificate purporting to be a certificate of membership of the Royal Pharmaceutical Society, or, with intent to deceive, lends or allows any issued certificate to be used by another person, or makes or copies a certificate, will be guilty of an offence, and will be liable, on conviction, to a fine, and by continuing fines. Failure to return to the registrar a certificate of registration as a pharmaceutical chemist, on cessation of the right to hold it, also amounts to an offence, punishable on conviction by a fine, and by continuing fines. Under s. 18, any registrar wilfully making false entries to the register or the annual register of pharmaceutical chemists will be guilty of an offence, punishable on conviction by a term of imprisonment.

Under s. 17, Pharmacy Act 1954, the Council may, out of the property of the Society, and out of any property comprised in the benevolent fund, make provision for the relief of distressed persons, being:

(a)   members;

(b)   persons who at any time have been members or have been registered as pharmaceutical chemists or as chemists and druggists;

(c)   widows, orphans, or other dependants of deceased persons who were at any time members or registered as aforesaid; and

(d)   students.

Section XV of the by-laws makes further provision for benevolent funds, establishing and making provision for three different funds, the Benevolent Fund, the Orphan Fund and the Birdsgrove House Fund. The first of these is applicable, at the discretion of the Council, towards the purposes outlined in s. 17, Pharmacy Act 1954. The Orphan Fund is to be applied for similar purposes to those of the Benevolent Fund except that it is to be applied towards the relief of distressed persons who are the orphan children of deceased persons who were at any time members and not otherwise. The Birdsgrove House Fund is again to be applied for similar purposes as the other two except that the fund is applicable towards the establishment and maintenance of convalescent homes for the relief of distressed persons who are current or past members of the widows, orphans or other dependants of deceased past members.

12.3   FITNESS TO PRACTISE

The Pharmacists (Fitness to Practise) Act 1997 amended the Pharmacy Act 1954 to allow for the establishment of a new committee of the Royal Pharmaceutical Society of Great Britain to consider allegations against registered pharmaceutical chemists of unfitness to practise due to ill health. The new provisions also enable the committee to impose practising conditions on, or suspend from registration, registered pharmaceutical chemists whose ability to practise it finds to be seriously impaired due to ill health.

A new s. 13A is inserted into the Pharmacy Act 1954 which provides for the appointment of the health committee of the Royal Pharmaceutical Society of Great Britain. Under the provisions of a new sch. 1B, the health committee consists of a chairman and deputy chairman appointed by the Privy Council and six other members appointed by the Council. The members appointed by the Privy Council must be registered medical practitioners at the time of their appointment, and at least three of the other members must be registered pharmaceutical chemists at the time of their appointment.

The chairman and deputy chairman hold office for five years and may be eligible for reappointment. Other members hold office for such period as may be determined by the Council. Any member may resign by giving the appropriate notice. Any member who is subject to a practice or suspension order will automatically cease to be a member of the health committee.

In any case, the function of the health committee is performed by three members, of whom one will be the chairman or the deputy chairman, with the others being selected by the chairman from among the members appointed by the Council. One of these others must be a registered pharmaceutical chemist. The health committee is assisted in its functions by legal assessors. These legally qualified persons have the statutory function of giving advice on questions of law arising in connection with any matter which the committee is considering. Provision is made for the payment of fees and expenses to members of the health committee and to legal assessors.

Provision is made in a new s. 13B, Pharmacy Act 1954 for a preliminary investigation by the Council of an allegation to the effect that the ability of a registered pharmaceutical chemist to practise is seriously impaired because of their physical or mental condition. Where such an allegation is made to the Council, they must notify the pharmaceutical chemist of the allegation and invite observations within 28 days, or within a shorter period where the Council considers the allegation to be well founded and it is necessary to protect members of the public without delay.

The Council is also under a duty to take such steps as are reasonably practicable to obtain as much information as possible about the case, and consider, in the light of the information which it has been able obtain, and any observations duly made to it by the pharmaceutical chemist, whether in its opinion there is a case to answer. Where the Council concludes that there is a case to answer, it must notify the pharmaceutical chemist of that conclusion and refer the allegation to the health committee. Where the Council concludes that there is no case to answer, the pharmaceutical chemist involved must be notified of that conclusion.

Where an allegation is referred to the health committee under the circumstances outlined in the previous paragraph, the health committee is under a duty to consider it, under the provisions of a new s. 13C, Pharmacy Act 1954. Where, after having considered the allegation, the health committee is satisfied that it is well founded, the committee must make one of two specific orders. The first, known as a 'conditions of practice order', imposes conditions which the pharmaceutical chemist must comply with while practising as a pharmaceutical chemist, for a period to be specified in the order. The second, known as a 'suspension order', directs the registrar to suspend the pharmaceutical chemist's registration for a period to be specified in the order. The periods specified in a conditions of practice order or a suspension order will not exceed three years.

Under the provisions of a new s. 13G, Pharmacy Act 1954, the Council of the Royal Pharmaceutical Society may make regulations as to the procedure to be followed on consideration of an allegation against a pharmaceutical chemist under s. 13C (and for review of any order made under s. 13D to be discussed below). The regulations must include provision for the service of notice on the pharmaceutical chemist, the opportunity for the pharmaceutical chemist to present a case, legal representation at any hearing, the conduct and form of any such hearing, the attendance of witnesses and the production of documents and the admissibility of evidence. At the time of writing, no such procedural regulations have been made by the Council.

Where the health committee makes a suspension order with respect to a pharmaceutical chemist, it may also make an order directing the registrar to suspend the pharmaceutical chemist's registration with immediate effect. This latter order, known as an 'interim suspension order', is provided for under the provisions of a new s. 13F, Pharmacy Act 1954. The health committee may only make an interim suspension order when it is satisfied that it is necessary to do so in order to protect members of the public.

Under the provisions of a new s. 13D, Pharmacy Act 1954, the health committee is given power to review a conditions of practice order or a suspension order, made in respect of a pharmaceutical chemist, at any time while the order has effect. In particular the health committee is under a duty to review such an order on the written application of a pharmaceutical chemist. Such an application will not be considered where an application to review, made within the previous twelve months, was unsuccessful.

When a suspension order is reviewed by the health committee, it may confirm, revoke, or vary the suspension order, replace the order with a conditions of practice order or make a conditions of practice order with which the pharmaceutical chemist must comply, on the resumption of any practice at the end of the period of suspension. Variation may include the extension or reduction of the period specified in the order, or the imposition of additional conditions, or removal or alteration of existing conditions in a conditions of practice order. In any case, the period specified in the order may not be extended by more than three years.

In exercising any power to make, confirm, vary or revoke a conditions of practice order or a suspension order, the health committee must ensure, under the provisions of a new s. 13E, Pharmacy Act 1954, that any conditions imposed, or period of suspension, is the minimum which it considers necessary for the protection of the public.

The making (and confirmation, review, variation, and revocation) of conditions of practice orders and suspension orders impose new duties on the Registrar of the Royal Pharmaceutical Society of Great Britain. These duties are dealt with under a new s. 13H, Pharmacy Act 1954. Notes of conditions of practice orders and suspension orders (both interim and full) must be entered into the register together with details of any revocation or variation on review, or on appeal. Where interim suspension orders cease to have effect, notes of them are deleted from the register. A pharmaceutical chemist who is subject to a suspension order or an interim suspension order is treated as if their name was not registered for most purposes under the Medicines Act 1968, the Misuse of Drugs Act 1971, the Poisons Act 1972 and the National Health Service legislation.

For the purposes of a new s. 13J, Pharmacy Act 1954, a conditions of practice order, a suspension order, the variation of an order on a review, or the replacement of an order with another order under review, are all 'appealable decisions'. This means that an appeal against such a decision may be made, within 28 days of notification of it, to an appeal tribunal.

Appeal tribunals are established for this purpose by the Privy Council. The provisions of sch. 1C to the Pharmacists (Fitness to Practise) Act 1997 apply in relation to such tribunals. An appeal tribunal consists of three members of whom one is the chairman, one must be a registered medical practitioner, and one must be a registered pharmaceutical chemist. Members of the appeal tribunals are drawn from a panel of members appointed by the Privy Council and consisting of a chairman and deputy chairman, two registered medical practitioners, and two registered pharmaceutical chemists.

Members of the Council, Statutory Committee, office holders and employees of the Royal Pharmaceutical Society of Great Britain are ineligible for membership of the panel of members. To be qualified as the chairman or deputy chairman, an individual must have certain legal qualifications. The appointment of the chairman and deputy chairman must also be approved by the Lord Chancellor and the Lord Advocate. Members of the panel hold office for a period of five years and are eligible for reappointment at the end of their period of office. Members of the panel may resign at any time by giving notice in writing, Privy Council. The Privy Council may also remove any member of the panel from office for inability to perform duties or for misbehaviour. Any member of the panel who is subject to a conditions of practice order or suspension order will also cease to be a member.

A new s. 13K, Pharmacy Act 1954 provides for the procedure for hearing and determining appeals. Appeals are to be by way of a rehearing of the case with the Council of the Royal Pharmaceutical Society of Great Britain acting as respondent to the appeal. The Council is also given power to make regulations for the procedure to be followed on appeal. The regulations must make provision for the manner in which the appeal is to be made, the opportunity for the pharmaceutical chemist involved to put a case at a hearing, legal representation at any hearing, the conduct and form of any such hearing, the attendance of witnesses and the production of documents and the admissibility of evidence. At the time of writing, no such procedural regulations have been made by the Council.

Under the provisions of a new s. 13L, Pharmacy Act 1954, an appeal tribunal may confirm, revoke, or vary a conditions of practice order or a suspension order, replace a suspension order with a conditions of practice order or make a conditions of practice order with which the pharmaceutical chemist must comply, on the resumption of any practice at the end of the period of suspension. Variation may include the extension or reduction of the period specified in the order, or the imposition of additional conditions, or removal or alteration of existing conditions in a conditions of practice order. In any case, the period specified in the order may not be extended by more than three years. Any decision of the appeal tribunal may be made by a majority of its members.

In exercising any power to make, confirm, vary or revoke a conditions of practice order or a suspension order, the appeal tribunal must ensure under the provisions of s. 13E, Pharmacy Act 1954, that any conditions imposed, or period of suspension, is the minimum which it considers necessary for the protection of the public. The appeal tribunal may award costs or expenses.

12.4 PROFESSIONAL DISCIPLINE

Section 7, Pharmacy Act 1954 provides for the appointment of a committee of the Royal Pharmaceutical Society to be known as the Statutory Committee. Further provisions relating to the constitution and procedure of the Statutory Committee are to be found in sch. 1 to the 1954 Act.

The Statutory Committee consists of six members. The chairman, who must be a person having practical legal experience, is appointed by the Privy Council. The remaining five members are appointed by the Council of the Royal Pharmaceutical Society. An individual may be appointed to membership of the Statutory Committee whether or not they are also a member of the Royal Pharmaceutical Society or the Council of the Royal Pharmaceutical Society. At least one member must be a pharmacist resident in Scotland.

A term of office for a member is five years with outgoing members being eligible for reappointment. Any member may resign office by giving notice in writing and provision is made for removal of a member for inability to perform duties or for misbehaviour. The quorum of the Statutory Committee is three, of whom the chairman must be one. The Statutory Committee acts by majority vote of the members present, with the chairman having a casting vote.

Under paragraph 5(1) of sch. 1, Pharmacy Act 1954, the Statutory Committee is given the power to make regulations as to the procedure to be followed by it in exercising its jurisdiction under the Pharmacy Act 1954, subject to approval by the Privy Council. The main regulations made under this power are now the Pharmaceutical Society (Statutory Committee) Order of Council 1978 (S.I. 1978/20).

Under reg. 3, where the Secretary of the Statutory Committee receives information from which it appears that:

(a) a registered pharmaceutical chemist, or a person employed by a pharmaceutical chemist in the carrying on of business, has been convicted of a criminal offence, or has been guilty of misconduct; or

(b) a body corporate carrying on a retail pharmacy business has been convicted of an offence under the relevant Acts; or

(c) a member of the board or any officer of or person employed by a body corporate carrying on a retail pharmacy business has been guilty of an offence, or been guilty of misconduct; or

(d) a representative or person employed by a representative in the retail pharmacy business has been convicted of a criminal offence, or been guilty of misconduct; or

(e) a person applying to be registered as a pharmaceutical chemist has been convicted of a criminal offence, or has been guilty of misconduct; or

(f) a person whose name has been removed from the register under s. 12, Pharmacy Act 1954 or a person employed by that person in the carrying on of business, has been convicted of a criminal offence, or been guilty of misconduct;

the secretary must submit the information, or a summary of the information to the chairman of the Statutory Committee.

Where the information is in the nature of a complaint charging misconduct, the chairman may require that any allegation of fact is substantiated by a written statement signed by a responsible person or, if necessary, by a statutory declaration, stating the source of the information and the grounds for believing its truth. In addition, the chairman may direct the secretary to invite the person concerned to submit in writing any answer or explanation.

After considering the information, any evidence in support of it, and any answer or explanation submitted by the person affected, the chairman may take any of the following forms of action:

(a)   the chairman may decide that the case will not proceed any further where he or she has formed the opinion that the case is not within the jurisdiction of the Statutory Committee, the complaint is of a frivolous character or owing to lapse of time or other circumstances, the complaint may properly be disregarded;

(b)   the chairman may, after consultation orally or by letter with the other members of the Statutory Committee, decide that the case will not proceed further but that the secretary should send a reprimand to the person affected and issue a caution as to future conduct, where the chairman is of the opinion that the conviction or misconduct is not of a serious nature or is, for any other reason, of such a character that the matter can be disposed of without an inquiry;

(c)   in any other case, the chairman must direct the secretary to take the necessary steps for the holding of an inquiry by the Statutory Committee.

The chairman is under a duty to report to the Statutory Committee any case where there is a direction that no inquiry is to be held.

Prior to the holding of an inquiry, the secretary instructs a solicitor to investigate the facts of the case, and to present, or brief counsel to present, the case to the Statutory Committee at the inquiry. Such instruction is not necessary where the complainant elects to present their own case to the Statutory Committee. Any instructed solicitor may report that the available evidence is insufficient to prove the conviction or misconduct. In such a case, the Statutory Committee must consider such a report and decide whether an inquiry should be held.

Where directions have been given for an inquiry to be held, the secretary will give 28 days' notice to the affected person of the date, time and place of the inquiry. The notice must in the prescribed form and must be sent in the prescribed manner, and provision is made for reduced periods of notice, for adjournment or postponement of the inquiry and for the inspection, and service of information and evidence.

The inquiry must be held in public and the person affected and the complainant may be represented by a solicitor or counsel, or in the case of a body corporate, by a director or other officer. An inquiry may proceed in the absence of the person affected where the Statutory Committee is satisfied that the requisite notice was served.

The order of proceedings is that the statement of the case against the person affected and the production of evidence in support of it will be presented first. This will be followed by the statement of the case of the person affected and the production of evidence in support of that. Finally there will be a reply to the case of the person affected which will not be allowed where the person affected has produced no other evidence. Provision is made for the giving of evidence, the putting of questions by members of the Statutory Committee and for the further adjournment of a case where the inquiry has commenced. At the conclusion of the hearing, the Statutory Committee deliberates in private and may decide:

(a) whether the conviction or misconduct alleged is proved;

(b) if so, whether the conviction or misconduct is such as to render the person affected unfit to remain on the register;

(c) if so, whether the registrar should be directed that the name be removed from the register; and

(d) whether any reprimand or admonition should be addressed to the person affected.

The Statutory Committee may decide to postpone its decision or any part of it. When the decision is made, it must be announced in public by the chairman and the secretary must communicate the decision to the person affected, the complainant, and the registrar, where appropriate.

Since its jurisdiction was first established, the cases dealt with by the Statutory Committee cover a wide range of subject-matter. Its findings on individual cases are published on a regular basis in the pages in the *Pharmaceutical Journal*. For example, two cases reported on 30 January 1999, relate to a striking-off order, subject to appeal, on the basis of excessive sales of codeine linctus, and the refusal of an application for restoration of a pharmacist's name to the register until the Statutory Committee was satisfied that she was no longer suffering from alcohol abuse. Other common cases relate to supervision, theft, unlawful sales, unsatisfactory premises, and dispensing mistakes.

Under s. 10, Pharmacy Act 1954, any person aggrieved by a direction of the Statutory Committee may, within three months of notification of it, appeal to the High Court. The Royal Pharmaceutical Society may appear as the respondent in any such appeal. The High Court may, on any such appeal, make any such order as it thinks fit, including an order as to costs. The order of the High Court in these circumstances is final. Again, there have been a number of important appeals heard under this jurisdiction. The resultant decisions form important precedents in determining future Statutory Committee cases, and other appeals to the High Court.

12.4.1 Applications for restoration to the register

Applications may also be made to the Statutory Committee for restoration of the name of the applicant to the register, or variation or revocation of any direction given by the Statutory Committee. Any application made under these provisions must be supported by a statutory declaration made by the applicant and must be accompanied by at least two certificates of the applicant's identity and good character. One of these certificates must be given by a registered pharmaceutical chemist and the other must be given by a registered pharmaceutical chemist, a registered medical practitioner, a justice of the peace or a legally qualified holder of a judicial office.

Where the name of the applicant for restoration was removed on a complaint made a person who appeared before the Statutory Committee, notice of the application for restoration must be served on that person, and they must be allowed to make any representations to the Statutory Committee. In turn, any such written representations and comments must be passed on to the applicant.

In considering an application, the Statutory Committee may take into account any information, which it has in its possession, concerning the applicant's conduct during the period which has elapsed since the original direction was given. Any adverse report contained in such information may be sent to the applicant. Applications for restoration to the register are now usually held in public. Unless the Statutory Committee decides to grant the application without a hearing, it must give the applicant an opportunity to appear before it in person or by a legal representative, and of adducing evidence. The decision of the Statutory Committee on such an application is communicated to the applicant, to any objector and to the registrar.

12.5 PROFESSIONAL RESPONSIBILITY WITHIN THE NATIONAL HEALTH SERVICE

12.5.1 NHS complaints procedure

In the mid-1990s, concern about the structure of the complaints and discipline procedures within the National Health Service led to the establishment of a committee, under the chairmanship of Professor Alan Wilson, to consider proposals for reform and restructuring. The committee's initial report, *Being Heard* (London: Department of Health, 1994) led, in turn, to a further period of consultation on the conclusions and proposed recommendations. Following this, the government, in March 1995, published a further document, *Acting on Complaints,* (London: Department of Health, EL (95) 37). Finally, the government produced detailed guidance on the form, structure and implementation of the new complaints system in March 1996, in *Complaints... Acting... Improving; Guidance on Implementation of the NHS Complaints Procedure* (London: NHS Executive, March 1996). Further guidance on the implications of the new complaints procedure for pharmacists is provided by the Department of Health in *Complaints... Acting... Improving; Guidance for Community Pharmacists and other providers of NHS Pharmaceutical Services* (London: Department of Health, NHS Executive 1996).

The new complaints procedure is separated from the disciplinary procedure which is described in more detail in 12.5.3. The complaints procedure is two-tiered with the expectation that most complaints will be dealt with at 'local' level through a process of 'local resolution'. The second tier, at health authority level, may involve a procedure called 'independent review'.

In the case of complaints against pharmacists, the new local resolution complaints process was introduced via the National Health Service (Pharmaceutical Services) Amendment Regulations 1996 (S.I. 1996/698). These regulations introduced significant changes to the terms of service of chemists by, amongst other things, inserting new paragraphs 10A and 10B relating to complaints. Chemists are under a duty to establish, and operate, a procedure to deal with any complaints made by or on behalf of any person to whom the chemist has provided pharmaceutical services. A chemist must co-operate with any investigation of a complaint by the health authority in accordance with the procedures which it operates under directions given by s. 17, MA 1968, whether the investigation follows one under the chemist's complaints procedure or not.

The co-operation required includes answering questions reasonably put to the chemist by the health authority, providing any information relating to the complaint reasonably required by the health authority, and attending any meeting to consider the complaint (if held at a reasonably accessible place and at a reasonable hour, and due notice has been given), if the chemist's presence at the meeting is reasonably required by the health authority. There are further requirements relating to the complaints procedure, outlined in a rider to the new paragraphs 10A and 10B:

(a) The complaints procedure to be established by a chemist may be such that it also deals with complaints made in relation to one or more other chemists.

(b) The complaints procedure to be established by a chemist who provides pharmaceutical services from more than one set of premises may be such that it relates to all those premises together.

(c) A complaints procedure shall apply to complaints made in relation to any matter reasonably connected with the chemist's provision of pharmaceutical services and within the responsibility or control of:

(i) the chemist;

(ii)   where the chemist is a body corporate, any of its directors or former directors;

(iii)   a former partner of the chemist;

(iv)   any pharmacist employed by the chemist;

(v)   any employee of the chemist other than one falling within (iv),

(d)   A complaint may be made on behalf of any person with his consent, or:

(i)   where he is under 16 years of age:

(1)   by either parent, or in the absence of both parents, the guardian or other adult person who has care of the child; or

(2)   where he is in the care of an authority to whose care he has been committed under the provisions of the Children Act 1989 or in the care of a voluntary organisation, by that authority or voluntary organisation; or

(ii)   where he is incapable of making a complaint, by a relative or other adult person who has an interest in his welfare.

(e)   A complaint may be made as respects a person who has died by a relative or other adult person who had an interest in his welfare, or where he was as described in (d)(i)(2), by the authority or voluntary organisation.

(f)   A complaints procedure shall comply with the following requirements:

(i)   the chemist must specify a person (who need not be connected with the chemist and who, in the case of an individual, may be specified by his job title) to be responsible for receiving and investigating all complaints;

(ii)   all complaints must be:

(1)   recorded in writing;

(2)   acknowledged, either orally or in writing, within the period of three days (excluding Saturdays, Sundays, Christmas Day, Good Friday and bank holidays) beginning with the day on which the complaint was received by the person specified under (i), or where that is not possible, as soon as reasonably practicable; and

(3)   properly investigated;

(iii)   within the period of 10 days (excluding Saturdays, Sundays, Christmas Day, Good Friday and bank holidays) beginning with the day on which the complaint was received by the person specified under (i) or, where that is not possible, as soon as reasonably practicable, the complainant must be given a written summary of the investigation and its conclusions;

(iv)   where the investigation of the complaint requires consideration of any records relating to the person as respects whom the complaint is made, the person specified under (i) must inform him or the person acting on his behalf if the investigation will involve disclosure of information contained in those records to a person other than the chemist or a director, partner or employee of the chemist; and

(v) the chemist must keep a record of all complaints and copies of all correspondence relating to complaints, but such records must be kept separate from any records relating to the person by whom the complaint was made.

(g) At each of the premises at which the chemist provides pharmaceutical services he must provide information about the complaints procedure and give the name (or title) and address of the person specified under (f)(i).

The health authority may be asked to trigger the second stage of the new complaints process, where the local resolution procedure has failed, or where the complainant wishes to bypass it directly. To assist in the resolution of complaints at this second tier, health authorities are required to establish an internal complaints process. This process includes the appointment of a complaints manager and a convener.

The general role of the complaints manager is to oversee the complaints procedure. The detailed responsibilities and functions of the complaints manager, which may be to investigate, or advise, or both, are determined by the board of each relevant health authority. The role of the convener, who is a non-executive director of the health authority concerned, is to look at complaints and decide whether to agree to a request for an independent review of the complaint. It is stressed in the guidance that health authority action will be flexible and will not need to follow strict procedures. The convener will have several options including:

(a) referring the complaint back to the pharmacy for further action under the local resolution procedure if it appears that this procedure has not been exhausted;

(b) arranging conciliation, where it appears that this might be helpful, using health authority provided conciliation services;

(c) setting up an independent review panel to investigate the complaint;

(d) taking no further action where it is clear that everything which could have been done has been done; or

(e) advising the complainant of his or her right to approach the Health Service Commissioner.

In making a decision under (c), the convener is assisted by an independent lay chairman nominated by the Secretary of State for Health from a list held by the regional office of the NHS Executive. If clinical or professional advice is required, it will be provided by independent practitioners nominated by local practitioner committees, and based outside the health authority area.

Where it is decided to establish an independent review panel, it will be composed of three members, an independent lay chairman, nominated as above, the convener, and another independent lay member, nominated by the Secretary of State from the regional office list. Where the complaint is wholly or partly related to clinical matters, panels must be advised by at least two independent clinical assessors, nominated by the local practitioner committees. The independent clinical assessors' role is to advise, and make a report, or reports, to the panel on the clinical aspects of the complaint.

The role of the independent lay panel chairman is to help the convener by providing independent advice and support during the convening period, and to chair the panel where established. Once the convener's decision has been made to establish an independent review panel, and its terms of reference have been set, the responsibility for leading the organisation of the panel's business falls to the chairman.

The function of the independent review panel is to investigate the complaints set out in the convener's terms of reference, taking into account the complainant's grievance as recorded in writing to the convener, and to make a report setting out its conclusions, with appropriate comments and conclusions. The panel decides on how to conduct its own proceedings subject to the rules:

(a)   that the panel's proceedings must be in private;

(b)   that the panel must give both the complainant and any person complained against a reasonable opportunity to express their views on the complaint;

(c)   that the chairman's decision on procedure is final, in the event of any disagreement; and

(d)   that when being interviewed, by any members of the panel or by the assessors, the complainant and any other person interviewed may be accompanied by a person of their choosing, who may, with the agreement of the panel chairman, speak to the panel members or assessors, except that no person interviewed may be accompanied by a legally qualified person acting as an advocate.

The advice of the NHS Executive is that the panels will not be obliged to engage in lengthy evidence-gathering procedures, nor will they be obliged to conduct formal hearings. The panels are to have flexibility to look at each complaint in the way which best suits the individual circumstances, the aim being to resolve the complaint as constructively as possible. Panels may decide to hear from each party through separate meetings, or alternatively, to bring them together.

The panel's final report should set out the results of its investigations, outlining its conclusion, with any appropriate comments or suggestions. The panel may not make any recommendations or suggestions in its report relating to disciplinary matters. The final report will be sent to the complainant, the patient (if a different person from the complainant), any person named in the complaint, the clinical assessors, the trust or health authority chairman and chief executive, the practitioner concerned, and any one of a number of other individuals, depending on the nature and form of the complaint.

Following receipt of the panel's report the chief executive of the trust or health authority must write to the complainant informing any action which the trust or health authority is proposing to take as a result of the panel's deliberations, and the right of the complainant to take the grievance to the Health Service Commissioner if they remain dissatisfied.

12.5.2 National Health Service Commissioner

Statutory provision for the office of Health Service Commissioner (or Ombudsman as the office was originally termed) has existed since 1973. The current legislative framework is contained in the Health Service Commissioners Act 1993, which was amended in 1996 through the Health Service Commissioners (Amendment) Act 1996. The function of the Commissioners is to provide a complaints procedure which operates parallel to the existing complaints procedure, but which is to be invoked only when the existing procedure has been exhausted.

Section 1 of the 1993 Act, as amended, continues the office of Health Service Commissioners for England, Wales and Scotland. Detailed provision concerning appointment is contained in sch. 1 to the 1993 Act. Sections 2, 2A and 2B outline the bodies which are subject to investigation by the Health Service Commissioners. The list includes most of those bodies responsible for the provision of health services. The amendments to s. 2, introduced by the 1996 Act, mean that those responsible for the provision of pharmaceutical services under the National Health Service legislation, are also subject to investigation by the Health Service Commissioners.

The general remit of the Commissioners to investigate failure in service and maladministration is set out in s. 3. As already noted, complaints will not be considered where the existing complaints procedure has not been exhausted, nor where there are other proceedings, including legal proceedings, pending. The prohibition against the investigation of complaints relating to the exercise of clinical judgment, contained in s. 5 of the 1993 Act, was substantially removed by the 1996 amendments.

Sections 8–10 of the 1993 Act, as amended, make provision for the form and structure of complaints. Complaints must be in writing, must usually be made by the person aggrieved, and must be made within one year of notice of the matters alleged in the complaint. Before proceeding to investigate the complaint, the Commissioner must be satisfied that notice of it has been brought to the appropriate health service body and that that body has been afforded a reasonable opportunity to investigate and reply to the complainant. Health service bodies may themselves refer a complaint to the Commissioner, in certain defined, limited circumstances.

Where the Commissioner proposes to conduct an investigation pursuant to a complaint, he or she must afford an opportunity to the health service body, or any other person affected by the complaint, an opportunity to comment on the allegations. Investigations must be conducted in private. Otherwise, the procedure is for the Commissioner to determine, as he or she thinks appropriate in the circumstances. The Commissioner may, in particular, obtain such information, and make such inquiries as he or she thinks fit. The Commissioner may determine whether representation, including legal representation, is appropriate, and may order the attendance and examination of witnesses and the production of documents. The Commissioner may certify an offence to the court where a person, without lawful excuse, obstructs the exercise of his or her functions.

The Commissioner must send a copy of the report of the results of the investigation to the complainant, any person who assisted with the complaint, the health service body, and any other person concerned with the complaint. Similarly, where the Commissioner decides not to conduct an investigation, a statement of the reasons for that decision must also be sent to the appropriate persons. The Commissioners' decisions are subject to judicial review in the courts, but otherwise are judicially unenforceable.

If, after conducting an investigation, it appears to a Commissioner that the person aggrieved has sustained an injustice or hardship by way of failure of service or maladministration, and the injustice or hardship has not been and will not be remedied, he or she may lay before Parliament a special report on the case. The Commissioner is also under a duty to make annual reports, to be laid before each House of Parliament, on the performance of his or her functions under the Act.

12.5.3   National Health Service disciplinary procedures

12.5.3.1   Discipline committees   Under the provisions of reg. 3(1) of the National Health Service (Service Committees and Tribunal) Regulations 1992 (S.I. 1992/664), as amended by the National Health Service (Service Committees and Tribunal) Amendment Regulations 1996 (S.I. 1996/703), every Health Authority must have:

(a)   a medical discipline committee;
(b)   a dental discipline committee;
(c)   an ophthalmic discipline committee;
(d)   a pharmaceutical discipline committee; and
(e)   a joint discipline committee;

and may, where it sees fit, have two or more of any of those committees. These committees are known as discipline committees. Three or more health authorities may appoint discipline committees jointly.

Schedule 2 makes provision for the constitution of discipline committees. The discipline committee consists of:

(a)   a chairman; and
(b)   no more than three lay persons appointed by the health authority; and
(c)   no more than three professional persons appointed by the health authority from a list of nominees provided by the relevant local representative committee.

The joint discipline committee consists of:

(a)   a chairman; and
(b)   ten other members of whom:

(i)   two must be lay persons appointed by the Health Authority;
(ii)   two must be doctors appointed by the medical discipline committee;
(iii)   two must be dentists appointed by the dental discipline committee;
(iv)   two must be pharmacists appointed by the pharmaceutical discipline committee;,
(v)   two must be ophthalmic medical practitioners or opticians appointed by the ophthalmic discipline committee.

As respects each committee, not fewer than three lay persons and not fewer than three professional persons are to be appointed as deputies, according to the same provisions as apply to the appointment of members of that committee other than the chairman. Where a member of such a committee other than the chairman is absent, a deputy appointed according to the same provisions as that member may act in his or her place.

The chairman of a committee must be a solicitor or barrister appointed by the health authority. Provision is made for the replacement of a chairman not acceptable to a majority of the other members of the committee. A person appointed as chairman of a committee who is already a member of that committee must, on appointment as chairman, cease to be a member otherwise than as chairman and a new member must be appointed to take his or her place. A person must be appointed to act as deputy for the chairman of any committee and may, in the absence of the chairman, act in the chairman's place.

The health authority may make standing orders with respect to the term of office of any members and deputy members of any committee. The term of office of any member or deputy member of such a committee is not to exceed one year. A chairman of a committee who is not a member of the health authority may attend and take part in any proceedings of the health authority at which a report of that committee is being considered, but may not vote. A person who is a member of a committee must cease to hold office:

(a)   where he or she is the chairman or a lay member, on his or her ceasing to be a lay person;

(b)   where he or she is a member not mentioned in (a), on his or her ceasing to be a professional person.

'Lay member' means, in relation to a discipline committee or joint discipline committee, any member (other than the chairman) who is a lay person. In turn, 'lay person' means a person who is not and never has been:

(a)   a doctor, a dentist, an ophthalmic medical practitioner, an optician or a chemist; nor

(b)   a registered dispensing optician within the meaning of the Opticians Act 1989; nor

(c)   a registered nurse, a registered midwife or a registered health visitor; nor

(d)   an officer of, or otherwise employed by, any health authority, or a community health council.

Under reg. 4(1), where an appropriate health authority receives information which it considers could amount to an allegation that a practitioner has failed to comply with his or her terms of service it must decide either to take no action or to take one or both of the following courses of action:

(a)   to refer the matter to another health authority for investigation by that health authority's appropriate disciplinary committee;

(b)   to refer the information to, as it considers appropriate, the National Health Service Tribunal, the relevant professional body or the local police authority.

Under reg. 6(1) where the disciplinary matter concerns an allegation which has been the subject of a complaint, the appropriate health authority must refer it within 28 days of the allegation having ceased to be the subject of a complaint which is being investigated. Where the disciplinary matter does not concern an allegation which has been the subject of a complaint, the appropriate health authority must refer it within 13 weeks after the event or matter which is the subject of the allegation. The 28 day time limit may be extended for a further 28 days in certain limited circumstances. Schedule 4 has effect with respect to the procedure for investigating disciplinary matters.

Where a disciplinary matter is referred to the appropriate discipline committee, the appropriate health authority must:

(a)   send notice of the referral to the practitioner who is the subject of the matter within two working days of the referral;

(b)   send a statement of case to the discipline committee and the practitioner within 28 days of the referral.

The statement of case must include:

(a)   details of each provision of the practitioner's terms of service with which it is alleged there has been a failure to comply;
(b)   copies of all relevant documentary evidence;
(c)   the name and address of any witness whom the appropriate health authority intends shall give evidence at a hearing before the discipline committee and a copy of any statement made by any witness.

Where the disciplinary matter concerns the conduct of an employed pharmacist, a notice must be sent to the employee within two working days of the referral, asking whether the employee wishes to be treated as a party to the investigation, together with further details of the case. Employees who do not wish to participate in proceedings may nonetheless make comments on the relevant matters.

The health authority which has appointed the discipline committee must in writing:

(a)   inform the parties:

(i)   that there will be a hearing;
(ii)   of the names of the members and deputy members of the discipline committee;

(b)   send to the parties copies of any further correspondence relevant to the disciplinary matter; and
(c)   request in writing each party to forward to the investigating committee within 14 days from the date of the request, copies of any documentary evidence and the names of any witnesses which that party proposes to produce or call at the hearing.

The health authority which has appointed the discipline committee must give to the parties and the secretary of the relevant local representative committee of the appropriate health authority, not less than 21 days' notice in writing of the date, time and place of the hearing and must include with the notice to each party a copy of any documents supplied by the other party and a request to that party to notify the discipline committee in writing whether or not he or she intends to attend the hearing. The chairman of the discipline committee may, upon the application of any party, postpone the hearing.

The health authority which has appointed the discipline committee must, not less than seven days before the date fixed for the hearing, supply to each member of the discipline committee and to the relevant local representative committee for the area of the appropriate health authority, copies of the appropriate health authority's statement of case, of any response of the practitioner, of any comments of an employee and of any further observations or correspondence between the parties.

The hearing before the discipline committee must be in private. The persons allowed to be present are:

(a)   no more than one member or officer of the appropriate health authority and the practitioner;

(b)   any person permitted to accompany a party;

(c)   not more than one person who is a member or officer of the relevant local representative committee for the area of the appropriate health authority and who is authorised by that committee to attend the hearing on its behalf as an observer only;

(d)   any person whose attendance is required for the purpose of giving evidence to the discipline committee;

(e)   not more than two officers of the health authority which has appointed the discipline committee, who have been authorised by that health authority to attend for the purpose of assisting the discipline committee in the discharge of its functions;

(f)   where the parties all consent, and the discipline committee considers it appropriate, any other person.

A party may be accompanied at the hearing by one other person who may assist him or her in the presentation of their case but, if that other person is a barrister or solicitor, they are not permitted to address the committee or put questions to witnesses. No officer or member of any health authority or of any of its committees is permitted to accompany the practitioner. Any person permitted to attend the hearing for the purpose of giving evidence must, unless the discipline committee otherwise directs, be excluded from the hearing except while actually giving evidence.

The procedure for the hearing is provided for in regs. 6 and 8 and sch. 4. There is provision for adjournment in appropriate cases, for the making of submissions and the presentation of evidence. At any hearing of a discipline committee other than a joint discipline committee the quorum consists of a chairman, two lay members and two members who are professional persons. The proceedings at any meeting of a discipline committee must be suspended if, and for so long as the number of members present falls below the quorum or the number of lay members who are present exceeds, or is exceeded by, the number of other members (apart from the chairman) who are present. Where there is an equality of votes among members of a discipline committee, the chairman has a casting vote, but is not otherwise entitled to vote.

Following the hearing, the discipline committee must present to the appropriate health authority a report in writing which is to contain:

(a)   details of the material evidence given to it;

(b)   its findings on all relevant questions of fact;

(c)   the inferences which, in the view of the discipline committee, may properly be drawn from such findings of fact as to whether or not the practitioner has failed to comply with his or her terms of service;

(d)   its reasons for drawing such inferences; and

(e)   its recommendations as to the action which should be taken by the appropriate health authority.

Under reg. 8(1), the appropriate health authority, after due consideration of a report presented to it by the discipline committee, must:

(a)   accept as conclusive the findings of fact made by that committee;

(b)   accept as conclusive the inferences from those findings of fact which that committee considered could properly be drawn from those findings as to whether the practitioner has failed to comply with any of the terms of service detailed in the appropriate health authority's statement of case;

(c)   determine, having regard to any recommendation made by the discipline committee either:

(i)   that no further action should be taken in relation to the report; or

(ii)   that action should be taken in relation to the practitioner.

If the appropriate health authority decides either not to adopt the recommendation of the discipline committee or to take any action not recommended by that committee, it must record in writing its reasons for that decision.

Where it has been determined that a practitioner to whom the report of the discipline committee relates has failed to comply with any of his or her terms of service, the appropriate health authority may:

(a)   determine that an amount is to be recovered from the practitioner, whether by way of deduction from his or her remuneration or otherwise;

(b)   determine that the practitioner should be warned to comply more closely with his or her terms of service in future.

The appropriate health authority must give notice in writing of its determination to the practitioner, any person who is treated as a party, the discipline committee and the Secretary of State, and must include with the notice a copy of the report of the discipline committee, a statement of any reasons recorded by the health authority and a statement as to the rights of appeal to the Secretary of State. Under the provisions of Part III of the Directions as to the

Functions of the Family Health Services Appeal Authority, the Secretary of State's appellate functions are exercised by the Family Health Service Appeal Authority (Establishment and Constitution) Order 1995 (S.I. 1995/621).

Under reg. 9(1) of the 1992 Regulations an appeal may be made to the Secretary of State by a practitioner against a finding of fact, or an adverse inference drawn from a finding of fact, or any determination by a health authority to take action, or in respect of a determination by a health authority that an overpayment has or has not been made in respect of his or her remuneration. A notice of an appeal must be in writing and sent to the Secretary of State within 30 days beginning on the date on which notice of the appropriate health authority's decision was given, and must contain a concise statement of the grounds of appeal upon which the practitioner intends to rely in respect of each ground of appeal.

The Secretary of State considers the appeal on the basis of such evidence as was available to the discipline committee and any further evidence adduced on the appeal, and must:

(a) make such findings of fact as thought fit; and
(b) draw such inferences from those findings as thought fit; and
(c) determine whether or not the practitioner has failed to comply with any one or more of the terms of service and determine what action should be taken in relation to that practitioner.

If the Secretary of State, after considering a notice of appeal and any further particulars furnished by the practitioner, is of the opinion that the notice and particulars disclose no reasonable grounds of appeal, or that the appeal is otherwise vexatious or frivolous, he or she may determine the appeal by dismissing it forthwith. Otherwise, the Secretary of State must send a copy of the notice of appeal, and of any further particulars furnished by the practitioner, to the appropriate health authority, and must invite that authority to submit its observations on the appeal within 28 days of being sent the copy of the notice of appeal. Where such observations are made, a copy of those observations must be sent to the practitioner who must be invited to submit comments on the observations within 21 days of being sent that copy.

The Secretary of State must hold an oral hearing to determine the appeal and must appoint three persons to hear the appeal, of whom one must be a barrister or a solicitor, who acts as chairman; and where the practitioner is a chemist, two registered pharmacists. The Secretary of State must appoint a day for the hearing and must give the practitioner and the appropriate health authority not less than 21 days' notice in writing of the day, time and place of the hearing. Only the practitioner, representative of the health authority, witnesses and representatives may be admitted to a hearing.

The persons hearing the appeal must draw up a report and present it to the Secretary of State who must take it into consideration and determine the appeal. The Secretary of State must give notice in writing to the practitioner and the health authority of the determination and must include with the notice a statement of reasons for the determination. Where the Secretary of State determines that a practitioner has failed to comply with one or more of the terms of service, the Secretary of State must determine whether any, and if so what, amount is to be recovered from the practitioner, whether by way of deduction from remuneration or otherwise. Any sum which falls to be recovered by a health authority is, to the extent that it is not recovered by deduction from the practitioner's remuneration, a debt owed by the practitioner to that health authority.

12.5.3.2 National Health Service tribunal Section 46(1), National Health Service Act 1977, as amended, makes provision for the establishment of a tribunal to inquire, amongst other things, into cases where representations are made that the continued inclusion of a person's name in a list of persons undertaking to provide pharmaceutical services would be prejudicial to the efficiency of the services in question. Provision for the constitution, form and procedure of the tribunal is provided for in sch. 9 to the 1977 Act. Under s. 49 power is given to make regulations covering the tribunal's procedure. That power has been exercised through Part III of the National Health Service (Service Committees and Tribunal) Regulations 1992 (S.I. 1992/664), as amended.

The chairman of the tribunal is appointed by the Lord Chancellor and sits with two other members. One of these is appointed by the Secretary of State following consultation with associations representative of the health authorities. The other member is appointed, where a case relates to the pharmaceutical list, from a panel of registered pharmacists.

Representations to the tribunal that the continued inclusion of a person's name in a pharmaceutical list would be prejudicial to the efficiency of the services in question must:

(a) be made in writing;

(b) be signed by the complainant or on the complainant's behalf by some person authorised by the complainant; and

(c) include a preliminary statement of the alleged facts and the grounds upon which the complainant intends to rely.

The complainant must, if so required by the tribunal, send to it, within 30 days of being so required, a further statement setting out the alleged facts, the grounds on which the representations are made, where a fact is not within the personal knowledge of the person signing the representations, the source of the information and why it is considered to be true; and such further particulars as the tribunal may require.

Where an inquiry is to be held, the tribunal must give to the respondent and complainant notice in writing, in the form set out in sch. 8, that the tribunal intends to hold an inquiry as to the representations made by the complainant. It must also require the complainant, within a time specified in the notice, to send to the tribunal a copy of any document proposed to be put in evidence. The tribunal must send to the respondent a copy of the preliminary statement provided by the complainant, a copy of any further statement, copies of documents which have been provided by the complainant and a notice informing the respondent that he or she may, by a statement in writing, admit or dispute the truth of all or any of the allegations appearing in a statement.

The inquiry must be held by way of an oral hearing, in accordance with the provisions of sch. 9. Notice of the date, time and hearing must be sent to the parties within specific time limits. Provision is made for postponement and adjournment, the admittance of parties to the hearing, representation, and the conduct of the hearing,

Where the grounds on which representations are based are solely that the respondent has been convicted of a criminal offence and the respondent states in writing that he or she admits the conviction and does not want an oral hearing, the tribunal may consider the case on the basis of such documentary evidence submitted to it. At the conclusion of the inquiry the tribunal must, as soon as practicable, issue a decision in writing, signed by the chairman, containing:

(a)   its findings of fact;
(b)   its conclusions;
(c)   any directions it decides to give;
(d)   a statement of the reasons for its decision; and
(e)   any order it decides to make as to costs.

The tribunal must send a copy of its decision to the respondent, the complainant and the Secretary of State; and the Secretary of State must send a copy of the decision to any health authority which appears to be concerned. Where the decision contains a direction of removal of a name from a list, the tribunal must include with the decision a notice to the respondent of a right of appeal to the Secretary of State.

A respondent wishing to appeal against a decision of the tribunal must, within 30 days of being sent the notice, give to the Secretary of State notice of appeal in writing containing a statement of the grounds of appeal on which he or she intends to rely. There must be an oral hearing of the appeal, and the Secretary of State must appoint two people to hear the appeal and report on it. One of these two people must, in a case involving the pharmaceutical list, be a pharmacist. The provisions of sch. 9 apply with respect to the hearing of an appeal. An appeal may, at any time before the date appointed for the hearing, be withdrawn by the appellant giving notice in writing of withdrawal to the

Secretary of State; and where an appeal is withdrawn the Secretary of State must confirm the tribunal's direction.

Otherwise, the Secretary of State must consider the report of the person hearing the appeal, make a decision on the appeal, and give notice in writing of that decision to the appellant, the tribunal, the complainant and any health authority which appears to be concerned. The notice must include a statement of the Secretary of State's reasons for the decision and where the person hearing the appeal has made an order as to costs, details of that order.

An application for a direction that a person shall no longer be disqualified for inclusion in any list may be made to the tribunal or to the Secretary of State. Such an application must be in writing, be signed by or on behalf of the applicant, contain a statement of the grounds on which it is made, and include a copy of each document which the applicant proposes to put in evidence. Regulations 29 and 30 provide for the procedure for the determination of such applications by the tribunal and Secretary of State, which are similar to the foregoing provisions relating to representations for removal.

Following a determination of the application, the Secretary of State must publish any direction of the Tribunal, any confirmation or revocation by the Secretary of State of such a direction of the Tribunal and any imposition or removal of a disqualification.

12.6   CONCLUSION

It is clear that an integral part of being professional and, in particular, being a health care professional, requires the development and promotion of virtues and ideals. These ideals promote the notions of merit and distinction, compassion and integrity. Professions require their members to accord to such ideals and to promote their use in practice.

Professional obligations are important to professions for a number of reasons. First, is important to remember that the aspiration towards virtues such as integrity, honesty, compassion etc. is a necessary precursor to entry to the profession, and helps to identify those with the necessary attributes to act in accordance with the objectives of the profession. Secondly, the recognition and clear definition of the required professional standards defines the parameters of professional practice, and allows professionals to seek to achieve those levels and implement them in their own working procedures and routines. Finally, professional standards allow the profession to gauge and determine the extent to which its individual members are achieving the levels identified and expected of them when they first entered the profession, and which they were expected to realise in professional practice.

As this chapter has shown, the pharmacy profession, with its long history, has been to the fore in the creation and maintenance of ideals and objectives expected of those desiring to join it, and the concurrent sanctions associated with failure to achieve the necessary levels in implementing those standards in practice. The professional pharmacist will treat professional administrative responsibility seriously. The implications of the failure to do so are obvious. Administrative or professional sanction can be more reproving than civil or criminal censure. It can deprive an individual of the attributes of professionalism, result in peer-reproach and castigation, and eliminate, at one stroke, the ability to continue to contribute to health care professionalism and to earn a livelihood.

This chapter has also sought to reinforce the significance of the relationship which pharmacy has with the National Health Service, by describing the implications of a failure to adhere to the internal norms and standards expected of all of those, doctors, pharmacists, nurses, dentists, who are contracted to provide professional health care services. Again, the significance of this aspect of professional pharmacy practice is obvious. The relationship between pharmacy and the NHS is symbiotic. Failure to accept the obligations associated with the relationship could lead to its termination.

THIRTEEN

Professional responsibility — responsibility for failures in drug therapy

13.1 INTRODUCTION

So far we have examined the variety of roles which the pharmacist undertakes in relation to the provision of health care. We have concluded that the pharmacist, together with other members of the primary health care team, has a distinct role in the sale and distribution of medicinal products. What is clear from this analysis is that the pharmacist, unlike the other two participants in the drug distribution process, has direct distributive contact with the patient in relation to all categories of medicinal drug product.

We have also recognised that the pharmacist's professional role has necessarily changed and altered in recent years. The practice of pharmaceutical care is now obliging the pharmacist to share responsibility for the design, implementation and monitoring of a therapeutic plan which seeks to achieve a set of desired therapeutic objectives. We now also know that pharmacists are expected to carry out their various professional roles, and the duties and obligations which arise from them, in a careful and reliable manner. This is what we have referred to as professional responsibility.

The scope of this chapter will be to explore the implications of a failure to act in a professional and responsible manner with respect to the sale and distribution of medicinal products. It is quite clear that a significant proportion of medical negligence claims are directly related to errors in prescribing, monitoring or administering medicinal products. In turn, the severity of injury caused by medication errors, or failures in drug therapy as we shall term it, is equally significant and can include permanent injury or death.

It is important to that remember the scope of professional responsibility described in this chapter also complements the range of duties and obligations which the pharmacist undertakes in relation to the sale and supply of medicinal drug products, as outlined in chapters five to nine.

13.2   PROBLEMS WITH DRUG THERAPY

Brushwood ('The Professional Capabilities and Legal Responsibilities of Pharmacists: Should "Can" Imply "Ought"?' (1996) 44 *Drake Law Review* 439) concludes that the importance of the role of drug therapy in medical treatment cannot be underestimated. He states that, for the most part, modern drug therapy works well, although problems do arise with it. Licensing and approval does not necessarily mean that a drug is problem free. Even proper diagnosis of a patient's condition, followed by the appropriate selection of a patient's medication, will not ensure a successful outcome from drug therapy. Toxicities and therapeutic failures can occur from either the chemistry of the drug or the chemistry of the patient, or both.

It is generally accepted that there are three main types of drug defect — manufacturing defects, design defects and marketing defects. Manufacturing defects are caused by errors which arise during the production process and may affect all, some or only one drug product. Contamination of the drug with another product would be a good example of a manufacturing defect. Design defects arise because the design process itself is imperfect although the manufacturing process is not. Such a defect will necessarily affect all drug products manufactured to the design. Marketing defects arise because of a failure to give an adequate warning of the dangers of the product or adequate guidance for its safe use.

Such failures and poor outcomes from drug therapy often lead to legal action and an attempt to discover who or what is responsible for the harm which has been done to the patient. Quite clearly there are a number of participants in the drug distribution business who may be responsible for such harm. Our analysis of the process of drug distribution undertaken so far, shows that the main participants in the procedure are the manufacturer of the drug, the doctor, and the pharmacist. A patient who has suffered harm as a result of a failure from drug therapy may consider litigation against any one, or a combination of these individuals.

In turn, an individual manufacturer, doctor or pharmacist, sued by a patient, may lay the blame for the failure of the drug therapy at the door of one of the other participants in the drug distribution process. The professional responsibility of a pharmacist for the distribution of drug products may only be understood by exploring the parallel responsibility of the manufacturer and doctor.

13.3   RESPONSIBILITY OF MANUFACTURER FOR DRUG THERAPY FAILURE

The manufacturer's initial role in the drug distribution process is to develop the drug product through a variety of stages — discovery, test, trial and licence. The manufacturer's secondary role is to market the drug product to health care professionals and patients and the final role is to distribute and/or sell the drug product to patients. Distribution and sale may be undertaken either directly through over the counter or pharmacy medicine sales, or via a health care professional through prescription only medicine disbursement.

It is important to note, therefore, that the manufacturer does not have direct distribution contact with the patient. Over the counter and pharmacy medicine sales are usually conducted by a pharmacist or other distributor with legal authority to sell. Prescription only products are distributed through two intermediaries — the prescribing health care professional and the dispensing pharmacist. This has a direct consequence for the patient's remedies against the manufacturer, should the product be defective and cause injury. The interjection of an intermediary (or two) necessarily affects the legal relationship between patient and manufacturer.

Direct liability becomes indirect liability and the patient loses the advantage of consequential legal remedies such as would be available under the sale of goods legislation. The right to make a product liability claim in contract is confined to an injured person who actually buys the goods himself or herself. The contract claim can be brought against the supplier of goods only. In contract there would, as between buyer and seller, normally be implied conditions and warranties as to the quality of the goods. Liability arises even though there is no fault. However the rules of privity of contract would prevent anybody other than the contracting party from relying on them. The patient who is injured by a defective drug product is not without a legal remedy against the manufacturer, but has to enter the minefield of tortious, and other remedies, in order to establish liability.

13.3.1   Manufacturers' duty of care with respect to products

It is important to note that the common law in the United Kingdom treats drug products in precisely the same way as other consumer products. There is no separate body of law to deal with liability for injuries caused by defective pharmaceutical products. A patient injured by a defective drug product is therefore in exactly the same legal position as a consumer injured by a defect in the consumer product which they have purchased.

In this jurisdiction manufacturers of products, including drug products, have a duty to exercise ordinary and reasonable care not to expose the public to an unreasonable risk of harm from the use of their products. It was not until 1932 that it was recognised that a general duty of care was owed by manufacturers to consumers. This was established by the House of Lords in the case of *Donoghue* v *Stevenson* [1932] AC 562. The importance of this decision in the field of product liability lies in the fact that, in his judgment, Lord Atkin described the duty of a manufacturer in the following terms:

> . . . a manufacturer of products, which he sells in such a form as to show that he intends them to reach the ultimate consumer in the form in which they left him with no reasonable possibility of intermediate examination, and with the knowledge that the absence of reasonable care in the preparation or putting up of the products will result in an injury to the consumer's life or property, owes a duty to the consumer to take that reasonable care.

This judgment has been subject to significant interpretation, analysis and application since 1932. It is clear that products will now include drug products and the duty also extends to any container or package in which it is distributed and to any labels, directions or instructions for use which accompany it (*Watson* v *Buckley* [1940] 1 All ER 174, *Holmes* v *Ashford* [1950] 2 All ER 76 and *Vacwell Engineering Co. Ltd* v *BDH Chemicals Ltd* [1971] 1 QB 88).

In *Donoghue* v *Stevenson*, Lord Macmillan was of the view that a manufacturer's liability should end when the manufacturer had parted with the product. It is now accepted (Newdick, 'The Development Risk Defence of the Consumer Protection Act 1987' (1988) 47 CLJ 455) that this is a narrow view and that manufacturers are under specific duties to issue adequate warning notices after putting the product into circulation and, if necessary, to issue a recall programme. We have already seen that the licensing rules also impose a requirement that there exists an adequate recall programme.

Lord Atkin's original analysis of the nature of the duty owed by manufacturers contains the words 'with no reasonable possibility of intermediate examination'. It is generally accepted that an intermediate examination may absolve the defendant manufacturer from liability where it can be shown that the examination ought to have revealed the defect or, importantly in relation to drug products, to have provided a warning which will allow the consumer to use the product safely. For such a defence to 'bite', there must, at least, be the probability that an intermediate examination will take place, a fact which the plaintiff need not prove. We have already noted that, in the drug distribution process, drug products will pass from the manufacturer, through the hands of at least one, and possibly two, intermediaries.

As part of the general duty of care, the manufacturer is required to provide adequate information about the product, including warnings, so that the product may be used safely. If the manufacturer supplies an adequate and proper warning to the user of the product and the user ignores the warning, then the manufacturer will be under no liability to the user. The question of what is an adequate and proper warning will be determined according to criteria such as the nature of the product, the degree of hazard inherent in it and the location and prominence of the warnings.

In the United Kingdom, a manufacturer may discharge the duty to supply information and warnings by supplying the information or warning to an intermediary. The case of *Holmes* v *Ashford* [1950] 2 All ER 76 was concerned with the supply of a hair dye by the manufacturers to hairdressers. The manufacturers included a warning that the dye could be harmful to certain individuals and that tests ought to be carried out before use. The claimant who contracted dermatitis after the dye was used on her hair failed in her claim against the manufacturer. Tucker LJ made these comments (at p. 80) about the supply of warnings to an intermediary:

In my view, if [the manufacturers] give a warning which if read by [an intermediary], is sufficient to intimate to [the intermediary] the potential dangers of the substance with which he is going to deal, that is all that can be expected of them. I think that it would be unreasonable and impossible to expect that they should give warning in such form that it must come to the knowledge of the particular customer who is going to be treated . . . The most that can be expected of the manufacturers of goods of this kind is to see that [the intermediary] is sufficiently warned.

13.3.2 Manufacturer's duty of care and drug products

How do these general principles apply to the specificity of drug products? There is no authoritative judicial pronouncement on this issue but several leading academic commentators in the United Kingdom have made it clear that in the field of medicinal products — at least those medicinal products available on prescription — the manufacturer's duty to warn is discharged by the provision of information to intermediaries (Miller and Lovell, *Product Liability*, London, Butterworths, 1977 and Clark, *Product Liability*, London, Sweet & Maxwell, 1989).

The 'informed intermediary doctrine' has been judicially recognised in the United States of America for some time. A good summary of the current position in that jurisdiction is to be found in the case of *Pitman* v *The Upjohn Company* (1994) Westlaw 663372 (Tenn. 1994). In its discussion of the manufacturer's liability, the court recognised that drug manufacturers have a duty to exercise ordinary and reasonable care not to expose the public to an unreasonable risk of harm from the use of their products. This included a requirement to market and distribute the products in a way which minimised the risk or danger.

However the court also recognised that under the 'informed intermediary doctrine' the manufacturer of an unavoidably risky prescription drug has no duty to warn patients directly and can fully discharge its duty to warn by providing the doctor with adequate warnings of the risks associated with the use of its drug. The question of the adequacy of a warning was one of fact to be decided in accordance with certain criteria.

As noted above, although there is no authoritative judicial pronouncement on this issue, we can conclude that, in general terms, the 'informed intermediary doctrine' applies in the United Kingdom. The manufacturer of an unavoidably risky prescription drug has no duty to warn patients directly and can fully discharge its duty to warn by providing the doctor and pharmacist with adequate warnings of the risks associated with the use of its drug.

Evidence supporting the 'informed intermediary doctrine' is to be found in the legislation which controls the licensing of drug products in the United Kingdom. As we have already seen, in section 4.16, under s. 96, Medicines Act 1968, the licence holder of a drug product may not promote a drug product to doctors through advertisements or other representations unless those doctors have been provided with a copy of the pharmaceutical manufacturer's data sheet about the drug product in the prescribed form within the preceding fifteen months.

The doctor will thus be compulsorily supplied with information about drug products by the drug manufacturer and is likely to obtain further information about the drug product from other authoritative sources such as the *Data Sheet Compendium* prepared by the Association of the British Pharmaceutical Industry, the *British National Formulary* and the *Monthly Index of Medical Specialities*.

In order for the manufacturers to discharge their duty to warn under the 'informed intermediary doctrine' the information which is supplied to the doctor and pharmacist must be adequate. Adequacy will be a question of fact to be judged according to criteria such as the magnitude of the risk and the seriousness of the injury which might result. A claimant who has been injured by a defective drug product and who wishes to sue a manufacturer in negligence would therefore need to show that no warning was given at all or that the warnings which were given were not adequate.

13.3.3   Breach of the manufacturer's duty of care

Newdick outlines the degree or standard of care which is expected of manufacturers of products at common law ('The Development Risk Defence of the Consumer Protection Act 1987' (1988) 47 *CLJ* 455 at p. 457):

Negligence does not require standards of absolute product safety from manufacturers. The extent of their duty to guard against defects has depended on a consideration of the nature of the risk presented by an activity, in terms of its likelihood and severity and the probable effectiveness of precautions. The greater the danger, the more that must be done to avoid or minimise it. If a particular manufacturer possesses more extensive knowledge of the risks presented by an undertaking than his competitors, he will be judged according to the more demanding standards of his own knowledge. On the other hand if he has less knowledge, he may be required to employ consultants to assist in the identification, or management, of the danger.

Newdick reinforces this view by stating that a manufacturer must keep abreast of leading developments and with increasing development comes an increasing obligation to remain familiar. In relation to particularly dangerous products, there may be a positive obligation to discover knowledge particular to that product. Finally, Newdick is of the view that, while a manufacturer might have regard to the standards currently adopted in the industry, adherence to those standards will not absolve liability where they have become outmoded.

In many cases, the task of proving that a defendant drug manufacturer did not reach the appropriate standard may be a difficult one for the claimant. It is difficult as it involves a detailed investigation of the defendant's processes of manufacture, design and testing, a comparison with industry standards, and a contrast with procedures adopted by other producers in the same field. The claimant will need to employ an expert witness or witnesses who can analyse these processes and procedures and pinpoint any lack of care which may have caused the defect in the product and therefore caused the injury. If the claimant is unable to prove a breach of duty, the loss may have to be borne without compensation unless there is another available legal basis for the claim.

Brazier (*Medicines, Patients and the Law*, London, Penguin, 1992) is of the view that a claimant's greatest difficulty in any claim against a drug company for a drug defect injury will be in proving that the drug caused the injury. The link between cause and effect in other product liability cases can be established clearly and quickly. With drug products, there may be significant delay in effect. Brazier notes that delay in effect is only one of the claimant's problems. The claimant may have difficulty in showing that the injury was caused by the defect in the drug taken rather than arising from some natural cause.

Newdick, in the article cited above, points to a second problem in causation which relates to the identification of the manufacturer of the drug product alleged to be defective and alleged to have caused the injury. That problem often arises because the drug has been prescribed under its generic, rather than its brand name, or because a number of different brand name drugs have been prescribed over a period of time. Newdick states that the courts take a strict view of the establishment of liability in these cases. The claimant must prove the claim on the balance of probabilities. The production of two defendants, when it is clear that only one is responsible, defeats the claim.

13.3.4 Obtaining compensation from the manufacturer

We have already seen in section 10.3.3 that, for a claimant to obtain damages in negligence he or she must show that loss has been suffered as a result of the defendant's breach. In reality this involves two separate issues — the issues of causation and remoteness of damage. The claim will fail if the link between the manufacturer's breach of duty and the claimant's loss cannot be proved. In turn, the manufacturer is only liable to compensate a patient for the type of damage which was reasonably foreseeable as a result of the defect in the drug therapy.

Where the patient has successfully established all of the elements of the negligence claim against the manufacturer, the claim may still fail because the manufacturer may raise a defence such as contributory negligence, or voluntary assumption of risk. Alternatively the claim might fail because it is commenced outside the statutory limitation periods. The implications of these aspects of a negligence claim were discussed in chapter ten.

However it is important to remember that a patient who is injured as a result of failures in drug therapy, and who is able to overcome the broad range of legal hurdles outlined above, may receive substantial compensation, including damages for physical injury, psychological injury, and economic loss, including loss of earnings.

13.3.5   Strict liability for failures in drug therapy

Following reports from a number of sources, including the Pearson Commission (*Royal Commission on Civil Liability and Compensation for Personal Injury*, 1978, Cmnd 7054), the Law Commission, the Scottish Law Commission (*Liability for Defective Products*, 1977, Cmnd 6831, Law Com No. 82, Scot Law Com No. 45), and the Council of Europe (*European Convention on Product Liability in regard to Personal Injury and Death*, 22 January 1977), a Directive on Product Liability 85/374/EEC ([1985] OJ L210/29) has been agreed, ratified and adopted by the member states.

The directive had a two-fold purpose of establishing a uniform system of product liability within the EU in order to remove distortions of trade and competition which arise because of the differences between the laws of member states in the field of product liability; and to solve the problem of a fair apportionment of the risks inherent in modern technological production.

There were lengthy negotiations between the member states on the terms of the directive. This gave rise to a number of optional provisions in the final text of the directive and means that full harmonisation of some aspects of product liability law throughout the EU has not been achieved.

The directive was implemented in the United Kingdom in the Consumer Protection Act 1987 and in Northern Ireland in the Consumer Protection (Northern Ireland) Order 1987. The legislation makes it clear that liability arises where damage is caused, either wholly or partly, by a defect in a product. In order to succeed in a claim, the claimant must prove:

(a)   that the product was defective; and
(b)   that the defect caused damage.

The definition of 'product' in the legislation is sufficiently wide to include drug products. 'Damage' includes death or personal injury, or any loss or damage to property. 'Personal injury' includes any disease or other impairment of a person's physical or mental condition.

Liability falls primarily on the 'producer', 'own brander', importer or, in certain circumstances, supplier of the product. The producer will usually be the manufacturer of the product but may also include the manufacturer of raw materials and components. An 'own brander' is someone who puts a name, trade mark or other distinguishing mark on the product. An importer of a product into a member state of the EU, from a place outside the EU, in order to supply it to another in the course of a business, may also be liable under the legislation. Finally, any supplier who cannot identify the person who produced the product, or supplied it may also be liable in certain defined circumstances. This will occur where the injured party requests the supplier to identify the producer, own-brander or importer of the product and the supplier fails to provide this information within a reasonable time.

Under the legislation, there are three types of product defects:

(a)   a manufacturing defect occurs when the product fails to comply with the manufacturer's product specifications and consequently deviates from the norm;

(b)   a design defect occurs when the product specifications are themselves at fault and present a hazard; and

(c)   a duty to warn defect refers to the producer's responsibility to provide appropriate warnings and instructions to enable the consumer to use the product safely.

The legislative provisions state that a product will be regarded as defective when the safety of the product is not such as persons generally are entitled to expect. Further guidance is given as to the factors which will be relevant in deciding whether a product is defective. These include:

(a)   the presentation of the product, including instructions and warnings;

(b)   the use to which it could reasonably be expected to be put; and

(c)   the time when the product was supplied.

Brazier (*Medicines, Patients and the Law*, at p. 177) has suggested that the issue of determining when a drug product falls within the definition of defective will be far from easy. Newdick ('The Development Risk Defence of the Consumer Protection Act 1987') is of the view that serious difficulties attach to a test which describes the defectiveness of a drug in terms of warnings and reasonable expectations. Current definitions of defectiveness are constructed to deal with all types of consumer products while drug products present particular difficulties in relation to risk and effects.

Newdick believes that there is an over-emphasis on the role of warnings and that it is unreasonable to assume that a patient has consented to the risk in question. He states that an examination of the broad categories of risks which may be presented by drugs, and the professional obligation to warn, suggests that the current tests are 'too crude and arbitrary'. The notion of defectiveness then necessarily leans towards the concept of fault, which the new legislation was trying to eliminate.

The defendant in a case under the consumer protection legislation has a number of possible defences:

(a)   that the defect was attributable to the defendant's compliance with a legal requirement;

(b)   that the defendant did not supply the goods to anyone;

(c)   that the defendant had not supplied the goods in the course of business and had not own-branded, imported into the EU or produced the goods with a view to a profit;

(d)   if the defendant is a producer, own brander or importer into the EC, then he or she can escape liability by proving that the defect was not present in the product at the time he or she supplied it. If he or she does not fall into any of these categories then he or she must show the defect was not present in the product at the time it was last supplied by any person of that category;

(e)   the development risks defence provides that, given the state of scientific and technical knowledge at the time the product was put into circulation, no producer of a product of that kind could have been expected to have discovered the defect if it had existed in his or her products while they were under his or her control;

(f)   where the defendant is a producer of a component product, he or she will have a defence if he or she can show that the defect in the finished product is wholly attributable to its design or to compliance with instructions given by the producer of the finished product; and

(g)   more than 10 years has elapsed since the product was first supplied.

Under the first defence, compliance must be with a statutory requirement rather than a voluntary code and the defect must be attributable to that compliance. The non-supply defence will absolve the defendant from liability during the research and development stage or in other extreme circumstances, such as the theft of the product. The fourth defence will negate liability where something has happened to the product between manufacture and supply.

The 'development risks' or 'state of the art' defence is the most contentious of all of the legislative defences. The United Kingdom was instrumental in having this defence included in the final draft of Directive 85/374/EEC. Member states were eventually allowed to derogate from it, if they wished. The United Kingdom, like most EU countries, has included the defence in its enacting legislation.

The Pearson Commission and the Law Commission had argued against the inclusion of such a defence. It has been suggested that the government of the day was persuaded by arguments from industry including the claims that innovation would be discouraged and that the cost of insurance against development risks would be astronomical.

The defence was considered recently by the European Court of Justice in a case brought against the United Kingdom by the European Commission (*European Commission* v *United Kingdom* [1997] All ER (EC) 481). The European Commission contended that the wording of the provisions including the defence in the UK legislation, which was different from the wording contained in the original directive, introduced a subjective assessment by placing an emphasis on the conduct of a reasonable producer, having regard to the standard precautions in use in the industry in question. This had the effect of broadening the ambit of the defence in that the original wording was based on an objective test. The net effect was to reduce the strict liability imposed by the directive into liability for negligence.

The European Court of Justice rejected the Commission's arguments. The Court was of the view that, on its proper construction, the 1987 legislation placed the burden of proof on the producer but placed no restriction on the state of scientific and technical knowledge which was to be taken into account. Neither did it suggest that the availability of the defence was dependent on the subjective knowledge of a producer taking reasonable care in the light of the standard precautions taken in the industrial sector in question.

The Court was of the view that the directive, as originally drafted, did raise difficulties of interpretation, which would have to be resolved by the national courts. The courts of the United Kingdom were obliged by the 1987 legislation to interpret the relevant provisions in conformity with the directive. This finding places the emphasis on the national courts to define the ambit of the 'development risks' defence through an interpretation of the relevant national provisions. That interpretation has not yet taken place and until it does, academic comment on the ambit of the defence can only remain conjecture.

There is an absolute prohibition on the limitation or exclusion of liability under the legislation.

13.4   RESPONSIBILITY OF DOCTOR FOR DRUG THERAPY FAILURE

Although the position is changing, the doctor (as general practitioner) will be the primary source of health care advice for the vast majority of patients. The doctor's role in health care practice is to use his or her knowledge, training, clinical experience and acquired subjective and objective evidence from the patient, to assess the patient's health care problem and to develop and implement a therapeutic plan to alleviate the difficulty. Knowledge, training and clinical experience will necessarily include information and expertise in the practice and expected outcomes of drug therapy. That knowledge may have been acquired through initial and continuing education, clinical practice or, importantly, through the marketing endeavours of the manufacturers of drug products.

The development of the therapeutic plan will often involve the writing of prescriptions for prescription only drug products. Occasionally it may also involve the actual distribution of prescription only drug products, either in an emergency situation, or because of the particular geographical location of the health care practice. However, although the position is changing, the doctor's expectations of the patient are to assist the implementation and outcome of the therapeutic plan by presenting the prescriptions to be dispensed and to take the prescribed drug product as instructed. The doctor's expectations of the pharmacist are to interpret the contents of the prescription, check its validity, dispense the prescription and give appropriate verbal or written instructions as to how to take the medicine.

It is important to note, therefore, that while the doctor has direct clinical contact with the patient, it is often the case that he or she does not have direct drug distribution contact. The sale of drug products on a general sale list and the sale of pharmacy medicines are usually conducted by a pharmacist or other distributor with legal authority to sell. Prescription only drug products are distributed through an intermediary — the dispensing pharmacist. We shall see below in section 13.5 that this fact may have a significant impact on the distribution of responsibility for defective drug products and failures in drug therapy.

In turn, the doctor acts as an intermediary between the manufacturer of the drug product and the patient. We have already seen (in 13.3.2) that the fact of the presence of an intermediary between manufacturer and patient (consumer) has led to the development of the rule that a manufacturer may discharge the essential element of the duty to provide adequate information about the product, including warnings, so that the product may be used safely, by the provision or supply of that information to the intermediary.

13.4.1 A brief note on contract

Patients may consult their doctor on a private basis, or through the National Health Service. The vast majority of patients choose the latter option. Two main questions arise from this. The first is whether the legal relationship between a doctor and patient who is being treated within the National Health Service is contractual in nature. The second relates to a similar analysis of the legal relationship between doctor and patient outside the National Health Service.

In the important case of *Pfizer Corporation* v *Ministry of Health* [1965] AC 512, the House of Lords held that, where services are being provided pursuant to a statutory obligation, there is no contractual relationship (see also Bell, 'The Doctor and the Supply of Goods and Services Act 1982' (1984) *Legal Studies* vol. 4, 175).

Lord Reid summarised the position (*Pfizer Corporation* v *Ministry of Health* at p. 536):

The appellant's argument is that when the patient pays [the prescription charge] and gets the drug there is a sale of the drug to him by [the doctor] or the chemist and that [the prescription charge] is the price ... But in my opinion there is no sale in this case. Sale is a consensual contract requiring agreements, express or implied. In the present case there appears to me to be no need for any agreement. The patient has the statutory right to demand the drug on payment of [the prescription charge] ... And if the prescription is presented to a chemist he appears to be bound by his contract with the appropriate authority to supply the drug on receipt of such payment. There is no need for any agreement between the patient and either [the doctor] or the chemist, and there is certainly no room for bargaining ... It appears to me that any resemblance between this transaction and a true sale is only superficial.

The reasoning in *Pfizer* was followed in *Appelby* v *Sleep* [1968] 2 All ER 265. This view of the legal relationship between doctor and patient under the National Health Service was accepted by the Pearson Commission (*Royal Commission on Civil Liability and Compensation for Personal Injury*, 1978, Cmnd 7054). At paragraph 1313, it was noted:

Under the National Health Service ... there is no contract between patient and doctor and a claimant must rely on an action in tort.

It is equally clear that a contract *does* exist between the doctor and patient who is seeking treatment on a 'private' basis or whose health care is being paid for by someone else, such as an insurance company or employer. Difficulties arise in determining the precise nature and scope of the contractual relationship.

The contract will also have terms, express and implied. Express terms are those which are expressly stated and agreed between the parties at the time the contract is entered into. In the context of a medical contract, the express terms *might* be found in a consent form, signed by both parties. Kennedy and Grubb (*Medical Law: Text and Materials*, London, Butterworths, 1994) correctly point out that the parties to a medical contract cannot expressly agree to terms which would be contrary to public policy, or would otherwise be unlawful, an example being a contract to sell an organ or body part.

Two cases — *Eyre* v *Measday* [1986] 1 All ER 488 and *Thake* v *Maurice* [1986] 1 All ER 497 — have discussed the nature of terms to be implied in contracts between doctors and patients. In *Eyre* v *Measday*, Slade LJ defined one such implied obligation as follows (at p. 495):

... I think that there is no doubt that the [claimant] would have been entitled to assume that the defendant was warranting that the operation would be performed with reasonable care and skill. That, I think, would have been the inevitable inference to be drawn, from an objective standpoint ... The contract did, in my opinion, include an implied warranty of that nature.

In *Thake* v *Maurice* Neill LJ was of the view that in a contract to perform a vasectomy operation, the defendant was subject to an implied duty to carry out the operation with reasonable care and skill.

One interesting aspect of the nature and scope of contracts between patients and doctors which has been discussed by the United Kingdom courts is whether there is an obligation, express or implied, that the success of the therapeutic procedure will be guaranteed. Kennedy and Grubb rightly draw the distinction between a requirement that a contract be performed properly — meaning, probably, with the inclusion of an implied term that it will be carried out with reasonable care and skill — and the demand of a doctor that he or she guarantee success.

The courts in the United Kingdom have not been prepared to find that a doctor has guaranteed a particular result. In *Thake* v *Maurice*, Nourse LJ stated (at p. 512):

> ... a professional man is not usually regarded as warranting that he will achieve the desired result. Indeed, it seems that that would not fit well with the universal warranty of reasonable care and skill, which tends to affirm the inexactness of the science which is professed. I do not intend to go beyond the case of a doctor. Of all sciences medicine is one of the least exact. In my view a doctor cannot be objectively regarded as guaranteeing the success of any operation or treatment unless he says as much in clear and unequivocal terms.

Other jurisdictions have allowed claimants to obtain damages for breach of contract where the doctor has guaranteed a particular result and has failed to achieve it. In *Sullivan* v *O'Connor* (1973) 296 NE 2d 183 (Cal Sup Ct), a cosmetic surgery case in California, the court allowed the claimant to recover damages for breach of contract, but stressed that recovery would not be automatic in every case. There was a difference between statement of opinion and firm promises.

In *La Fleur* v *Cornelis* (1979) 28 NBR (2d) 569 (New Brunswick), a Canadian cosmetic surgery case, the claimant succeeded in establishing a breach of contract as well as succeeding in an action for negligence. The court found that the terms of the contract had been clearly established between the parties. There was no need to consider the implications of an implied warranty of success, as the defendant surgeon had expressly indicated that the proposed surgery would be successful.

13.4.2   Liability of doctor in the civil law of tort

As noted in 13.4.1, the patient who is treated within the National Health service has no contractual legal relationship with the doctor. To succeed in gaining compensation for injuries alleged to have been caused by an error of the doctor, the National Health Service patient claimant will have to sue in the law of tort. In general terms, patients injured by an error of the doctor usually allege one of two things. The first is that the doctor has been careless in diagnosis and treatment. This could mean that, in the development and implementation of the therapeutic plan, the doctor has omitted to take relevant evidence into account, or has missed relevant symptoms, or has not checked medical records, or has failed to keep up to date with recent developments in therapy, or has carelessly written a prescription.

The second allegation is usually that the patient has not consented to the therapeutic plan which the doctor has devised and implemented. Here the patient often alleges that he or she was unaware of the risks involved with the therapeutic plan, had not consented to those risks, and would not have proceeded with the therapeutic plan had the risks been known.

A doctor owes a patient a number of duties in tort in relation to the development and implementation of therapeutic plans. So, for example, the doctor has a duty to diagnose and treat correctly (*Barnett* v *Chelsea and Kensington Hospital Management Committee* [1968] 1 All ER 1068). A doctor who fails to carry out these duties in a careful manner, or who fails to act, will be liable in negligence and will have to pay compensation to any patient injured as a result. The concept of duty in medical negligence has been recognised by the courts for some time, at least as far back as *R* v *Bateman* [1925] LJKB 791.

The action in medical negligence is not without its problems. While the existence of a duty of care will usually be conceded by a doctor, hospital or health authority sued by a patient, difficulties arise in establishing the appropriate standard of care, that the doctor was in breach of that standard and that the injury was caused by the careless act or omission in question. Some of those difficulties, and the further defences which might be asserted by the doctor, have been outlined in the discussion of the manufacturer's duty of care in section 13.3.

We have also already seen, in 10.4, that there are two significant cases relating to a doctor's duty of care and the writing of prescriptions — *Dwyer* v *Roderick and others* (1983) 80 Law Society Gazette 3003, and *Prendergast* v *Sam & Dee Ltd* (1989) 1 MLR 36. It is clear from these cases that the law, through the tort of negligence, will readily impose liability on doctors (and other health care professionals) who have been careless in their professional work. Although the implications in the above cases may seem obvious from the facts, their seriousness should not be underestimated by those health care professionals involved.

As noted above, the allegation by an injured claimant may often be that he or she has not *consented* to the therapeutic plan which the doctor has devised and implemented. Here the claimant often alleges that he or she was unaware of the risks involved with the therapeutic plan, had not consented to those risks, and would not have proceeded with the therapeutic plan had the risks been known.

Consent lies at the heart of all medical treatment. It is settled law that an adult patient with sufficient mental and physical capacity may withhold consent to medical treatment. The principle, which is based on the concept of the right to self determination, was well summarised by Butler-Sloss LJ in *Re T* [1992] 4 All ER 649 at pp. 664–5:

> A man or woman of full age and sound understanding may choose to reject medical advice and medical or surgical treatment either partially or in its entirety. A decision to refuse treatment by a patient capable of making the decision does not have to be sensible, rational or well considered . . . Doctors therefore who treat such a patient against his known wishes do so at their peril.

The consequences of that peril are a civil suit for trespass to the person or a variety of criminal charges. Doctors and other health care professionals are therefore under a duty to ensure that the patient has consented to the proposed therapeutic plan. Where the design and implementation of the therapeutic plan involves drug therapy, through the actual supply of drug products or, more usually, the writing of a prescription for prescription only drug products to be dispensed by someone else, the doctor will have to be sure that a valid consent is forthcoming. Ferguson (*Drug Injuries and the Pursuit of Compensation*, London, Sweet & Maxwell, 1996) puts the problem quite well (at pp. 68–9):

> Ideally the doctor will have spent some time . . . outlining to the patient the diagnosis, proposed treatment, and any important hazards associated with that treatment. In medical cases we are not, generally, faced with a complete lack of consent . . . In an ideal world the doctor could be relied upon to ensure that the patient is given relevant warnings and risk information. The reality is likely to fall short of this; not infrequently, patients leave their doctors' surgeries without knowing what has been prescribed for them. It is clear that there would have been minimal discussion of any risks associated with the medication in such cases.

In our discussion (section 13.3) of the civil liability of the manufacturer for defective drug products, we noted that the manufacturer of an unavoidably risky prescription drug has no duty to warn patients directly and can fully discharge its duty to warn by providing the doctor and pharmacist with adequate warnings of the risks associated with the use of its drug.

If the 'informed intermediary doctrine' discharges the duty of the manufacturer towards the patient, the focus then turns to the doctor (and pharmacist) who has been supplied with the information. To begin with, what should a doctor in the United Kingdom do with the wide variety of information which has been supplied to him or her? The law in the United Kingdom takes the same view about the supply of information to patients by doctors about drug use as it does about the supply of information about all forms of medical treatment.

The famous case of *Bolam* v *Friern Hospital Management Committee* [1957] 2 All ER 118 makes it clear that a doctor will not be negligent if he or she acts in accordance with a practice which is in accordance with a responsible and competent body of relevant medical opinion. The rule concerning the supply of information about medical treatment was clearly set out by the Court of Appeal in *Sidaway* v *Governors of the Bethlem Royal Hospital* [1984] 1 QB 493 at p. 512:

> What information should be disclosed and how and when it should be disclosed is very much a matter of professional judgment, to be exercised in the context of the doctor's relationship with a particular patient in particular circumstances.

The reasoning was confirmed on appeal to the House of Lords ([1985] 1 All ER 643). Applying this general principle about the supply of information concerning all medical treatment to the specificity of adequate information or warnings about drug use, a potential claimant would need to show that the provision of information is not in accordance with accepted, responsible and competent practice with the medical profession.

As it currently stands such a task may be onerous. In the case of *Blyth* v *Bloomsbury Health Authority* [1993] 4 Med LR 151, the claimant had seen a consultant in relation to her pregnancy. It was established that she had no, or insufficient immunity to rubella. The proposal was that although it was too late to vaccinate her against rubella at that stage of her pregnancy, it was necessary to do so after the birth of her baby in order to protect her and the baby (who, too, was vaccinated) against the risk of infection. In addition, since the vaccine itself could cause adverse symptoms to a foetus should she become pregnant again within three months, it was necessary that she should have some contraceptive protection during this period. The claimant had a previous history of problems with Minilyn, a combined pill containing oestrogen and progesterone.

The general practice at the hospital during this period was to use Depo-Provera for the purpose of long-term contraceptive protection. It was a progesterone only contraceptive and it was thought that it would not have the same adverse consequences as the Minilyn which she had used previously. The claimant alleged that she had been ill-informed and ill-advised when she was in hospital about the possible side-effects of Depo-Provera; that if she had been informed more fully about the possible side-effects, she would not have agreed to take the Depo-Provera injection and that she suffered from manifold side-effects as a result of the injection of Depo-Provera.

The Court of Appeal held that the duty owed to the claimant by her doctor was to use the doctor's professional judgment to decide what information to give to the patient even where the patient asks specific questions about specific treatments. In determining whether the doctor has exercised that judgment correctly he or she is to be judged against the standards of the profession as laid down in *Bolam* and *Sidaway*.

13.5   RESPONSIBILITY OF PHARMACIST FOR DRUG THERAPY FAILURE

The pharmacist's role in the drug distribution process is best understood by reference to the classification of drug products. The pharmacist, unlike the other two participants in the drug distribution process, has direct distributive contact with the patient in relation to all three categories of medicinal drug products. The pharmacist may recommend and/or sell general sale list medicines, has direct control over the sale and supply of pharmacy medicines, and is directly responsible for the distribution of the vast majority of prescription only medicines. It is clear that such an allocation of responsibility has direct consequences for the civil liability of the pharmacist should problems occur with the distributed drug products.

13.5.1   The pharmacist's liability in contract

It is clear that the sale of general sale list medicines and pharmacy medicinal products are subject to the laws and principles applicable to the sale of all other consumer products. To begin with, this means that the sale is subject to the normal rules of contract law. A detailed analysis of all of those rules is beyond the scope of this textbook. However it is clear that liability may attach to the pharmacist under such general principles.

For example, pre-contractual discussions may take place in relation to the sale and supply of medicinal products as would happen in relation to other consumer products. A customer might ask the pharmacist for advice in relation to the choice of a medicinal product and specify that it is required for a particular purpose or for a particular individual. In turn, the pharmacist may make statements or representations concerning the product and its uses, prior to sale. For example, a pharmacist may state that a particular drug product is safe for use, or that it will provide a remedy for a particular ailment. If the pre-contractual statement turns out to be untrue, and the patient is injured as a consequence, he or she may seek a remedy in contract from the pharmacist.

Contract law classifies pre-contractual statements in one of three ways: as advertising talk or boasts; as terms of the contract; or as representations of fact. Where the statement is classified as mere advertising talk, and it turns out to be untrue, the law offers no individual civil remedy to the injured party. Where the statement is classified as a term of the contract, and it turns out to be untrue, contract law offers a civil remedy for breach of contract. Finally, where the statement is classified as a representation of fact, and turns out to be untrue, contract law offers a civil remedy for misrepresentation.

Much will turn on the classification of the pre-contractual statement and much will depend on the injured party proving difficult aspects of the breach or the misrepresentation. However, misrepresentation, if proved, may cover statements made recklessly, carelessly and even innocently. It is also important to remember that liability in contract law is strict. Once the breach or misrepresentation is proved, then damages are payable for all of the consequences of the breach, subject to the rules on remoteness. Damages will be payable for physical or psychological injury, for example, consequent on the breach or misrepresentation. As such, the action for misrepresentation or breach of contract is an attractive one for a claimant patient.

The pharmacist's potential liability as a retailer of goods does not stop with general principles of contract law. In order to redress the imbalance in contracting power between the seller and buyer in a consumer sales contract, Parliament has intervened to offer protection to the seller. This has resulted in the passing of the Sale of Goods Act 1979 which received significant amendment through the Sale and Supply of Goods Act 1994. Again, a detailed analysis of the provisions of these important Acts of Parliament is beyond the scope of this textbook. For the moment, there are some aspects of sale of goods law worthy of consideration.

Section 1 of the 1979 Act defines a contract for the sale of goods as 'a contract whereby the seller transfers or agrees to transfer the property in goods to the buyer for a money consideration called the price'. Pharmaceutical goods are clearly within the definition of 'goods' for the purposes of the legislation and include the container or packaging in which the products are supplied (*Geddling* v *Marsh* [1920] 1 KB 668), and any instructions which are provided (*Wormell* v *RHM Agriculture* (East) Ltd [1986] 1 All ER 769).

The main purpose of the 1979 Act is to imply terms into contracts for the sale of goods, the most important of which are as follows.

Section 13(1) provides that 'where there is a contract for the sale of goods by description there is an implied condition that the goods shall correspond with the description'. Goods ordered through a catalogue, or a new car ordered from the manufacturers through a dealer, will always be sold by description, because this is the only way to identify what is required. Even goods seen and specifically chosen by the customer can be sold by description, and a customer is entitled to expect, for example, that goods chosen from the shelf in a pharmacy will correspond to the description on the container or packet.

The word 'description' covers a wide variety of matters. Statements as to quantity, weight, ingredients and even packing have been held to be part of the description. Compliance with the description must be complete and exact.

Unlike the obligations imposed by ss. 12, 13 and 15, which apply to all sales of goods, s. 14 applies where the seller sells in the course of a business. As a general rule, a seller owes no obligations as regards the quality or suitability of his or her goods but, where s. 14 applies, there are a number of important exceptions to this general rule.

Section 14(2), inserted by s. 1 of the Sale and Supply of Goods Act 1994, provides that 'where the seller sells goods in the course of a business, there is an implied term that the goods supplied under the contract are of satisfactory quality'. By s. 14(2)(A), goods are of 'satisfactory' quality if they meet the standard that a reasonable person would regard as satisfactory, taking account of any description of the goods, the price (if relevant) and all the other relevant circumstances. By s. 14(2)(B), quality of goods includes their state or condition, and fitness for purpose, appearance and finish, freedom from minor defects, safety and durability are all aspects which can be taken into account in assessing quality.

This obligation regarding satisfactory quality does not apply to any matter making the quality of the goods unsatisfactory which is (a) specifically drawn to the buyer's attention before the contract is made, or (b) where the buyer examines the goods before the contract is made, which that examination ought to reveal. The second of these obligations is often misunderstood; there is no obligation on the buyer to examine the goods, and if he or she chooses not to do so, he or she is entitled to the full protection of s. 14(2).

Section 14(3) provides that:

> where the seller sells goods in the course of a business and the buyer, expressly or by implication, makes known . . . to the seller . . . any particular purpose for which the goods are being bought, there is an implied condition that the goods supplied are reasonably fit for that purpose, whether or not that is a purpose for which such goods are commonly supplied, except where the circumstances show that the buyer does not rely, or that it is unreasonable for him to rely, on the skill or judgement of the seller . . .

This subsection only applies, therefore, if the buyer has expressly or impliedly made known to the seller the purpose for which he or she requires the goods. Where the goods only have one or two obvious uses, it will readily be assumed that the buyer has impliedly indicated that he or she wants them for their normal purpose. Thus, if someone buys food, he or she will be taken to indicate that he or she wants it to be reasonably fit for eating.

The goods supplied need only to be reasonably fit, however, and then only for the purposes made known. The subsection contains one exception to this implied condition, namely, where the circumstances show that the buyer does not rely, or that it is unreasonable for him or her to rely, on the seller's skill or judgment. This may apply, for example, where the buyer is an expert in such goods, and gives detailed specifications as to what he or she requires.

You will see that the most important of these implied terms are conditions. A condition is a more important term of a contract, breach of which by the seller will enable the buyer to refuse further performance of the contract and to recover any money or other property which they have paid for the goods.

Under the Unfair Contract Terms Act 1977, in a consumer contract the seller may also not limit or exclude his or her liability for breach of the implied terms concerning description, quality or fitness for purpose. Liability for breach of these terms may be excluded or limited in business contracts where it is reasonable to do so.

The provisions of the Sale of Goods Act 1979 have significant consequences for pharmacists as retailers of general sale list and pharmacy medicines. A patient who purchases general sale list or pharmacy medicines does so under a sale of goods contract and is entitled to all of the protection outlined above. Injury as a result of a defect in a general sale list or pharmacy medicine drug product will allow the patient to sue for breach of the sale of goods contract. The cause of action will usually be breach of one, or a number of the implied terms. Damages will be payable for physical or psychological injuries suffered if they are consequential on the breach.

It is very important to stress that liability is strict under such an action. A pharmacist may well claim that the drug product was sold to the patient in the same form and structure as it arrived in the pharmacy and that any defect was attributable to another defendant. Such a claim will not excuse the individual contractual liability of the pharmacist to the patient. However it may allow the pharmacist to sue the party alleged to have been responsible for the defect in the drug product, or join them as a co-defendant in a claim made by the patient.

The pharmacy profession in the United Kingdom has considered the specific issue of the sale of non-prescribed medicines, pharmacy and general sale list medicines. As part of the practice advice which supplements the Royal Pharmaceutical Society's *Code of Ethics*, there is a requirement that there should be a written protocol in each pharmacy covering the procedure to be followed in that pharmacy when a medicine is supplied or advice on treatment of a medical condition is sought. In addition, each member of staff whose work in a pharmacy includes the sale of medicines should have completed a course at NVQ level in retail operations.

Further, as part of the general legal advice offered by the Royal Pharmaceutical Society of Great Britain, it is suggested that medicines' sales protocols should comply with certain standards outlined in the *Standards of Good Professional Practice*. These include standards on the request for advice on treatment of symptoms or a condition, request for a medicine by name, the pharmacist's involvement in the sale of non-prescribed medicines, special purchasers or users and medicines requiring special care.

These issues may go some way towards the assessment of whether a pharmacist has acted recklessly or carelessly in making pre-contractual statements in relation to the sale of non-prescribed medicines and they will have a direct bearing on the defence of any pharmacist sued for misrepresentation. However, the fact of acting carefully, and in conformity with a profession's accepted standards will generally be of no defence to the general action for breach of contract and for breach of the terms of a contract implied under the sale of goods legislation.

13.5.2   The pharmacist's liability in tort

The action in contract relates most closely to manufacturing and design drug defects, leading to problems inherent in the drug product itself. Marketing defects, on the other hand, arise because of a failure to give an adequate warning of the dangers of the product or adequate guidance for its safe use. The action in contract may not be appropriate for failure in drug therapy due to an omission to give a warning of the dangers associated with it. The question then arises as to whether pharmacists owe a duty to warn in the civil law of tort.

Equally the action in contract correlates more closely with the sale of non-prescribed drugs which are always supplied to a patient pursuant to a contract. Pharmacists are directly responsible for the distribution and supply of prescription only medicine drug products to patients. The manufacturer will have had an impact on the development and marketing of the drug product. The doctor may have decided that the prescribing of the drug product will form part of the therapeutic plan for the patient. However it is the pharmacist who will ultimately put the drug product into the hands of the patient.

It is clear that there can be no liability in contract for injuries caused by a defective drug product distributed to the patient via a prescription. To repeat what was said in 13.4.1, in the important case of *Pfizer Corporation* v *Ministry of Health* [1965] AC 512, the House of Lords held that, where services are being provided pursuant to a statutory obligation, there is no contractual relationship. Does the pharmacist in the United Kingdom owe any duty in tort to the patient in relation to the supply of prescription only medicines?

We have already seen in 10.4 that it is well-established in United Kingdom law that the relationship between the pharmacist and the patient is one which gives rise to a duty of care in certain circumstances. In each of the cases of *Collins* v *Hertfordshire County Council* [1947] 1 KB 633, *Dwyer* v *Roderick* (1983) Law Society Gazette 3003 and *Prendergast* v *Sam & Dee Ltd* (1989) 1 MLR 36, the courts were prepared to hold that pharmacists possess expertise regarding the supply of medicinal products and reliance is placed on them by patients for that expertise.

The cases confirm that the relationship between pharmacist and patient is one which gives rise to the imposition of a duty of care. The net result is that the pharmacist must be aware that he or she should not tacitly accept what they see, or perceive to see, on the written prescription before them. They are under a legal duty of care to draw on their skill and knowledge of drugs to inquire into the surrounding circumstances of the case.

Now it is an established fact that a pharmacist does owe a duty of care, any patient harmed as a result of a pharmacist's involvement in drug therapy, will have to show that the pharmacist was in breach of that duty, that the injuries were consequent on that breach, and that the action has been commenced in time. As noted above, these aspects of the tort of negligence are not easy to prove, but it is not impossible. The awards of damages in *Collins*, *Dwyer*, and *Prendergast* were significant.

In addition to a requirement that the pharmacist must show technical accuracy, the law will consider that a pharmacist, as a professional, has sufficient knowledge, through education and training and supply of information by the manufacturer, to counsel patients about drug therapy. In addition the pharmacist has a duty to provide such counselling and a failure to do so which results in injury to the patient will result in liability. That was the conclusion of the court in the United States case of *Pittman* v *The Upjohn Company* (1994) Westlaw 663372 (Tenn. 1994), already discussed in section 10.5, and it is our view that a similar conclusion would be reached by the courts in the United Kingdom.

An important factor for the court in *Pittman* was the inclusion of an 'information for patients' section in the drug's package insert. The conclusion for pharmacists in the United States from the court's analysis of the significance of the insert is that to ignore the contents of the insert is perilous. The question of the inclusion of package inserts has taken on a greater significance in the United Kingdom since the alteration in the rules regarding the provision of information leaflets with drug products, as outlined in section 9.9.

Pharmacists have been concerned about the practical questions which arise from this change in the law, namely whether each patient receiving stock from a split original pack should be entitled to an information leaflet; whether an information leaflet must be supplied if stock is dispensed from a bulk pack; whether multiple copies of leaflets will be available or whether photocopying of leaflets will be permitted.

Pharmacists should also be concerned about the legal implications of this change in the law. What is clear is that if leaflets containing information and warnings are supplied by manufacturers to pharmacists in order that the pharmacist might pass on the information to patients, then a failure to provide the information attracts the potential for liability should that failure result in injury. If patient information leaflets are supplied by the manufacturer they should be passed on to the patient and their contents noted and explained to the patient at the time of delivery. To that extent, the conclusions of the court in *Pittman* regarding the peril of ignoring package inserts is as applicable in this jurisdiction.

There has been a further recognition by the legal advisers of those injured as a result of failures in drug therapy that pharmacists have duties and responsibilities beyond the filling of prescriptions and that liability for failure to perform these expanded roles may result in the award of damages. These duties reflect current trends in pharmacy practice which emphasise pharmacist responsibility for patient care through drug therapy. Failure to act responsibly in the new professional role, with resultant failure in drug therapy outcomes, is likely to result in an extension of pharmacist liability.

13.6   CONCLUSION

The purpose of this chapter has been to analyse the implications of a failure to act in a professional and responsible manner with respect to the sale and distribution of medicinal products. We began by concluding that, for the most part, modern drug therapy works well. However, problems do arise with drug therapy. Such failures and poor outcomes from drug therapy often lead to legal action and an attempt to discover who or what is responsible for the harm which has been done to the patient.

Quite clearly there are a number of participants in the drug distribution business who may be responsible for such harm. A patient who has suffered harm as a result of a failure from drug therapy may consider litigation against any one, or combination, of these individuals. In turn, an individual manufacturer, doctor or pharmacist, sued by a patient, may lay the blame for the failure of the drug therapy at the door of one of the other participants in the drug distribution process.

We have explored the civil liability of the manufacturer, doctor and pharmacist for injuries caused by defects in drug products. Cases against manufacturers of drug products for compensation for injuries caused by defects in those drug products do not tend to be successful in the United Kingdom. This is largely to do with the problems of proving breach of a duty and causation. The 'learned intermediary' doctrine absolves many manufacturers of liability where they can prove that adequate warnings were provided to a third party intermediary. The inclusion of the 'state of the art' defence in the reforming consumer protection legislation is likely to exacerbate rather than lessen the problems.

Equally, cases against prescribing doctors for compensation for injuries caused by failure to warn about drug products do not tend to be successful, unless the error falls into the 'gross' category as outlined in some of the cases above. The reason for that is largely to do with the analysis of the law on doctor liability, and in particular the problems which attach to the issue of informed consent, outlined above.

Attention therefore focuses on the final participant in the drug distribution process — the dispensing pharmacist. For most patients, the pharmacy is the place where they are likely to receive their drug products. Under the current classification, pharmacists have responsibility for the distribution of all three classes of drug product and have sole responsibility for the distribution of one of these. That prerogative is the result of long-standing negotiation by the pharmacy profession. Pharmacists should be rightly proud of this unique role which they play in the provision of drug therapy as part of health care.

However the role carries significant legal implications. The patient who purchases general sale list or pharmacy medicines from a pharmacist does so under a sale of goods contract. All of the general principles of contract law are applicable to such contracts and we have noted certain specific consequences for pharmacists of that fact. More importantly we have agreed that all of the principles of sale of goods law are also applicable to such sales with the result that pharmacists may find themselves strictly liable for the consequences of the breach of an implied term in the contract. Liability under contract law is strict and pharmacists may not be absolved by blaming the defect on others in the drug distribution process.

The lack of a contractual relationship between a pharmacist and patient in relation to prescription only medicine drug products under the National Health Service means that the patient who is injured by a defect in a drug product, and who alleges that the fault for that injury lies with the doctor, must sue in tort. That form of action is also appropriate for a patient who alleges injury as a result of a failure to warn of the dangers of a drug product or adequate guidance for its safe use.

We have seen that the relationship between the pharmacist and the patient is one which gives rise to a duty of care in certain circumstances. In each of the cases examined the courts were prepared to hold that pharmacists possess expertise regarding the supply of medicinal products and reliance is placed on them by patients for that expertise. The evidence has also shown that legal advisers are bringing actions for failure to warn and that this trend will mean that the issues will soon be discussed and deliberated upon in the higher courts.

Pharmacy has concluded a prime position for the profession in the provision of health care, drug therapy, and in relationships with individual patients. Other health care professionals, with similar roles, have taken steps to absolve themselves of liability should failures in health care occur. Careful performance of function and discharge of role will also absolve pharmacists of liability and that is the best advice possible. However pharmacy should also note that those responsible for giving advice to litigants have noted the pharmacist's prime position in the distribution of drug products, and are taking action accordingly.

FOURTEEN

The pharmacist and confidential information

14.1 INTRODUCTION

In the course of their professional practice pharmacists will receive a great deal of information, both informal and informal. That information may come from a wide variety of different sources, both official and unofficial, may be personal or general in its nature, and may be given with or without the qualification of confidence. A great deal of information concerning the treatment regimes of patients is exchanged or disclosed in the pharmacy environment. The information interchange does not necessarily need to be directly related to health care. Although the position is changing, the pharmacy remains a source of exchange of information about many aspects of the community in which it is located. Whether it falls into the category of gossip, chat, rumour, innuendo, or hard fact, much is said and imparted within the walls of the community pharmacy. Pharmacists may also be requested to disclose information which they have in their possession. Again, the request may be formal or informal, or official or unofficial. Further, all of this information may not imparted directly to the pharmacist. It may given indirectly to a technician or sales assistant, or shared with other members of the pharmacy team.

So, for example, in a single (but horrendous!) day, a pharmacist may receive a prescription telling him or her that a patient is receiving new treatment for the treatment of a sexually-transmitted disease; may be informed by another pharmacist that a colleague may be developing a dependency on alcohol; may be informed by a patient that another patient in the practice has been taken into hospital with a serious illness; may be told by a patient to whom drugs have been given that he or she intends to take them all to end their life; may be informed by a sales assistant that young customers have been seeking to purchase solvent based products; may be asked by irate and angry parents to confirm or deny that their fifteen-year-old daughter has been asking for contraceptive advice; may be asked by a legal representative to divulge the contents of a patient's medication records for the purposes of pending court proceedings or may be asked by a data collection company to download computerised records of general practitioner prescribing habits.

What does a pharmacist do in each of these situations? What are the legal and ethical requirements relating to the receipt and disclosure of information? The purpose of this chapter is to seek to give legal and ethical guidance on the duties and obligations which pharmacists owe in relation to confidential information. The duty of confidence has a legal and ethical reality where the rules and principles seek to maintain a balance between the right to expect confidences to be maintained against the right to obviate such a duty where the individual or public interest demands it. The chapter will explore the dynamics of the legal and ethical duty to maintain confidences and analyse the situations where the legal and ethical principles permit relaxation.

The legal and ethical principles are framed in terms of confidential information and the legal and ethical duty is said to be one of confidence. This limitation in terminology does not mean that there are no legal or ethical requirements concerning non-confidential information. The law and ethics of confidence set the framework for the receipt and disclosure of all information.

Finally, it is important to correlate the legal and ethical notion of confidentiality with that of privacy. Ethically the concepts are very closely linked. The moral justifications for maintaining confidences draw much from similar principles in privacy. It could be argued that privacy is designed to protect information from invasive interference from anyone, including those to whom the information has not been disclosed, for example, preventing a 'hacker' from accessing a computerised databank of patient medication records. Confidentiality, on the other hand, could be said to impose a duty on an individual or group of individuals to whom information has voluntarily been given, in the expectation that it will not be disclosed except with the consent of the informant, for example, disclosure by an individual to a pharmacist that he or she is suffering from a life-threatening illness. Ethically, though, the parallel theories of privacy and confidentiality are very closely linked.

Legally, the concepts of privacy and confidentiality are disparate. As we shall see below, the law recognises and protects confidences, only allowing breach of this general rule in exceptional circumstances. As it presently stands, however, there is no legal right to privacy in the United Kingdom although the position may change in the next few years with the introduction of specific legislation on the subject. A variety of different legal methods are used to protect privacy, but it continues to be missing as a distinct legal concept.

14.2 THE DUTY OF CONFIDENTIALITY

The law now recognises that an obligation of confidentiality will arise where information of a confidential nature is entrusted to another in circumstances where that other is relied on to keep the confidence. Failure to keep the confidence may lead to action for breach of confidence.

The first discussion of the elements of action in breach of confidence was by Megarry J in *Coco* v *A N Clarke (Engineers) Ltd* [1969] RPC 41. He thought that there were three elements required if a case for breach of confidence was to succeed. First the information must have the necessary quality of confidence about it. Secondly the information must have been imparted in circumstances importing an obligation of confidence, and finally, there must be an unauthorised use of the information.

This analysis of the action for breach of confidence was cited with approval and adopted by the court in *Attorney-General* v *Guardian Newspapers (No. 2)* [1988] 3 All ER 545, often known as the *Spycatcher* case. The explication of the elements of the duty of confidence by Lord Goff in this case (at pp. 658–9) is now considered to be the most precise:

> ... a duty of confidence arises when confidential information comes to the knowledge of a person (the confidant) in circumstances where he has notice, or is held to have agreed, that the information is confidential, with the effect that it would be just in the circumstances that he should be precluded from disclosing the information to others ... The extent of this broad general principle reflects the fact that there is such a public interest in the maintenance of confidences, that the law will provide remedies for their protection.

The duty of confidence owed by pharmacists to their patients, and others, has been explored recently by the High Court in the case of *R* v *Department of Health, ex parte Source Informatics Ltd* [1999] All ER (D) 563.

The facts were that Source Informatics Ltd had issued a request to general practitioners and pharmacists seeking their consent to obtain certain information relating to the treatment provided for patients, and to allow them to collect data on the prescribing habits of general practitioners. Source Informatics Ltd believed that this information would be of commercial value to drug companies, and would provide useful data for those interested in monitoring prescribing patterns. The proposal was that, with the consent of the GPs, the pharmacists would, for a fee, and using software provided by Source Informatics Ltd, download onto disc the name of the GP and the identity and quantity of the drugs prescribed, but no information which could identify the patient.

On learning of the proposal, the Department of Health issued a policy document to health authorities, in which it expressed concern that what was contemplated could amount, in law, to a breach of the duty of confidence, and that any GP or pharmacist seriously considering acceding to the requests, would be incurring legal risks. The Department of Health strongly discouraged participation in the proposal and advised any GP or pharmacist to take their own legal advice.

The basis for the Department's concern was that anonymisation, even if it could be guaranteed, did not remove the duty of confidence towards the patients who were the subject of the data. Apart from the risk of identification, the patient would not have entrusted the information to the GP or pharmacist for it to be provided to Source Informatics Ltd. According to the Department, the patient would not be aware of, or have consented to, the information being given to the data company, but would have given it to be used in connection with care and treatment, and other wider National Health Service purposes. Finally, the Department had severe reservations that the disclosures by GPs or pharmacists would be in the public interest, thereby triggering the recognised legal corollary that the duty of confidence might, in certain circumstances, be outweighed by the public interest in its disclosure. Rather the Department was of the view that it might be contrary to the public interest if the data company was selling on the information on doctors' prescribing habits to the pharmaceutical industry.

As a result of the distribution by the health authorities of the policy document, most doctors and pharmacists refused to participate in Source Informatics Ltd's proposals. The basis of the legal action was a claim that the guidance provided was wrong in law, and that disclosure by doctors and pharmacists to a third party of anonymous information did not constitute a breach of confidentiality. In the Queen's Bench Division, Latham J found that Source Informatics Ltd's proposal did involve a breach of confidence which was capable of founding an action, and that the Department of Health was therefore entitled to give guidance in the form of the policy document in question, and to recommend that any pharmacist interested in the proposal should seek legal advice.

Although much of the judgment in this case involves an analysis of the role of detriment in a breach of confidence action, the decision is extremely significant for the practice of pharmacy. The judgment represents the first significant analysis of the extent of the duty of confidence owed by pharmacists to their patients, and helps to clarify, for pharmacists, how to implement the principles of law into professional health care practice.

Latham J began by confirming that all of the parties involved in the action accepted and agreed that the first two elements of the action for breach of confidence had been satisfied:

> . . . it is not disputed that the information in the prescription handed to the pharmacist has the necessary quality of confidence about it; nor is it disputed that in receiving the information, the pharmacist is under a duty of confidence in relation to it.

Earlier, in dealing with the legal submissions of counsel on behalf of the Source Informatics Ltd, the judge summarised how the duty arises:

> ... when the patient hands in the prescription to the pharmacist for the pharmacist to dispense the relevant drugs, the contents of the prescription are confidential information. The confidence is partly that of the GP as the prescriber, and partly that of the patient. As far as the patient is concerned, it identifies the fact that he is taking drugs; and the nature of the drugs he is taking could identify his mental or physical condition.

This aspect of the judgment, although dealt with promptly and routinely by the judge, is very significant for pharmacists. It tells them that the contents of prescriptions handed to them are confidential. The base position, therefore, is that such information should be managed with caution. Pharmacists should take careful note of this finding and adapt their professional practice accordingly.

What are pharmacists permitted to do with such confidential information and does the confidence which permeates prescriptions extend to other information which the pharmacist receives? What is clear from further aspects of the judgment in this case is that the passing of the information to others, such as the data collecting agency in the present case, would amount to an unauthorised use by the pharmacist of confidential information. Without the consent of the patient, which was neither expressly nor impliedly present in the case in question, the passing on of the information, whether anonymised or semi-anonymised, amounted to a breach of confidence. Further there was no public interest in allowing the established confidence to be obviated for the purposes of using the information for commercial uses. On the contrary, according to Latham J, this was one type of situation where there was a public interest in ensuring that confidences were kept:

> ... for some, the sensitivity, as they see it, of the information may be such that they would feel that any use of the information without their consent, would be unconscionable. In other words it would be a breach of the trust which they were reposing in the pharmacist ... It is important that those who require medical assistance should not be inhibited in any way from seeking to obtain it. As I have indicated, I believe that there may be some patients who feel very strongly that the pharmacist should not give any information obtained from the prescription without their consent. This will enable them to make a decision as to whether to allow the information to be used.

The implications of this finding are clear. Confidential information may only be used for the purposes for which it is given. In the case of information in prescriptions, it amounts to a use for care and treatment, and possibly, for wider National Health Service purposes. Pharmacists should note carefully that the judgment not only confirms that there is no public interest which obviates the duty of confidence with regard to prescription information, but it also goes further in confirming that there is a public interest in ensuring that the confidence is kept. This reinforces the nature of the obligation owed by the pharmacist with regard to the information contained in prescriptions, and supports the view that all confidential information should be treated with caution.

Does the duty of confidence extend to other information? An argument could be made that the decision in *ex parte Source Informatics Ltd* should be restricted to its own facts, and that the duty of confidence is restricted to information contained in prescriptions. We would caution against such a conclusion for two reasons. The first lies in the strong general comments of Latham J relating to the significant public interest in the preservation of confidences by pharmacists. This would strengthen the view that the duty extends to other confidential information. Further, the judge went on to make other important comments about the role and function of pharmacists and the relationship which they have with their patients:

> Pharmacists provide a service to the community as a whole. It is a matter of real importance that they retain the trust of the public. For them to breach their patients' confidence ... does not seem to me to be acceptable.

These comments are further suggestive of the extension of the duty of confidence to all information obtained by pharmacists about their patients. The views of the judge in this regard are reassuring. Judicial recognition of professional functions is important and reinforces claims to such professional roles. Pharmacists should welcome this development.

It is important to note that the courts have recognised that it may be justified to disclose confidential information in the public interest. This possibility was recognised by the Department of Health in the policy guidance which it had issued in the case of *ex parte Source Informatics Ltd*, and an analysis of the role of the public interest in the duty of confidence was discussed in the judgment in that case.

In the case of *X* v *Y* [1988] 2 All ER 648, the issue arose as to whether a newspaper could publish an article, allegedly identifying doctors who were continuing to practise in the National Health service despite having being diagnosed as being HIV positive. The court held that disclosure of the identity of the doctors could not be justified as being in the public interest. The judge was strongly of the view that the maintenance of confidence in such circumstances was of paramount importance to patients and doctors alike. Patients who had grounds for believing that such confidence had been breached might be reluctant to come forward for, or continue their treatment. The public interest in the freedom of the press, and in knowing about the employment practices of health authorities, was substantially outweighed when measured against the public interests in relation to loyalty and confidentiality.

In *W* v *Egdell* [1990] Ch 359, the right of a psychiatrist to send a confidential report, prepared in the interests and at the request of a patient but adverse to the patient in opposing transfer with a view to discharge from a secure hospital, to the Home Secretary, was discussed. The patient had killed five people and wounded two others, and had a long-standing interest in firearms and explosives. The court held that confidence could, in this case, be breached in the public interest. The nature of the killings had to give rise to the gravest concern for the safety of the public, and the authorities responsible for the patient's treatment were entitled to the fullest relevant information concerning his condition.

It is difficult to know how the principle of public interest would be applied in pharmacy confidence cases. However the judgment in *ex parte Source Informatics Ltd* gives us a number of clues. As was noted above, Latham J was strongly of the view that the passing on of confidential prescription information to the data processing company for commercial gain could not be justified in the public interest. Further he found, as a corollary, that the facts presented in the case represented the type of situation where there is a public interest in ensuring that confidences are kept.

The judgment strongly reinforces the view that it will be extremely difficult to justify, from a legal perspective, the obviating or modifying of the duty of confidence, on the grounds of public interest. It is possible to argue that the potential for commercial gain, which was at the heart of the facts in *ex parte Source Informatics Ltd*, as a public interest ground, could never permit the revision of the duty of confidence. The fact that the judge went further and suggested that the public interest lay, in fact, in ensuring that public confidences are kept, is indicative of a judicial attitude towards restriction of the use of the public interest argument in this area. It is submitted that the facts would have to demonstrate strong public interest grounds before any pharmacist would consider breaching the duty of confidence by passing on confidential information.

It is also important to note that Parliament has intervened in relation to the issue of confidentiality and health care, and has also indicated that in certain circumstances confidences may be breached.

Under the provisions of the National Health Service (Venereal Diseases) Regulations 1974 (S.I. 1974/29), health authorities are under a duty to take all necessary steps to secure that any information capable of identifying an individual obtained by officers of the authority, with respect to persons examined or treated for any sexually transmitted disease, is not disclosed to anyone, except to a medical practitioner, or person employed by a medical practitioner, for the purposes of treatment or prevention.

Section 11, Public Health (Control of Diseases) Act 1984 compels a medical practitioner to forward details concerning a patient suffering from a notifiable disease to the appropriate local authority. The details include the name, age, and sex of the patient and the address of the premises where the patient is, details of the disease itself, the day, if any, of admission to hospital, the address of the premises from which the patient was admitted to hospital, and a statement of opinion of whether or not the disease from which the patient is, or is suspected to be, suffering was contracted in the hospital. An list of original notifiable diseases was contained in s. 10 of the 1984 Act. This list has now been added to by the Public Health (Infectious Diseases) Regulations 1988 (S.I. 1988/1546), as amended. Failure to adhere to the requirements of the legislation may amount to a criminal offence punishable on summary conviction by a scale fine.

Under reg. 5 of the Abortion Regulations 1991 (S.I. 1991/499), a notice of a termination of a pregnancy, or other related information, required to be furnished to the Chief Medical Officer, for the purposes of the regulations, must not be disclosed to anyone else. Disclosure may, however, be made to a number of different individuals. Disclosure may be made to officers of the Department of Health, authorised by the Chief Medical Officer, or to the Registrar General or an authorised member of his or her staff, for the purpose of carrying out their duties.

Disclosure may be made to the Director of Public Prosecutions, a member of the Director's staff, to a police officer not below the rank of superintendent or a person authorised by him or her, for the purposes of investigating whether an offence has been carried out under the abortion legislation. The certificate or information may also be disclosed pursuant to a court order where court proceedings have already begun. Disclosure may also be made for the purposes of bona fide scientific research, or to the practitioner who terminated the pregnancy, or to a practitioner, with the consent in writing of the woman whose pregnancy was terminated. Finally, disclosure may be made when requested by the President of the General Medical Council, to the President or a member of the President's staff, for the purpose of investigating whether there has been serious professional misconduct by a practitioner.

Finally, ss. 9, 11 and 12, Police and Criminal Evidence Act 1984 (articles 11, 13 and 14 of the Police and Criminal Evidence (Northern Ireland) Order 1989) allow for the obtaining of materials, including medical records which would normally be excluded on the grounds of confidence, by the police on application to a judge. The materials may include human tissue or tissue fluid which has been taken for the purpose of diagnosis or medical treatment and which is held in confidence.

Obtaining the consent of an individual to disclose information about them will be a defence to an action for breach of confidence. The usual remedy sought for a breach of confidence is an injunction.

14.3 PATIENT ACCESS TO REPORTS

A patient may seek or demand access to reports which he or she knows have been compiled about him or her by pharmacists. Patients may wish to have such reports for a variety of reasons, from simple curiosity or perhaps to use as evidence in legal proceedings. The parents of a child patient may demand to see access to the child's records for the purposes of confirming or denying suspicions or allegations.

Under the provisions of para. 36 of sch. 2 of the National Health Service (General Medical Services) Regulations 1992 (S.I. 1992/635), ownership of National Health Service medical and hospital records lies with health care professionals and with health authorities and so an individual patient does not have an automatic right to access to such records. The position is less clear cut with the patient who has entered into private arrangements with a health care professional or institution. Ownership of, and access rights to health care records would be subject to the terms and conditions of the individually negotiated contract.

At common law, the issue of patient access to records and reports was considered in the social work case of *In Re D (Infants)* [1970] 1 WLR 599. In this case two children had been judicially committed to the care of a county council who had boarded them out to foster parents. The mother of the children applied to the court for custody of the children and in turn the county council sought to make the children wards of court. During the wardship proceedings the mother's lawyer applied to the court for disclosure of the case records kept by the county council.

The Court of Appeal held that the case records which had been compiled and kept by the local authority were private, confidential and privileged records. This meant that there was no legal requirement to produce the notes and records during the wardship proceedings. The privilege attaching to the documents derived from public policy. In particular, Harman LJ was of the view that public policy demanded that those who compiled and kept records of this nature should not have to be continually looking over their shoulders for attack on their views and opinions.

The case of *R v Mid-Glamorgan FHSA, ex parte Martin* [1995] 1 All ER 356, concerned a patient who had long-standing psychiatric problems. As part of his treatment, the patient received support from a social worker to whom he formed an emotional attachment. The social worker was withdrawn from the course of treatment as part of the clinical management of his case. The patient sought to have sight of his records of diagnosis, and in particular, of the reasons behind the decision to withdraw the social worker from the clinical management team.

The decision post-dated the introduction of the Access to Health Records Act 1990, which will be discussed in greater detail below. Nonetheless there was extensive analysis and discussion of the existence of a common law right to access to medical records. In the course of his judgment, and having reviewed the leading authorities, Popplewell J, came 'to the clearest possible conclusion' that there is no right at common law in a patient to access to any records.

It is important to note that Parliament has now given individuals certain rights of access to records whether of a general nature or relating to an individual's medical history. As we shall see below, the Data Protection Act 1998 allows individuals access to certain electronic data concerning them.

More importantly, the Access to Medical Reports Act 1988 (Access to Personal Files and Medical Reports (Northern Ireland) Order 1991) establishes a right of access by individuals to information relating to themselves maintained by certain authorities, and reports relating to themselves provided by medical practitioners for employment or insurance purposes. While the rights are restricted to medical practitioners, defined under the legislation as those registered under the Medical Act 1983 and therefore, in essence, doctors, the legislation is important in setting the framework for access to medical reports.

Section 3 of the 1988 Act imposes a requirement that no one may apply to a medical practitioner for a medical report relating to any individual for employment or insurance purposes unless that individual has been informed of the proposal and has consented to it. Under the provisions of s. 4, an individual who has given consent is entitled to state that he or she wishes to have access to the report before it is supplied. Where this is the case, the medical practitioner, subject to certain limitations, must not supply the report unless the individual concerned has been given access to it.

Section 7 of the 1988 Act gives an exemption from the access to medical reports provisions where the supply of the data would, amongst other things, be likely to cause serious harm to the physical or mental health of the individual who is seeking access to the data.

The Access to Health Records Act 1990 (Access to Health Records (Northern Ireland) Order 1993) gives an individual the right to access to information, held both manually and electronically by health professionals. The definition of health professional includes registered pharmacists.

Under the provisions of s. 3 of the 1990 Act, applications for access to a health record, or any part of a health record, may be made by a patient, a person authorised in writing to apply on the patient's behalf, a person having parental responsibility for a child patient, a person appointed to act on behalf of a patient incapable of managing their own affairs or the personal representative of a deceased patient. A 'health record' is defined as consisting of information relating to the physical or mental health of an individual who can be identified from that information, and which has been made by or on behalf of a health professional in connection with the care of that individual. Access is restricted to records created after 1 November 1991, the date of commencement of the legislation. However, access to earlier records may be allowed where this is necessary in order to make intelligible any subsequent reports.

Where an application is made by a parent of a child patient, access must not be given, under s. 4(2), unless the holder of the record is satisfied that the patient has consented to the making of the application, or that the patient is incapable of understanding the nature of the application and the giving of access would be in the child's best interests.

Detailed provision is made for time limits for giving access to records and for the charging of fees, particularly in relation to copying. Under the provisions of s. 3(3), where any information contained in a record or extract, accessible under the legislation, is expressed in terms which are not intelligible without explanation, such an explanation must be given, at the same time as the granting of access.

Again it is possible for a health professional to refuse access to such information on the grounds that, in the view of the health professional, access would cause serious harm to the physical or mental health of the individual concerned or where it would be likely to identify another person to whom the data relates.

Finally, under the provisions of s. 6 of the 1990 Act, patients who consider that any information contained in a health record is inaccurate, may apply to the holder of the record, without the payment of a further fee, for the necessary correction to be made. A correction may be made where the holder of the health record is satisfied that the information is inaccurate. Where the holder is not so satisfied, a note of the request for correction, and the reasons for it, must be included with the record.

14.4   DATA PROTECTION

The Data Protection Act 1998 is designed to give effect to the Data Protection Directive 95/46/EC. It completely replaces the existing legislative scheme relating to data protection which had been embodied in the Data Protection Act 1984, and in parallel secondary legislation. The 1998 Act embodies many of the principles and rules which had existed in the earlier 1984 legislation but also makes certain significant changes.

The general purpose of the 1998 Act is again to allow individuals ('data subjects') to be informed whether personal data relating to them is being processed by others ('data controllers', formerly 'data users'), to be given a description of that data, the purposes for which it is held and details of the recipients or classes of recipients to whom the data may be disclosed. A new change also allows data subjects to be provided with the data in an intelligible form, and where the personal data is used for evaluative purposes, such as performance at work, creditworthiness, or reliability or conduct, and could constitute the sole basis for decision-making, the data subject has the right to be informed of the logic involved in the decision-making.

Data subjects are also given new rights to prevent processing likely to cause damage or distress, to prevent processing for the purposes of direct marketing, to prevent decision-making solely on the basis of automatic processing and the right to ask a court for the rectification, blocking, erasure or destruction of inaccurate data.

The definition of 'personal data' has also been altered in the 1998 Act to include not only electronically stored information but also manual data in a 'relevant filing system' structured so that 'specific information relating to a particular individual is readily accessible'. While this change will greatly increase the duties and obligations of data controllers, two factors allow for adaption to the changes. The first lies in the commencement dates for the provisions of the Act itself, and the second, and more important, lies in the inclusion of 'transitional relief' provisions within the legislation which allows temporary exemptions from the manual data provisions from the commencement of the Act until October 2001, and potentially until October 2007.

A data controller is not obliged to supply any information unless the request is in writing and, except in prescribed cases, is accompanied by the requisite fee. Further the data controller must have sufficient information to allow for the identification of the individual concerned. Special provisions exist for the disclosure of information which also leads to the identification of a third party.

All data controllers, that is those involved in the processing of personal data, are required to register with the Data Protection Commissioner (formerly the 'Data Protection Registrar'). Processing is given a wide definition. Registration involves the notification of certain personal particulars and details of the data being processed, its purposes, potential or actual recipients and any claimed exclusions from the legislative requirements. The processing of personal data without registration is unlawful and amounts to a criminal offence.

Data controllers are under a duty to comply with the data protection principles in relation to all personal data with respect to which they are data controllers. As with the 1984 legislation there are eight data protection principles, although the wording and ethos is slightly different. Personal data must be:

(1)   processed fairly and lawfully;

(2)   obtained only for one or more specified and lawful purposes, and must not be further processed in any matter incompatible with that purpose;

(3)   adequate, relevant and not excessive in relation to the purpose or purposes for which they are processed;

(4)   accurate and, where necessary, kept up to date;

(5)   kept for no longer than is necessary;

(6)   processed in accordance with the rights of data subjects under the 1998 Act;

(7)   protected against unauthorised or unlawful processing and against loss, or destruction or damage, by the taking of appropriate technical and organisation measures;

(8)   transferred to a country or territory outside the European Economic Area only if that country or territory ensures an adequate level of protection for the rights and freedoms of data subjects in relation to the processing of personal data.

The Data Protection Commissioner is given wide powers and duties under the legislation, particularly in relation to the enforcement of the legislative provisions and requirements. The Commissioner will be able to issue enforcement notices on being satisfied that data controllers have contravened the data protection principles. The Commissioner may also issue information and special information notices where further detailed information is required. Failure to comply with such notices amounts to an offence. There are, however, special appeal procedures to a Data Protection Tribunal. The Data Protection Commissioner is also given wide powers to prepare and disseminate codes of practice and is under a duty to make and lay reports before Parliament.

The 1998 Act provides for the possibility of a wide range of exemptions from the legislative requirements, for example, in the areas of national security, crime and taxation etc. The range of potential exemptions is greater in the 1998 Act than it was in the 1984 legislation. Of particular interest to health care professionals, including pharmacists, is s. 30 which allows the Secretary of State, by order, to exempt from the subject information provisions, or modify those provisions in relation to, personal data consisting of information as to the physical or mental health or condition of the data subject.

This exemption is not new. Under the authority of the 1984 Act, the Data Protection (Subject Access Modification) (Health) Order 1987 (S.I. 1987/1903) allowed for exemptions in relation to personal data which would be likely to cause serious harm to the physical or mental health of the data subject. It is highly likely that equivalent secondary legislation will be made under the power given by s. 30 of the 1998 Act.

The pharmacy profession in the United Kingdom has given careful consideration to the legislative requirements relating to data protection. Detailed advice contained in the practice advice section of *Medicines, Ethics and Practice*, published by the Royal Pharmaceutical Society of Great Britain, on pharmacy computer systems contains specific guidance on security of information. This has detailed advice to ensure that pharmacy computer systems comply with the provisions of the data protection legislation in general and its principles in particular. It is important to remember that the *Code of Ethics* also requires that pharmacists must comply with the guidance in codes of practice where applicable. Failure to meet the standards could also form the basis of a complaint of misconduct.

14.5 PHARMACISTS AS COMPELLABLE WITNESSES

In all types of lawsuits, each party to a claim may seek to obtain documentary or other evidence to try the case and may ask a court, in certain circumstances, to order the other side, or indeed a third party, to produce this evidence. Such an order is an example of a number of organisational rules and regulations which circumscribe the substantive areas of civil and criminal law and which may themselves may be enforced through force of law, e.g., the Supreme Court Act 1981. The threat of such enforcement is often hidden in the language used to describe the order, e.g., 'subpoena' literally meaning 'under pain'.

It could be the case that a pharmacist could be served with such an order. It requires him or her to produce the relevant documentary evidence or to testify orally at the stipulated time. It is not an order belonging to the other party to the claim nor is it an order against the pharmacist. It is an order of the court which is to hear the claim and is designed to ensure that all possible evidence is brought to the attention of the court.

If a pharmacist chooses to ignore the order and refuses to appear in court or does appear but refuses to testify, the judge in charge of the court may require that pharmacist to be brought before him or her to explain his or her actions. During such an explanation the pharmacist may claim that he or she is refusing to testify and/or reveal the contents of notes or records because he or she believes them to be confidential or privileged. We have already seen (in 14.3), in the case of *In Re D*, that the courts may be prepared to consider such an argument and refuse to compel an individual to produce such documentation.

However, if a pharmacist is unable to persuade the court to extend the privilege to him or her and continues to refuse to abide by the terms of the subpoena and testify, a judge may then find her in contempt of court and impose a penalty. This penalty may include fines, imprisonment, or both. The language of these orders and the nature of the action enforcing them sums up the law's attitude towards them. Continuing to ignore such orders will leave a pharmacist in contempt of the authority of the law manifested through the court. A pharmacist will have to consider carefully a course of action in refusing to testify. A pharmacist may have a sense that he or she is bound by a moral duty of confidentiality not to disclose information about a patient or patient's condition or treatment to people outside the health care team. From a legal point of view the implications of non-compliance are obvious.

As noted in the introduction to this chapter, the pharmacy profession in the United Kingdom has paid particular attention to the issue of confidentiality. That analysis has led to the inclusion of a specific principle in the *Code of Ethics* of the Royal Pharmaceutical Society of Great Britain. This principle, and its associated obligations and detailed advice, will be discussed in greater detail in 14.8.

The guidance on the obligations associated with the principle relating to confidentiality deals specifically with the question of confidentiality and the disclosure of information for legal purposes. Pharmacists are advised that where disclosure is directed by a coroner, judge, or other presiding officer of a court, it may provide an exception to the general obligation to restrict access to information relating to a patient, and the patient's family, to those who, in the pharmacist's judgment, need that information in the interests of the patient or in the public interest. This advice is qualified by the further guidance that disclosure should only be to the person presiding. Confidential information should not be disclosed to a solicitor or court official except as directed by the presiding officer or with the consent of the patient concerned.

14.6   CONFIDENTIALITY AND INFORMANTS

Occasionally, pharmacists receive a great deal of confidential information about their patients from private individuals, sometimes in confidence. For example, a pharmacist may be told, in confidence, that a child under the age of sixteen to whom contraceptive advice has previously been given, is having a sexual relationship with an adult. Alternatively, a pharmacist may be told that a patient is selling prescription drugs, obtained from the pharmacy, on the streets to those with a drug dependency. A further question of confidentiality arises in this context. Can you protect the source of your information against requests to reveal their identity?

This issue arose in the social work context, in the case of *D v NSPCC* [1978] AC 171. The Society had received a complaint from an informant about the treatment of a 14-month-old girl and sent an inspector to the child's home to investigate. The child's mother brought an action against the Society for damages alleging negligence in failing properly to investigate the complaint and the manner and circumstances of the inspector's call which had caused her severe and continuing shock. The Society denied that it had been negligent and argued that there should be no disclosure of any documents which revealed, or might reveal, the identity of the informant. The Society argued that the proper performance of its duties required that the absolute confidentiality of information given in confidence should be preserved, that if disclosure were ordered its sources of information would dry up and that disclosure would be contrary to the public interest.

The House of Lords refused to compel the NSPCC to reveal the identity of its informant through disclosure of the documents. It held that a similar immunity from disclosure of their identity in civil proceedings to that which the law allowed to police informers, should be extended to those who gave information about neglect or ill-treatment of children to a local authority or the NSPCC. One judge, Lord Edmund-Davies, held that where a confidential relationship exists and disclosure would be in breach of some ethical or social value involving the public interest, then the court has a discretion to uphold a refusal to disclose relevant evidence provided it considers that, on balance, the public interest would be better served by excluding such evidence. The public interest in this case was the effective functioning of a statutory organisation authorised to bring legal proceedings to protect children's welfare.

14.7   CONFIDENTIALITY AND CHILDREN

Those pharmacists whose work brings them into contact with children may find that the children impart confidential information to them. For example, a child may seek advice about the best methods for contraception, and thereby indicate that he or she is having a sexual relationship with an adult. Indeed the child may indicate a willingness to speak only on the basis that the information will not be divulged elsewhere, particularly to its parents. Obviously this will create particular problems for pharmacists because they will not wish to lose the trust of the child but may feel that the information ought to be passed to others, including perhaps the child's parents.

The approach which the law would take on this matter would be based on the child's capacity to form a relationship of confidence with the pharmacist. The basis for this proposition is *Gillick* v *West Norfolk and Wisbech AHA* [1985] 3 All ER 402. Here the House of Lords ruled that a medical practitioner could give contraceptive advice to a girl aged under 16, without the consent, or even knowledge, of her parents where, essentially, the girl was capable or competent to understand the advice. Other factors, such as the inability to persuade the girl to inform her parents, the likelihood of sexual intercourse, the effect of a refusal on the girl's physical and mental health, and her best interests, were also to be taken into account.

As a result, the law will favour disclosure of information where the child is incompetent of forming a relationship of confidentiality only allowing non-disclosure where there are justifiable reasons for so doing. It has been suggested that this approach is in keeping with the basic principle that the paramount concern of the law is with the welfare of the child and that on the face of it, the welfare of a child is usually best served by others knowing what has been divulged.

The corollary is that a duty of confidentiality will be owed to a child who is competent to form a relationship of confidentiality with the pharmacist. However it is clear that the duty of confidentiality may be lawfully be broken. *In Re M* [1990] 1 All ER 205, a child had made an allegation of sexual abuse against a foster parent but when removed from the foster parents' home asked that the foster parents should not be told of the allegation. The local newspaper wished to publish a story condemning the local authority for removing the child without a valid explanation. The local authority sought an injunction restraining the newspaper from printing a story which revealed the identity of the child and which commented on the case.

The Court of Appeal granted the injunction to prevent the child being identified but allowed the newspaper to comment in relatively general terms on the issue. In so doing, the Court of Appeal discussed the duty of confidentiality and when and how it might be breached. Butler–Sloss LJ said (at p. 213):

A child cannot be sheltered from the consequences of the information disclosed and the person to whom the confidences have been made must give the child a truthful description of the likely outcome. He or she cannot promise what cannot be delivered. Whatever assurances . . . may be given to a child, he or she has to be told that at some stage . . . the carers will have to be told.

As noted in the introduction to this chapter, the pharmacy profession in the United Kingdom has considered closely the issue of confidentiality. That analysis has led to the inclusion of a specific principle in the *Code of Ethics* of the Royal Pharmaceutical Society of Great Britain. This principle, and its associated obligations and detailed advice, will be discussed in greater detail below.

The guidance on the obligations associated with the principle relating to confidentiality deals specifically with the issue of confidentiality and children. Pharmacists are advised that where the patient is a child, they may have to decide whether to release information to a parent or guardian without the consent of the child but in the child's best interests. Aware of the principles which emerged from the *Gillick* case, pharmacists are further advised that much will depend on the maturity of the child concerned and the child's relationship with parents or guardian.

The Royal Pharmaceutical Society of Great Britain has also recognised the relationship between the issue of confidentiality and the sensitive question of contraceptive advice, particularly for girls under the age of sixteen. Pharmacists are advised, when undertaking contraceptive advice, or pregnancy testing, to make efforts to establish the age of the girl. If the girl is under the age of sixteen, the pharmacist should strongly urge her to seek advice from her general practitioner, parent or similar responsible adult. In deciding whether to provide contraceptive advice, pharmacists are further advised that regard should be paid to the maturity of the girl and the consequences of unprotected intercourse taking place.

In addition, information concerning a positive pregnancy test result should not normally be referred without the girl's consent. Pharmacists are advised that if they believe that there may be a risk to the life of the girl or her pregnancy following the receipt of this information, it may be judged necessary to inform a responsible person without the girl's consent.

The issue of confidentiality and children is a potential minefield for the professional pharmacist. When one adds the very delicate questions of contraception and pregnancy to the equation, the problems are exacerbated. Pharmacists should be fully aware of their professional and legal obligations in this area, and should implement the appropriate principles in practice. In this regard, the advice given by the Royal Pharmaceutical Society of Great Britain, based on the principles in the cases of *Gillick* and *Re M*, is extremely sound. It is important to remember that breach of the professional principles may form the basis of a complaint of misconduct. Breach of the legal principles could result in substantial court action which may attract a great deal of public interest.

14.8   THE ETHICS OF CONFIDENTIALITY

It is widely accepted that a central tenet of health care professionalism is the maintenance of appropriate professional-patient relationships. Appropriate health care relationships include, amongst other things, an obligation of confidentiality. Veracity, privacy and fidelity could be said to be some of the other duties owed in such relationships. An analysis of the basis, meaning, limits and potency of the duty of confidentiality is essential for health care professionals wishing to develop and maintain appropriate patient relationships.

The basis for the obligation of confidentiality's primary status as an integral aspect of health care relationships is, first, that it promotes the goals of health care for, without the assumption that imparted information will be concealed by health care professionals, many patients would be reluctant to disclose further details, thereby preventing accurate diagnosis, prognosis and treatment. Secondly, the duty of confidentiality respects essential health care principles such as autonomy and privacy, and parallels the equivalent obligation of fidelity and trust. The duty of confidentiality is also a requisite for the formation and preservation of the health care profession itself. A primary attribute of health care professions is the ability to adhere to a duty of confidentiality.

The duty of confidentiality has a distinct ethical reality. Principles of medical ethics, in all of their forms, place confidentiality, with its inherent notions of autonomy, privacy, integrity, and trust, high on the agenda for health care professionals. It has been accepted for quite some time that the individual codes of ethics of health care professions should reflect the prominence of this ethical and legal duty. The pharmacy profession, both in the United Kingdom and elsewhere, has enthusiastically adopted this principle and has been to the forefront among health care professions in ensuring promotion of the duty of confidence as an imperative aspect of pharmacy professionalism, and its effective implementation into professional pharmacy practice.

The salience of the duty of confidence is reflected in the fact that it is included as a principle in the *Code of Ethics* of the Royal Pharmaceutical Society of Great Britain. Principle four requires pharmacists to respect the confidentiality of information acquired in the course of professional practice relating to a patient and the patient's family. Pharmacists are advised that such information must not be disclosed to anyone without the consent of the patient or appropriate guardian unless the interest of the patient or the public requires such disclosure. It is submitted that the definition of the duty in the *Code of Ethics* in this manner strongly reflects the legal duties of confidence which are owed by pharmacists, and which have been described above. It is important to note, however, the comments of Latham J in *ex parte Source Informatics Ltd* (see 14.2), on the circumstances in which the duty of confidence might be obviated in the public interest.

Principle four encompasses a series of further obligations. This include an obligation to restrict access to information relating to a patient, or the patient's family to those who, in the pharmacist's judgment, need that information in the interests of the patient or in the public interest. Further guidance on this obligation outlines a series of potential exceptions to the need to keep information, which includes both manual and electronically held information, confidential. Exceptions may be made where the information is to be shared with other health care professionals involved in the care and treatment of the patient, and who would be unable to continue to provide that care and treatment without the information. Information may also be disclosed by virtue of a legal requirement to do so, either arising under a right of access through statute, or for the purpose of court proceedings. A further potential exception relates to the disclosure for the purpose of a medical research project which has been approved by a recognised ethical committee. This exception would require to be reassessed against the legal principles outlined by Latham J in *ex parte Source Informatics Ltd*, as discussed in 14.2.

Finally, exceptions from the professional duty may exist where disclosure is justifiable on the grounds of public interest, for example to assist in the prevention of, detection of, or prosecution for serious crime, where disclosure could prevent a serious risk to public health, or where it is necessary to prevent serious injury or damage to the health of a third party. Without labouring the point, the guidance (in the *Code of Ethics*) on these obligations needs to be viewed with caution in light of *ex parte Source Informatics Ltd*. In fairness to those who have drafted the guidance, they have recognised the limitations which ought to be placed on these exceptions by qualifying one of them with the word 'rarely' and by indicating, in more general terms, that it will be necessary to assess the risk and seriousness of the potential consequence of failure to disclose as against the rights of the patient to confidentiality.

Pharmacists are also under a duty to ensure that anyone who has access to information relating to a patient or to a patient's family is aware of the need to respect its confidential nature and does not disclose such information without reference to, and only with the consent of, the patient. This obligation is clearly designed to cover those others within professional pharmacy practice, e.g., technicians, sales assistants, who may become privy to confidential information. Quite clearly the extent of the duty of obligation needs to be reinforced with them. It is important to emphasise, however, that the duty rests finally with the pharmacist, as part of the obligations owed as a professional. Any breach of the duty of confidence by a member of staff in the pharmacy practice might, however, have distinct employment implications.

Where a pharmacist judges it necessary to disclose information relating to a patient and the patient's family, he or she is under a further duty to ensure that the content should be limited to the minimum necessary for the specific purpose involved.

Specific guidance is given on the disclosure of information relating to those who are incapable of giving consent, because of age or physical or mental handicap. Some of this guidance has already been discussed above in 14.7. Pharmacists are advised that the assessment of the best interests of the patient, for the purposes of disclosure of confidential information, should take into account any known wishes of the patient, the patient's next of kin, any other relative and anyone with powers of attorney. In mental health and mental handicap cases, pharmacists are advised that the Mental Health Act Commission should be informed of the disclosure.

Specific obligations are created concerning the maintenance of information on computers. Pharmacists are under a duty to ensure that pharmacy computer systems which include patient specific data must incorporate access control systems which should be implemented to minimise the risk of unauthorised or unnecessary access to the data. Further guidance on this obligation advises pharmacists to be aware, and take all practical steps possible to guard against the risks, of unauthorised access to information held on pharmacy computer systems. Pharmacists are further advised that they should take particular care to ensure that computer systems linked to the Internet or other networks incorporate measures designed to eliminate the risk of unauthorised access to confidential data.

The pharmacy profession in the United Kingdom has anticipated the potential for the facts which arose in *ex parte Source Informatics Ltd*, by including specific obligations and guidance on the use of information for other purposes. Pharmacists are warned that information acquired by a pharmacist in the course of professional practice other than that relating to patients may also be confidential, and must be treated by the pharmacist as such. Pharmacists are further advised that, in particular, information relating to the prescribing practices of identifiable doctors or doctors' practices, and other prescribers, is confidential and must not be disclosed, other than for necessary purposes of the NHS, unless the prescriber has given informed written consent to the disclosure. Subject to further analysis of the disclosure of the information for 'the necessary purposes of the NHS', this obligation reflects very well the extent and range of the obligations owed by pharmacists, as outlined in *ex parte Source Informatics Ltd*.

However, one further piece of guidance will certainly have to be reassessed in light of the principles emerging from that case. As it presently stands, pharmacists are advised that none of the obligations or further guidance precludes the collation of date from patient records, on condition that it is presented anonymously, for the purposes of research or as information to an interested commercial source. Quite clearly this guidance is contrary to the principles of law in *ex parte Source Informatics Ltd*, where the judge held that such courses of action could amount to a breach of the legal duty of confidence.

This last qualification aside, the manner in which the pharmacy profession in the United Kingdom has managed the crucial issue of the pharmacist's duty of confidence has been very effective. The inclusion of the duty as a fundamental principle in the *Code of Ethics*, and the range and detail of the advice and guidance which has been offered, reflects the significance of the duty to the profession and assists the process of the implementation of the obligation into practice. The constructive management of this issue is a definite strength for the profession and rightly deserves commendation.

14.9 CONCLUSION

The duty of confidentiality means that, as a pharmacist, you must be sure that all information which you receive, both in your professional practice and otherwise, is treated as confidential. It is equally clear that your duty has to be balanced against the rights of your patients and others, arising through legislation and case law, in gaining access to information for specific purposes. Account will also have to be taken of the fact that you may be ordered to produce certain information and that ignoring such an order may result in the imposition of penalties. Specific attention will also have to be paid to sensitive information, particularly that relating to children, and that which may have an impact on other individuals or on the public in general. The community nature of the pharmacy also necessitates the consideration of the exchange or repetition of personal information, particularly that which is based on rumour or innuendo.

The legal and ethical aspects of the control of information, including its receipt and disclosure, are likely to increase in importance over the next few years. The possibility of the introduction of specific rules on privacy, as part of an overall policy of open access, is likely to increase the range of duties and obligations owed by health care professionals in this area. The growth in health care litigation has resulted in a parallel rise in requests (or demands) for access to health care records and reports. Finally, the advent of new technologies has seen the development of new sources and forms of information which increasingly are subject to legislative and regulatory control, and which require further ethical analysis.

The pharmacy profession in the United Kingdom has worked hard to manage the issue of confidentiality, set in context its place as an essential tenet of professionalism, and given detailed advice on the implementation of the duties and obligations into professional practice. The principles, obligations, advice and guidance, reflect the pharmacist's legal and ethical duties and obligations with regard to information. Pharmacists would be well advised to pay close attention to them. The consequences of failure to do so are obvious.

FIFTEEN
The conduct of business

15.1 INTRODUCTION

A general theme of this book has been to show that the pharmacist is a health care professional sharing responsibility for the competent provision of pharmaco-therapy for the purposes of achieving definite outcomes that improve or maintain a patient's quality of life. However, the pharmacist has a parallel, distinctive trading role, involving the expectation of commercial profit directly from the distribution of products and services. The pharmacy profession is not unique in this regard. Other professions have a plurality of roles of which the aspiration towards commercial profit is one. However, the pharmacist is probably atypical of health care professionals in having a distinctive business orientation.

Certain of the products sold for profit by the community pharmacist are medicinal drugs distributed to patients as part of the wider professional health care role. Aspects of that part of the commercial role of pharmacists was explored in chapter thirteen. The sale of other commodities, e.g., perfumes, cosmetics, hair dryers, bears little relation to that role. Even the expectation of commercial profit from the distribution of medicinal products can create different compulsions and motivations. Often this divergence leads to tensions and conflict, leaving a pharmacist in an ethical dilemma.

Despite this, it is clear that pharmacy has a distinctive commercial reality. Commerce, in turn, has a distinctive legal reality, and the purpose of this chapter is to explore certain aspects of the legal reality of business. That purpose will be achieved by first exploring the legal aspects of establishing a business. The organisation and structure of a business has specific and distinct legal consequences, and the attributes of the most common forms will be examined. The conduct of business is carried out through the format of exchange, and the law of exchange is the law of contract; so a further section of the chapter will explore aspects of the law of contract. That exploration will form an essential background to two further areas of the law relating to the conduct of business — the rules and regulations relating to the sale of goods and the provision of goods on credit. The former forms an essential element of the day-to-day conduct of business in a pharmacy. The latter is increasing in importance, even for a pharmacist, as more and more consumers seek to purchase goods and services on credit. The commercial pharmacist, in seeking to enter into business relationships with others, has to meet those customers, usually through inviting potential buyers onto business property and so the chapter will finally explore the significant rules relating to the legal duties owed towards visitors to premises.

There are two caveats in relation to this chapter. First, in a textbook such as this, it will only be possible to give a general overview of the rules and regulations relating to the conduct of business. There are many aspects of this important area which cannot be discussed in detail. For example, the consideration of the registered company as a form of business organisation mentions the possibility of insolvency. There are complex and intricate rules on the process of insolvency which are beyond the scope of this book. Those who are interested in an academic discussion of this, and other areas, are referred to specialised textbooks on the subject. Those who actually find themselves faced with the legal reality of an insolvency, or other specific aspect of the conduct of a business, should refer themselves to a lawyer.

Secondly, there are other legal aspects of the conduct of a business which have not been addressed in detail. For example, the pharmacist as the owner of business property would need to be aware of the planning and environmental regulations associated with commercial property ownership. Again the detail of such issues is beyond the scope of this particular text. Research elsewhere, or specific legal assistance should provide the required answers.

15.2   THE ORGANISATION OF BUSINESS

Those involved in the conduct of business use a number of phrases and terms to describe the organisational status of their enterprise. So, for example, we often hear individuals state that they own a company, or are running a firm or that their business name is 'X & Co'. The interchanging use of these expressions disguises a particular legal significance. In law, the terms have distinct and definite meanings, and the organisation of a business in a particular way has distinct (and separate) legal consequences. Those legal consequences pervade all aspects of the choice of business organisation from formation through to termination and beyond.

The factors determining the choice of business organisation are not limited to the legalities. Other considerations — economic, social, strategic, marketing

— play an equally important part. It is important to pay close attention to the literature on such factors. Indeed these elements probably play an even greater role in the choice of business organisation. It is important, however, to remember that the legal structure and organisation of business is significant, particularly in managing the consequences of business failure.

Any discussion of the structural organisation of business focuses on three main types of categorisation — the sole trader, the partnership, and the company. It is also often stated that the three classifications are hierarchical in nature. The sole tradership is where any aspiring business person starts with the eventual aim of corporate status. While there is some credence to be attached to such organisational theory, it disguises the fact that each form has its own particular attributes. It must be emphasised that the legal implications of formulating a business in a certain way should not be underestimated.

15.2.1 The sole trader

Setting up in business as a sole trader is the most usual method adopted by individuals who wish, initially, to set up in business on their own. From the legal perspective, there are no formalities to be adopted in actually formulating a business as a sole tradership. As noted above, there may be other strict legal formalities, e.g., in the use of a professional name or title, in acquiring business property, or obtaining planning permission to adapt and modify such property. Legally, though, there is nothing to prevent an individual from declaring that he or she is in business as a sole trader.

The conduct of business is also without strict legal formality. There is no requirement to have annual (or indeed any) meetings, nor is the sole trader obliged to make annual returns of accounts or business dealings. Any profit obtained in the business belongs solely to the proprietor who also retains ultimate control over the day-to-day management and future direction of the business. The proprietor may also, without interference, decide when and how the business should be terminated or dissolved.

For example, the sole trader may decide, after a period in business, to sell it as a going concern to another commercial organisation. Again, apart from the usual legal procedures involved in the selling and transfer of business assets, including stock, goodwill, and commercial property, there are no specific formalities required in the transfer of a sole tradership. Equally, should an individual decide to dissolve or terminate the business, because of commercial failure or retirement, there are no strict legal formalities to be undertaken.

Problems, with distinct legal consequences, may arise where the business is dissolved with debts owing to creditors. Should the sole trader be unable to meet the business debts, a number of legal procedures may be invoked by the creditors involved. These include the informal simple request for payment, through to the commencement of more formal legal procedures against the sole trader. The latter can, and often does include actions in the court, the enforcement of judgments through a variety of different warrants and orders, composition with creditors, schemes and voluntary arrangements and petition-ing for bankruptcy. The bankruptcy procedures may even be invoked by debtor sole traders themselves, as a method of relieving some of the undoubted burden of dealing with the consequences of business failure.

One of the main disadvantages of operating in business as a sole trader, which significantly balances (or even outweighs) the advantage of lack of legal formality in formulation, conduct and termination noted above, is that in seeking to recover debts owing to the business, the law draws no distinction between the individual and their business as a sole trader. This often means that an individual's personal property, house, car etc., will be aggregated with the business property for the purposes of the settlement of business debts owing to creditors. Such difficulties are compounded by the fact that the intrinsic nature of the sole tradership means that there are no partners, or others, with whom to share the financial burden.

15.2.2 The partnership

The partnership is an appropriate form of business structure for a larger organisation. A partnership usually arises where a sole trader is experiencing business growth sufficient to allow for expansion through the acquisition of other trading partners. A sole trader might wish to attract further investment income or individual expertise to expand into new areas of trade and find that there are other like-minded traders wishing to do the same. Equally a sole trader might discover that the only method of achieving development is to amalgamate with rival traders, eliminating the problems of competition and business stagnation which inevitably might result. The partnership is equally an apposite form of business structure for this situation.

Legal control over partnerships is much more strict than that for a sole tradership. A Partnership Act was passed in 1890 and still outlines the fundamental rules applicable to partnerships today. The 1890 Act defines a partnership as 'the relationship which subsists between persons carrying on business in common with a view to profit'. The definition is set in terms of relationship which does not necessarily mean a legal relationship. Whether a partnership agreement has been entered into or not, two or more persons who are involved in the actual running of a business, not preparing for it, or not acting informally without a view to profit, will be regarded as being a partnership. Except in certain limited circumstances applicable to particular professions, the maximum number of partners allowed is 20.

The partnership, as a form of business organisation, has distinct advantages. While certain formalities are involved, these are less strict than those for a company. As with the sole tradership, the partners own the business property, and retain ultimate control over the day-to-day running of the business and its future direction. Responsibility for the management of the business and its potential liabilities, is shared between the partners, and one individual does not have to assume sole responsibility for the consequences of business failure. The addition of other partners to the business increases the potential for the acquisition of capital and further growth.

The absence of a requirement for legal formality in the establishment of a partnership disguises the fact that the process is often very legalistic and formal. The formation of a partnership usually involves the drawing up, normally by a lawyer, of a partnership agreement. The partnership agreement should make provision for the amount of property and capital brought into the business by each partner, the rights of each partner to a share of the profits, the obligation of each partner to contribute to the business debts, the powers of the partners to bind the partnership in contract, the responsibilities of each partner in the day-to-day management of the business, individual partners' rights, and the rights, obligations and duties on termination of the partnership.

Where there is no partnership agreement, or where there is an agreement which does not provide for one of the matters noted above, the provisions of the Partnership Act 1890 will apply. The legislation implies that all partnership property, and profits of the business are to be shared equally between the partners. In addition, all partners will have the right to manage the business, and new partners may not be introduced without the consent of the existing partners.

The preferred option is to have an agreement which clearly outlines the relevant position, duties and obligations of all of the parties. This is particularly important in relation to the power of individual partners to bind the partnership in contract. Unlike the position with sole traders, third parties will often deal with individual partners acting on behalf of the partnership, rather than with the partnership itself. In the absence of any agreement to the contrary, of any evidence of actual authority to act, and of any knowledge of a lack of authority, a third party may hold the partnership to be bound to any contract carried out in the usual manner, and connected with the business. The parameters of this principle have been explored in depth by the courts, both before and since 1890, and it is subject to certain limitations. However the broad nature of the doctrine reinforces the imperative of making provision for the contractual liability of partners in the partnership agreement.

The Partnership Act 1890 makes specific provision for the duties which each partner owes to each other and to the partnership in general. These include the duty to disclose all matters relating to the partnership, the duty to account for all personal profits and benefits, the duty not to compete and the duty to take reasonable care in the performance of duties. Again, it is usual for these important matters to be provided for in the partnership agreement. The agreement should also make provision for the dissolution of the partnership and the realisation and distribution of assets. In the absence of such provision, dissolution will usually take place on the death or bankruptcy of one of the partners, on the giving of notice of intention to leave by one of the partners, the expiry of a fixed term partnership, or by order of the court. The Insolvent Partnerships Order 1994 (S.I. 1994/2421) makes specific provision for insolvent partnerships.

Finally it is important to note that it is possible in restricted circumstances to establish a limited partnership. The Limited Partnerships Act 1907 provides for the establishment of limited partnerships in which one or more of the partners has limited liability for the partnership debts. Such limited partnerships must be registered with the Registrar of Companies, who must be supplied with specific details of the nature of the business. In return for limited liability, the limited partner has no power to bind the business and is not permitted to take part in the management of the enterprise. The death of a limited partner, or the giving of notice by a limited partner, does not automatically dissolve the partnership.

Some of the main disadvantages of forming a partnership are that the requirement to share decision-making, control and the profit of the business, means, as a corollary, that individual management is lost. Equally the transfer of a share in the partnership is only permissible with the agreement of the other partners. In addition, and in parallel with the position with sole traders, the liability of the partners to contribute to the debts of the partnership is personal so that personal property will be aggregated with business property for the purpose of settlement of business debts.

15.2.3   The company
The term 'company' is used quite frequently in commercial circles to describe a wide variety of different types of business organisations. In reality, it has a detailed and technical legal meaning. The company is an attractive form of business structure for those seeking to expand a business, and who see the potential for even further growth. It is equally attractive for those individuals who wish to limit their liability to contribute towards the debts of the business in the event of financial failure. The desire is to separate legally the concept of individual and business, something, as we have noted, which is not always possible with sole traderships and partnerships.

Companies are classified in a variety of different ways. For example, it is possible to become a company through royal charter or through the passing of an Act of Parliament. The most common format, and the one which is most familiar in business, is a registered company. This means that the company has been registered with the Registrar of Companies under the provisions of the Companies Act 1985, as amended. As noted above, one of the main attractions of forming a registered company is the possibility of limiting liability and so the vast majority of registered companies fall into this category. It is possible to have unlimited companies but their intrinsic nature has meant that they are relatively rare.

Registered companies may be limited by shares or by guarantee. A company limited by shares means that once the members have paid the full nominal value of their shares, together with any premium, the members cannot be asked to contribute any more towards the cost of the business debts, on a winding-up. Of course, the members may lose the value of their share holding but will not be required to contribute any more. Such limitation is confined to the members. The company, as a separate legal person, is still required to settle its debts. When a company is limited by guarantee, the members agree, at the time of formation, to contribute a specific amount to the company's debts on a winding-up. That is the extent of the members' liability and the company is again not covered by the restriction.

Registered companies may also be public or private. A public company must have a nominal issued share capital of at least £50,000 and the name of the company must include the words 'public limited company' or 'plc'. There must be a membership of at least two and the company is required to register with the Registrar of Companies. Any company which is not a public company is a private company by legislative default.

A company is registered by application to the Registrar of Companies in the required format. A number of documents must accompany the application of which the articles of association, the memorandum of association, the statutory declaration of compliance with the statutory requirements, and the statement of the company's first directors and secretary, are the most important. The articles of association provide for the internal management of a company and cover the nature and types of shares, the transfer and forfeiture of shares, company meetings, rights of members, appointment of directors and their rights, powers and duties and matters relating to the company accounts.

The memorandum of association is one of the most important documents relating to the company and sets out the company's name, details of the registered office, the objects of the company, details of the company's liability, its capital and association. The objects clause used to have a particular significance in that it set out the objects for which the company had been formed. Any transaction entered into which was outside the stated objects could be stated to be *ultra vires*, beyond the power given in the objects and thus void. The net effect of the *ultra vires* rules has been limited by the tactic of drafting objects clauses in a wide manner, so as to permit a wide range of business activities, and by subsequent amendments to the companies' legislation to comply with European Community directives.

There are detailed company law rules on the running of a company as a business. These rules provide for the raising of capital, the issue of shares and debentures, the rights of members, including minority members, the appointment, remuneration, meetings, and control of directors, the maintenance of books and records and the annual submissions of these to the Registrar of Companies. There are also detailed rules on the duties of directors and their authority to bind the company.

Companies may come to an end in a variety of different ways. Particular attention is paid to the winding-up of a company, both on a voluntary and involuntary basis. The Insolvency Act 1986 makes specific provision for different types of insolvency procedures and practitioners.

As noted above, the main advantage of the registered company as a form of business organisation is the effect of corporate personality. The company becomes an individual legal person separate from its members, has a continual existence independent of changes in its membership, may own its own property, and may bring and defend legal actions in its own name. In addition, the potential for the acquisition of limited liability by members of the company, the possible increase in capital by the issue of further shares, and the relative ease in transfer of ownership of shares, are further benefits relevant to the adoption of the registered company as a business structure.

The major disadvantages are that there are specific legal formalities to be adhered to in order to establish the company by registration in the first place and further procedures to be complied with on an annual basis, in terms of returns to the Registrar of Companies. Company law is also very complicated and intricate and it is virtually impossible to conduct the business of running a registered company without substantial input from lawyers. Finally, control over the day-to-day management of the business, and its future direction is shared with and may be lost to other members and interests. Registered companies tend to be personally anonymous.

15.3 A BRIEF NOTE ON BUSINESS NAMES AND BUSINESS PROPERTY

We have already noted in s. 8.3.1.2, that the use of professional titles in pharmacy is strictly controlled by a series of pharmacy laws. Pharmacists setting up in business as pharmacists would need to pay particular attention to such professional requirements. In addition to these requirements, commercial law imposes specific obligations on the use of certain names and titles.

A sole trader who wishes to trade in his or her own name will face no major, statutory restriction. However, the provisions of the Business Names Act 1985, will apply to those sole traders who wish to trade under a business name. A business name is one which does not consist only of the surname of the sole trader, together with any forename or initials. The Business Names Act 1985 introduces specific controls over the choice of business name and disclosure of the background to any chosen business name. Choice of a business name is restricted. For example, there can be no adoption of a name which appears to be connected to central or local government authorities, except with permission, or which uses words such as 'charity' or 'royal'. Obscene names are also prohibited. Where a business name is being used, the name and address of the true owner must be disclosed on all literature, including letters, orders, invoices, business cards, and be displayed in all business premises so that it can be easily seen and read. Failure to comply with these provisions amounts to a criminal offence.

Similar rules on the choice of names apply to partnerships. In addition, the names and addresses of all members of a partnership must be displayed on all literature, including letters, orders, invoices, business cards, and be displayed in all business premises in a notice so that it can be easily seen and read. The requirement as to the display of the names and addresses is relaxed in relation to those partnerships with more than twenty partners. The names and addresses of all partners must be given to anyone who is undertaking business with the partnership and who asks for such details. Under the provisions of company law, partnerships are allowed to use the terms 'company' or 'and company'. The term 'limited' or 'ltd' is strictly controlled and may not be used even by a limited partnership. Strict criminal penalties attach to failure to comply with this latter requirement.

The provisions of the Business Names Act 1985 are supplemented by the Companies Act 1985, in relation to the adoption and use of names by companies. There are detailed rules on the form of company names, including the use of the terms 'limited' or 'ltd', and the above-mentioned connections with central or local government or other organisations. A name will not be accepted if it is the same as, or similar to one already entered into the index of names maintained by the Registrar of Companies. There are additional procedures for voluntary and compulsory changes of name. The name of the company must be displayed on all literature, including letters, orders, invoices, business cards, cheques and receipts and be displayed outside the registered office and in all business premises so that it can be easily seen and read. Again strict penalties attach to a failure to comply with these requirements. Companies using business names which are different from the corporate name are subject to the same business name legislative requirements (and sanctions) as apply to partnerships.

The tort of passing-off is often used to protect a trader's business or trading goodwill where that is likely to be damaged by confusion or deceit created by another trader. In its most usual form, passing-off occurs when one trader leads the public to believe that his or her business, products or services are those of another trader. As a result, the law on passing-off is often used by traders who feel that their particular trade or service mark or shape or get-up is being used without authority to cause confusion and deception. The protection offered by this branch of the law tends to go further than that provided by the trade marks legislation in that a greater range of forms of identity may be covered.

However it is often more difficult, time-consuming and expensive to prove passing-off. It is necessary to establish that a trader's goods have acquired a reputation in the market and are known by some distinguishing feature. It is then necessary to show that the defendant has adopted this distinctive feature in relation to his or her own products and as a result the public have been confused or have been deceived into buying the product believing it to be that of the plaintiffs. Nevertheless, it would be inadvisable to call a new pharmacy 'Butes' the Chemist'.

The pharmacist, in business, is going to have specific dealings in business property. The law divides all property, including business property, into real and personal property. Real property includes land, buildings and fixtures. Personal property includes leasehold interests in land, tangible objects (such as stock, shelving, cash registers, personal computers) and intangible property, such as business goodwill, copyright, patents, designs, trade marks).

There are detailed laws relating to both real and personal property which are too intricate to be dealt with in a textbook such as this. Pharmacists who encounter issues relating to aspects of dealing with personal property, from planning and environmental issues through to the infringement of an intellectual property right, or sale of fixtures and fittings, are referred to specialist textbooks in this area, or legal advisers with professional expertise.

15.4   THE LAW OF CONTRACT

15.4.1   Formation of a contract

What is a contract? When we are asked to define a contract we usually come up with the word 'agreement'. Agreement plays an important part in a contract and in contract law. However a contract cannot be restricted simply to the notion of agreement. It is much more complex than that. For example, we all make agreements every day of the week. We might agree to wash the car or mow the lawn. We might also agree to sell our car. Not all of these agreements are contracts, however. A contract, therefore, is an agreement which the law will recognise. The law will recognise an agreement as being a contract when that agreement has certain specific characteristics.

The first characteristic of a valid, legally binding contract is an intention to create legal relations. Contract law says that those who make an agreement must have intended to be legally bound it. There will be no contract if the parties did not intend it to be legally enforceable in the courts. The law presumes that those who make friendly or social or domestic agreements did not intend to be legally bound by them. This will mean that most agreements of this type will not be legally binding and enforceable in the courts unless one party to the agreement can produce evidence to the contrary.

On the other hand the law presumes that when businesses are involved in making commercial agreements, either with other businesses or with a consumer, that they *did* intend to be legally bound by them. This will mean that most agreements of this type will be legally binding unless one party can produce evidence to the contrary. The law takes the view that businesses ought to know what they are doing and so it will take strong evidence to prove that they did not intend to be legally bound by their agreements.

The second characteristic of a valid, legally binding contract is that there must be agreement. Naturally, if the parties did not agree there cannot be a contract. Agreement is made up of two elements — offer and acceptance. Many people think that contracts need to be in writing and that the offer and acceptance must be contained in a written document. This is not true. We all make contracts every day which are not in writing. A verbal offer and acceptance is sufficient. Contracts will be put into writing where they are valuable or are meant to last a long time and contracts concerning land and consumer credit agreements must be put into writing. Other than that it is important to remember that most contracts are verbal ones.

The offeror is the person in a contract who makes an offer; the offeree is the person to whom an offer is made — that might be an individual, a specific group or the whole world. An offer is an indication by one person that he or she is prepared to contract with one or more others, on certain terms, which are fixed, or capable of being fixed, at the time the offer is made.

We have all seen situations in which it appears that offers are being made. Often the word offer is used to describe these situations. However the law will take a different view of some types of situations and has declared that these are not offers in the legal sense of the word.

Preliminary negotiations, or expressions of interest will be regarded as invitations to treat, or invitations to make an offer rather than offers themselves. Displays of goods in shops, or shop windows, will generally be regarded as invitations to treat, not offers. This was discussed in a famous case involving a pharmacy, *Pharmaceutical Society of Great Britain* v *Boots* [1953] 1 All ER 482. Where goods are displayed in a self-service store or in a shop window, the offer is made by the customer when the goods are taken to the counter or till for payment. The acceptance takes place when the price of the goods is put through the till or cash machine. Until the price is put through there is no acceptance. This means that the shop-owner may refuse to sell at the price indicated on the goods.

An offer may also be distinguished from an advertising boast which no one would be expected to take seriously. It is important to note that there is a thin dividing line between advertising boasts and offers. Many people will say many things during discussions about an agreement. The law has stated that merely giving information is not an offer. You may have seen advertisements for tenders in the newspapers where a company or organisation invites businesses to bid for work or the supply of services. An invitation to tender for work will normally constitute an invitation to treat, with the responses being offers. In auctions the bids are offers, which are accepted by the fall of the hammer. An auction advertised as being 'without reserve', however, implies an obligation to sell to the highest bidder.

It is possible for the offeror to withdraw or revoke the offer at any time up to acceptance. He or she is entitled to do this even if he or she has promised to keep the offer open for a specified period. This has led to many problems in contracts for the sale of land where some parties have attempted to introduce a subsidiary agreement to keep the offer or negotiations open for a specified period. If the offeror imposes a time limit for acceptance and the offeree does not accept within that time, the offer will lapse and come to an end. If no express time limit is imposed the offer will lapse after a reasonable time. Once the offeree has rejected the offer, he or she cannot later go back and purport to accept it. A counter-offer amounts to a rejection. Rejection, like offer and withdrawal of an offer, is only effective when the offeror learns of it.

Acceptance is an unconditional agreement to an definite offer. Acceptance must take place while the offer is still open. It must be an absolute and unqualified acceptance of the offer or it may amount to a rejection. Acceptance may take the form of words spoken or written or it may be implied by conduct. There must be some positive act of acceptance, however. Silence is usually not enough. This rule has been applied to the receipt of unsolicited goods although the position is now covered by the Unsolicited Goods and Services Act 1971. Someone who receives unsolicited goods will become the owner of the goods unless the sender collects them within six months; the recipient can, by notice to the sender, reduce this period to thirty days. Acceptance by conduct is also possible, for example where a supplier delivers goods which have been ordered.

An unusual old rule of contract law states that a letter of acceptance, properly addressed and stamped, is effective from the moment of posting, even if it never arrives. This rule is subject to the conditions that there must be some evidence of posting, that the parties must have contemplated use of the post and the rule will not apply where the offer has required actual communication. There is no authority on the effect of this rule on acceptance by private courier. 'Instantaneous' communications, such as telex, take effect at the point of receipt. Again, there are no precise rules in relation to e-mail, telephone answering machines or faxes and in particular, the precise time at which messages are read.

The third essential characteristic of a valid, legally binding contract is the presence of consideration. Consideration means that only bargains, and not simple promises, should be enforced. Consideration might be described broadly as something given, promised or done in exchange

Most people find the concept of consideration difficult to understand because they equate an exchange of promises with offer and acceptance. However in law they are different concepts and practically can be so as well. To give an example, in a pharmacy the purchaser will offer to buy and promise to pay and the pharmacist will accept the offer to buy and promise to deliver. All of these things usually happen together but they can be separated.

Consideration can be executory or executed. Executory consideration is a promise yet to be fulfilled, and most contracts start in this way. Executed consideration is the completed performance of one side of the bargain. The law does not recognise past consideration where one party makes a promise to someone else after they have carried out a transaction for them. For example, I might promise this week to give my ten-year-old car to my sister-in-law who has started a new job. On Saturday she wins the lottery and promises to give me £5,000 for the car. In law this will be regarded as a mere expression of thanks for a past kindness or as a designated gift, and no contract will arise. However where the claimant has performed services for the defendant without any agreement for remuneration but with the assumption that the services were ultimately to be paid for and with a promise from the defendant to that effect, then an action might lie for breach of the promise.

Normally, only a person who has given consideration may sue on a contract. I may promise to pay £1 to my wife, if my wife will give a book to my friend. If my wife refuses to deliver the book, I may sue, but my friend, who has given no consideration, cannot sue. This is known as privity of contract.

Certain acts and promises are deemed incapable in law of supporting an action for breach of contract by the person who has supplied them. Here it is possible to distinguish between whether the act or promise supplied by the claimant is an adequate recompense for the defendant's promise, and whether the act or promise amounts to sufficient consideration.

It has long been established that the courts will not enquire into the adequacy of consideration. This means that the courts will not ask whether the price which has been promised is, in fact, enough or adequate for the goods or services which have been promised in return. It has often been said that the courts will not make a man's (or woman's) bargain for him (or her).

Even though a bargain has been struck, the consideration may be deemed to be insufficient. Here the essential question is whether the courts can discover the promise or performance of something more than what one party is already bound to do. The cases may be grouped into four classes.

The first is where a public duty is imposed upon the claimant by law. We are all occasionally obliged to carry out certain public duties by force of the law. For example, we might be obliged to turn up at court under a subpoena and we all have to pay our taxes. If one party attempts to use an existing legal obligation as a promise under a contract then the law will say that this is not enough or is insufficient.

The second is where the claimant is bound by an existing contractual duty to the defendant. There is no consideration if all that the claimant does is to perform an obligation imposed by a previous contract with the defendant although the legal basis for this principle has recently come in for considerable further discussion. Despite this, the principle has been applied in a variety of ways to the settlement of debts. The general rule is that an agreement where one party promises to pay part of a debt owed to another in return for the other's promise to forego the balance of the sum due is not binding because of a lack of consideration. To use an example, if a supplier is owed £1,000 by a pharmacist and agrees to take £750 in full and final settlement, the agreement is unenforceable by the pharmacist as there is no consideration for the supplier's promise to accept the lesser sum. The pharmacist is already obliged to pay the full amount and, in law, the supplier receives no benefit from accepting less.

However the rule has exceptions. The rule does not apply where the debtor does something different, such as giving something else in payment or paying at an earlier date. In addition, a promise made by a party that he or she will not insist on his or her strict contractual rights may be relied upon by the other party under a doctrine known as equitable estoppel. Therefore a gratuitous promise by one party to suspend rights under the contract will prevent that party from proceeding to enforce them until reasonable notice of the intention to resume them has been given. The rule is very specialised and is subject to many qualifications.

It is a common practice for creditors of a debtor to make an arrangement with him or her whereby each agrees to accept a stated percentage of the debt in full satisfaction. As an example, if a pharmacist owes £1,000 to supplier A, £2,000 to supplier B and £3,000 to supplier C, and cannot pay, the creditors may agree to accept a 'dividend' of 50p in the pound in settlement of each debt, which will amount to £500 to A, £1,000 to B and £1,500 to C. Such an arrangement is called a composition agreement and the courts have long held such an arrangement to be binding, so that none of the creditors can sue for the full amount.

The final situation where the courts have had to consider the issue of sufficiency of consideration is where the claimant is bound by an existing contractual duty to a third party. In some cases two parties make a contract to provide a benefit for a third party. If one of them makes a further promise to that third party, to provide the benefit they have already contracted to provide, then that further promise may be binding.

In discussing formation of a contract, it is important to examine the legal rules relating to the contents of a contract. First, it is important to remember that many things are said by the parties to a contract before the contract is actually entered into. The law classifies these pre-contractual statements as either representations or terms of the contract. The distinction between representations and terms is important because of the remedies which are available if the representation turns out to be untrue or the term is broken. The remedies for an untrue representation are more limited.

In order to decide whether a pre-contractual statement is a representation or a term, the courts have said that the principal test is the intention of the parties, and the courts will consider the importance of the issue to the parties, whether the contract was put into writing, relative skill and knowledge of parties, and the lapse of time between statement and contract.

Contract terms are classified in different ways as follows. A condition is a more important term of a contract, breach of which entitles the aggrieved party to repudiate the contract and/or claim damages. On the other hand a warranty is a less important term of the contract, breach of which entitles the aggrieved party to damages alone. It is important to remember that warranty in this sense has a different meaning from its use as a guarantee of products. A trend has emerged whereby the courts will only classify a term of the contract as being a condition or warranty after it has been broken. Depending on how serious the consequences of the breach of the term are, the term might be classified as either a condition or a warranty. Such terms are referred to as innominate terms.

Contract terms might also be classified as express or implied terms. Express terms are those identified and agreed by the parties at the time of contracting, either in writing or orally. Terms may also be implied by the court, by custom, in fact, or by law. In some types of contracts, detailed terms are implied by Act of Parliament. The best-known examples of intervention by Parliament are in the areas of consumer law and some of these are discussed in 15.5.

Exclusion clauses are those types of contractual terms which attempt to exclude or limit the liability of one party to the contract. Such clauses are usually inserted into agreements by one party with a stronger bargaining position. While it may be acceptable for parties negotiating on an equal footing to exclude or limit their liability for breach of contract, both the courts and Parliament have been reluctant to allow exclusion clauses which a stronger party has imposed upon a weaker. Control over the use of exclusion clauses has come from both the courts and from Parliament.

In attempting to nullify the effect of exclusion clauses, the courts ask two questions. The first is whether the clause is part of the contract. Where a contract is made by signing a written document, the general rule is that the signer is bound by everything which the document contains, whether he or she read it or not. If it contains an exclusions clause, the other party is taken to agree to this when he or she signs. However, if misrepresentations were made as to the effect of the document before the claimant signed, this might prevent reliance on the exclusion clause.

Where terms are contained in an unsigned document, as when an individual is given a ticket, the person seeking to rely on them must show that the other party knew or should have known that the document was a contractual one which would be expected to contain terms. The other party must also show that everything reasonable had been done to bring the terms to the notice of the other party. Any attempt to introduce an exclusion clause after the contract has been made is ineffective.

The second issue which the courts will address in relation to exclusion clauses is how they might be interpreted. Under the *contra proferentem* rule, if there is any ambiguity as to the meaning of an exclusion clause the courts will construe it in a way unfavourable to the person who put it into the contract. Under the repugnancy rule, if an exemption clause is in direct contradiction to another term of the contract, it is repugnant to it and can be struck out. Finally, exemption clauses only protect a party when that party is acting within the terms of the contract.

Parliament has also intervened in the control of exclusion clauses by passing the Unfair Contract Terms Act 1977. The title of the Act is very misleading as its provisions deal not only with terms in contract but also with purported exclusions of tortious liability by means of non-contractual notices. Some types of contract (e.g., concerning land, insurance contracts) are altogether outside its scope. In other cases it generally only applies to 'business liability'.

The general effect of the legislation is to make some exclusion clauses absolutely void, and to make other clauses valid but subject to a reasonableness test. Any clause which attempts to exclude or restrict liability for death or personal injury resulting from negligence is absolutely void. Therefore any notices to the effect that 'the company is not liable for loss of life or injury however caused' or 'no liability is accepted for death or injury to persons using the equipment' would now be unlawful.

Exclusion clauses which seek to exclude or restrict liability for loss other than personal injury are valid but are subject to the requirement of reasonableness. This provision is intended to cover attempts to exclude other forms of liability, e.g., damage to, or loss of, property in a pharmacy. The legislation also indicates that liability for breach of the obligations arising from s. 12, Sale of Goods Act 1979 (as amended) and s. 8, Supply of Goods (Implied Terms) Act 1973 cannot be excluded by reference to any contract term. The legislation also indicates that liability for breach of the obligations arising from ss. 13, 14 or 15, Sale of Goods Act 1979 (as amended) or ss. 9, 10 or 11, Supply of Goods (Implied Terms) Act 1973 cannot be excluded or restricted by reference to any contract term, where one of the parties acts as a consumer. As against a person dealing otherwise than as a consumer, such as a business, liability can be excluded or restricted but only in so far as the term satisfies the requirement of reasonableness.

Under s. 7, similar terms to those mentioned above are implied into any contracts under which either the ownership or possession of goods passes, e.g., contracts for work and materials, contracts of exchange and contracts of hire. Likewise the inability to exclude liability in respect of breach of such terms is similar to that in contracts for the sale of goods.

By s. 11(1), Unfair Contract Terms Act 1977, the question of whether an exemption clause in a contract satisfies the requirement of reasonableness is to be decided by reference to whether the clause is fair and reasonable having regard to the circumstances at the time when the contract was made. The reasonableness of an exemption clause in a contract for the sale of goods, hire-purchase, hire, work and labour and exchange is to be decided by applying the guidelines outlined in sch. 2. The question of whether an exemption notice in a tortious situation satisfies the requirement of reasonableness is to be decided by reference to all the circumstances which are in existence at the time liability arises.

The Unfair Terms in Consumer Contracts Regulations 1994 (S.I. 1994/3159) place controls over unfair standard terms in consumer contracts. They apply alongside the Unfair Contract Terms Act 1977 and the common law, but are not limited to exclusion clauses. The test of unfairness is based on good faith, and the balance between the parties. Certain clauses are listed in sch. 3 to the Regulations as potentially unfair. The regulations also impose a requirement of intelligibility in relation to all terms in consumer contracts. The regulations also impose new supervisory duties on the Director-General of Fair Trading in relation to complaints that a contract term drawn up for general use is unfair.

15.4.2 Vitiating factors

A vitiating factor is something which affects the validity of a contract even after it has been made. This means that a contract might be set aside because of some defect in it. The first vitiating factor is misrepresentation.

Before a contract is made, at the negotiating stage, statements may be made by a seller of goods to the prospective buyer, concerning e.g., the age, description, brand, quality of the goods. These statements may be classified as either traders' boasts, representations of fact which induce the buyer to make the contract with the seller, or terms which are incorporated into the contract. Whether a statement is a representation or a term of the contract is an issue of fact and so hard and fast rules cannot be laid down. Some broad tests have been developed however.

Once it has been decided whether a statement is a representation or a term, the remedy for the first comes under the heading of misrepresentation and for the second, breach of contract. There is no individual civil remedy where a trader's advertising boast turns out to be untrue.

Misrepresentation may be defined as a false statement of fact which is made by one party to another party inducing that other party to make a contract with him or her. Some aspects of that definition need to be looked at in more detail. Statement includes not only written and verbal methods of communication but also facial expressions and gestures. However silence cannot amount to misrepresentation except in five limited instances. Therefore, generally, there is no obligation upon anybody to say anything about goods or services which are being used — *caveat emptor* means that it is the duty of the buyer to find out all they can about what is being contracted for.

The exceptions where silence will amount to misrepresentation are often called contracts *uberrimae fidei*, or contracts of the utmost good faith. These are certain contracts in which disclosure of material facts is required by law. Here silence can amount to misrepresentation, in the sense that non-disclosure of some material fact by one of the parties to the contract will give rise to a remedy to the injured party. The categories of contract of the utmost good faith are extremely limited: one example is a contract of insurance.

The false statement must be one of fact. False statements of law, statements of opinion as long as that opinion is honestly held, and statements of future intention are therefore not included. In addition, the false statement of fact must have been relied on by the party complaining of misrepresentation. It must actually have played an important part in the person's decision to enter into the contract.

There are three main types of misrepresentation. The first of these is fraudulent misrepresentation which is the most serious form of misrepresentation and has been recognised by the common law for some time. Fraud is only proved if the claimant can prove that the defendant made the statement with knowledge of its falsity, or without a belief in its truth, or recklessly, not caring whether it is true or false. However it is extremely difficult to prove fraudulent misrepresentation because the defendant can show that he or she had an honest belief in the truth of the statement. Therefore until 1967, whether a misrepresentation was innocent or negligent, there was no remedy in law.

In 1967 the Misrepresentation Act was passed giving rise to two other types of misrepresentation in the law of contract. A purely innocent misrepresentation is a false statement made by a person who had reasonable grounds to believe that the statement was true, not only when it was made but also at the time the contract was entered into. A negligent misrepresentation is a false statement made by a person who had no reasonable grounds for believing the statement to be true. The onus of proving that the statement was not made negligently, but that there were reasonable grounds for believing it to be true, is on the person making the statement.

The remedy for fraudulent misrepresentation is damages for the tort of deceit and/or rescission of the contract. The remedy for negligent misrepresentation is damages and/or rescission of contract. For innocent misrepresentation, the principal remedy is rescission of the contract, but a court may award damages instead. Rescission allows innocent parties to end the contract because of the misrepresentation which misled them. It is available for most types of misrepresentation. Unlike damages it is an equitable remedy which cannot be claimed as of right but is awarded at the discretion of the court. It is subject to several limitations. The court must be satisfied that both parties to the contract can revert to the pre-contract state of affairs.

The second type of vitiating factor is mistake. Mistake in the legal sense has a very specialised and technical meaning unlike its everyday use. Before looking at what mistake *does* mean, it is necessary to look at three main situations in which the law will give no remedy on the grounds of mistake, even though one person in the agreement feels that he or she has had a rough deal. These are: a mistake as to the effect or operation of a bargain; a mistake as to the quality of goods; and a mistake as to the value of property. Therefore it is vital for a party to a contract to be satisfied as to value, quality, bargain, description etc.

There are however some situations where the law does recognise mistakes of law. The first of these is common mistake. This occurs where both parties are mistaken as to the existence of the subject matter of the contract at the time of the contract. This might occur where the subject-matter of the contract has been destroyed, or perished, or has been sold off. The second recognisable form of mistake is mutual mistake. This occurs where the parties are at cross-purposes. If the parties are not agreed about what is being bought there can be no contract; there has been no meeting of the minds between the parties.

The third type of mistake is unilateral mistake regarding identity. This is a mistake by one party to the contract regarding the true identity of the other contracting party. All of the cases on this point have concerned a 'rogue' who has stated that he is another person, gaining a financial advantage by obtaining goods on credit, by deception, selling the goods on to an innocent third party, and disappearing. 'Identity' is therefore an issue, particularly for the innocent party. In order for the innocent party to plead a defence of unilateral mistake, he or she must establish the following:

(a)   that he or she only intended to contract with the person named and not with the rogue;

(b)   that the person named is a real person with whom preferably he or she has had dealings in the past;

(c)   that the contract was preferably made by correspondence and not face to face.

If these facts are established, then the innocent party may sue the further innocent third party for the tort of conversion. This latter action involves the first party proving that they have a better claim to ownership (or title) to goods than the person who actually has them in their possession. If a better claim to title can be established, the goods must be returned.

Finally the law may give a remedy, in very limited circumstances, under the doctrine of *non est factum*. Literally translated this means 'it is not my deed'. As we have seen, normally a person who signs a document is bound by all the terms in the document, whether it has been read or not. However in certain circumstances, even though a document has been signed, it can be set aside by proving certain very narrow conditions.

So if one succeeds in one's plea of mistake on the above principles, the contract will be void. This may mean that money and property transferred cannot be received unless one can prove better ownership to them than the party who actually has the property in their possession. No property or ownership passes after a void contract.

The next form of vitiating factor is duress. Duress relates to contracts induced by violence or the threat of violence. At common law it was always thought that duress had to be directed against the person and that other types of threats could not amount to duress. The courts have now begun to recognise threats to break an existing contract as amounting to duress under the doctrine of economic duress. The law as regards economic duress is still very uncertain however.

The equitable concept of undue influence has a close relationship with duress. Equity may allow an individual relief from a contract that had been entered into because improper pressure had been placed on one of the parties. The courts will intervene where a relationship (either continuing, or in relation to a particular transaction) between the two parties has been exploited by one party in order to gain an unfair advantage.

Where there is a fiduciary relationship between the parties the law will presume that there has been undue influence and provided that the person complaining can show that the contract is disadvantageous to him or her, the onus will be on the other party to show that there was no undue influence. In some situations, for example, between solicitor and client or doctor and patient, a fiduciary relationship is deemed to exist automatically. However the courts have also been prepared to acknowledge that a fiduciary relationship can also arise outside of these particular categories.

Where there is no fiduciary relationship between the parties the burden of proof of undue influence lies on the person who is complaining of it. They will have to show that they would not have entered into the contract but for the influence which has been exerted on them. There have been a number of recent cases which have looked at the situation where a wife acts a surety for her husband's business debts by agreeing to re-mortgage the matrimonial home with a bank or other lending institution. In this situation a bank may have a duty to ensure that the wife (or other co-habitee) receives independent advice before it can enforce the contract in its favour.

The effect of undue influence on a contract is to render it voidable rather than void. It follows that the victim must take steps to avoid the contract by rescinding it.

A contract is illegal if the parties are prohibited by law from entering into it. 'Illegality' covers all contracts which are considered to be contrary to 'public policy'. Some examples of illegal and void contracts are contracts which constitute a criminal offence, contracts to commit a tort, contracts promoting sexual immorality, contracts to oust the jurisdiction of the courts, and wagering contracts. Contracts in restraint of trade are those contracts which seek to prevent employees from going to work for other employers or from setting up in rival businesses or which tie a seller of products to one particular brand (solus agreements). These agreements will initially be treated as void unless it can be shown that they are reasonable. Reasonableness will be determined by asking whether the business interest is one which should be protected, how long the restraint is going to last and how wide a geographical area is covered by the restraint. The fact that one restraint in the contract is void does not mean that the rest of the contract may not be treated as being valid. The courts may be able to cut out or sever the void restraint and leave the rest of the contract standing.

In general, an adult, sane and sober person, male or female, married or unmarried has full contractual capacity and can enter into any type of contract apart from those which the law forbids. Special rules, however, apply to partnerships, unincorporated associations or clubs, companies, those suffering from mental incapacities and those who are drunk at the time of entering into the contract.

Special rules also apply to those below a certain age. At common law persons under the age of 21 were categorised as 'infants' and had only a limited capacity to contract. Section 1, Family Law Reform Act 1969 reduced the age to 18 and permitted the use of the term 'minor' as an alternative to 'infant'. The capacity of a minor to contract is still regulated by the common law, modified only by the Minors' Contracts Act 1987 and the Minors' Contracts (NI) Order 1988.

Certain minors' contracts are deemed by the law to be valid. These include contracts for 'necessaries' which have been delivered on credit. What is a necessary will depend, however, on the characteristics of the individual minor. Beneficial contracts of employment and education are also valid provided that, taken as a whole, they are for the benefit of the minor at the time the contract was made.

If a minor acquires an interest in something permanent, either land or shares, the minor is bound until he or she repudiates the contract while under the age of 18 or within a reasonable time after attaining the age of 18. What amounts to a reasonable time depends on all the circumstances of the case. Until it is repudiated the contract is valid in every respect and the minor is liable under it. The most obvious example is a contract made by a minor for a lease.

All other contracts which do not come within the above two definitions are not binding on the minor but are binding on the adult. The contract becomes binding on the minor only if, after attaining majority, the contract is ratified.

The law is capable of producing injustice where a minor has obtained property under a contract which is not enforceable against him or her. The minor may get the property for nothing and the adult party, who may be in no way at fault, is the loser. This may be so even where the minor has lied about his or her age. The minors' contracts legislation now affords a limited measure of redress to the adult party. By s. 3 of the 1987 Act, where a contract, made after the commencement of the Act, is unenforceable against a defendant because he or she was a minor when it was made, the court may, if it is just and equitable to do so, require the minor to transfer to the adult any property acquired by the minor under the contract, or any property representing it. The adult party might also still rely on the equitable doctrine which required a fraudulent minor to return property obtained by deception and which was still identifiable in the minor's possession.

15.4.3 Termination of a contract
Contracts do not last for ever and may come to an end in a variety of ways. The first, and most common, method of termination is by performance. A contract comes to an end by performance when both parties have fulfilled all their obligations under the contract in every respect. However, if one party (or both) has omitted to perform obligations, the contract will be discharged not by performance but by breach. The common law is very harsh in this respect and holds that very minor departures from the contract amount to breach of contract and not performance. Because this harsh common law rule could work injustice in some cases, the courts have developed a number of exceptions.

Secondly, as a contract is set up by agreement it can be ended by mutual agreement, subject to a number of rules. If the contract was set up by a deed the parties' agreement to terminate must also be done by deed, usually a deed of discharge. Executory contracts, i.e., where neither side has performed any obligations under the contract as yet, may be terminated by a mutual verbal agreement to that effect. Executed contracts, i.e., where at least one party has performed obligations under the contract, may not be terminated by agreement alone. Some fresh consideration for that discharge is also needed.

Where, after a contract has been made, something happens which is outside the fault and/or control of either party to the contract and which makes further performance of the contract impossible, illegal or completely pointless, the contract is said to be frustrated and both parties are discharged from it. Neither party has been responsible for the discharge of their contract.

Self-induced frustration is really a form of breach of contract in that one party has by his or her own actions made the contract impossible to perform. It is wise to insert a term into business contracts spelling out what happens in the event of a normally 'frustrating' event. Such clauses usually known as force majeure may be open to challenge both in the courts and under the Unfair Contracts Act 1977.

If a contract is frustrated the effects are governed either by the terms of the contract, the common law, or the Law Reform (Frustrated Contracts) Act 1943. At common law, frustration always discharges the contract. The parties may not salvage anything even if they wish to do so, although they may set up a new contract. Unless there is a total failure of consideration losses lie where they fall. Property can be claimed back if there is a total failure of consideration in that parties did not get what they bargained for at all. Because of the harshness of this rule the Law Reform (Frustrated Contracts) Act 1943 was passed.

The 1943 Act does not apply to certain contracts (including insurance contracts), and the common law rules continue to apply to such agreements. The aim of the 1943 Act is to share out losses in a just and equitable way after frustration of the contract, rather than one party having to bear all or most of the loss at common law. There are two main rules. Under s. 1(2), all sums of money paid or payable to any party before the frustrating event must, in the case of sums paid, be recoverable and in the case of sums payable, cease to be so payable. However, if the party owed the money has incurred expenses, the court may allow him or her to keep any payment *or* claim the cost of expenses. Under s. 1(3), if there is no clause for advance payment (i.e., money is not due until goods are supplied or work is done) but one party has received a valuable benefit, excluding money, before the contract was frustrated, the court may award the other party such compensation as they think fit.

If the performance is not complete, then subject to the exceptions outlined above and to the doctrine of frustration, there will be breach of contract. One then has to decide how serious the breach is because this affects one's remedies.

As already stated in 15.4.1, the more important terms of the contract are called conditions. Breach of a condition usually gives the injured party the choice of repudiating or affirming the contract. Repudiating the contract means ending the contract, so that neither party is bound, and claiming damages. Affirming the contract means choosing to let the contract stand despite the breach of condition. Damages may be claimed in certain circumstances but the right to repudiate will be lost after a party has affirmed the contract despite the breach.

The less important terms which are incidental to the main purpose of the contract are called warranties. Breach of a warranty usually gives the injured party the right to sue for damages for actual loss. It does not entitle the injured party to regard himself or herself as freed from the contract.

This discussion of conditions and warranties has revealed two remedies which are available in the event of breach of contract, namely damages and repudiation. These are often referred to as common law remedies which are available as of right to a claimant who makes out a good case. Other remedies for breach are referred to as equitable remedies which are given out at the discretion of the court and which include specific performance and injunction.

Specific performance is an order of the court compelling a party in default to perform the contract according to its terms. The remedy is a discretionary one and is subject to a number of limitations. It will not be awarded: where damages would be an adequate remedy; where the claimant's conduct has been unfair; where the claimant has delayed unduly in bringing the legal action; where it would cause hardship to the defendant; to enforce a contract for personal services; where the court would be involved in constant supervision of the contractual acts.

An injunction is an order restraining a party from acting in a particular way. It must not, however, become an indirect method of enforcing a contract for which specific performance would not be available.

Damages may be classified as liquidated or unliquidated. Sometimes the parties will agree in advance what damages are to be paid in the event of a breach of contract. Such a clause is called a liquidated damages clause. The court will usually be prepared to adhere to the parties stated wishes unless it finds that the clause does not adequately reflect a true apportionment of the damages and instead amounts to a penalty. The types of clauses which are usually deemed to be penalties include those where the agreed damages are large in comparison with the loss suffered, where the agreed damages provide for a much greater sum than the contract price, and where the contract stipulates that the same sum will be paid in the event of breaches of contract of unequal seriousness.

Unliquidated damages are those damages which are assessed by the courts, either where there is no liquidated damages clause or where such a clause has been struck down by the courts as amounting to a penalty. Unliquidated damages can be sub-classified further. First, ordinary damages are those which are assessed by the court in respect of loss arising naturally from a breach of contract. In deciding whether to award ordinary damages, the court will ask whether reasonable persons would expect the particular type of loss to arise from the breach. If this is so then damages will be allowed. If not, the loss will be too remote.

Secondly, special damages may be awarded where both parties know that the particular loss was likely to result from a breach of contract. The knowledge of the parties themselves is more important here than the knowledge of reasonable persons. Special damages will not be recoverable if the party in breach did not know that the particular loss was likely to result and the damages will be too remote a consequence of the breach. Recovery is limited to those losses which were within the reasonable contemplation of the parties as not unlikely to result from the breach.

Exemplary damages are those which are designed to punish the defendant and act as a deterrent for others in future. They are rarely given out. Nominal damages are awarded to a claimant who has technically established that there has been a breach of contract by the defendant but where the claimant has suffered very little loss as a result.

15.5   THE SALE OF GOODS

We have already seen that contract provides the mechanism for the effective conduct of economic exchange in business. The most common and significant form of business contract is that for the sale of goods. Every day millions of such contracts are negotiated and effected in tens of thousands of businesses in the United Kingdom. The prosaic nature of the sale of goods contract and the potential for exploitation by those big businesses with a monopoly over the provision of goods has meant that the law has paid close attention to this important issue. Intervention has taken the form of specific legislation with the primary purpose of protecting the consumer in a sale of goods contract. The fact that such legislation exists, and has been on the statute books since 1893, reflects both the significance of such contracts and the desire of the legislators to prevent manipulation.

The community pharmacy is a business where the contract for the sale of goods has a particular significance. For example, we have already seen, in chapter eight, that a wide range of drug products classified as general sale list and pharmacy medicines are distributed through pharmacies. The legal mechanism for the dissemination of such products is the contract for the sale of goods. Some of the implications of this relationship were explored in chapter thirteen.

However the significance of the contract for the sale of goods is not restricted to the distribution of drug products. The pharmacy is the commercial locus for the sale of a wide variety of other products from films for cameras through to perfumes, aftershave and hair dryers. The legal device employed for the distribution of such products is the contract for the sale of goods. The pharmacist, as both a health care professional and a business person, has to understand the significance of the legal rules which surround the sale of goods and the important consequences of failure to adhere to such regulation.

15.5.1   The sale of goods legislation
Section 1, Sale of Goods Act (SGA) 1979, as amended, defines a contract for the sale of goods as 'a contract whereby the seller transfers or agrees to transfer

the property in goods to the buyer for a money consideration called the price'. Such a definition restricts the application of the legislation to cash contracts. We shall see below that equivalent safeguards are provided for non-cash arrangements such as the provision of credit.

The primary purpose of the sale of goods legislation is to safeguard the consumer, perceived as the party to the legal arrangement to be in the weaker bargaining position. The method by which such protection is achieved is through the implication of terms into the sale of goods contract. The SGA 1979, as amended, sets out various implied obligations, some of which the parties are free to vary, some not. The legislation takes the unusual step of classifying the implied terms as either conditions or warranties, reinforcing the significance of the protection offered.

The main implied conditions are: that the seller has the right to sell, under s. 12(1)(a); that goods sold by description correspond with the description, under s. 13; that goods sold in the course of the business are to be reasonably fit for their purpose, under s. 14(3); that goods sold in the course of the business are to be of satisfactory quality, under s. 14(2); that where goods are sold by reference to sample the bulk of goods will correspond with sample in quality, under s. 15(2)(a); that the buyer will have reasonable opportunity of comparing bulk with sample, under s. 15(2)(b); and that the goods will be free of any defect, making their quality unsatisfactory, which would not be apparent on reasonable examination of the sample, under s. 15(2)(c). The main implied warranties are: that the buyer is to have quiet possession of the goods; and that the goods are free from undisclosed third party claims (both under s. 12(1)(b)).

You will see that the most important of these implied terms are conditions. This will mean that breach of the contract by the seller will enable the buyer to refuse further performance of the contract and to recover any money or other property which they have paid for the goods.

You will also note that the terms relating to the right to sell the goods, that the goods must correspond with their description and that the goods must correspond with their sample, apply to all sales of new and secondhand goods. The remaining implied terms, relating to satisfactory quality and fitness for purpose, will only apply where the seller sells in the course of a business. These terms will not apply, therefore, in relation to private sales of new or secondhand goods between private individuals.

15.5.2 What do the implied terms mean?

By s. 12(1) of the SGA 1979, if the seller has no right to sell the goods (because he or she had stolen them or only held them on hire-purchase, for example), then he or she will be liable to the buyer for breach of condition. The buyer can recover the full price which he or she paid, even if he or she has had the use of the goods for some time.

Section 12(2) also implies two warranties into contracts of sale, namely that the goods are free from any encumbrance (such as a mortgage) not disclosed or made known to the buyer before the contract is made, and that the buyer will enjoy quiet possession of the goods.

Section 13(1) provides that 'where there is a contract for the sale of goods by description there is an implied condition that the goods shall correspond with the description'. Goods ordered through a catalogue, or a new car ordered from the manufacturers through a dealer, will always be sold by description, because this is the only way to identify what is required. Even goods seen and specifically chosen by the customer can be sold by description, and a customer is entitled to expect, for example, that goods chosen from the shelf in a pharmacy will correspond to the description on the container or packet. The word 'description' covers a wide variety of matters. Statements as to quantity, weight, ingredients and even packing have been held to be part of the description. Compliance with the description must be complete and exact.

Unlike the obligations imposed by ss. 12, 13 and 15, which apply to all sales of goods, s. 14 applies where the seller sells in the course of a business. Usually the phrase 'in the course of a business' presents no difficulty, e.g., as where an individual buys from a shop or pharmacy.

As a general rule, a seller owes no obligations as regards the quality or suitability of goods but s. 14 provides a number of important exceptions. Section 14(2) (as inserted by s. 1, Sale and Supply of Goods Act 1994) provides that 'where the seller sells goods in the course of a business, there is an implied term that the goods supplied under the contract are of satisfactory quality'.

By s. 14(2)(A), goods are of 'satisfactory' quality if they meet the standard that a reasonable person would regard as satisfactory, taking account of any description of the goods, the price (if relevant) and all the other relevant circumstances. By s. 14(2)(B), quality of goods includes their state or condition and fitness for purpose, appearance and finish, freedom from minor defects, safety and durability.

This obligation regarding satisfactory quality does not apply to any matter making the quality of the goods unsatisfactory which is (a) specifically drawn to the buyer's attention before the contract is made, or (b) where the buyer examines the goods before the contract is made, which that examination ought to reveal. The second of these obligations is often misconstrued. There is no *obligation* on the buyer to examine the goods, and if the buyer chooses not to do so he or she is entitled to the full protection of s. 14(2).

Section 14(3) provides that:

where the seller sells goods in the course of a business and the buyer, expressly or by implication, makes known . . . to the seller . . . any particular purpose for which the goods are being bought, there is an implied condition that the goods supplied are reasonably fit for that purpose, whether or not that is a purpose for which such goods are commonly supplied, except where the circumstances show that the buyer does not rely, or that it is unreasonable for him to rely, on the skill or judgment of the seller . . .

This subsection only applies, therefore, if the buyer has expressly or impliedly made known to the seller the purpose for which the goods are required. Where the goods only have one or two manifest uses, it might readily be assumed that the buyer has impliedly indicated that they are wanted for their usual purpose. Thus, if someone buys analgesics, it will be taken to indicate that they are wanted to be reasonably fit for killing pain.

The goods supplied need only to be reasonably fit, however, and then only for the purposes made known. The subsection contains one limited exception to this implied condition, that is, where the circumstances show that the buyer does not rely, or that it is unreasonable for the buyer to rely, on the seller's skill or judgment. This may apply, for example, where the buyer is an expert in such goods, and gives detailed specifications as to what is required.

By s. 15, if goods are sold by sample, there are implied conditions (a) that bulk will correspond with the sample in quality, (b) that the buyer will have a reasonable opportunity of comparing the bulk with the sample, and (c) that the goods will be free from any defect, making their quality unsatisfactory, which would not be apparent on reasonable examination of the sample.

A sale will be by sample if there is an express or implied term to this effect.

Under the Unfair Contract Terms Act 1977 the seller of goods cannot exclude or limit liability for breach of the implied terms regarding title in any form of sale of goods contract. In a consumer contract the seller may also not limit or exclude his or her liability for breach of the implied terms concerning description, quality or fitness for purpose. Liability for breach of these terms may be excluded or limited in business contracts where it is reasonable to do so.

15.5.3 Remedies for breach of the sale of goods contract: the buyer's remedies

Where a seller breaks one of the express or implied obligations under the contract, the buyer may have any one of a number of remedies. Where the term broken by the seller is a condition, the buyer has rights to reject the goods and treat the contract as repudiated. We have already noted that most of the terms implied by ss. 12 to 15 are conditions.

However, the time within which the goods can be rejected may be very short. Section 11(4) provides that, in the vast majority of sale of goods contracts, the rights to reject the goods and treat the contract as repudiated are lost as soon as the buyer has accepted the goods, or part of them. It is important to note that this does not mean that the buyer is without a remedy. The right to reject the goods is lost but the right to sue for damages is not. Therefore, it is important to identify whether or not the buyer has accepted the goods, because this will determine whether the buyer can reject for breach of condition or simply sue for damages.

By s. 34 the buyer is not to be deemed to have accepted the goods until he or she has had a reasonable opportunity of examining them for the purpose of ascertaining whether they are in conformity with the contract and, in relation to sale by sample, of comparing the bulk with the sample.

Section 35 sets out certain circumstances in which the buyer will be deemed to have accepted. Primarily this will be when he or she intimates to the seller that he or she has accepted them, or when the goods have been delivered to him or her and he or she does any act in relation to them which is inconsistent with the ownership of the seller or when, after the lapse of a reasonable time, he or she retains the goods without intimating to the seller that he or she has rejected them.

These rules are based on the ordinary equitable ones whereby a party who 'affirms' the contract thereby loses his or her right to rescind it. The first and third rules are fairly simple: the remedies are lost if the buyer expressly accepts the goods, or if the goods are retained for more than a reasonable time, this being a question of fact. The right to reject perishable goods, for example, may be lost within hours. The second rule arises when the buyer treats the goods as belonging to him or her, for example by consuming or re-selling them.

The buyer must have a reasonable time to examine the goods after delivery and is not deemed to have accepted the goods merely because he or she has asked for, or agreed to their repair under an arrangement with the seller. This addition to the section, which was made by the Sale and Supply of Goods Act 1994, means that the buyer who receives defective goods will no longer run the risk of losing the right of rejection for breach of condition simply because the seller is allowed to make some attempt to put the defect right.

Finally, it should be repeated that all of these rules affect only the buyer's rights to reject the goods and end the contract. Where the buyer has lost these rights, or where the breach is a breach of warranty, he or she can still sue the seller for damages.

Damages can always be claimed as of right, although where no real loss has occurred the amount may be nominal. The measure of damages and the question of remoteness are the same as in contract generally; ss. 51 and 53, SGA 1979, provide rules very similar to those put forward in ordinary contract law, the basic rule being that 'the measure of damages is the estimated loss directly and naturally resulting, in the ordinary course of events, from the seller's breach of contract'. Section 52 preserves the remedy of specific performance in contracts for the sale of goods but, as noted elsewhere, this will only be awarded where the article sold is rare.

Other sections of the SGA 1979 deal with rejection where too much or too little is tendered, or partly defective goods are tendered; with instalment contracts; and with non-delivery.

15.5.4 Remedies for breach of the sale of goods contract: seller's remedies

The seller has two possible remedies against a buyer of goods, namely an action for the price, and damages for non-acceptance. Under s. 49, SGA 1979, where property has passed to the buyer and he or she wrongfully refuses or neglects to pay, the seller may bring an action for the price. Where the buyer wrongfully neglects or refuses to accept delivery of the goods and to pay for them, the seller may bring an action for damages for non-acceptance, under s. 50.

An unpaid seller may exercise three possible remedies against the goods: lien, stoppage *in transitu* and resale. Section 41, SGA 1979 allows an unpaid seller to exercise a lien over the goods. This is a right for the seller to retain goods until the buyer pays the price. There are a number of conditions before lien can be exercised and the right to exercise it may be lost in various ways, under s. 43.

Stoppage *in transitu* is covered by s. 44 and is available where the seller is unpaid, and the buyer is insolvent, and the goods are in transit. If these three conditions are satisfied the seller may resume possession of the goods until the buyer pays the price.

Resale is provided for under s. 48. As the goods are the buyer's goods the seller generally has no right to sell them to somebody else but s. 48 does allow the seller to resell where the goods are perishable, and where the unpaid seller gives notice to the buyer of his or her intention to resell and the buyer does not then pay within a reasonable time. The unpaid seller may sell the goods and still claim damages from the buyer for breach of contract.

15.5.5   Passing of ownership in a sale of goods contract

The legislative definition of a sale of goods contract provides that the seller must transfer the property in the goods or agree to transfer it to the buyer. Therefore the buyer becomes the owner of the goods. However, property or ownership may not be transferred immediately but when the parties intend it to pass. This becomes important in relation to the risk of loss or damage to the goods. In ss. 17 and 18, there are particular rules to ascertain the intention of the parties.

Under s. 17, property in specific or ascertained goods passes to the buyer when the parties intend it to. Their intention can be discovered from the express terms of the contract or by implied terms. 'Specific or ascertained goods' means goods identified and agreed upon at the time a contract is made. As a corollary, 'unascertained goods' means those goods not identified at the time of the contract. Further legislative definitions include those for 'future goods' which are goods to be manufactured or acquired by the seller after making the contract and 'deliverable state'. Goods are in a deliverable state if the buyer is bound to take delivery of them because, for example, they comply with contract description in every respect.

The rules contained in s. 18 will come into play if there is no clear intention from the terms of the contract as to the time at which the property in the goods is to pass to the buyer. Section 18 provides a number of rules as follows:

> Where there is an unconditional contract for the sale of specific goods, in a deliverable state, the property in the goods passes to the buyer when the contract is made, and it is immaterial whether the time of payment or the time of delivery, or both, be postponed.

Where there is a contract for the sale of specific goods and the seller is bound to do something to the goods, for the purpose of putting them into a deliverable state, the property does not pass until such thing is done, and the buyer has notice that it has been done.

Where there is a contract for the sale of specific goods in a deliverable state but the seller is bound to weigh, measure, test, or do some other act with reference to the goods for the purpose of ascertaining the price, the property does not pass until such act or thing be done, and the buyer has notice that it has been done.

When goods are delivered to the buyer on approval or 'on sale or return' or other similar terms the property therein passes to the buyer, when he or she signifies approval or acceptance to the seller or does any other act adopting the transaction, or if he or she does not signify approval or acceptance to the seller but retains the goods without giving notice of rejection then, if a time has been fixed for the return of the goods, on the expiration of such time and, if no time has been fixed, on the expiration of a reasonable time. What is a reasonable time is a question of fact.

Where there is a contract for the sale of unascertained or future goods by description and goods of that description and in a deliverable state are unconditionally appropriated to the contracts, either by the seller with the assent of the buyer, or by the buyer with the assent of the seller, the property in the goods thereupon passes to the buyer. Such assent may be express or implied, and may be given either before or after the appropriation is made.

Where, in pursuance of the contract, the seller delivers the goods to the buyer or to a carrier or other bailee or custodian for the purpose of transmission to the buyer, and does not reserve the right of disposal, he or she is deemed to have unconditionally appropriated the goods to the contract. The goods must be 'ascertained' before this rule can operated.

These rules may be varied by a contrary intention in the contract, express or implied, or by a trade custom or by a course of previous dealing. Some businesses have tried to oust the operation of these rules by express terms in the contract with varying rates of success.

Those who are not the owners of goods cannot pass title to them to somebody else. This rule is referred to by the Latin maxim, *nemo dat quod non habet* (no one gives who possesses not) and is preserved by s. 21, SGA 1979. There are several situations where a person who does not own the goods may nevertheless pass ownership to somebody else. These are referred to as the exceptions to the *nemo dat* rule and are too detailed to be examined here.

15.6   THE PROVISION OF GOODS ON CREDIT

In 15.5 we examined the legal rules which circumvent the provision of goods by direct cash sale. In so doing we emphasised the standard nature of the sale of goods contract and the desire of the legislators to protect the consumer from over-exploitation by business. The sale of goods for cash remains the most common form of business transaction, equally applicable to the pharmacy business as to any other.

Increasingly, though, both consumer and business seek to rely on the use of credit as a means of financing the provision of goods. This is particularly the case where the goods are expensive and the consumer wishes to spread the payments for them over a period of time. Equally there has been a considerable increase in the use of other types of credit facilities, from in-store charge cards through to charge cards, which are used by both the consumer and commerce as a means of transacting business.

As might be imagined, the increasing use of credit facilities, and the potential for further exploitation of the consumer has also attracted the attention of the legislators. There are significant and important rules relating to the provision of goods on credit. The principal legislation regulating the control of credit is the Consumer Credit Act 1974. It is important that the pharmacist is aware of the parameters and implications of these legislative provisions, both in relation to transactions with consumers, and in relation to arrangements with other businesses such as suppliers or wholesalers.

15.6.1   Definitions

The main provisions of the Consumer Credit Act 1974 apply to regulated agreements which may be either a consumer credit agreement or a consumer hire agreement. Some other types of credit agreement, including mortgage lending, are completely exempt from the provisions of the 1974 Act. A consumer credit agreement is a credit agreement by which the creditor provides the debtor with credit not exceeding £25,000. A consumer hire agreement relates to the hiring of goods to an individual for a period of more than three months, for not more than £25,000 and which is not a hire-purchase agreement.

Section 10 of the 1974 Act provides that credit may be either running account credit which is credit up to an agreed limit or fixed sum credit which is credit of a definite amount. An example of running account credit would be a bank overdraft. An example of fixed sum credit would be a bank loan.

Section 11 classifies credit agreements according to the purpose for which the credit is given. Restricted-use credit may be used for a stipulated purpose. Unrestricted-use credit is as it is described and may be used for any purpose. An example of restricted-use credit would be a hire-purchase agreement. An example of unrestricted-use credit would be an overdraft facility.

Sections 12 and 13 of the 1974 Act provide a further classification based on the relationship between the creditor, the debtor and the supplier. A debtor-creditor-supplier agreement is where credit is provided to finance a transaction between a debtor and a supplier. The credit may be supplied by an outside creditor or by the supplier. In each case the agreement is still called a debtor-creditor-supplier agreement. A debtor-creditor agreement is any agreement to supply credit which is not a debtor-creditor-supplier agreement. An example of a debtor-creditor-supplier agreement would be a hire-purchase agreement. An example of a debtor-creditor agreement would be a bank loan.

A conditional sale is an agreement for the sale of goods whereby the price is payable by instalments and where ownership remains with the seller until all of the instalments are paid (and any other conditions are satisfied). A credit sale is an agreement for the sale of goods where the purchase price is payable by five or more instalments and which is not a conditional sale agreement. Ownership in the goods passes at once.

You will see from the above that any one type of agreement will fall into a number of the above definitions. For example, a hire-purchase agreement is a fixed-sum, restricted-use, debtor-creditor-supplier agreement!

15.6.2 Making the credit agreement

Any person or body wishing to carry on consumer credit business must first obtain a licence from the Director-General of Fair Trading, who must be satisfied that the applicant is a fit person to engage in such activities. Regulations state the ways in which licensees must conduct their business, in particular as to books and records to be kept and information to be furnished to those with whom they deal. There are detailed provisions regarding research, variation, suspension and revocation of licences and anyone who carries on consumer lending without a licence commits a criminal offence. Loans by unlicensed lenders are enforceable against the borrower only at the discretion of the Director-General of Fair Trading.

Advertising of credit, for the purposes of a business carried out by the advertiser, is strictly controlled under the 1974 Act. Regulations, the Consumer Credit (Advertisement) Regulations 1989 (S.I. 1989/1125), exist as to the form and content of such advertisements, to ensure that, having regard to its subject-matter and amount of detail included in it, each advertisement conveys a fair and reasonably comprehensive picture of the nature of the credit offered, and the true cost. If any advertisement contains false or misleading information, or fails to comply with the regulations, the advertiser commits a criminal offence. It is also an offence to advertise goods or services or credit where the advertiser does not also hold himself or herself as willing to sell for cash.

Canvassing people, other than on business premises, to persuade them to borrow money is also an offence, as is giving or sending an unsolicited credit-token. Quotations by those offering credit, as to the terms upon which they will do business, are also subject to controls as to form and content.

There are formal legislative requirements relating to the form and content of credit agreements. Before the agreement is made the lender must give specified information to the borrower in the prescribed manner. This requires disclosure, in writing, of the cash price and credit charge. The agreement itself must comply with the following requirements.

It must be in writing, signed by the debtor personally and by or on behalf of the creditor. Signature of a form in blank, leaving it to a supplier or agent to fill in the details, is not enough. The document must be in the prescribed form, and contain the prescribed information, the debtor's rights and duties, the protection and remedies available under the 1974 Act, and the amount and rate of the total charge for credit. Notice of the rights of cancellation must be given in all cancellable agreements.

Copies of the agreement must be given to the debtor. The debtor must always receive, immediately, a copy of the form which has been signed. If the form then has to be sent away for completion by the creditor, the debtor must also be given a copy of the completed agreement within seven days of its completion, so that it can be verified that no alterations have been made since its signature. In the case of a cancellable agreement, this second copy must be sent by post and contain details of the debtor's rights to cancel.

Non-compliance with these formalities renders the agreement improperly executed and therefore unenforceable against the debtor without an order of the court. The court must refuse to enforce the agreement, where it was not in writing at all, where the debtor has not been given a copy up to the time of commencement of proceedings, and where a cancellable agreement does not contain the required notice.

The prospective debtor can withdraw from the proposed agreement at any time before it is made, that is, normally at any time before signature by the creditor. Withdrawal can be by notice, written or oral, to the creditor, or any agent or supplier who was involved in negotiations leading up to the agreement.

A 'cancellable' agreement is one which the debtor signs other than on the premises of the creditor or any dealer with whom the customer originally negotiated. The right to cancel arises after the agreement is made. The debtor can serve notice of cancellation at any time up to the end of the fifth day following the day when the second copy of the agreement was received. Notice must be in writing, and it can be served on the creditor, any dealer or other person involved in any negotiations, or any person specified in the statutory notice of the right to cancel. The effect of cancellation is to end the agreement. The debtor, therefore, has a limited 'cooling-off' period in which to reconsider any hasty agreement and a right to escape from it after second thoughts. Goods or a loan obtained under the agreement must be returned.

15.6.3 Terms of the agreement

As with the legislation concerning contracts for the sale of goods, the Consumer Credit Act 1974 contains specific provisions relating to the terms of the credit agreement. This protection takes two main forms. First, the 1974 Act implies certain terms into consumer credit agreements, concerning description, quality, fitness for purpose etc., which parallel those for sale of goods contracts, discussed in section 15.5.1. Secondly, the 1974 Act makes specific provision for terms which might be regarded as extortionate.

The implied terms incorporated into consumer credit agreement under the Consumer Credit Act 1974 (sch. 4), as amended, include implied conditions that the creditor has the right to sell the goods, that goods supplied by description will compare with that description, that goods must be of satisfactory quality, that goods must be reasonably fit for the purpose, and that where goods are supplied by reference to sample the bulk of goods will correspond with the sample in quality, the debtor will have reasonable opportunity of comparing the bulk with the sample, and that the goods will be free of any defect, rendering their quality unsatisfactory, which would not be apparent on reasonable examination of the sample. The 1974 Act also implied two minor warranties relating to third party rights in relation to the goods.

Again, it is important to note that these implied terms are conditions. As with sale of goods contracts, breach of these conditions will allow the debtor to repudiate the agreement and claim damages. The consumer credit legislation does not, however, contain parallel provisions to those contained in the sale of goods legislation, as discussed in section 15.5.3, which limit the right to repudiation following acceptance of the goods. This will mean that the right to end a consumer credit agreement, for breach of one of the implied conditions, will potentially be stronger under a consumer credit agreement than a sale of goods arrangement.

The provisions as to extortionate bargains apply to all credit agreements where the borrower is an individual, partnership or unincorporated association, and irrespective of the amount borrowed. By s. 137, Consumer Credit Act 1974, if the court finds a credit bargain extortionate it may re-open the agreement so as to do justice between the parties. This can be done on application by the debtor to the court. A bargain is 'extortionate' if it requires the debtor to make payment which is grossly extortionate or otherwise grossly contravenes ordinary principles of fair trading. Regard must be had to matters such as interest rates, the debtor's age, experience, business capacity and health, the degree to which he or she was under financial pressure, the creditor's relationship to the debtor, the degree of risk accepted by the creditor and the cash price quoted for the goods or service.

15.6.4 Termination of the agreement

By s. 94 of the 1974 Act, the debtor under a regulated consumer credit agreement is entitled at any time to pay off the balance of what is owed, on giving notice to the creditor of an intention to do so. At any time, the creditor must, on request in writing from the debtor, give the latter a statement of the amount currently required to discharge the debt, together with particulars showing how the amount is worked out. If the creditor fails to comply with such a request within a prescribed period the agreement may not continue to be enforced during the default, and if the default continues for one month a criminal offence is committed.

Notice by the creditor to the debtor is necessary before the creditor can terminate a regulated agreement, or enforce rights either under the agreement, or on breach. By ss. 87–9, where the debtor has broken the agreement, for example, by defaulting in payment, the creditor must first serve a written notice of default in the proscribed form. The notice must specify the nature of the alleged breach, give at least seven days in which to remedy the breach or pay compensation, and explain the consequences of failure to comply. Until the notice expires, the creditor cannot take any steps to enforce any rights. In particular, the creditor cannot terminate the agreement, demand earlier payment, recover possession of any goods or land, or treat any of the debtor's rights as terminated, restricted or deferred.

If the debtor complies with the notice, this is the end of the matter, and the breach is to be treated as if it had never occurred. Otherwise, the creditor may now take action subject to certain controls. An enforcement order may be made by the court on the application of the creditor if the debtor defaults and fails to comply with the notice served on him or her. Sections 129 and 130, however, give the court wide powers to allow the debtor an extension of time where it appears just to do so. This can be done either in the action by the creditor, or on a special application by the debtor after notice has been served.

In addition to his or her right to pay off the debt early under s. 84 the hirer under a hire-purchase agreement has a right under s. 99 to terminate the agreement at any time, on giving notice to the creditor or any other person entitled or authorised to receive payments under the agreement. This right applies equally to conditional sale agreements, but not to credit sale.

On termination, the hirer or buyer must return the goods, and pay off any arrears. To guard against possible loss under the agreement, due to depreciation in the value of the goods by the time of termination, creditors often include 'minimum payment' clauses into hire-purchase agreements, requiring the hirer, on termination or breach, to bring the total payments under the agreement up to a percentage of the hire-purchase price. Section 100, Consumer Credit Act 1974 contains statutory limits on minimum payment clauses. Unless the agreement provides for a minimum payment, none will be due. If the agreement does provide for such a payment on termination or breach, it must not exceed the amount (if any) by which one half of the total price exceeds the aggregate of the sums paid and due immediately before termination. If the court is satisfied that the actual loss suffered by the creditor is less than the above amount, the court may order payment of the actual loss only. On the other hand, if the debtor has contravened an obligation to take reasonable care of the goods, the debtor's payments must be increased by the sum necessary to compensate the creditor.

It used to be held, at common law, that where the hirer under a hire-purchase agreement was late in paying any instalment, the creditor could immediately end the agreement for breach of condition, and take back the goods. Hire-purchase agreements used to give the creditor a right of access to the debtor's premises for the purpose of such taking back. The debtor, in turn, could not recover what had been paid. The position concerning default and taking back is now rigorously controlled by the 1974 Act.

By s. 92, the creditor is not entitled to enter any premises to take goods subject to a regulated hire-purchase agreement without first seeking an order of the court. Entry in breach of this provision is actionable as a breach of statutory duty. By ss. 90 and 91, when at least one-third of the hire-purchase price has been paid, then unless the debtor terminates the agreement, the goods become 'protected goods', and must not be taken back without an order of the court. On application of the creditor for the return of the goods, the court may give the debtor additional time to pay. Even if the court does order return of the goods, the debtor still has the right, up to the moment when the goods reach the creditor, to pay off the whole balance of the hire-purchase price. The goods then become the debtor's property.

If the creditor does take back protected goods without a court order, the agreement immediately terminates, the debtor is released from all liabilities, and can recover from the creditor all that has previously been paid under the agreement.

15.7   CRIMINAL LIABILITY IN THE CONDUCT OF BUSINESS

There are a number of pieces of legislation which create specific criminal offences which have a direct bearing on the conduct of business. The first of these is the Trade Descriptions Act 1968.

Section 1(1) of the 1968 Act provides that any person who, in the course of a trade or business, applies a false trade description to any goods, or supplies or offers to supply any goods to which a false trade description is applied, is guilty of an offence. The offences created by s. 1 are offences of strict liability, meaning that no guilty intent need be proved by the prosecution. A number of defences, to be discussed below, may be raised by the defendant, however.

Under s. 2, trade description includes any indication as to quantity, size, method of manufacture, composition, fitness for purpose, further physical characteristics, testing by any person and the results of such testing, approval by any person or conformity with a type, place and date of manufacture, the name of the manufacturer, or the history of the goods. By virtue of s. 3, a trade description is false if it is false or misleading to a material degree. For the purpose of the 1968 Act, a trade description may be made either in writing or orally or may be contained in an advertisement.

Section 14 makes it is an offence for a person in the course of trade or business to make a false statement either knowingly or recklessly about any services, accommodation or facilities. Unlike the offence relating to the making of false statements, this offence is not one of strict liability and the prosecution will have to adduce evidence of knowledge of the falsity or that the statement was made recklessly. Recklessness means making a statement regardless of whether it is true or false and whether or not the person making it had reasons for believing that it might be false.

A person accused of an offence under the 1968 Act may plead any of a number of defences provided by the Act. Under s. 24 it may be pleaded that the offence was due to a mistake, or reliance on information supplied, or the act or default of someone else, or an accident, or some other cause beyond the control of the defendant and that he or she took all reasonable precautions and exercised all due diligence to avoid the commission of such an offence by himself or herself or any person under his or her control.

Section 24 also provides that if a person is charged with an offence under the 1968 Act of supplying or offering to supply goods to which a false trade description is applied, he or she may plead, as a defence, that he or she did not know, and could not with reasonable diligence have ascertained, that the goods did not conform to the description or that the description had been applied to the goods.

Finally, under s. 25 of the 1968 Act a person who is charged with an offence committed by the publication of an advertisement for publication in the ordinary course of business and who did not know and had no reason to suspect that its publication would amount to an offence, has the defense of innocent publication of an advertisement.

Enforcement of the legislative provisions relating to the misdescription of goods and services lies with trading standards officers in each local authority area. The officers have powers to make test purchases and to enter premises and inspect and seize goods and documents. A person convicted under the Act is liable on summary conviction to a fine not exceeding £5,000, and on conviction on indictment to a fine or imprisonment for a term not exceeding two years, or both.

The Trade Descriptions Act 1968, and other specific legislative provisions, used to contain controls over false and misleading price indications. These are now provided for in Part III of the Consumer Protection Act 1987. Under s. 20(1) of the 1987 Act, a person is guilty of an offence if, in the course of any business, he or she gives (by any means whatever) to any consumers an indication which is misleading as to the price at which any goods or services are available (whether generally or from any particular person). Liability extends into statements which become misleading after they were initially made, because of a change of circumstances, unless the person concerned has taken reasonable steps to prevent consumers from relying on the statement.

A 'consumer' is defined by s. 20(6) of the 1987 Act, as including any person who might wish to be supplied or provided with the goods or services, for private use or consumption, or otherwise than for any business. 'Price' means the aggregate of the sums to be paid by the consumer. Section 21 gives detailed guidance on when a price, or method of determining the price, might be misleading. This includes an indication:

(a)   that the price is less than in fact it is;

(b)   that the applicability of the price does not depend on other facts or circumstances when in fact it does;

(c)   that the price covers other matters in respect of which an additional charge is made;

(d)   that the price may be increased or reduced when it in fact it will not; and

(e)   that the facts or circumstances by which an individual might be expected to judge the validity of a comparison are not, in fact, what they are.

Offences under the legislation may only be committed by persons acting in the course of a business. Employees cannot therefore be made individually liable under the legislation, even when they are personally responsible for the misleading price indication.

Section 24 of the 1987 Act provides a number of defences to individuals prosecuted under the legislation. First, it is a defence to show that the acts or omissions constituting the alleged offence were authorised under further regulations made under the 1987 Act. Details of some of these regulations are discussed below. The second possible defence is that the price indication was published in a book, newspaper, magazine, film, radio or television broadcast, but not in an advertisement. Thirdly, it is possible for those involved in the advertising business to show that the misleading price was contained in an advertisement submitted to them for publication and that there were no grounds for suspecting that the publication would involve the commission of an offence. Fourthly, it is also possible to prove, as a defence, that the price had been recommended to all suppliers of the goods or services, that the price was misleading because the supplier did not follow the recommendation, and that it was reasonable for the person recommending the price to assume that the recommendation was being followed.

Enforcement of the legislative provisions relating to misleading price indications lies with the trading standards officers in each local authority area. The officers have powers to make test purchases and to enter premises and inspect and seize goods and documents. A person convicted under the 1987 Act is liable on summary conviction to a fine.

Under s. 25 of the Consumer Protection Act 1987, the Secretary of State is given power, after consultation with the Director-General of Fair Trading, to approve codes of practice designed to give practical guidance with respect to the provisions on misleading price indications, and promoting good practice in this area. Contravention of the code of practice does not, in itself, give rise to any civil or criminal liability, but in any proceedings against a retailer, any contravention of, or compliance with a code, may be relied on by either party. The most apposite code of practice on pricing, issued under these provisions, is provided for in the Consumer Protection (Code of Practice for Traders on Price Indications) (Approved) Order 1988 (S.I. 1988/2078).

Section 26 of the Consumer Protection Act 1987 gives power to the Secretary of State to make detailed regulations about all aspects of price indications. Regulations made under this power include the Price Indications (Method of Payment) Regulations 1991 (S.I. 1991/199) which impose obligations on retailers to guarantee that customers are made aware of any changes in the price consequential on the method of payment.

15.8 PRODUCT SAFETY

Section 10, Consumer Protection Act 1987 created an express offence of supplying (or offering or agreeing to, or exposing or possessing for supply) any consumer goods which fail to comply with the general safety requirement. Section 10 has now been disapplied by the important General Product Safety Regulations 1994 (S.I. 1994/2328), designed to implement the Directive on General Product Safety, 2/59/EEC ([1982] O.J. L228/24). The 1994 Regulations do not apply to any product where there are specific provisions in EC law governing all aspects of the safety of the product. To the extent that the safety of medicinal drug products for human use is already covered by EC law, the 1994 Regulations will not apply. However, the provisions *do* apply to all other products, many of which are for sale by retail in community pharmacies.

Regulation 7 imposes a general safety requirement on producers of products who are prohibited from placing a product on the market unless it is a safe product. Regulation 8 imposes duties on the producer of products to provide information to consumers with the relevant information to assess the risks inherent in a product, where such risks are not immediately obvious. Under reg. 9, requirements are imposed on distributors to ensure that the general safety requirements are met. In particular, a distributor must not supply a dangerous product, and must participate, within limits, in monitoring the safety of products placed on the market.

Products which comply with specific rules of United Kingdom health and safety law are deemed to comply with the general safety requirement. Enforcement of the legislative provisions is through the weights and measures authorities, who are given powers to issue suspension notices and to obtain information. Certain criminal offences are created by the legislative provisions, punishable on summary conviction by the imposition of a scale fine, or a term of imprisonment. A limited due diligence defence is provided for under reg. 14.

The Price Marking Order 1991 (S.I. 1991/1382) implements Directive 79/581/EEC ([1979] OJ L158/19), as amended by Directive 88/315/EEC ([1988] OJ L142/23), and Directive 88/314/EEC ([1988] OJ L142/19), on consumer protection in the indication of the prices of foodstuffs and non-foods respectively. The 1991 Order applies to goods sold by retail and to advertisements for such goods. With limited exceptions, the 1991 Order imposes a requirement that the selling price of such goods, whether sold in shops or otherwise, is indicated in writing. It also requires that the unit price must be indicated for goods sold from bulk, pre-packed in pre-established quantities, and pre-packed in variable quantities.

Article 8 sets out the manner of indicating the price. Prices indicated should, in general, be the final price to the consumer. Prices are required, under art. 9, to be indicated inclusive of VAT or other taxes, and if the consumer must pay for ancillary goods or services, the price of these must be included, under art. 10, in the price of the goods or stated separately.

15.9   ETHICS AND THE CONDUCT OF BUSINESS

As noted in the introduction, certain of the products sold for profit by the community pharmacist are medicinal drugs distributed to patients as part of the wider professional health care role. The sale of other commodities, including perfumes, cosmetics, hair dryers, for example, bears little relation to that role. The expectation of commercial profit from the distribution of medicinal products can create different compulsions and motivations. Often this divergence leads to tensions and conflict, leaving a pharmacist in an ethical dilemma. In such a case, the conduct of business has an ethical reality.

Part of that ethical reality has been addressed by the profession itself. We have already noted, in chapter eight, that the principles of the *Code of Ethics* of the Royal Pharmaceutical Society of Great Britain, impose specific obligations on pharmacists relating to the supply of general sale list and pharmacy medicines. Those principles provide an ethical dimension to the retail sale of medicinal drug products as part of the professional health care role.

The *Code of Ethics* has also addressed certain other aspects of the conduct of business. Principle Seven indicates that a pharmacist, or pharmacy owner, should, in the public interest, provide information about available professional services. As part of this principle, any such publicity must not claim or imply any superiority over the professional services provided by other pharmacists or pharmacies, must be dignified and must not bring the profession into disrepute. The detailed obligations, which follow on from this principle, stress that the distribution and content of publicity for professional services should impress upon the public that medicines are not ordinary articles of commerce. The professional guidance accompanying these obligations also emphasises the need for the separation of the publicity for professional services from all other publicity, including advertising techniques for commercial goods, and stresses that such techniques are not appropriate for professional services.

It is important to remember that breach of the principles contained in the *Code of Ethics* may form the basis of a complaint of professional misconduct. The obligations and duties outlined in the principles of the *Code of Ethics* have been supplemented by a range of practice advice issued by the Council of the Royal Pharmaceutical Society of Great Britain. The practice advice includes guidance on the sale of non-prescription medicines and other sales.

For example, pharmacists are advised that, as part of the professional responsibility for the welfare of patients and the public, they should not encourage the sales of ordinary confectionery by impulse purchase at till points or at the medicines counter. This advice is based on the evidence that the consumption of sweets containing sugar, especially by children, contributes to dental caries. Further, the Royal Pharmaceutical Society of Great Britain advises that care should be taken, by those with a licence to sell alcohol, that alcohol products sold through a registered pharmacy are not promoted in such a manner as to encourage abuse. Those pharmacists who sell alcohol are also advised that they have a professional responsibility to provide counselling, if requested, and to provide educational information on the dangers of alcohol abuse.

The Council of the Royal Pharmaceutical Society of Great Britain also recognises that the sale of certain inappropriate products may have a detrimental effect on the good standing of the profession, and risks bringing the profession into disrepute. The Council advises that it would not wish to be prescriptive in listing inappropriate products but would consider that products such as pornographic literature and videos are inappropriate for sale in pharmacies. The Council goes on to state that there would be some products whose sale would adversely affect the standing of the profession in the eyes of the public and would be incompatible with the professional health care services provided from pharmacy premises.

Despite this, the Council recognises the economic reality that the majority of pharmacies sell a range of products some of which are not related to professional services. The Council is concerned that customers' perception of pharmacy might be adversely affected if they are unable to distinguish between the professional area and other parts of the pharmacy premises. A pharmacist is therefore obliged to ensure that the professional area within pharmacy premises is readily identifiable. Even when such identification takes place, the sale of certain inappropriate products could ground an allegation of misconduct, as representing behaviour capable of bringing the profession into disrepute.

Finally, the Council of the Royal Pharmaceutical Society of Great Britain advises that the sale of lottery tickets is not an activity conducive to the development and promotion of the pharmacy as a centre for health care. For this reason, the Council firmly advises that pharmacy owners will damage the public's and opinion formers' perception of the pharmacy as an important source of professional health care advice if lottery ticket machines are located in pharmacies.

The Council has formed a view that it cannot, by virtue of the terms of the Charter of the Royal Pharmaceutical Society of Great Britain, declare the activity of selling lottery tickets to be unethical. However it repeats its advice that any trading activity which interferes with the proper performance of the duties of the pharmacist, or the efficient provision of a comprehensive pharmaceutical service from a pharmacy, would constitute misconduct. The fact that large queues for the purchase of lottery tickets often form, particularly on draw days, would amount to an interference with the proper provision of a pharmaceutical service, in a typical, modest size pharmacy. Those pharmacists who decide, despite this strong advice, to install lottery ticket machines are advised that they must be located away from the professional area of the premises, and pharmacists working in these pharmacies must ensure that their professional duties are not interrupted or adversely affected by ticket sales.

The ethical reality of the dual trading/professional role of the pharmacist was explored, in part, in *Dickson* v *The Pharmaceutical Society of Great Britain* [1966] 3 All ER 404 (Chancery Division), [1967] 2 All ER 558 (Court of Appeal), [1968] 2 All ER 686 (House of Lords). The rulings in the case were, of course, designed to explore the issues associated with the tensions associated with the duality of pharmacy role and function.

On 25 July 1965, a special general meeting of the Pharmaceutical Society of Great Britain (as it then was), passed a motion, the effect of which, if carried out, would be that existing pharmacies must not, except with the approval of the Council, extend their existing range of trading activities, and that new pharmacies must confine their trading activities within certain limits. The Society intended to implement the motion through its inclusion in the Society's *Code of Ethics*.

The motion had its roots in the *Report on the General Practice of Pharmacy*, published in 1961, following the appointment of a committee to study the state of pharmaceutical practice in 1954. Following publication of the report, there was disquiet in some parts of the profession over possible lowering of standards through the extension of the trading role of pharmacists beyond pharmaceutical goods. The motion was carried, at a meeting attended by over 6,000 members (out of a potential 29,000 members), by a large majority. Following this, Dickson, who was a member of the society and the retail director of Boots Pure Drug Co. (as it then was), issued a writ against the Society, claiming, amongst other things, that the motion, if passed, would operate as a rule in restraint of trade affecting the members of the Society engaged in the retail pharmacy trade.

Pennycuick J, in the Chancery Division of the High Court, gave judgment for Dickson, holding that the motion constituted a restraint of trade which could be supported only if the defendants had established reasonableness in the interests of the parties, and as they had not done so, the restraint was contrary to public policy. His ruling was upheld by the Court of Appeal (where the judgment of Lord Denning is the most easy to read, and explains the provisions in the most appropriate manner). On the restraint of trade issue, the Court of Appeal ruled that the restraint imposed by the new rule had not been agreed by all of the members, and was thus an involuntary restraint in relation to them, and would be invalid unless justified. Further it had not been shown that the selling of non-traditional goods distracted pharmacists from their pharmaceutical work or affected adversely the status of the profession, or the number and quality of new entrants to the profession. Accordingly, the restraint was not reasonable in the interests of the profession and not reasonable in the public interest.

On further appeal to the House of Lords, the decisions of both the High Court and the Court of Appeal were upheld. The House of Lords, in a carefully considered set of speeches ruled, amongst other things, that the restrictions imposed by the motion were in restraint of trade and had not been justified as reasonably necessary for achieving the objects of the Society's charter. It should be noted that all three courts also ruled on the questions of whether the issues raised by the case were justiciable, that is whether their validity could be determined by the court, and whether the motion (and the resultant rule of conduct) was *ultra vires*, or beyond the powers of the Society.

The decisions in *Dickson* are significant for a number of reasons. First, they confirm that the pharmacist has a distinct trading, or business role. Secondly, they determine that the dual roles of health care professional and trader do not necessarily conflict. Thirdly, they provide that the Royal Pharmaceutical Society of Great Britain, while retaining a power to regulate the conduct of the members of the profession, has no power to interfere with the pharmacist's trading role by the issue of restraints. Fourthly, the decisions reassess the function of the Royal Pharmaceutical Society of Great Britain, and the part to be played by the *Code of Ethics*, in the regulation of professional conduct. The judges are confirming that while the *Code of Ethics* has compelling force, it does not form the basis for applying compulsion. Further, any attempt to introduce new rules of conduct for the members of the profession by the Royal Pharmaceutical Society of Great Britain, is subject to the jurisdiction of the courts to inquire into the validity of the rule.

The decision in *Dickson* may have settled the issue of the strains between the professional and trading or business role from a legal perspective. Further, aspects of the ethical reality of the duality of role have been addressed in the profession's *Code of Ethics*. However, as was emphasised in chapter eleven, the systematic addressing of ethical issues, and the resolution of ethical questions and dilemmas form part of the professional responsibility of pharmacists. The process of ethical decision-making, as an integral part of the professional role, cannot be restricted to the development of an ethical code, adherence to its general principles, and compliance with judicial pronouncements, however authoritative. The ethical reality of a duality of role for the pharmacist, with its inherent tensions and conflicts, has yet to be pragmatically considered and managed by the pharmacy profession in the United Kingdom.

15.10 VISITORS TO PHARMACY PREMISES

The law imposes specific duties and obligations on the occupiers of premises towards those who come onto those premises, including both lawful and non-lawful visitors. A lawful visitor is one who comes onto premises with the express or implied permission of the occupier, or by force of law. Express permission is a relatively straightforward concept. Visitors who become lawful by coming onto premises with implied permission would include customers or sales persons coming into pharmacy premises. A non-lawful visitor, or trespasser, is a person who comes onto property without express or implied permission or who remains on property after such permission has been withdrawn.

The duties owed to lawful visitors are now contained in the Occupiers' Liability Act 1957, which imposes a common duty of care on the occupier towards such visitors. It is important to note that the duty is imposed on the occupier of the property. The occupier will often also be the owner of the property. However liability, for failure to meet the common duty of care, may also be imposed on an occupier who is not the owner where it can be shown that the occupier has immediate supervision and control of the premises. So, for example, a pharmacist who holds a tenancy of business premises by way of commercial lease, may be liable under the 1957 Act. Occasionally, liability may be imposed on both an occupier and an owner, where both have a degree of supervision and/or control.

The duty is to take such care as in all the circumstances of the case is reasonable to see that the visitor will be reasonably safe in using the premises for the purpose for which he or she is permitted or invited to be there. The occupier will not be liable where the visitor is using the premises for unauthorised purposes, for example, by entering a room clearly marked 'private' or 'unauthorised access denied'.

The legislation anticipates that there will different categories of visitors and that the degree and satisfaction of the duty of care owed will depend on the characteristics of each visitor. So, for example, a higher duty is owed towards children. Equally, the purpose of the visit and individual attributes of the visitor are relevant in assessing the degree of care owed towards adult visitors. It can be expected that experts who are on premises for a particular purpose and who have a particular expertise will appreciate the special risks associated with their work. An electrician invited onto pharmacy premises for the purposes of repairing a fault is taken to be aware of, and accept the degree of risk associated with, opening a fuse box.

The 1957 Act, as originally drafted, permitted the exemption of liability by occupiers from the duty owed to visitors. However, as we have already noted in section 15.4.1, under ss. 1 and 2 of the Unfair Contract Terms Act 1977, it is not now possible to exclude or modify the duty owed in so far as death or personal injury is concerned. The occupier may limit liability for other loss or damage, for example to property, provided that it is reasonable to do so.

However an occupier may take certain steps towards limiting the potential for liability under the legislation by taking reasonable steps to warn the visitor of specific dangers. The warning, however, must be adequate to enable the visitor to be reasonably safe. So what would be deemed to be an adequate warning for an adult may not necessarily be so for a child, or person with a disability. In addition, the law recognises that children are attracted towards certain dangers and particular precautions must be taken accordingly.

As noted above, a non-lawful visitor or trespasser is someone who enters on the property of another without lawful authority or who was a lawful visitor and is remaining on property following the withdrawal of permission. The common law traditionally held that the occupier owed no duty towards trespassers who were obliged to take premises as they were found together with any dangers or risks. However problems arose with the application of such a strict principle to all categories of non-lawful visitors. No difference was acknowledged between the innocent child coming onto property to retrieve a toy and the non-innocent burglar coming onto premises to steal.

Now, the position relating to trespassers is governed by the Occupiers' Liability Act 1984 (Occupiers' Liability (Northern Ireland Order)) 1987. If the occupier has reasonable grounds to believe that a danger exists on his or her premises, and the consequent risk is one against which in all the circumstances he or she may reasonably be expected to offer some protection, then he or she will owe a duty to trespassers, and other uninvited entrants, whom he or she has reasonable grounds for supposing may be in the vicinity. The duty is to take such precautions as are reasonable in all the circumstances to see that they do not suffer injury (due to the state of the premises or to things done or omitted to be done on them).

The duty may be discharged, in an appropriate case, by taking reasonable steps to warn of the danger or to discourage persons from incurring the risk. It is important to note that the extent of the duty owed to trespassers is very limited and is largely dependent on constructive knowledge of their presence by the occupier.

15.11 CONCLUSION

The purpose of this chapter has been to explore the legal reality which surrounds the pharmacist's distinctive commercial role, involving the expectation of commercial profit directly from the distribution of products and services. The wealth of legal material analysed reflects the significance of the structure of business, the importance of the commercial relationship to the efficient running of the economy, and the degree of protection afforded to the consumer participating in daily business transactions.

The pharmacist should not be daunted by the extent of the regulation of business. Many of the controls will work to the pharmacist's advantage by clearly defining structures, delineating responsibilities and limiting potential liabilities. Adopting a strict, legalistic approach to the conduct of business is distinctly beneficial. Equally pharmacists should not be alarmed at the degree of protection offered to the consumer entering into commercial transactions.

The legal safeguards were introduced to prevent the exploitation of those with unequal bargaining strength. The pharmacy business has a degree of monopoly, negotiated over a period of time, in the provision and sale of certain commercial products, particularly certain medicinal products. It is necessary, therefore, for pharmacists to accept that the advantage of the monopoly carries parallel responsibilities and obligations. The potential for commercial profit in the pharmacy business is often resultant on the professional health care roles. The patient seeking the professional health care services of the pharmacist may, at the same time, be equally persuaded to purchase commercial items. The atypicality of this duality of role intensifies the level of duty which is owed.

The pharmacist's distinctive trading function sits beside the pharmacist's primary, health care professional role, in sharing responsibility for the competent provision of pharmaco-therapy for the purposes of achieving definite outcomes that improve or maintain a patient's quality of life. As noted in the introduction to this chapter, the convergence of health care and commercial health care roles is uncommon in health care professions and the divergence of behaviour, involving competing compulsions and motivations, can create tensions and potential for conflict. While the issue of plurality of role may have been considered by the courts, the inherent pressures and frictions have not been systematically explored and managed by the pharmacy profession in the United Kingdom. Until that has been done, the distinctive trading role will continue to sit uneasily with the health care role, leaving the profession subject to further analysis and criticism.

SIXTEEN

The pharmacist and employment

16.1 INTRODUCTION

The employment relationship forms an essential and integral aspect of the effective conduct of commerce, and such, forms a basic requirement for the maintenance and management of a productive economy. Without the employment of labour, businesses cannot expand, sole traders do not become partnerships, and companies cannot operate at all.

The employment relationship is equally important to the practice of pharmacy. At its most basic, pharmacists cannot usually undertake their important health care functions unless and until employed by someone to do so. Even those pharmacists who initially, or subsequently become self-employed, usually require the labour of others, assistants, technicians, etc., to provide a comprehensive and effective pharmacy service. As with other businesses, the growth of a pharmacy business requires the employment of labour, and the employment relationship lies at the heart of the employment of labour. The employment of labour has a distinct legal reality. The purpose of this chapter, therefore, is to describe, in detail, the essential aspects of that legal reality.

The legal reality of the employment relationship is increasing in significance. In 1999 alone, the Government announced plans for, or enacted into law, proposals for limiting the hours which individuals might work, the minimum amount of wages which they are entitled to receive, and for protecting those employees who make disclosures about illegal or suspicious employment practices. Those laws come on top of a wide range of employment laws giving protection against further detriment in employment, against discrimination on the grounds of sex, marital status, religious belief, political opinion, disability, race, giving employees the right not to be unfairly dismissed and awarding substantial compensation where an employee is unfairly dismissed, safeguarding the rights of pregnant employees, recognising trade unions and their activities, and granting significant redundancy payments. These laws have been implemented, essentially through legislation. However, both the courts and the EC are now having a significant impact on the development of United Kingdom employment law, adding to a comprehensive and detailed set of rules and regulations which govern employment practices.

At some stage in their professional careers, pharmacists are going to be classified as employees or employers. The employee and employer relationship is essentially based on the contract of employment. This chapter will therefore begin with an analysis of the laws governing the employment contract. The operation of the employment contract rarely attracts legal attention until it breaks down. Indeed, many specialist textbooks on employment law focus more exclusively on the termination of an employment contract than on its formulation and implementation. The successful negotiation of an employment contract, with an inherent evaluation and recognition of employment rights, avoids the necessity for further legal implications on the breakdown of the employment relationship or termination of the employment contract. Despite this, many contracts of employment break down in animosity and resentment, with subsequent assertion of legal rights. It is essential therefore to analyse the dynamics of the termination of the employment relationship from a legal perspective, and to describe, in detail, the rules relating to dismissal, and the implications for employer and employee when the dismissal is found to be unfair.

As noted above, Parliament has been active in the formulation of laws relating to the employment relationship. These have taken the form of a series of pieces of legislation, essentially guaranteeing and protecting a number of individual employment rights. The theory behind the introduction of such laws is that the employee, by necessity having to sell his or her labour to an employer with a monopoly over the availability of employment, particularly in times of recession, has unequal bargaining strength in negotiating the terms of employment. Parliament's intervention is to balance that strength and afford employees the rights which they cannot negotiate themselves. After a pause in such philanthropic legislative activity in the 1970s and 1980s, the cause of the employee has again been taken up and proposals have been introduced for a new series of laws. A large section of the chapter, therefore, is taken up with an analysis of the variety of legal rights which arise in the employment relationship.

The discussion so far has focused on the civil aspects of the employment relationship, concentrating on individual rights enforceable through the civil law. The employment relationship has also a distinct criminal law reality, particularly in relation to the scheme of law governing health and safety at work. An analysis of these aspects of the employment relationship is essential.

A number of further general points need to be made about the content of this chapter. The chapter describes the legal reality of the employment relationship.

The myriad laws which make up that legal reality can, on first analysis, be daunting and, indeed, off-putting. It is important to remember that the consideration of the legal reality of the employment relationship in advance of the negotiation of an employment contract can obviate the need for further legal implication and incrimination. Most contracts of employment operate, in law and in practice, effectively and harmoniously. In this regard, the assumption of voluntary arrangements, which recognise and reflect the legal rights of both employer and employee, ensures the practical management of employment and eliminates the requirement for further recourse to law. For example, the voluntary negotiation of rights and payments resultant on a redundancy suspends the need for a detailed analysis of redundancy law.

As noted above, the scheme of law governing the employment relationship is extensive. The content of this chapter necessarily reflects and describes that scheme in general terms. For example, it is not possible to discuss the law on discrimination in all of its detail. Those with further academic interest in the detail of the law are referred to the extensive range of textbooks on this subject. Advice for both employers and employees is also available from a wide range of specialist agencies and departments established to implement specific employment legislation. For example, the Equal Opportunities Commission will give advice on sex discrimination law and the Health and Safety Commission will advise on health and safety legislation. It is important to remember, however, that employment law is both technical and detailed. Specific problems should be addressed to specialist employment lawyers. The consequences of not doing so can be significant.

Finally, a brief note on terminology. Until recently, the legislation, and academic and other comment on it, tended to use the phrases employer and employee. New phrases are beginning to drift into employment law and practice. For example, recent legislation uses the term worker instead of employee. The former industrial tribunals are now termed employment tribunals. As far as possible, this chapter retains the phrases employer and employee.

16.2 THE CONTRACT OF EMPLOYMENT

Most employment rights, established and protected by the law, are restricted to employees. An employee is defined by s. 230, Employment Rights Act 1996 as an individual who has entered into or works under (or, where the employment has ceased, worked under) a contract of employment.

The fact that an individual is an employee, working under a contract of employment, does not usually cause legal, or other difficulties. The problems associated with the status of part-time workers have also now been resolved by the Employment Rights Act 1996, which imposes no restrictions on the number of hours for which an individual is employed, thereby ensuring that the further employment protections, outlined in the legislation, extend to part-time employees as well.

The importance of establishing the status of employee, the existence of a contract of employment, and the legal relationship of employer and employee, lies in distinguishing an employee from an individual who is self-employed or an independent contractor. The employment rights, established by the law, are not owed to those 'employed' as independent contractors, who must make their own provision for protection. Such provision might be established through the contract with the 'employer', under which the services of the independent contractor are to be supplied. The legal status of independent contractor is also important in relation to the issue of vicarious liability, already considered in 10.2.

An everyday and obvious example of an independent contractor is a window cleaner. A window cleaner might be 'employed' by a community pharmacist to clean the windows of the pharmacy premises regularly, as part of the duty outlined in Principle Eight of the *Code of Ethics* of the Royal Pharmaceutical Society of Great Britain. Even though a legal relationship is created with the window cleaner, the relationship is not that of employer and employee, for the purposes of creating employment rights. The pharmacist owes no obligation relating to unfair dismissal, maternity or trade union rights.

Various tests have been developed to determine whether a worker is an employee working under a contract of service or an independent contractor working under a contract for services. These include the existence of a relevant financial association, including the deduction of income tax, and the payment of social security contributions and pensions, and the provision of written particulars of the main terms of employment. Other common law tests relate to the extent to which an individual's employment is controlled or organised by the employer. Such legal tests are not exhaustive, however. Where the issue is in dispute it is for the courts to decide, applying the relevant legal criteria, whether a potential applicant is in fact an employee.

16.2.1 The terms of the employment contract

The basis of the employment relationship is the law of contract. It is important to note that the detailed rules of the law of contract, explained in detail in chapter fifteen, are as applicable to the contract of employment as to any other contract. A contract of employment is formed when an employer makes an offer of employment to a potential employee and that offer is accepted. The terms of the contract define the rights and duties of both parties. These terms are usually made up of express, implied, statutory and incorporated terms.

Express terms, which may or may not be written, are those terms which actually agreed by the employer and employee, at the time of entering into the contract. Incorporated terms are those terms agreed by collective bargaining between a trade union and an employer (e.g., wages, holidays) which are incorporated into the contracts of employment of each employee covered by the collective agreement.

Statutory terms are those terms implied into a contract by statute or legislation, e.g., equal pay legislation. Many of these statutory terms will be discussed below. Finally, implied terms may exist by the operation of custom and practice in an industry. More significantly, however, the courts have held that certain implied terms are intrinsic to every contract of employment. The most important of these are that an employee will obey all lawful and reasonable orders, take reasonable care in his or her work, not wilfully disrupt the employer's business and be honest, and act in good faith.

On the part of the employer, the implied terms are that the employer will pay agreed wages, take reasonable care for the employee's safety and health not require an employee to do illegal acts, not act in a manner likely to destroy the relationship of trust or confidence, and inform an employee of employment benefits available where the benefits have not been negotiated with the individual.

The implication of these terms has taken place over a considerable period of time. The extent of their applicability, and their meaning in individual contexts, have been determined by the courts in a series of cases. It is impossible to define clearly the parameters of lawful and reasonable orders, for example. The significance of that phrase, and the nature of the duties and obligations owed under it, can only be determined by looking at the individual facts on relevant circumstances.

16.2.2 Written statement of terms
As noted above, a contract of employment does not have to be in writing and may come into existence by oral agreement. Many employees do not have a written contract of employment, and are often unaware of the main terms of their employment. To counteract this problem, s. 1, Employment Rights Act 1996, obliges an employer to provide all employees, within two months of commencing employment, with a written statement of certain major terms of the contract of employment. The written statement may be given in instalments but must be given in full during the statutory period. This written statement is not the contract of employment but it may amount to much the same thing by being the only, or best evidence of it, especially if the employee has signed a copy. Therefore it is important to check that the particulars given are correct. The written statement must include a number of matters, including:

(a) the names of the employer and the employee;

(b) the date on which the employment began;

(c) the date on which the employee's period of continuous employment began, taking into account any employment with a previous employer which counts towards that period;

(d) the scale and rate of remuneration, and the method of calculating remuneration;

(e) the intervals at which remuneration is paid (i.e., weekly, monthly or other specified intervals);

(f)   any terms and conditions relating to hours of work;

(g)   any terms and conditions relating to holiday entitlement, including public holidays and holiday pay, the particulars being sufficient to enable the employee's entitlement to accrued holiday pay on termination of employment to be calculated;

(h)   any terms and conditions relating to incapacity for work due to sickness or injury, including any provision for sick pay;

(i)   any terms and conditions relating to pensions and pension schemes;

(j)   the length of notice which the employee is obliged to give and entitled to receive to terminate the contract of employment;

(k)   the title of the job which the employee is employed to do or a brief description of the work entailed in the employment;

(l)   where the employment is not intended to be permanent, the period for which it is expected to continue or, if for a fixed term, the date when it is to end;

(m)   either the place of work, or where the employee is required or permitted to work at various places, an indication of that and of the address of the employer;

(n)   any collective agreements which directly affect the terms and conditions of employment, including, where the employer is not a party, the persons by whom they were made; and

(o)   where the employee is required to work outside the United Kingdom for a period of more than one month, details of the required work period, currency of remuneration, any additional remuneration or other benefits and any terms and conditions relating to the return to employment in the United Kingdom.

The written statement must also include a note specifying any disciplinary rules applicable to the employee or referring the employee to the provisions of a document specifying such rules which is reasonably accessible. The note should also specify a person to whom the employee can apply if dissatisfied with any disciplinary decisions, a person to whom the employee can apply for the purpose of seeking redress of grievances, and give full details of the manner in which such applications may be made, including the relevant steps to be taken. Most of these requirements relating to disciplinary proceedings need not be complied with where the relevant number of employees in the employee's employment is less than twenty. Sound advice is that full details of disciplinary proceedings should be given to all employees.

The written statement may refer the employee for particulars of any of the required matters relating to sickness, incapacity, pensions to any document which is reasonably accessible by the employee. A similar referral, or to any collective agreement affecting the terms and conditions of employment, may be made in relation to the required particulars concerning notice. Any change in the particulars contained in the written statement must be notified, in writing, to the employee, within one month of the change in question.

Failure by an employer to supply a written statement of the main terms and conditions of employment may be referred by an employee to an employment tribunal, under s. 11 of the 1996 Act. A similar application may be made where there is doubt concerning the content of certain of the particulars. An application or complaint to an employment tribunal can be made either while still employed or within three months of leaving employment. The employment tribunal, upon receipt of such an application, will determine what particulars ought to have been included or referred to in such a statement. Any such determined particulars are deemed to be included or referred to in a statement.

16.3 TERMINATION OF EMPLOYMENT

The employment relationship can end in a number of different ways. It may come to a conclusion by the mutual agreement of the parties, the expiry of a fixed term contract, or as a result of the employer's insolvency. Alternatively the contract of employment can be terminated by either the employer or the employee.

The law has given a significant range of protection to employees on termination. These rights must be read subject to the introduction of new methods of resolving employment disputes introduced by the Employment Rights (Dispute Resolution) Act 1998. These legislative provisions allow for the establishment of appeal procedures by employers and provide for alternative procedures for determining employment disputes through independent arbitration and conciliation procedures. The new provisions do not abrogate the individual rights of employees on dismissal but promote the use of flexible, voluntary (but binding) elective procedures. The extent to which an employee has taken advantage of such procedures, or been prevented by the employer from benefiting from such procedures, may be taken into account by employment tribunals.

16.3.1 Minimum notice
Section 86, Employment Rights Act 1996 provides that both employers and employees have rights to minimum periods of notice.

An employee who has been in continuous employment for one month or more is entitled to receive at least one week's notice if the employment has been for less than two years. Thereafter the employee is entitled to receive at least one week's notice for each completed year of service, subject to a maximum of twelve weeks' notice after twelve or more years. An employee who has been in continuous employment for at least one month is required to give not less than one week's notice.

Any provision for shorter notice in any contract of employment has effect subject to these statutory minimums, but does not prevent either party from waiving a right to notice on any occasion, from accepting a payment in lieu of notice, or from affecting the right of either party to the contract to treat the contract as terminable without notice by reason of the conduct of the other party.

Sections 87 to 91, Employment Rights Act 1996 give certain rights to an employee during the period of notice, whether the notice was given by the employee or the employer. Where the employee had normal working hours under the contract of employment in force during the period of notice, and during any part of those normal working hours, the employee is ready and willing to work but no work is provided by the employer, the employee is incapable of work because of sickness or injury, the employee is absent from work wholly or partly because of pregnancy or childbirth, or the employee is absent in accordance with the terms of employment, the employer is liable to pay the employee for the part of the normal working hours covered by those particular circumstances.

Any payments made to the employee in respect of the relevant period of notice by way of sick pay, statutory sick pay, maternity pay, statutory maternity pay or otherwise, go towards meeting the employer's liability under these provisions. Where notice was given by the employee, the employer's liability does not arise unless and until the employee leaves the service of the employer in pursuance of the notice.

If an employee does not have normal working hours under the contract of employment in force at the period of notice, the employer is liable to pay the employee, for each week of the period of notice, a sum not less than a week's pay. The employer's liability, under these provisions, is conditional on the employee being ready and willing to do work of a reasonable nature and amount to earn a week's pay. That latter obligation does not apply to any period in which the employee is incapable of work because of sickness or injury, during which the employee is absent from work wholly or partly because of pregnancy or childbirth, or during which the employee is absent from work in accordance with the terms of employment. Any payments made to the employee in respect of the relevant period of notice by way of sick pay, statutory sick pay, maternity pay, statutory maternity pay or otherwise, go towards meeting the employer's liability under these provisions. Where notice was given by the employee, the employer's liability does not arise unless and until the employee leaves the service of the employer in pursuance of the notice.

An employer is not liable to make any payment in respect of a period during which the employee is absent from work with the leave of the employer granted at the request of the employee, including any time off taken in accordance with the legislative provisions relating to public duties, looking for work and making arrangements for training, ante-natal care, occupational pension schemes, and employee representatives. Further, no payment is due in consequence of a notice to terminate a contract given by an employee, if, after the notice is given and on or before the termination of the contract, the employee takes part in a strike of employees.

If, during the period of notice, the employer breaks the contract of employment, payments received under the legislative provisions relating to the period of notice, in respect of the period after the breach, go towards mitigating the damages recoverable by the employee for loss of earnings. If the employee breaks the contract during the period of notice, and the employer rightfully treats the breach as terminating the contract, no payment is due to the employee in respect of that period falling after the termination. Finally, if an employer fails to give the required notice, the rights to payments during the period of notice are taken into account in assessing liability for breach of the contract.

16.3.2 Written statement of reasons for dismissal

Under the provisions of s. 92, Employment Rights Act 1996, an employee is entitled to be provided by the employer with a written statement giving particulars of the reasons for the employee's dismissal where:

(a) the employee is given by the employer notice of termination of the contract of employment;

(b) the employee's contract of employment is terminated by the employer without notice; or

(c) the employee is employed under a fixed term contract and that term expires without being renewed under the same contract.

Entitlement is restricted to those employees who have been continuously employed for two years or more prior to the effective date of termination. Equally, an employee will only be entitled to such a written statement of the reasons for dismissal where it is requested. However neither of these requirements apply to a dismissal of an employee at any time while she is pregnant, or after childbirth in circumstances in which her maternity leave ends by reason of the dismissal.

Written statements of reasons for dismissal are admissible in any proceedings. An employee may make a complaint to an employment tribunal on the ground that the employer has unreasonably failed to provide a written statement or that the particulars of reasons given in purported compliance with that requirement are inadequate or untrue. Where an employment tribunal finds such a complaint to be well founded, it may make a declaration as to what it finds the employer's reasons were for dismissing the employee, and make an award that the employer pay the employee a sum equal to two weeks' pay.

16.3.3 Unfair dismissal

Under ss. 94, 108 and 109, Employment Rights Act 1996, an employee, who has been continuously employed for two years before the termination of employment, has the right not to be unfairly dismissed. Employees will lose this right upon reaching retirement age. There is no qualifying period of continuous employment if any employee is dismissed for trade union membership or activity or for non-membership of a union. Dismissals as a result of discrimination are equally not subject to any qualifying periods or age requirement, as are dismissals on grounds of assertion of statutory rights and in health and safety cases.

There are a number of distinct legal aspects to unfair dismissal. First, an employee must be dismissed. Under s. 95, Employment Rights Act 1996, an employee is dismissed only in the following circumstances:

(a)   when the contract under which the employee is employed by the employer is terminated by the employer, with or without notice;

(b)   where the contract of employment is for a fixed term, and that term expires without being renewed;

(c)   when the employee terminates that contract, with or without notice in circumstances such that he or she is entitled to terminate it with or without notice by reason of the employer's conduct.

The form of dismissal under (c) is sometimes referred to as 'constructive' dismissal. The Employment Rights Act 1996 refers to the following additional forms of dismissal:

(d)   if the employer gives notice to the employee to terminate the contract of employment, and before the end of the period of notice, the employee gives an indication that the contract should be terminated early, the employee is taken to be dismissed, and the reason for the dismissal is taken to be the reason for which the original notice was given; and

(e)   where an employee has the right to return to work following a period of maternity leave, and has exercised that right, but is not permitted to return to work, she is taken to be dismissed for the reason for which she was not permitted to return.

The finding of dismissal in (e) is subject to a number of important exceptions relating to the number of employees in the employment, the reasonable practicality of permitting a return to work, and the unreasonable refusal by the employee of suitable and appropriate alternative work.

The fact of dismissal does not automatically mean that it is unfair. Under s. 98, Employment Rights Act 1996, it is for the employer to establish the reason for dismissal and that the dismissal was for one of a number of reasons outlined in the legislation, or some other substantial reason of a kind such as to justify the dismissal of the employee. The legislative reasons are that the dismissal is related to capability or qualifications, conduct, redundancy, or statutory prohibition. The determination of whether the dismissal is then fair or unfair, having regard to the reason shown by the employer, will depend on whether in the circumstances, including the size and administrative resources of the employer's undertaking, the employer acted reasonably or unreasonably in treating it as a sufficient reason for dismissing the employee. In making such a determination, the tribunal will be able to take into account the equity and substantial merits of the case.

The legislation makes it clear that some reasons for dismissal are automatically unfair. These include discrimination, refusal to work on Sundays, union activity and membership, health and safety, carrying out the duties of a trustee of an occupational pension scheme assertion of statutory rights, redundancy and pregnancy and childbirth, and the making of a protected disclosure.

An employee will be regarded as having been dismissed for a substantial reason of a kind justifying dismissal, in circumstances where the employee was hired as a maternity leave replacement employee, or to cover for an employee suspended on medical grounds, and was informed, in writing, that the employment would be terminated on the resumption of work by the employee on maternity leave, or suspended on medical grounds.

In determining the reason for an employee's dismissal, whether the reason was of a kind justifying dismissal, and whether an employer acted reasonably in treating the reason as a sufficient reason for dismissal, no regard is taken of any pressure which was exercised on the employer by the calling, organising, procuring or financing of a strike or other industrial action.

16.3.4 Remedies for unfair dismissal

A complaint of unfair dismissal must be made to a tribunal within three months of the termination of employment, or within such further period as the tribunal considers reasonable in a case where the tribunal is satisfied that it was not reasonably practicable for the complaint to be presented before the end of that period of three months.

Where the tribunal finds that the grounds for complaint are well-founded, it will explain to the complainant what orders may be made under s. 113, Employment Rights Act 1996, and will ask the complainant whether he or she wishes such an order to be made. If no order is made under s. 113, the tribunal will make an award of compensation calculated under ss. 118–27 of the 1996 Act.

The orders which may be made under s. 133 are an order for reinstatement and an order for re-engagement. Reinstatement takes effect as if an applicant has never been dismissed and involves full restoration of pay and other benefits, seniority and pension rights. An order for re-engagement may be made where the tribunal thinks that reinstatement is not suitable, practicable or appropriate. This might occur where relationships in one particular department within the employment have broken down. Re-engagement allows the employer to offer the employee a different but comparable job or another suitable job.

The tribunal will consider, as its first priority, an order for reinstatement. In so doing it will take into account whether the complainant wishes to be reinstated, whether it is practicable for the employer to comply with an order for reinstatement, and whether the complainant caused or contributed to the dismissal. If the tribunal decides not to make an order for reinstatement, it is then obliged to consider an order for re-engagement. Similar considerations as for an order for reinstatement are taken into account. The fact that an employer has replaced the dismissed employee with a permanent replacement is an irrelevant consideration for either order, except in certain limited circumstances.

Where the tribunal makes an order for reinstatement or re-engagement which is not fully complied with by the employer, the tribunal will make an award of compensation to be paid to the employee, the amount of which will be such as the tribunal thinks fit having regard to the loss sustained by the complainant in consequence of the failure to comply fully with the order. This might occur where the employee is reinstated but has lost accrued pension or seniority rights. Where the employee is not reinstated or re-engaged at all, pursuant to an order of the tribunal, the tribunal will make an award of compensation for unfair dismissal and an additional award of an appropriate amount.

It is important to note that although the legislation places great emphasis on securing the reinstatement or re-engagement of the dismissed employee, few awards of reinstatement or re-engagement are made. This is largely because the employment relationship has usually broken down irreparably, and the tribunal will be reluctant to force reluctant employers and employees to work with each other. It could be said, therefore, that there is no legal right to return to work. Employees who are unfairly dismissed by an employer who refuses to reinstate or re-engage them will find that their only remedy is monetary compensation.

16.3.5 Compensation

As noted in 16.3.4, an award of compensation for unfair dismissal will be made where the tribunal has decided that an order for reinstatement or re-engagement is not appropriate, or where such orders have been made but have not been complied with. In reality the award of monetary compensation is the most common remedy for unfair dismissal. The basis for the calculation of the amount of monetary compensation is set out in ss. 118–27, Employment Rights Act 1996.

Two types of awards may be made, although in certain cases special awards may also be added. Under s. 119, a basic award of compensation is calculated in the same way as the statutory redundancy payment, based on age, pay, and length of service. Under s. 123, the tribunal may make also a compensatory award. This award will be of such an amount as the tribunal considers just and equitable in the circumstances, having regard to the loss sustained by the complainant in consequence of the dismissal. It includes provision for expenses, and loss of accrued benefits.

Both awards may be reduced if the tribunal decides that the employee contributed to the dismissal, and the basic award may be reduced where the tribunal find further that the complainant unreasonably refused an offer of reinstatement. An employee is also under a statutory duty to mitigate his or her loss by, for example, seeking employment elsewhere. In addition, under the provisions of the Employment Rights (Dispute Resolution) Act 1998, a compensatory award may be reduced if an employee has failed to take advantage of any notified, in-employment appeal procedure established by the employer. Alternatively, a special award of compensation may be made where the employer does not allow the employee to make use of such procedures.

Section 125 of the Employment Rights Act 1996 provides for special compensation for employees dismissed for automatically unfair reasons, and where the complainant has asked for an order for reinstatement or re-engagement, which has been refused by the tribunal.

Where compensation is payable for an act which amounts to both unfair dismissal and discrimination, the tribunal must not award compensation for any matter which has already been considered under other proceedings. In essence, a double payment of compensation is not permissible.

16.3.6 Interim relief

Under s. 128, Employment Rights Act 1996, interim relief is a procedure applicable to an employee who is dismissed for union activity and membership, health and safety, carrying out the duties of a trustee of an occupational pension scheme, or acting as an employee representative. An employee must apply to an employment tribunal within seven days of the termination of the employment.

A preliminary hearing then takes place and if the tribunal considers that the dismissed employee's unfair dismissal application is likely to succeed, it may make an order for reinstatement or re-engagement, if the employer states that he or she is willing to reinstate or re-engage the employee. If the employer refuses to re-employ or the employee reasonably refused to be re-employed, the tribunal can make an order for the continuation of the contract of employment. This has the effect of ensuring that the employee remains on full pay, and retains full employment rights, until the tribunal makes its final decision. The tribunal may determine the rate and method of payment for the interim period.

16.4 EMPLOYMENT PROTECTION RIGHTS DURING THE CONTRACT OF EMPLOYMENT

In addition to legislation concerning equal pay, sex, marital, disability and religious or political discrimination, to be discussed below, there exists a wide range of legislation which provides employment protection rights for employees.

16.4.1 Wages

16.4.1.1 Minimum wage Following the recommendations of the Low Pay Commission (*The National Minimum Wage*, London: HMSO, Cm 3976,

June 1998), the Government has passed the National Minimum Wage Act 1998, and the National Minimum Wage Regulations 1999 (S.I. 1999/584).

The 1998 Act sets out the basic structure for the introduction of an entitlement to the national minimum wage. It provides the primary legislative basis for the determination of the appropriate hourly rate of remuneration, the exclusion of, and limited modifications for certain classes of persons. The 1998 Act also cements the pivotal position of the Low Pay Commission in the initial, and subsequent, prescription of the appropriate rate of the national minimum wage.

The 1998 Act imposes specific duties on employers to keep records demonstrating that they have paid their employees at least the rate of the national minimum wage. Employees are given the right to require employers to produce any relevant records, on service of the relevant notice, and subsequently, to have the right to inspect and examine those records and copy any part of them. Failure to permit access to the relevant records will ground a complaint to an employment tribunal.

Sections 13 and 14 of the 1998 Act allow for the appointment of officers for the purposes of monitoring compliance with the provisions of the legislation. Such officers will have powers to require the production of records, the furnishing of further explanations relating to such records and any further additional information, and at all times to enter any relevant premises in order to exercise any statutory power. Any information obtained as a result of the exercise of these powers by officers is restricted by ss. 15 and 16 to certain uses.

Non-compliance with the legislative provisions entitles a worker to be paid, under the contract of employment, an additional amount of remuneration, equivalent to the difference between the actual remuneration received and that which would have been received under the national minimum wage. Officers appointed under ss. 13 and 14 are given further powers to issue enforcement notices to employers requiring the employer to implement minimum wage remuneration and pay back any unpaid wages for previous failures to comply. Employers who are served with an enforcement notice have a right of appeal to an employment tribunal.

Where a served enforcement notice is not complied with by an employer, officers are given the right, under s. 20 of the 1998 Act, to sue on behalf of a worker, in order to recover any sums which are due. In addition, those officers may serve a penalty notice on a non-compliant employer requiring the employer to pay a financial penalty to the Secretary of State. The amount of the financial penalty is calculated at a rate equal to twice the hourly amount of the national minimum wage for each worker to whom the failure relates for each continuing day of failure. Appeals against penalty notices lie to an employment tribunal.

Under s. 23 of the 1998 Act, a worker is given an additional employment right, the right not to be subjected to any detriment by any act, or any deliberate failure to act, by the employer on the ground that the employee took any action to secure a benefit under the legislation, that the employer was prosecuted under the legislation as a result of action taken by or on behalf of the worker, or that the worker qualifies, or might qualify, for the minimum wage. Employees who feel that they have suffered such a detriment are given the right to make a complaint to an employment tribunal.

Section 25 of the 1998 Act inserts a new s. 104A into the Employment Rights Act 1996, providing that an employee who is dismissed will be regarded as having been unfairly dismissed if the reason, or principal reason, for the dismissal was the taking of any action to enforce or secure a benefit under the national minimum wage legislation, that the employer was prosecuted under the legislation as a result of action taken by or behalf of the worker, or that the worker qualifies, or might qualify, for the minimum wage.

Section 31 of the 1998 Act creates a range of offences relating to the national minimum wage, including offences relating to the refusal or wilful neglect to remunerate a worker at the national minimum wage, offences relating to records and further information, and the obstruction of officers. Such offences are punishable on summary conviction by the imposition of a scale fine. A limited due diligence defence is provided for by s. 31(8). As noted above, the legislation provides for the exclusion of, and limited modifications to, the provisions for certain classes of persons.

The legislative provisions for the implementation of a national minimum wage are completed by the National Minimum Wage Regulations 1999 (S.I. 1999/584). These regulations, which came into force on 1 April 1999, set the hourly rate of the national minimum wage at £3.60, and prescribe the working hours in respect of which workers must be paid the national minimum wage. The regulations also provide for which payments by employers to workers are to be taken into account in determining whether the national minimum wage has been paid for those hours and require employers to keep records sufficient to establish that they are paying their workers at least the rate of the national minimum wage.

The 1999 Regulations provide that certain categories of workers are not entitled to the national minimum wage. These include workers under the age of 18, those apprentices who are under 19 or in the first year of apprenticeship and are under the age of 26, and workers on certain Government schemes providing them with training, work experience or temporary work, or assisting them to obtain work.

Regulation 13 of the 1999 Regulations provides for particular classes of workers to be entitled to the national minimum wage at a lower rate. The hourly rate is £3 for workers aged 18 or more but less than 22, and £3.20 during the first six months of employment for those older workers who agree to undergo a specified amount of accredited training during those six months.

The remainder of the 1999 Regulations provides for the method of determining whether at least the rate of the national minimum wage has been paid; establish, for each description of work that may be done by a worker, the hours for which the worker must be paid the national minimum wage and say how the total number of those hours in a pay reference period is to be determined; prescribe what payments made by the employer to a worker are to be taken into account in ascertaining whether the worker has been paid at least the national minimum wage in a pay reference period; and complete the legislative provision for the requirement on employers to keep records sufficient to show that they have paid their workers at least the rate of the national minimum wage.

16.4.1.2 Protection of wages Part II of the Employment Rights Act 1996 makes provision for the protection of wages. Under s. 13, an employer is not permitted to make deductions from the wages of an employee, unless that deduction is required or authorised by statutory provision (income tax or national insurance contributions, for example), or the employee has previously signified in writing an agreement or consent to the making of such a deduction (superannuation or trade union levies, for example). Section 15 of the 1996 Act provides a parallel right not to have to make payments to the employer, subject to the same conditions.

Overpaid wages or expenses may be lawfully deducted and specific provision is made for the deduction for cash shortages and stock deficiencies in the retail trade, subject to detailed limitations. Employees may make a complaint to an employment tribunal, concerning unlawful deductions from wages, within a period of three months from the date of deduction. Where the employment tribunal determines that such a complaint is well-founded, it will make a declaration to that effect, and will order the repayment of any unlawfully deducted amounts.

16.4.2 Hours

The Working Time Regulations 1998 (S.I. 1998/1833), implement Directive 93/104/EC ([1993] OJ L307/18), on certain aspects of the organisation of working time, and certain provisions concerning working time in Directive 94/33/EC ([1994] OJ L216/12), on the protection of young people at work. Young people means those between the ages of 15 and 18. We shall see below, in section 16.6.1 that the protection of children at work is provided for under separate legislation.

Regulations 4 to 9 impose obligations on employers concerning the maximum average weekly working time of workers, the average normal hours of night workers, the provision of health assessments for night workers, and rest breaks to be given to workers engaged in certain kinds of work. Under reg. 5, individual workers may agree that the maximum average weekly working time should not apply to them. Employers are also under a duty, under reg. 9, to keep records of workers' hours of work. Enforcement of these provisions is undertaken through the Health and Safety Executive and local authorities.

Workers are also given individual rights under the 1998 Regulations. Workers are entitled to a rest period in every 24 hours during which they work for their employers and longer rest periods each week or fortnight. Workers are also entitled to a rest break in the course of a working day and to a period of annual leave. Enforcement of these provisions is through proceedings before an employment tribunal.

The Employment Rights Act 1996 is also amended to include a right for workers not to be subjected to any detriment for refusing to comply with a requirement contrary to the working time provisions, or to forgo a right conferred by these provisions. Workers have a right to pursue a claim that they had been subjected to a detriment through an employment tribunal. The dismissal of an employee on the basis of any such refusal will automatically become unfair.

Regulations 18 to 27 provide for particular regulations not to apply, either in relation to workers engaged in certain kinds of work, or where particular circumstances arise. These provisions have recently been invoked in relation to the working hours of hospital doctors. The 1998 Regulations also provide for groups of workers and their employers to agree, or modify, or exclude the application of certain regulations.

16.4.3 Sunday working

The Sunday Trading Act 1994 (The Shops (Sunday Trading &c.) (Northern Ireland) Order 1997) made provision for trading on a Sunday by repealing existing legislation which had imposed restrictions on such activity. The 1994 Act had included specific provisions giving rights to individual workers who might be contractually obliged, or be requested to work on a Sunday. Those individual rights are now contained in Part IV of the Employment Rights Act 1996.

The 1996 Act categorises workers for the purposes of the protections offered in relation to Sunday working. 'Protected' shop workers are those workers who were employed before the commencement of the Sunday Trading Act 1994, and those who presently work under a contract of employment which does not require work on a Sunday. An 'opted-out' shop worker is someone who is employed under a contract of employment which requires Sunday working but who opts out of such a requirement. Opting out is effected by the service of a written notice on the employer. Workers may also give up their right not to work on a Sunday by the service of an 'opting-in' notice. Such a notice must be in writing, must be signed and dated, and must state expressly that the worker does not object to Sunday working or, alternatively, indicates a wish to work on a Sunday. The worker must then enter into an agreement with the employer to work on a Sunday, or on a particular Sunday.

Under s. 42, Employment Rights Act 1996, employers are required to give every shop worker, within two months of the commencement of work, an explanatory statement outlining the basic right to opt out of Sunday working.

The legislation contains prescribed forms of written statements to be given to employees.

As will be seen below, dismissal of an employee will automatically be regarded as unfair if the reason or principal reason was that the employee refused or proposed to work on a Sunday. In addition, where an employee is a protected shop worker or an opted-out shop worker, that employee has the right not to be subjected to any detriment by any act of the employer done on the ground that the employee refused to work on Sunday. An employee who is a shop worker equally has the right not to be subjected to detriment by any act of the employer on the ground that the employee gave an opting-out notice to the employer.

16.4.4 Guarantee payments

Part III of the Employment Rights Act 1996 makes provision for guarantee payments for 'workless days' and 'workless periods'. A 'workless day' is defined as a day during which an employee would be required to work, in accordance with his or her contract of employment, but is not provided by work by the employer by reason of a diminution in the requirements of the employer's business, or any other occurrence affecting the normal working of the employer's business. A 'workless period' has a corresponding meaning.

Under the provisions of s. 28, Employment Rights Act 1996, an employee is entitled to be paid an amount by the employer for a workless day. This right does not extend to employees in a number of different circumstances. First, it does not apply to those employees who have not been continuously employed for at least a month before the day on which the guarantee payment is claimed. Secondly, it does not apply to those who have been working under a fixed term or fixed task contract for three months or less unless they have been continuously employed for a period of more than three months before the day on which the guarantee payment is claimed.

Thirdly, it does not apply if the failure to provide work is in consequence of a strike, lock-out or other industrial action involving any employee. Fourthly, an employee is not entitled to a guarantee payment if the employer has offered to provide alternative work for that day, which is suitable in all of the circumstances, and is unreasonably refused by the employee. Finally, an employee is not entitled to a guarantee payment if he does not comply with reasonable requirements imposed by his employer with a view to ensuring that services are available.

Section 30, Employment Rights Act 1996 provides the mechanism for the calculation of a guarantee payment. The amount of a guarantee payment will not exceed £15.35 a day and payment will normally only be made for a period of five days in any three months. A right to a statutory guarantee payment does not affect the right of an employee in relation to remuneration under a contract of employment.

An employee who alleges that the employer has failed to pay the whole or any amount of a guarantee payment to which the employee is entitled, may present a complaint to an employment tribunal, within a period of three months, or within such further period as the tribunal considers to be just and equitable where it is satisfied that it was not reasonably practicable for the complaint to be presented before the end of the period of three months. Where the employment tribunal finds that any such complaint is well-founded, it must order the employer to pay the employee the amount of guarantee payment which it finds is due.

16.4.5 Itemised pay statement

Under the provisions of s. 8, Employment Rights Act 1996 all employees have the right to be given an itemised pay statement every time they are paid. The statement must specify:

(a) the gross and net wages payable;
(b) the amounts of any fixed or variable deductions; and
(c) where parts of the net wage are paid in different ways the amount and method of each part payment.

If there are several fixed deductions, such as a trade union subscription, an employer, instead of listing each separately, can give a standing statement of fixed deductions. Such a statement must be in writing, and must give full details of all deductions, including amount, intervals and purpose. Amendments may be made to the standing statement by notice in writing to the employee and any such statement must be renewed at least every 12 months.

Failure by an employer to supply a written statement of the main terms and conditions of employment may be referred by an employee to an employment tribunal, under s. 11 of the 1996 Act. A similar application may be made where there is doubt concerning the content of certain of the particulars. The employment tribunal, upon receipt of such an application, will determine what particulars ought to have been included or referred to in such a statement. Any such determined particulars are deemed to be included or referred to in a statement.

If an employee does not get an itemised pay statement or disputes the content of the statement, he or she can apply to an employment tribunal for it to determine what should be included in the statement. If unnotified deductions have been made, the tribunal can order the employer to repay the amounts so deducted in the 13 weeks prior to the claim. An application to an employment tribunal can be made by an employee either while still employed or within three months of leaving employment.

16.4.6 Trade union membership and activities

A certain degree of protection and some enforceable rights have been given to employees who are trade union members and indeed to non-members.

Under the provisions of s. 61, Employment Rights Act 1996, an employee who is an employee representative, or a candidate in an election for the purposes of electing employee representatives, is entitled to be permitted by the employer to take reasonable time off work in order to perform the functions of such an employee representative or candidate. The employee who is permitted to take time off under these provisions, is also entitled to be paid remuneration for the time taken off at the appropriate hourly rate, to be calculated in accordance with the provisions of s. 62 of the 1996 Act.

An employee who feels that the employer has unreasonably refused to permit time off as required by s. 61, or has failed to pay the whole or any amount of remuneration under s. 62, may present a complaint to an employment tribunal, within a period of three months, or within such further period as the tribunal considers to be just and equitable where it is satisfied that it was not reasonably practicable for the complaint to be presented before the end of the period of three months. Where the employment tribunal finds that any such complaint is well-founded, it must make a declaration to that effect, and may order the employer to pay an amount equal to the remuneration to which the employee would have been entitled, had the employer not refused.

16.4.7   Time off to look for work or arrange training
Under the provisions of s. 52, Employment Rights Act 1996, an employee who is given notice of dismissal by way of redundancy, and who has been continuously employed for a period of two years or more, is entitled to be permitted by the employer to take reasonable time off before the end of the notice in order to look for new employment or make arrangements for training for future employment. The employee is also entitled to be paid remuneration by the employer for the period of absence at the appropriate hourly rate, to be calculated in accordance with the provisions of s. 53.

An employee who feels that an employer has unreasonably refused to permit time off as required by s. 52, or who feels that the employer has failed to pay the whole or part of any remuneration to which the employee is entitled under s. 53, may make a complaint within three months of the date on which it is alleged that the time off should have been permitted. An employment tribunal which feels that the complaint is well-founded may make a declaration to that effect, and order the employer to pay to the employee the amount which it finds is due, up to 40 per cent of a week's pay of that employee.

16.4.8   Time off for pension scheme trustees
Under the provisions of s. 58, Employment Rights Act 1996, an employer, in relation to a relevant occupational pension scheme, must permit an employee who is a trustee of the scheme to take time off during the employee's working hours for the purpose of performing any duties as such a trustee, or undergoing training relevant to the performance of those duties. What is reasonable is to be determined by a series of factors, including the amount of time off required, and the circumstances of the employer's business and the effect of the employee's absence on the running of that business. An employer who permits

an employee to take time off under these provisions, must also pay the employee for the time taken off pursuant to that permission, at a rate to be determined in line with the provisions of s. 59 of the 1996 Act.

An employee who has not been permitted to take time off under these provisions, or whose employer has failed to pay for that time off, may make a complaint to an employment tribunal, within three months of the date on which the failure occurred, or within such further period as the tribunal considers to be just and equitable where it is satisfied that it was not reasonably practicable for the complaint to be presented before the end of the period of three months. An employment tribunal which finds that the complaint concerning the failure to permit time off is well-founded may make an order to that effect and make an award of compensation to the employee. The amount of compensation will be such as the tribunal considers just and equitable in all the circumstances having regard to the employer's default in failing to permit time off to be taken by the employee, and any loss sustained by the employee which is attributable to the matters complained of. Where the tribunal finds that an employer has failed to pay an employee for permitted time off, it will order the employer to pay the amount which it finds to be due.

16.4.9 Suspension from work

Under the provisions of s. 64, Employment Rights Act 1996, an employee who is suspended for work on medical grounds is entitled to be paid by the employer remuneration during suspension for a period not exceeding 26 weeks. Suspension on medical grounds may be in consequence of the requirements imposed by the provisions of the Control of Lead at Work Regulations 1980, the Ionising Radiations Regulations 1985, the Control of Substances Hazardous to Health Regulations 1988, as amended, and the codes of practice issued or approved under the Health and Safety at Work Act 1974.

An employee will only be regarded as suspended from work if and for so long as he or she continues to be employed by the employer but is not provided with work or does not perform the work normally performed before the suspension. Exceptions from the entitlement to remuneration on the grounds of suspension on medical grounds apply to those who have not been continuously employed for more than one month before the date on which the suspension begins, those who have been working under a fixed term or fixed task contract for three months or less unless they have been continuously employed for a period of more than three months before the day on which the suspension begins, and to those who are incapable of work by reason of disease or bodily or mental disablement. The entitlement to remuneration does not apply also to those who are offered suitable alternative work, and have unreasonably refused to perform that work, or who do not comply with reasonable requirements imposed by the employer with a view to ensuring that services are available.

Under the provisions of s. 66, Employment Rights Act 1996, an individual is deemed to be suspended from work on maternity grounds if, in consequence of any relevant requirement or relevant recommendation, she is suspended from work by her employer on the ground that she is pregnant, has recently given birth, or is breastfeeding a child. An employee will be regarded as suspended from work on maternity grounds only if and for so long as she continues to be employed by her employer but is not provided with work or does not perform the work which she normally performed before the suspension.

Under s. 67, where an employer has available suitable alternative work for an employee, the employee has a right to be offered to be provided with the alternative work before being suspended from work on maternity grounds. For alternative work to be suitable, it must be of a kind which is both suitable in relation to her and appropriate for her to do in the circumstances, and the terms and conditions applicable to her for performing the work must not be substantially less favourable to her than her corresponding terms and conditions. An employee who is suspended from work on maternity grounds is entitled to be paid remuneration by her employer while she is so suspended, except where her employer has offered to provide her with work which is suitable alternative work, and the employee has unreasonably refused to perform that work.

The amount of remuneration payable by an employer to an employee who is suspended from work on medical or maternity grounds is to be a week's pay in respect of each week of suspension. Pro rata amounts will be paid in respect of part weeks. Entitlement to remuneration under these provisions does not affect any right of an employee under the employee's contract of employment. An employee may present a complaint to an employment tribunal, that his or her employer has failed to pay remuneration under the relevant provisions, within a period of three months from the date of the failure to pay, or has failed to provide an employee suspended on maternity grounds with suitable alternative work. An employment tribunal which finds that the complaint concerning the failure to pay remuneration is well-founded may make an order to that effect and make an award of compensation to the employee. The amount of compensation will be such as the tribunal considers just and equitable in all the circumstances having regard to the employer's infringement, and any loss sustained by the employee which is attributable to the matters complained of.

16.4.10 Maternity rights

16.4.10.1 Ante-natal care Under s. 55, Employment Rights Act 1996, an employee who is pregnant and who has, on the advice of a registered medical practitioner, registered midwife or registered health visitor, made an appointment to receive ante-natal care, is entitled to be permitted by her employer to take time off during her working hours in order to enable her to keep the appointment. Except for the first appointment during pregnancy, entitlement to time off for keeping such an appointment is dependent on the production of a medical certificate and appointment card confirming the facts of pregnancy and medical appointment.

The employee is also entitled to be paid for such time off work at the appropriate hourly rate, calculated in accordance with the provisions of s. 56 of the 1996 Act. If an employer refuses to give time off or fails to pay wages during time off the employee may complain to an employment tribunal. An application to an employment tribunal can be made either while the employee is still employed or within three months of leaving employment. Where the employment tribunal determines that the employer has unreasonably refused to permit the employee to take time off, or has failed to pay the employee for any time taken off, it may order the employer to pay equal amounts of remuneration to the employee.

16.4.10.2 Maternity leave Section 71, Employment Rights Act 1996 establishes a general right to maternity leave for employees. Such leave commences either on the date of notification by the employee or on the first day after the beginning of the sixth week before the expected date of childbirth. The maternity leave will continue for a period of 14 weeks from its commencement or until the birth of the child. Entitlement to maternity leave is dependent on the employee notifying her employer of the date on which she intends her period of absence from work to commence, not less than 21 days before the leave is due to commence. There must also be notification to the employer, in writing, within a similar period of the fact of the pregnancy and the expected date of childbirth. The employee must also produce a certificate, confirming the expected date of childbirth, should the employer request it.

Under the provisions of s. 79, a female employee who has the statutory right to maternity leave, and who has, at the beginning of the eleventh week before the expected week of childbirth, been continuously employed for a period of not less than two years, has a parallel right to return to her job, within 29 weeks after childbirth. The right is to return under her original contract of employment and on terms and conditions as favourable as if she had not been absent, and with accrued seniority and pension rights as if she had been continuously employed. To trigger the right, the employee must have given her employer notice of the intention to return, at the same time as giving formal notice of the fact of pregnancy and the expected date of childbirth. An employee who intends to return to work earlier than the end of her maternity leave period, must give her employer not less than seven days' notice of the date on which she intends to return.

Following childbirth, the employee may be required to furnish written confirmation of her intention to return. When she is able to resume her job she must give her employer 21 days' notice. There are three situations in which maternity leave can be extended:

(a)   an employer, for specific reasons, can delay the employee's return by up to four weeks;

(b)   an employee can delay her return by up to four weeks if she is ill and produces a medical certificate; and

(c)   if there is an interruption of work, due to industrial action, or some other reason, she can postpone the date of her return until 28 days after work resumes.

If the employee is not permitted by the employer to return to work, she can apply within three months to an employment tribunal under the unfair dismissal provisions. Alternatively, if due to redundancy her job no longer exists and her employer cannot offer her a suitable alternative job, she is entitled to a redundancy payment and can apply to an employment tribunal within six months.

Where an employee has both the statutory maternity rights and other maternity rights under a contract of employment, she may not exercise the two rights separately, but may take advantage of whatever right is, in any particular respect, the more favourable.

16.4.10.3   Maternity pay   Entitlement to statutory maternity pay is governed by relevant social security provisions, mainly the Social Security Contributions and Benefits Act 1992, and the Social Security Administration Act 1992, as amended. To be eligible to be paid statutory maternity pay, an employee must satisfy a number of conditions. She must have been continuously employed in an employed earner's employment for 26 weeks up to the fifteenth week before the expected date of childbirth. In addition, the employee's average weekly earnings in the eight weeks before the expected date of childbirth must have exceeded the lower earnings limit used for contribution purposes. Finally, the employee must have been pregnant at the eleventh week before the expected date of childbirth.

For those who qualify under these conditions, the rate of statutory maternity pay is 90 per cent of earnings or average earnings for a period of six weeks followed by a flat rate sum, equivalent to the weekly rate of statutory sick pay, for a period of 12 weeks. Those who are not entitled to statutory maternity pay (because they are self-employed or do not have the requisite degree of continuous employment), but who have made sufficient national insurance contributions for at least 26 weeks in the 66 weeks before the expected date of childbirth, will be entitled to a state maternity allowance for a period of 18 weeks. The rate of state maternity allowance is equivalent to the lower rate of statutory maternity pay.

Employers may be reimbursed 92 per cent of the cost of statutory maternity pay. Small employers may be reimbursed a greater amount under limited circumstances.

16.4.11   Time off for public duties
Section 50, Employment Rights Act 1996 entitles an employee to reasonable time off work without pay to perform certain public duties. Where the employee is a justice of the peace, the time off is for the purpose of performing

any of the duties of that office. Where the employee is a member of a local authority, statutory tribunal, police authority, board of prison visitors, relevant health or education body or environmental agency, the time off will be for the purpose of attending meetings of the body or any of its committees, or subcommittees, or discharging any of the functions of the body.

What is reasonable is to be determined by a series of factors, including the amount of time required, how much time the employee has already been permitted to have off under other relevant provisions, including time off for trade union duties and activities, and the circumstances of the employer's business and the effect of the employee's absence on the running of that business. An employee who has not been permitted to take time off under these provisions may make a complaint to an employment tribunal, within three months of the date on which the failure occurred, or within such further period as the tribunal considers to be just and equitable where it is satisfied that it was not reasonably practicable for the complaint to be presented before the end of the period of three months. An employment tribunal which finds that the complaint is well-founded may make an order to that effect and make an award of compensation to the employee.

16.4.12 Right not to suffer detriment

Part V, Employment Rights Act 1996 provides protection to employees from suffering detriment in employment due to participation in a variety of different activities. It is important to note that most of these protection provisions do not apply where the detriment in question amounts to a dismissal. In these situations, the dismissal provisions will apply.

The first of these circumstances relates to an employee who is involved with health and safety. Under s. 44 of the 1996 Act, an employee has the right not to be subjected to any detriment on the ground that:

(a) having been designated by the employer to carry out activities in connection with preventing or reducing risks to health and safety at work, the employee carried out any such activities;

(b) being a representative of workers on matters of health and safety at work, or member of a safety committee, in accordance with arrangements established under any enactment, or by virtue of being acknowledged as such by the employer, the employee performed such functions;

(c) being an employee at a place where there was no health and safety representative or safety committee, or where there was such a representative or committee, but it was not reasonably practicable to raise the matter by those means, the employee brought to the employer's attention, by reasonable means, circumstances connected with the employee's work which the employee reasonably believed were harmful or potentially harmful to health and safety;

(d) in circumstances of danger which the employee reasonably believed to be serious and imminent and which the employee could not reasonably have been expected to avert, the employee left (or proposed to leave) or (while the danger persisted) refused to return to the place of work or any dangerous part of the place of work; and

(e)   in circumstances of danger which the employee reasonably believed to be serious and imminent, the employee took (or proposed to take) appropriate steps to protect himself or herself or other persons from danger.

Whether steps which an employee took (or proposed to take) were appropriate is to be judged by reference to all the circumstances, including the knowledge of the employee and the facilities and advice available at the time.

Secondly, where an employee is a protected shop worker or an opted-out shop worker, that employee has the right not to be subjected to any detriment by any act of the employer done on the ground that the employee refused to work on Sunday. An employee who is a shop worker equally has the right not to be subjected to detriment by any act of the employer on the ground that the employee gave an opting-out notice to the employer.

Thirdly, an employee has the right not to be subjected to any detriment on the ground that, being a trustee of a relevant occupational pension scheme which relates to the employee's employment, the employee performed any functions as such a trustee. Fourthly, an employee has the right not to be subjected to any detriment on the ground that, being an employee representative, for the purposes of the relevant trade union legislation, or a candidate for election to the position of employee representative, he or she carried out the functions or activities as an employee representative, or as such a candidate.

Finally, an employee has the right not to be subjected to any detriment on the ground that the employee has made a protected disclosure. These provisions were inserted into the Employment Rights Act 1996 by the Public Interest Disclosure Act 1998, which came into force on 2 July 1998.

A protected disclosure is a qualifying disclosure made by an employee in certain defined circumstances. In turn, a qualifying disclosure means any disclosure of information which, in the reasonable belief of the employee, making the disclosure, tends to show that:

(a)   a criminal offence has been committed, is being committed or is likely to be committed;

(b)   a person has failed, is failing or is likely to fail to comply with any legal obligation;

(c)   a miscarriage of justice has occurred, is occurring or is likely to occur;

(d)   the health or safety of any individual has been, is being or is likely to be endangered;

(e)   the environment has been, is being or is likely to be damaged; or

(f)   information tending to show any matter outlined above is being or is likely to be deliberately concealed.

Qualifying disclosures become protected disclosures where they are made to an employer or other responsible person, to a legal adviser, Minister of the Crown, other prescribed person, or in other prescribed circumstances. These latter circumstances include disclosures subsequent to earlier disclosures to the employer, and disclosures of exceptionally serious failure.

An employee who feels that he or she has suffered a detriment, in the circumstances outlined above, may make a complaint to an employment tribunal, within a period of three months from the act to which the complaints relates, or within such further period as the tribunal considers to be just and equitable where it is satisfied that it was not reasonably practicable for the complaint to be presented before the end of the period of three months. On such a complaint, it is for the employer to show the ground on which any act, or deliberate failure to act, was done. Where an employment tribunal finds such a complaint to be well-founded, it may make a declaration to that effect, and may make an award of compensation to the complainant.

The amount of compensation will be such as the tribunal considers just and equitable in all of the circumstances having regard to the nature of the infringement, and loss which is attributable to the act, or failure to act. The loss will include any expenses reasonably incurred and any loss of accrued benefit. Any compensation may be reduced where the tribunal finds that the complainant caused or contributed to the act, and the complainant is also under a duty to mitigate any resultant loss.

16.5 REDUNDANCY

The law on redundancy covers two important issues relating to redundancy. The first relates to the obligation of an employer to consult about redundancies, and the second relates to the rights of an individual employee in the redundancy situation.

16.5.1 Individual redundancy payments

Part XI of the Employment Rights Act 1996 provides for individual employment rights in redundancy. Section 135 of the 1996 Act establishes a general right to a redundancy payment for any employee who is dismissed by the employer by way of redundancy, or is eligible for a redundancy payment by reason of being laid off or kept on short-time. However, the general right to a redundancy payment on dismissal is subject to a number of important exceptions:

(a) those who have not been continuously employed for a period of not less than two years;

(b) those who have reached the normal retiring age for an employee of that business, or the age of 65;

(c) those who are subject to approved, exempted agreements;

(d)   those holding certain public offices or who are employed in overseas government employment;

(e)   certain domestic servants in a private household;

(f)   those employed on fixed term contracts of two years or more and who have agreed in writing in the contract, or at any other stage in the contract, to forgo the right to a redundancy payment;

(g)   those who unreasonably refuse an offer of suitable alternative employment; those who accept an offer of suitable alternative employment have a trial period of four weeks during which they may terminate the new contract without losing individual redundancy rights; and

(h)   those who are on strike during the currency of an employer's notice of termination; special rules apply, however, where the strike commences after the redundancy notice has been given.

Exceptions also exist to the general right to a redundancy payment by reason of a lay-off or short time. These include the situation where the employer serves the employee who has claimed such a payment, with a counter-notice contesting any liability. No entitlement exists to a redundancy payment unless the employee on short-term or lay-off resigns from the employment. Equally no entitlement will arise where the employee is dismissed (although other employment rights will arise) or where there is a likelihood of full employment, during the subsequent 13 weeks.

Under s. 139, Employment Rights Act 1996, an individual who is dismissed (the meaning of which is outlined in ss. 136–8 of the Act) is taken to be dismissed by reason of redundancy if the dismissal is wholly or mainly attributable to the fact that the employer has ceased, or intends to cease, to carry on the business in which the employee was employed, or to cease to carry on that business in the place where the employee was employed. Equally dismissal by way of redundancy arises where the requirements of that business for employees to carry out work of a particular kind, or in the place where the employee was employed, have ceased or diminished or are expected to cease or diminish.

An employee is taken to be laid off for a week in circumstances where he or she is employed, and paid, under a contract of employment which depends on being provided with work, and no entitlement to remuneration arises because work has not been provided. An employee is taken to be on short-time for a week if by reason of a diminution in the work provided, the employee's remuneration for the week is less than half a week's pay.

Employees must make a written claim for a redundancy payment to their employer, or to an employment tribunal, within six-months from the termination of employment. The six-month period may be extended by an employment tribunal in limited circumstances. Any question relating to the right of an employee to a redundancy payment, or the amount of a redundancy payment, where, for example, the employer refuses to pay, or where the amount paid is not adequate or appropriate, will be referred to and determined by an employment tribunal. For the purposes of any such reference, an employee who has been dismissed will, unless the contrary can be proved, be presumed to have been dismissed by reason of redundancy.

An employee who makes a redundancy payment is further obliged to give the employee a written statement indicating how the amount of the payment has been calculated. An employer who fails to comply with this requirement, either at the time of the making of the redundancy payment, or on further application by the employee, is guilty of a criminal offence, punishable on summary conviction by the imposition of a fine.

The amount of the redundancy payment is calculated on the basis of the provisions of s. 162, Employment Rights Act 1996. A formulaic approach is taken, based on years of continuous employment, which is similar to that used for calculating the basic award of compensation payable as a result of an unfair dismissal.

16.5.2 Consultation requirements

The Collective Redundancies and Transfer of Undertakings (Protection of Employment) (Amendment) Regulations 1995 (S.I. 1995/2587), introduced as a result of a series of cases before the European Court of Justice, make specific provision for consultation before the introduction of redundancy. The 1995 Regulations amend the Trade Union and Labour Relations (Consolidation) Act 1992, to require employers to consult with the elected representatives of the employees or representatives of a recognised trade union where there are to be redundancies or the transfer of an undertaking, within a specified time period.

These requirements are limited to cases where at least twenty redundancies are being proposed. The purpose of the consultation is to discuss the avoidance of dismissals, the reduction of the numbers of employees to be dismissed, and to mitigate the consequences of dismissal. As part of the consultation process, written notice containing specified details of the proposed redundancies must be served on the employee representatives or trade union. In addition, the employer is obliged to serve notice of the proposed redundancies on the Department of Trade and Industry (Department of Economic Development in Northern Ireland), in a prescribed form, within specific time limits.

Failure to comply with the legislative requirements concerning consultation over redundancies renders the employer liable to both civil and criminal penalties. These may include the payment, following complaint to an employment tribunal, of a 'protective award' of remuneration to employees during a specified protected period.

16.6 DISCRIMINATION IN EMPLOYMENT

16.6.1 Minors

As we have already seen, in section 15.4.2, under common law rules an employment contract with someone under 18 years of age will only be enforced where the contract is 'substantially for the minor's benefit'.

Certain provisions concerning working time in Directive 94/33/EC ([1994] OJ L216/12), on the protection of children at work have been implemented in the United Kingdom by the Children (Protection at Work) Regulations 1998 (S.I. 1998/276).

16.6.2   Sex or marital status

The sex discrimination legislation (Sex Discrimination Acts 1975 and 1986 (Sex Discrimination (Northern Ireland) Orders 1976 and 1988) Equal Pay Act 1970 (Equal Pay (Northern Ireland) Act 1970)) makes it unlawful to discriminate against a person on grounds of their sex or marital status. There are three main types of discriminatory conduct. Direct discrimination occurs when an employer treats a person less favourably than another on grounds of their sex or marital status. Indirect discrimination is where an employer applies an unjustified employment-related requirement or condition (for example, age, height, educational qualifications) which cannot be complied with by particular individuals because of their sex or marital status. Victimisation occurs where an individual suffers further discriminatory detriment in their future employment after having brought a complaint of sex discrimination or having been associated with such a complaint.

All aspects of the employment relationship — advertisements and interviews, terms of the employment contract, opportunities for training or promotion, and selection for redundancy or dismissal — are covered by the sex discrimination legislation. Limited exceptions are provided by the legislation where the employer can show that the application of a particular condition, which would otherwise would be discriminatory, is a 'genuine occupational qualification' for the employment. An example would be restricting applications for attendants for male lavatories to men.

Complaints of unlawful sex discrimination are dealt with by an employment tribunal. Where the tribunal finds that the complaint is well-founded, it may make a recommendation, a declaration and/or an award of unlimited compensation. The application of the sex discrimination legislation is overseen by the Equal Opportunities Commission for Great Britain (EOC), (Equal Opportunities Commission for Northern Ireland). The EOC has specific powers with regard to the monitoring and investigation of the effect of the legislation in specific employments, and with dealing with other aspects of unlawful discrimination, including discriminatory advertisements, and may assist in the bringing of complaints before employment tribunals, and further, on appeal.

The equal pay legislation implies an equality clause into the terms and conditions of employees. This clause ensures that both men and women must be given contractual terms not less favourable than those of the opposite sex who are employed on 'like work', that is work which is the same or broadly similar, on work rated as 'equivalent', under a job evaluation scheme, and on work of 'equal value', that is in terms of the demands made on the workers. To assess the last, it is appropriate to look at factors such as skill, effort, and decision-making. Limited defences are available to the employer under the legislation, including a right to claim that the difference in pay is due to material differences.

As with sex discrimination cases, complaints concerning equal pay will be made to an employment tribunal. Where the tribunal finds the claim to be well-founded, it will make an award of monetary compensation, amounting to the difference between the remuneration of the complainant and a comparator, and arrears up to a specified amount.

16.6.3 Religious and political discrimination

The Fair Employment (Northern Ireland) Acts 1976 and 1989, which as their names suggest only apply in Northern Ireland, make it unlawful to discriminate on grounds of a person's religious belief or political opinion. As with sex discrimination, discrimination means direct or indirect discrimination, or victimisation. The legislation imposes obligations relating to all aspects of the employment relationship, including advertisements and interviews, terms and conditions of employment, training or promotion, and selection for dismissal or redundancy.

The legislation imposes further obligations on employers, including registration with the Fair Employment Commission for Northern Ireland (FEC). Employers are also obliged to monitor the religious composition of the workforce, carry out periodic reviews where it is clear that imbalances are evident, and may even be required to engage in aspects of affirmative action. The FEC has specific powers to review the operation of the fair employment legislation, and has power to investigate individual employments, and issue instructions for employers to undertake. In addition it may assist individual complainants in specific test cases. The FEC also publishes a code of practice for employers.

Complaints of unlawful religious or political discrimination are heard by a specialist tribunal — the Fair Employment Tribunal for Northern Ireland. It has extensive powers in relation to the remedies which it may award.

16.6.4 Race discrimination

The Race Relations Act 1976 (Race Relations (Northern Ireland) Order 1997) makes it unlawful to discriminate on grounds of a person's race. As with the other legislation on discrimination, direct discrimination, indirect discrimination, and victimisation are provided for by the legislation. Discrimination again will cover advertisements and interviews, terms and conditions of employment, training or promotion, and selection for redundancy or dismissal.

As with sex discrimination, limited exceptions are provided by the legislation where the employer can show that the application of a particular condition, which would otherwise would be discriminatory, is a 'genuine occupational qualification' for the employment.

Complaints of unlawful race discrimination are dealt with by an employment tribunal. Where the tribunal finds that the complaint is well-founded, it may make a recommendation, a declaration and/or an award of unlimited compensation. The application of the race discrimination legislation is overseen by the Commission for Racial Equality for Great Britain (CRE), (Commission for Racial Equality for Northern Ireland). The CRE has specific powers with regard to the monitoring and investigation of the effect of the legislation in specific employments, and with dealing with other aspects of unlawful discrimination, including discriminatory advertisements, and may assist in the bringing of complaints before employment tribunals, and further, on appeal.

16.6.5 The disabled

The Disability Discrimination Act 1995 outlaws discrimination in employment relating to recruitment, terms and conditions of employment, promotion, training, and selection for redundancy and dismissal. The employment provisions of the Act do not apply to an employer who has fewer than 20 employees. Limited defences are provided for in the legislation, allowing employers to show that the reason for the discrimination is material to the circumstances of the case and substantial.

Employers may also be liable, under the legislation, for failure to comply with a duty to make reasonable adjustments to working arrangements or the physical features of premises where the existing arrangements or features constitute a disadvantage to disabled persons. Discrimination may also take the form of victimisation of an individual who has brought a complaint of unlawful disability discrimination or who has been associated with such a complaint.

Complaints of unlawful disability discrimination are dealt with by an employment tribunal. Where the tribunal finds that the complaint is well-founded, it may make a recommendation, a declaration, an award of unlimited compensation, or an order indicating the specific steps which an employer must take to reduce the adverse effects complained of. The application of the disability discrimination legislation is overseen by the National Disability Council for Great Britain. The powers of the Council are not as extensive as those, EOC, FEC or CRE, but may be extended in the future.

16.6.6 Ex-offenders

The Rehabilitation of Offenders Act 1974 (Rehabilitation of Offenders (Northern Ireland) Order 1978) provides that after a period of time a criminal conviction is spent and should not be referred to. Whether a conviction is spent depends on the sentence passed. Sentences of more than two and a half years in prison are never spent, prison sentences of six months to two and a half years are spent after ten years, and prison sentences of less than six months are spent after seven years.

The legislation makes specific provision for questions by employers relating to a person's previous convictions as not applying to spent convictions, except certain convictions relating to sexual offences where the employment may involve contact with minors. In addition, a spent conviction or failure to disclose a spent conviction will not be a ground justifying dismissal, exclusion from employment, or other employment prejudice.

16.7 EMPLOYMENT TRIBUNALS

There has been much reference in this chapter to the role played by employment tribunals in the management of the employment relationship, and the protection and enforcement of individual employment rights. Employment tribunals used to be called industrial tribunals (they are still called industrial tribunals in Northern Ireland), and have an extremely important role to play in employment law and practice.

An employment tribunal comprises three persons, a legally qualified chairman and two lay representatives, one chosen from a panel nominated by employers' organisations (the Confederation of British Industry (CBI), for example), the other from a panel nominated by the trade unions. The jurisdiction of employment tribunals mainly concerns individual employment matters, but in some cases a trade union may complain to an employment tribunal, for example, where it has not been consulted in advance of redundancies or prior to the transfer of an undertaking.

16.7.1 Procedure at an employment tribunal

It is intended that employment tribunals by their practice and procedures should provide cheap, quick and informal methods of hearing complaints but in many cases, due to the complexity of the legislation, a different result is achieved. The employment tribunal has become very formalised, although the tribunal will do its best to assist unrepresented complainants. Legal aid is not available for the purposes of pursuing a complaint through the employment tribunal procedure. It is however possible to utilise the 'green form' scheme whereby advice and assistance can be obtained from a solicitor in advance of a tribunal hearing. The scheme is subject to a small monetary limit although this may be raised when expert opinion is needed.

The practice and procedure of the employment tribunal has been radically altered by the provisions, Employment Rights (Dispute Resolution) Act 1998. Certain cases may now be heard on the basis of written evidence alone, with the mutual consent of both employee and employer, or may be heard without the presence of the respondent, or may be heard, in limited circumstances, by chairman alone, or the chairman with only one lay member.

16.7.2 Challenging the decision of an employment tribunal

A party dissatisfied with the decision of an employment tribunal may challenge the decision in one or more of four ways:

(a)   request the tribunal to review its own decision. This can be done only in certain limited situations, where:

(i)   the decision was wrongly made as a result of an error on the part of the tribunal staff; or
(ii)   a party did not receive notice of the proceedings leading to the decision; or
(iii)   the decision was made in the absence of a party or person entitled to be heard, or new evidence has become available since the making of the decision provided its existence could not have been reasonably known or foreseen, or the interests of justice require such a review.

(b)   appeal, in England and Wales to an Employment Appeal Tribunal;
(c)   request the High Court using its supervisory jurisdiction over inferior courts to review the decision where it is contended that the rules of natural justice have been broken. Legal aid may be available at this stage; and
(d)   appeal by way of case stated on a point of law to the Court of Appeal. Again, legal aid may be available at this stage.

There is no Employment Appeal Tribunal in Northern Ireland, where disappointed parties to the action will have to pursue one of the other further remedies.

16.8   HEALTH AND SAFETY AT WORK

The general legislative scheme for health and safety at work is provided for by the Health and Safety at Work Act 1974. The general scheme is completed by a series of six sets of regulations, designed to implement, into United Kingdom law, a number of EC directives. The overall legislative scheme is designed to impose duties on employers to protect employees, and others, from harm in the workplace. The detail of the legislative duties and responsibilities is now to be found in the regulations, which seek to define the range of obligations owed clearly and explicitly. Employers and employees should pay particular attention to these.

The 1974 Act retains a significance in defining the general duties relating to health and safety at work. In addition, it sets out the structure, jurisdiction and powers of the Health and Safety Commission and the Health and Safety Executive.

16.8.1   The Health and Safety at Work Act 1974 — General duties
Section 2 of the 1974 Act imposes a duty on employers to ensure, so far as is reasonably practicable, the health, safety and welfare at work of all their employees. This general duty is supplemented by a series of specific duties relating to the provision and maintenance of plant and systems of work, the use,

handling, storage and transport of articles and substances, the provision of information, instruction, training and supervision, and the provision and maintenance of access and egress. Employers must prepare, and revise, a written statement of the policy with respect to the health and safety of employees, the organisation and arrangements for carrying out that policy, and the bringing of the statement to the notice of the employees. Provision is also made for the appointment of safety representatives from amongst the employees and for consultation with such representatives for the purpose of effective co-operation in promoting and developing measures to ensure health and safety at work.

Under s. 7 of the 1974 Act, there is a parallel general duty imposed on employees to take reasonable care for the health and safety of themselves, and of other persons who may be affected by the employees' acts or omissions at work. In addition, the employee is under a further duty to co-operate with the employer to ensure compliance or performance with any duty or requirement imposed on the employer under any relevant statutory provisions. Further, employees must not intentionally or recklessly interfere with or misuse anything provided in the interests of health, safety or welfare. Failure to comply with this latter requirement can amount to a criminal offence.

Under s. 3 of the 1974 Act, a duty is imposed on employers and self-employed persons to conduct their undertakings in such a way as to ensure, so far as is reasonably practicable, that persons not in their employment but who may be affected by the undertaking, are not exposed to risks to their health or safety. A further obligation is imposed under this section to furnish those persons not in their employment but who may be affected by the undertaking, with information about such aspects of the way in which the undertaking is conducted as might affect their health and safety.

Section 4 of the 1974 Act imposes duties on employers, and others, in relation to those persons, who are not employees, but who come onto their business premises. The duty is to ensure, so far as is reasonably practicable, that the premises, and means of access and egress from the premises, and any plant or substance in the premises, are safe and without risk to health. This important duty supplements the obligations owed, under civil law, to those who come onto premises, already discussed in 15.10. A similar obligation is imposed on landlords who retain the obligation to maintain or repair business premises under a tenancy agreement. Failure to comply with this requirement may also amount to a criminal offence.

Under s. 6 of the 1974 Act, general duties are imposed on those who design, manufacture, import or supply any article for use at work to ensure, so far as is reasonably practicable, that the article is so designed and constructed that it will be safe and without risk to health at all times when it is being set, used, cleaned or maintained. There are further duties with regard to the testing and examination of such articles to ensure compliance with these duties, and to the supply of adequate information about the use for which the article is designed or has been tested, and about any conditions necessary to make sure that the article will be safe and without risks to health when it is being set, used, cleaned or maintained.

A whole series of criminal offences is created by the legislation. These relate mainly to failure to undertake obligations or duties created by the 1974 Act, or failure to comply with specific legislative provisions. Where the commission of an offence is due to the act or default of another person, that other person is guilty of the offence and liable to be proceeded against. Where an offence committed by a company is proved to have been committed with the consent or connivance of, or to have been attributable to any neglect on the part of, a director, manager, secretary or other officer of the company, that person will also be guilty of the offence and is liable to be proceeded against.

Section 37 of the 1974 Act makes it clear that breach of any of the provisions of the legislation does not automatically confer a right of action in any civil proceedings. This prohibition does not prevent an employee, or others, from commencing a civil action in negligence, or for breach of the employment contract, in the civil courts.

16.8.2 The Health and Safety Commission and the Health and Safety Executive

The Health and Safety Commission and the Health and Safety Executive are created by s. 10 of the 1974 Act, which, together with sch. 2, also makes provision for membership, functions and jurisdiction. The general duties of the Commission are to promote and encourage the purpose of the legislation through the publication of codes of practice, to carry out research and publish its results, provide training and information, recommend proposals for the reform of the legislation, and to conduct enquiries.

The power of the Commission to direct investigations and inquiries is contained in s. 14 of the 1974 Act. Where there has been an accident, occurrence, situation or other matter, which the Commission thinks it necessary or expedient to investigate, including for the purpose of the making of new laws, the Commission may direct the Executive or any other person to investigate and report, or, with the consent of the Secretary of State, direct that an inquiry be held. Further detailed sections make provision for the conduct of such inquiries, including powers of entry and inspection, the summoning of witnesses and production of documents. Reports of inquiries may be published.

The general duty of the Executive is to enforce the provisions of the legislation. Enforcement is carried out through health and safety inspectors, appointed by enforcing authorities, under the provisions of s. 19 of the 1974 Act. Enforcing authorities include local authorities to whom powers of authority may be devolved. Health and safety inspectors are given extensive powers to assist in the enforcement of the legislation including the power to enter premises, make examinations and investigations, direct that examined premises be left undisturbed, take measurements, samples, photographs, and make recordings, cause dangerous products to be dismantled, take possession of and detain dangerous substances, require any person to answer questions and sign a declaration of the truth of the answers, and require the production and inspection of relevant documents and take copies of them, or entries in them.

Where the inspector has reasonable cause to believe that an article may be the cause of imminent danger, the inspector is given further power to enter premises, remove the article, and cause it to be made harmless, by destruction or otherwise. An inspector exercising this power is under a duty to make and serve a written report outlining the reasons for the removal and seizure.

Where an inspector is of the opinion that a person is contravening one or more of the relevant statutory provisions, or has contravened those provisions in circumstances that make it likely that the contravention will be repeated or will continue, that inspector may serve an improvement notice, requiring that person to remedy or rectify the contravention. Where an inspector is of the opinion that activities which are being, or are about to be, carried out involve a risk of serious personal injury, that inspector may serve a prohibition notice on the person who controls the activities. The prohibition notice must give reasons why the activities are considered unsafe and specify that the activities must cease until the matter is remedied or rectified.

Appeals against improvement or prohibition notices may be made to an employment tribunal within a specified statutory period. The effect of an improvement notice is suspended until the appeal is heard. A prohibition notice is not so suspended unless the tribunal so directs on an application to it. An employment tribunal may affirm or cancel a notice. Affirmation may be of the original notice or may be with such modifications as the tribunal thinks fit. Further appeals lie to the Divisional Court of the Queen's Bench Division of the High Court.

16.8.3   The health and safety regulations

As noted above, the general scheme for health and safety at work has now been complemented by a series of six sets of regulations, designed to implement, into United Kingdom law, a number of EC directives. The detail of the legislative duties and responsibilities is now to be found in the regulations, which seek to define clearly and explicitly the range of obligations owed. While these six set of regulations make up the main framework of health and safety laws in the United Kingdom, they are supplemented by a variety of other rules, e.g., the Health and Safety (First Aid) Regulations 1981 (S.I. 1981/917), the Reporting of Injuries, Diseases and Dangerous Occurrences Regulations 1995 (S.I. 1995/3163) and the Fire Precautions (Workplace) Regulations 1997 (S.I. 1997/1840). Close attention should also be paid to these rules.

16.8.3.1   The Management of Health and Safety at Work Regulations 1992 (S.I. 1992/2051)   These regulations give effect to Directive 89/391/EEC on the introduction of measures to encourage improvements in the safety and health of workers at work ([1989] OJ L183/1) ('the Framework Directive') and to Directive 91/383/EEC supplementing the measures to encourage improvements in the safety and health at work of workers with a fixed-duration employment relationship or a temporary employment relationship ([1991] OJ L206/19) ('the Temporary Workers' Directive').

Regulation 3 requires employers and self-employed persons to make assessments of the health and safety risks to which their respective undertakings give rise, for the purpose of ascertaining what they have to do to comply with their obligations under health and safety legislation. Regulation 3 also makes provision for the review and recording of the results of risk assessments. Regulation 4 imposes a duty on employers to make, give effect to and in certain cases record appropriate health and safety arrangements.

Employers are required under reg. 5, to ensure that their employees are provided with appropriate health surveillance. They are also required, under reg. 6, to appoint an adequate number of competent persons to assist them to comply with their obligations under health and safety legislation unless (in the case of a sole trader or a partnership) the employer concerned already has sufficient competence to comply with the relevant obligations without assistance.

Regulation 6, as well as defining 'competent person', also requires employers to make arrangements for ensuring adequate co-operation between the competent persons they appoint; and to provide the competent persons they appoint with the facilities necessary to enable them to carry out their functions, and with specified health and safety information.

Regulation 7 requires employers to establish and give effect to procedures to be followed in the event of serious and imminent danger to persons working in their respective undertakings, to nominate competent persons to implement those procedures in so far as they relate to the evacuation from premises of persons at work in their respective undertakings, and to restrict access to any danger areas occupied by them. This regulation also specifies in detail what the procedures referred to above must achieve and defines what is meant by 'competent person'.

Employers are required, under reg. 8, to provide their employees with specified health and safety information. Regulation 9 requires every employer and self-employed person who shares a workplace with any other employer or self-employed person to co-operate with that other person so far as is necessary to enable him or her to comply with his or her statutory health and safety obligations, co-ordinate the measures he or she takes in compliance with statutory health and safety obligations with the measures being taken in that regard by that other person, and take steps to provide that other person with specified health and safety information.

Regulation 10 requires employers and self-employed persons to ensure that the employers of any employees from outside undertakings who are working in their respective undertakings are provided with specified health and safety information, self-employed persons who are working in their respective undertakings are provided with specified health and safety instructions and information, and any employees from outside undertakings who are working in their respective undertakings are provided with specified health and safety instructions and information.

Employers are under a duty, under reg. 11, to consider their employees' capabilities as regards health and safety when entrusting tasks to them, and to ensure that in specified circumstances their employees are provided with adequate health and safety training. Regulation 11 also specifies when the training referred to above is to be provided and the circumstances in which it is to be repeated or adapted.

Regulation 12 imposes specific duties on employees. They are under a duty to use machinery, equipment, dangerous substances, transport equipment, means of production and safety devices in accordance with any relevant training and instructions, and to inform their respective employers or any specified fellow employees of dangerous work situations and shortcomings in those employers' health and safety arrangements.

Finally reg. 13 outlines a number of miscellaneous health and safety requirements. Employers and self-employed persons are required to provide temporary workers in their respective undertakings with health and safety information before they commence their duties. They are also under a duty to provide any employment business whose employees are to carry out work in their respective undertakings with specified health and safety information about the work to be done by those employees. Any employment business provided with information by an employer or self-employed person in pursuance thereof is to pass that information on to the employees to whom it relates.

Regulation 13 has been the subject of significant amendment through the Management of Health and Safety at Work (Amendment) Regulations 1994 (S.I. 1994/2865) and the Health and Safety (Young Persons) Regulations 1997 (S.I. 1997/135). The effect of these amendments is to introduce further health and safety protection for new and expectant mothers and young persons. These include additional requirements in regard to the assessment process in the case of new and expectant mothers and young persons and further specific duties in relation to these specific employees.

Regulation 15 provides that breach of a duty imposed by the regulations does not confer a right of action in civil proceedings. This repeats the general provision that failure to comply with a legislative health and safety requirement does not confer a right of action in civil proceedings. An exception exists in relation to civil action for breach of the new duties concerning new and expectant mothers.

16.8.3.2   The Workplace (Health, Safety and Welfare) Regulations 1992 (S.I. 1992/3004)   These regulations impose requirements with respect to the health, safety and welfare of persons in a workplace. They give effect as respects

Great Britain to Directive 89/654/EEC ([1989] OJ L393/1) concerning the minimum safety and health requirements for the workplace.

Requirements are imposed upon employers, persons who have, to any extent, control of a workplace, and persons who are deemed to be the occupiers of factories for the purposes of s. 175(5), Factories Act 1961. The regulations impose requirements with respect to:

(a) maintenance (reg. 5);

(b) ventilation of enclosed workplaces (reg. 6);

(c) temperature indoors and the provision of thermometers (reg. 7);

(d) lighting (including emergency lighting) (reg. 8);

(e) cleanliness of the workplace, furniture, furnishings and fittings; the ability to clean the surface of floors, walls and ceilings; and the accumulation of waste materials (reg. 9);

(f) room dimensions and unoccupied space (reg. 10 and sch. 1, Part I);

(g) the suitability of workstations (including workstations outdoors) and the provision of suitable seats (reg. 11);

(h) the condition of floors (reg. 12);

(i) the condition and arrangement of routes for pedestrians or vehicles (regs. 12 and 17);

(j) protection from falling objects and for persons falling from a height or falling into a dangerous substance (reg. 13);

(k) the material or protection of windows and other transparent or translucent walls, doors or gates and to them being apparent (reg. 14);

(l) the way in which windows, skylights or ventilators are opened and the position they are left in when open (reg. 15);

(m) the ability to clean windows and skylights (reg. 16);

(n) the construction of doors and gates (including the fitting of necessary safety devices) (reg. 18);

(o) escalators and moving walkways (reg. 19);

(p) the provision of suitable sanitary conveniences (reg. 20 and sch. 1, Part II);

(q) the provision of suitable washing facilities (reg. 21);

(r) the provision of a supply of drinking water and of cups or other drinking vessels (reg. 22);

(s) the provision of suitable accommodation for clothing and of facilities for changing clothing (regs. 23 and 24); and

(t) the provision of suitable facilities for rest and to eat meals (reg. 25).

16.8.3.3 The Health and Safety (Display Screen Equipment) Regulations 1992 (S.I. 1992/2792)   These regulations give effect as respects Great Britain to the substantive provisions of Directive 90/270/EEC on the minimum safety and health requirements for work with display screen equipment ([1990] OJ L156/14).

Regulations 2 and 3 impose specific requirements on employers relating to those workstations which, regardless of who has provided them, are used for the purposes of the undertaking by users. Regulation 2 requires each employer to make a suitable and sufficient analysis of those workstations, to assess the health and safety risks to which those operators or users are exposed in consequence of that use, to reduce those risks to the lowest extent reasonably practicable, and to review (and where necessary change) any such assessment. Regulation 3 requires each employer to ensure that any workstation meets the requirements laid down in the schedule to the regulations. The schedule lays down specific requirements relating to the display screen, the keyboard, the desk and chair, working environment and task design and software.

Regulation 4 requires each employer to plan the activities of users at work in the undertaking in such a way that their daily work on display screen equipment is periodically interrupted by such breaks or changes of activity as reduce their workload at that equipment.

Regulation 5 imposes duties on employers to ensure that users employed by the employers are provided with initial eye and eyesight tests on request, and at regular intervals thereafter and with the consent of the users concerned, with subsequent eye and eyesight tests. In addition, the employer must provide additional eye and eyesight tests on request, where the users concerned are experiencing visual difficulties which might reasonably be considered to be caused by work on display screen equipment, and appropriate special corrective appliances, where normal corrective appliances cannot be used and any eye and eyesight tests carried out on the users show such provision to be necessary.

Regulation 6 requires employers to ensure that users employed by them are provided with adequate health and safety training in the use of their workstations, and users at work in their undertaking are provided with adequate health and safety training whenever their workstations are substantially modified. Further, under the provisions of reg. 7, employers must ensure that operators and users at work in their undertakings are provided with adequate health and safety information, both about their workstations and about such measurements taken by the employers to comply with the other regulations as relate to the employees and their work.

16.8.3.4 The Personal Protective Equipment at Work Regulations 1992 (S.I. 1992/2966) These regulations impose health and safety requirements with respect to the provision for, and use by, persons at work of personal protective equipment. They require employers to ensure suitable personal protective equipment is provided for their employees and also require self-employed persons to ensure suitable personal protective equipment is provided for themselves. The circumstances in which personal protective equipment must be provided and minimum conditions of what is 'suitable' are specified in reg. 4. The regulations also impose requirements with respect to:

(a) compatibility of items of personal protective equipment where it is necessary to wear or use more than one item simultaneously (reg. 5);

(b)   the making, review and changing of assessments in relation to the choice of personal protective equipment (reg. 6);

(c)   the maintenance (including replacement and cleaning as appropriate) of personal protective equipment (reg. 7);

(d)   the provision of accommodation for personal protective equipment (reg. 8);

(e)   the provision of information, instruction and training (reg. 9); and

(f)   ensuring personal protective equipment is used (reg. 10(1)).

Requirements are imposed on employees and self-employed persons in respect of the use of personal protective equipment and in respect of returning it to accommodation provided for it under reg. 10(2)–(4). Employees are also required, by virtue of the provisions in reg. 11, to report to their employer the loss of, or any obvious defect in, personal protective equipment.

16.8.3.5   The Provision and Use of Work Equipment Regulations 1992 (S.I. 1992/2932)   These regulations give effect as respects Great Britain to Directive 89/655/EEC ([1989] OJ L393/13) on the minimum safety and health requirements for the use of work equipment by workers at work. They impose requirements upon employers in respect of work equipment provided for or used by their employees at work. The regulations make provision with respect to:

(a)   the suitability of work equipment (reg. 5);

(b)   the maintenance of work equipment and keeping up to date of any maintenance log (reg. 6);

(c)   steps to be taken where the use of work equipment is likely to involve a specific risk to health or safety (reg. 7);

(d)   information, instruction and training for persons who use work equipment and certain other employees (regs. 8 and 9);

(e)   conformity with European Community requirements (reg. 10 and sch. 1);

(f)   the protection of persons from dangerous parts of machinery and rotating stock-bars (reg. 11);

(g)   the prevention or control of exposure of any person to any risk caused by certain specified hazards (reg. 12);

(h)   protection from high or very low temperature (reg. 13);

(i)   controls (including emergency and other stop controls) and control systems (regs. 14 to 18);

(j)   the isolation of work equipment from sources of energy (reg. 19);

(k)   the stability of work equipment (reg. 20);

(l)   lighting at any place where work equipment is used (reg. 21);

(m)   taking measures to ensure that work equipment is so constructed or adapted that maintenance operations can be carried out in specified ways (reg. 22);

(n)   appropriate markings, warnings, or warning devices (regs. 23 and 24).

16.8.3.6 The Manual Handling Operations Regulations 1992 (S.I. 1992/ 2793) These regulations give effect as respects Great Britain to the substantive provisions of Directive 90/269/EEC on the minimum health and safety requirements for the manual handling of loads where there is a risk particularly of back injury to workers ([1990] OJ L156/9).

Regulation 4 imposes a general duty on employers, so far as it is reasonably practicable to do so, to avoid the need for their employees to undertake manual handling operations at work which involve a risk of their being injured. Where it is not reasonably practicable to avoid the need for employees to undertake any manual handling operations at work which involve a risk of their being injured, an employer must assess all such manual handling operations to be undertaken by them having regard to sch. 1 to the regulations, to reduce the risk of injury to those employees arising out of their undertaking any such manual handling operations to the lowest level reasonably practicable, and to provide any of those employees who are undertaking any such manual handling operations with certain information about the loads to be carried by them. Finally, under these provisions, employers must review any such assessment.

Employees are required, under reg. 5, while at work to make full and proper use of systems of work provided for their use by their employer in compliance with that employer's duty described above.

16.9 CONCLUSION

There are major misconceptions about the nature, scope and extent of employment law, shared by employer and employee alike. Employers have a negative view of the rationale behind employment protection and perceive employment protection laws to be pro-employee and anti-employer. In turn, many employees attempt to exploit such perceptions, attempting to reinforce an attitude that employment law is about safeguarding employees' rights and enforcing those rights through civil, and if necessary criminal, action in the courts.

A stark analysis of employment laws, as outlined in this chapter, might augment such popular misconceptions. The pharmacist employer, already faced with health care and business roles, with distinct legal realities, might baulk at the further reality of the law of employment, and wonder how the legal aspects of employment practice are to be fitted into other procedures and routines. Equally, the pharmacist employee might be strengthened in a conviction that the status of employee carries with it the greater legal protection.

To further such misconceptions is to miss the purpose of this chapter. As was noted in the introduction, the content of this chapter depicts the reality of employment law but not that of employment practice. The pharmacist employer (and pharmacist employee) takes the legal reality of employment law seriously, but is not intimidated by it, knowing that effective analysis, comprehension and implementation of employment law leads to constructive employment practice. Constructive employment practice includes an effective employment relationship, with an inherent recognition of employment rights. In turn, effective employment relationships are good for pharmacy business, good for pharmacy practice and good for the pharmacy profession.

Index